SHORTER
CLASSICS

of

EUGEN VON
BÖHM-BAWERK

Volume I

LIBERTARIAN PRESS
SOUTH HOLLAND, ILLINOIS, U.S.A.

By The Same Author . . .

CAPITAL AND INTEREST
(in three volumes *)

I
History and Critique of Interest Theories

II
Positive Theory of Capital

III
Further Essays on Capital and Interest

THE EXPLOITATION THEORY
(An Extract of Volume I)

VALUE AND PRICE
(An Extract of Volume II)

* Also published in one volume.

Acknowledgments

I THE AUSTRIAN ECONOMISTS
Henrietta Leonard translation printed in *The Annals* of the American Academy of Political and Social Science, Philadelphia, Pennsylvania, January 1891, pp. 361-384. Reprinted here by special permission of *The Annals*.

II WHETHER LEGAL RIGHTS AND RELATION-
SHIPS ARE ECONOMIC GOODS
The title of the German original is *Rechte und Verhält-nisse vom Standpunkte der volkswirtschaftlichen Gü-terlehre*, Verlag der Wagner'schen Universitäts-Buch-handlung, Innsbruck, Austria, 1881.

III CONTROL OR ECONOMIC LAW?
The title of the German original is "Macht oder öko-nomisches Gesetz?". This essay first appeared in *Zeit-schrift für Volkswirtschaft, Sozialpolitik und Verwal-tung*, Vienna, Austria, Volume XXIII, December 1914, pp. 205-271. Also reprinted in Volume I (1924) of *Gesammelte Schriften* by the same author (Hölder-Pichler-Tempsky A. G., Vienna). A translation was made in 1931 by John Richard Mez whose address was given as Eugene, Oregon. No copyright of this article is recorded in the United States copyright office.

IV UNRESOLVED CONTRADICTION IN THE MARX-
IAN ECONOMIC SYSTEM
The title of the German original is "Zum Abschluss des Marxschen Systems." This essay first appeared in *Staatswissenschaftliche Arbeiten — Festgaben für Karl Knies zur Fünfundsiebzigsten Wiederkehr*, Berlin, Haering, 1896, pp. 85-205. Translation by Alice Mac-donald, *Karl Marx and the Close of His System*, T. Fisher Unwin, London, 1898 (The Macmillan Company, New York, 1898) and Augustus M. Kelley, New York, 1949.

V THE ULTIMATE STANDARD OF VALUE
The title of the German original is "Der letzte Massstab der Güterwertes." This essay first appeared in *Zeit-schrift für Volkswirtschaft, Sozialpolitik und Verwal-tung*, Vienna, Austria, Volume III, 1894, pp. 185-230. A translation by C. W. Macfarlane was printed in *The Annals* of the American Academy of Political and So-cial Science, Philadelphia, Pennsylvania, September 1894, pp. 1-60. Reprinted here by special permission of *The Annals*.

General Foreword By Present Publisher

The essays combined in this book are not arranged in the chronological order in which they were written.

Böhm-Bawerk was 30 years old when he wrote "Whether Legal Rights and Relationships Are Economic Goods"; 40, when he wrote "The Austrian Economists"; 43, "The Ultimate Standard of Value"; 45, "Unresolved Contradiction in the Marxian Economic System"; and 63 (just before his death), when he wrote "Control or Economic Law?".

In general, where translations existed they have been followed, with only minor changes.

Paragraphs have frequently been reduced in size.

Side headings are all new, and are not to be ascribed to Böhm-Bawerk, nor the translators.

References have been modernized whenever that was feasible.

Appropriate acknowledgments to other publishers have been made elsewhere.

This publication is labeled *Volume I* to facilitate distinguishing it from a possible *Volume II*.

These essays are individually, and also collectively, overshadowed by Böhm-Bawerk's great three-volume work, CAPITAL AND INTEREST, but nevertheless they contribute independently and significantly to economic thought.

FREDERICK NYMEYER

September, 1961
South Holland, Illinois, U.S.A.

Contents

HIS EXCELLENCY EUGEN VON BÖHM-BAWERK
(1851-1914)
Professor of Political Economy, University of Vienna, Austria
Austrian Finance Minister: 1895, 1897, 1900-1904

ix

BIOGRAPHICAL SKETCH

OF EUGEN VON BÖHM-BAWERK

EUGEN VON BÖHM-BAWERK (February 12, 1851, Brünn, Austria-August 27, 1914, Vienna, Austria) was one of Austria's foremost economists and statesmen. His enduring fame rests on his lifelong defense of the science of economics and his stout resistance against the rising flood of interventionism and socialism. He was one of the first to see clearly the imminent destruction of our civilization through Marxism and all its related schemes of socialism. Böhm-Bawerk was a brilliant critic who also had the rare gifts of an originator.

He studied law at the University of Vienna and political science in Heidelberg, Leipzig, and Jena. In 1881 he was appointed professor of economics at the University of Innsbruck where he developed and defended the economic principles that Carl Menger and the classical economists had outlined.

His name as a statesman is associated with the best period of Austrian financial history. In 1889 he entered the Austrian Finance Department, where his abilities as an economist were needed for a projected currency reform. He was vice-chairman of the commission which led to the adoption of the gold standard with the krone as the unit. He was minister of finance in 1895, then again in 1897 and for the third time from 1900 to 1904. His tenure of office was characterized by far-sighted management, balanced budgets, stable currency and a successful conversion of the public debt. He also succeeded in abolishing the age-old special privilege of government subsidies to exporters of sugar. All this was achieved in spite of rising economic nationalism which was working continuously toward the disintegration of the Austro-Hungarian union. It was achieved in spite of the fact that Böhm-Bawerk was not associated with any political party. In 1904 he resigned from his position in protest against army irregularities in budgetary estimates and thereafter devoted his life to writing and teaching economics at the University of Vienna.

As an economist he won great fame by an unusual combination of qualities—extraordinary learning, independence of thought and judgment, dialectical skill, power of penetrating criticism, and mastery of exposition and illustration. An indefatigable scholar, he was marked by the ability always to go to the core of the subject. He showed lively interest in the problems of the Western democracies and in the controversies carried on in English and American journals to which he frequently contributed. His labors were prodigious. In his famous treatise, *Capital and Interest,* he not only expounded a complete theory of distribution but also a theory of social cooperation which exerted a profound influence on the thought of other economists. His most important works are the following:

1. KAPITAL UND KAPITALZINS comprising three volumes:
   I *Geschichte und Kritik der Kapitalzins-Theorien*
   (first edition, 1884; second edition, 1900; third edition, 1914; fourth edition, 1921)
   II *Positive Theorie des Kapitales*
   (first edition, 1889; second edition, 1902; third edition, 1909-1912; fourth edition, 1921)
   III *Exkurse zur "Positiven Theorie des Kapitales"*
   (Printed as appendices to the third edition of *Positive Theorie des Kapitales* in 1909-1912; printed as separate volume in 1921)
2. *Rechte und Verhältnisse vom Standpunkte der volkswirtschaftlichen Güterlehre,* Innsbruck, 1881
3. "Grundzüge der Theorie des wirtschaftlichen Güterwerts," in Conrad's *Jahrbücher für Nationalökonomie und Statistik,* new series, volume 13, 1886, pp. 1-88 and 477-541; reprinted in the "School of Economics Series of Scarce Tracts in Economic and Political Science," number 11, London, 1932
4. "The Austrian Economists," in the *Annals of the American Academy of Political and Social Science,* volume 1, 1891, pp. 361-384
5. "The Historical vs. the Deductive Method in Political Economy," in the *Annals of the American Academy of Political and Social Science,* volume 1, 1891, pp. 244-271
6. "Wert, Kosten und Grenznutzen," in Conrad's *Jahrbücher für Nationalökonomie und Statistik,* series III, 1892, pp. 321-367
7. "Der letzte Masstab des Güterwertes," in *Zeitschrift für Volkswirtschaft, Sozialpolitik und Verwaltung,* volume III, 1894, pp. 185-230; English translation under the title "The Ultimate Standard of Value," in the *Annals of the American Academy of Political and Social Science,* volume V, number 2
8. "The Positive Theory of Capital and Its Critics," published as a series of essays in the *Quarterly Journal of Economics* in 1895 and 1896 under the titles:
   "Professor Clark's Views on the Genesis of Capital," volume IX, pp. 113-131
   "General Walker Against *Capital and Interest,*" volume IX, pp. 235-256

"The Views of Mr. White, Mr. Bilgram, Professor Mac-Vane and Mr. Hawley," volume x, pp. 121-155

9. "Zum Abschluss des Marxschen Systems," in *Staatswirtschaftliche Arbeiten, Festgaben für Karl Knies,* Berlin, 1896, published in English under the title "Karl Marx and the Close of His System" by T. Fisher Unwin, London, 1898, and by Augustus M. Kelley, New York, 1949

10. "Einige strittige Fragen der Kapitalstheorie," Vienna, 1899, in *Zeitschrift für Volkswirtschaft, Sozialpolitik und Verwaltung,* volume VIII

11. "Macht oder ökonomisches Gesetz?" in *Zeitschrift für Volkswirtschaft, Sozialpolitik und Verwaltung,* volume XXIII, 1914, pp. 205-271, published in English under the title "Control or Economic Law?" by Consumers-Producers Economic Service, South Holland, Illinois, 1951

12. "Unsere passive Handelsbilanz," in *Neue Freie Presse,* issues of January 6, 8 and 9, 1914

F. X. Weiss has collected the more important minor works of Böhm-Bawerk in *Gesammelte Schriften,* two volumes, Vienna 1924-1926.

HANS F. SENNHOLZ

EUGEN VON BÖHM-BAWERK

I

The Austrian Economists*

Henrietta Leonard Translation

*First printed in *The Annals* of the American Academy of Political and Social Science, Philadelphia, Pennsylvania, January 1891, pp. 361-384. Reprinted here by special permission of *The Annals*.

Contents

Present Publisher's Preface To "The Austrian Economists"

In his essay on "The Austrian Economists" Böhm-Bawerk makes the arresting statement:

The most important and most famous doctrines of the Classical economists are either no longer tenable at all, or are tenable only after essential alterations and additions.

That critique orients the Classicists relative to the Austrians, who are the most important subdivision of the *Neo*classicists.

*   *   *

After the Classicists, two diverging trends become pronounced — (1) the Socialist, involving the ideas that man cannot be "free" of his material environment, and that the State should "plan" his life; and (2) the Neoclassical, which developed renewed appreciation of liberty and of the kind of economic organization of society which promotes prosperity. There is an irreconcilable difference between the Socialist and Neoclassical schools.

But what is here even more significant is the critique of the Classical school by the Neoclassical. The former had fixed its attention primarily on the *relationship of men to men.* There was an assumption underlying that, namely, that the *relationship of men to things* was not crucial, that it was simple, and that it needed no penetrating study.

The Neoclassicists declared that the *relationship of men to things* was fundamental and much more complex than had previously been realized. That view is clearly a derivative of the concept known under the name, *marginal utility.*

The Neoclassicists believed, rightly, that by that approach, they were re-laying the foundations of economics—correcting the errors of the Classicists and rebutting the fallacies of the Socialists.

In the essay which follows there is the almost obscure — but obviously important — sentence which reads as follows (the sentence italicized) :

> To be sure, the Classical economists well knew to what point all their explanations must be traced — to the care of mankind for its own well-being which (undisturbed by the incursion of altruistic motives) is the ultimate motive force of all economic action. *But owing to a certain circumstance, the middle term of the explanation, by means of which the actual conduct of men, in the establishment of prices of goods, of wages, rent, etc., ought to have been joined to the fundamental motive of regard for utility — this middle term was always wrong.*

That "middle term" is the relationship of men *to things,* as clarified by the law of marginal utility. It is not possible to think lucidly on the relationship of men to men without first adequately understanding the relationship of men to things. Because that relationship was not understood by the Classicists, they did not understand logically what followed from it, nor adequately understand the relationship of men to men.

*   *   *

The Neoclassical approach involves a genuinely "new look" at the world. Neoclassical cosmology is different — a modern and sophisticated cosmology that has been explicitly formulated in the field of the relation of men to things.

From basically different Neoclassical premises, new and revolutionary conclusions are developed on questions of value, price, cost, capital, interest, the "distribution" of the proceeds of joint production resulting from division of labor, etc.

To be ignorant of Neoclassical economics, in any era after Marx, is to be "invincibly unintelligent."

THE AUSTRIAN ECONOMISTS

The editors of this magazine have requested from my pen an account of the work of that group of economists which is popularly called the Austrian School. Since I am myself a member of the group, possibly I shall prove to be no impartial expositor. I will, nevertheless, comply with the request as well as I can, and I will attempt to describe what we Austrians are actually doing and seeking to do.

The Most Important Doctrines Of
Classical Economists Are No Longer Tenable

The province of the Austrian economists is *theory* in the strict sense of the word. They are of the opinion that the theoretical part of political economy needs to be thoroughly transformed. The most important and most famous doctrines of the classical economists are either no longer tenable at all, or are tenable only after essential alterations and additions. In the conviction of the inadequacy of the classical political economy, the Austrian economists and the adherents of the historical school agree. But in regard to the final cause of the inadequacy, there is a fundamental difference of opinion which has led to a lively contention over methods.

The historical school believes the ultimate source of the errors of the classical economy to be the false method by which it was pursued. It was almost entirely abstract-deductive, and, in their opinion, political economy should be only, or at least chiefly, inductive. In order to accomplish the necessary reform of the science, we must change the method of investigation; we must abandon abstraction and set ourselves to collecting empirical material — devote ourselves to history and statistics.

The Austrians, Although Primarily Interested
In Theory, Have Been Obliged To Defend
Their Views On Method

The Austrians, on the contrary, are of the opinion that the errors of the classical economists were only, so to speak, the ordinary diseases of the childhood of the science. Political economy is even yet one of the youngest sciences, and it was still younger in the time of the classical economy, which, in spite of its name "classical," given, as the event proved, too soon, was only an incipient, embryonic science. It has never happened in any other case that the whole of a science was discovered, at the first attempt, even by the greatest genius; and so it is not surprising that the whole

of political economy was not discovered, even by the classical school. Their greatest fault was that they were fore-
runners; our greatest advantage is that we come after.
We who are richer by the fruits of a century's research
than were our predecessors, need not work by different
methods, but simply work better than they. The historical
school are certainly right in holding that our theories should
be supported by as abundant empirical material as possible;
but they are wrong in giving to the work of collection an
abnormal preference, and in wishing either entirely to dispense with, or at least to push into the background, the
use of abstract generalization. Without such generalization
there can be no science at all.

Numerous works of the Austrian economists are devoted
to this strife over methods;[1] among them the *Untersuchungen über die Methode der Sozialwissenschaften*, by C.
Menger, stands first in deep and exhaustive treatment of
the problems involved. It should be noticed in this connection that the "exact," or, as I prefer to call it, the "isolating"
method recommended by Menger, together with the "empir-
ico-realistic" method, is by no means purely speculative or
unempirical, but, on the contrary, seeks and always finds
its foundation in experience. But although the strife of
methods, perhaps more than anything else, has drawn attention to the Austrian economists, I prefer to regard it as an
unimportant episode of their activity. The matter of importance to them was, and is, the reform of positive theory.
It is only because they found themselves disturbed in their
peaceful and fruitful labors by the attacks of the historical
school, that they, like the farmer on the frontier who holds
the plow with one hand and the sword with the other, have
been constrained, almost against their will, to spend part
of their time and strength in defensive polemics and in
the solution of the problems of method forced upon them.

[1]. Menger   : *Untersuchungen über die Methode der Sozialwissen-
schaften, 1883.* [The original German-language
text was republished in *Collected Works of Carl
Menger*, Vol. II, London School of Economics and
Political Science, University of London, 1933.
(Reprint No. 18).]

    Menger   : *Die Irrtümer des Historismus in der deutschen
Nationalökonomie, 1884.* [Republished in "Klein-
ere Schriften zur Methode und Geschichte der
Volkswirtschaftslehre," *Collected Works of Carl
Menger*, Vol. III, London School of Economics and
Political Science, 1935 (Reprint No. 19).]

    Menger   : "Grundzüge einer Klassifikation der Wirtschafts-
wissenschaften," in Conrad's *Jahrbuch für Nationalökonomie und Statistik*, N. F., Vol. XIX, 1889.
[Republished in "Kleinere Schriften zur Methode
und Geschichte der Volkswirtschaftslehre", *Collected Works of Carl Menger*, Vol. III, London

Features Of Austrian Theory Of Value —
Final Utility

What, now, are the peculiar features which the Austrian school presents in the domain of positive theory?

Their researches take their direction from the theory of value, the cornerstone being the well-known theory of final utility. This theory can be condensed into three unusually simple propositions. (1) The value of goods is measured by the importance of the want whose satisfaction is dependent upon the possession of the goods. (2) Which satisfaction is the dependent one can be determined very simply and infallibly by considering which want would be unsatisfied if the goods whose value is to be determined were not in possession. (3) And again, it is evident that the dependent satisfaction is not that satisfaction for the purpose of which the goods are actually used, but it is the least important of all the satisfactions which the total possessions of the individual can procure. Why? Because, according to very simple and unquestionably established prudential considerations of practical life, we are always careful to shift to the least sensitive point an injury to well-being which comes through loss of property. If we lose property that has been devoted to the satisfaction of a more important want, we do not sacrifice the satisfaction of this want, but simply withdraw other property which had been devoted to a less important satisfaction and put it in place of that which was lost. The loss thus falls upon the lesser utility, or — since we naturally give up the least important of all our satisfactions — upon the "final utility." Suppose a peasant has three sacks of corn: the first, a, for his support; the second, b, for seed; the third, c, for fattening poultry. Suppose sack a be destroyed by fire. Will the peasant on that account starve? Certainly not.

School of Economics and Political Science, 1935 (Reprint No. 19). English translation by Louise Sommer, "Toward A Systematic Classification of the Economic Sciences," Chapter I in *Essays in European Economic Thought*, D. Van Nostrand, New Jersey, 1960.]

Sax : *Das Wesen und die Aufgabe der Nationalökonomie*, 1884.

Philippovich : *Über Aufgabe und Methode der politischen Ökonomie*, 1886.

Böhm-Bawerk: "Grundzüge der Theorie des wirtschaftlichen Güterwerts," in Conrad's *Jahrbuch*, N.F., Vol. XIII, 1886, pp. 480ff. [Republished by London School of Economics and Political Science, 1932 (Reprint No. 11).] Review of Brentano's "Classische Nationalökonomie in the *Göttinger Gelehrten Anzeigen*, 1-6, 1889. Review of Schmoller's "Litteraturgeschichte" in Conrad's *Jahrbuch*, N. F., Vol. XX, 1890; translation in *Annals* of the American Academy, Vol. I, No. 2, October, 1890.

Or will he leave his field unsown? Certainly not. He will simply shift the loss to the least sensitive point. He will bake his bread from sack *c*, and consequently fatten no poultry. What is, therefore, really dependent upon the burning or not burning of sack *a* is only the use of the least important unit which may be substituted for it, or, as we call it, the final utility.

As is well known, the fundamental principle of this theory of the Austrian school is shared by certain other economists. A German economist, Gossen, had enunciated it in a book of his which appeared in 1854, but at that time it attracted not the slightest attention.[2] Somewhat later the same principle was almost simultaneously discovered in three different countries, by three economists who knew nothing of one another and nothing of Gossen — by the Englishman W. S. Jevons,[3] by C. Menger, the founder of the Austrian school,[4] and by the Swiss, Walras.[5] Professor J. B. Clark, too, an American investigator, came very near the same idea.[6] But the direction in which I believe the Austrians have outstripped their rivals, is the use they have made of the fundamental idea in the subsequent construction of economic theory. The idea of final utility is to the expert the open sesame, as it were, by which he unlocks the most complicated phenomena of economic life and solves the hardest problems of the science. In this art of explication lies, as it seems to me, the peculiar strength and the characteristic significance of the Austrian school.

The Vital Point: Final Utility Rests On Substitution Of Goods

And here everything turns upon one point: we need only take the trouble to discern the universal validity of the law of final utility throughout the manifold complications in which it is involved in the highly developed and varied economy of modern nations. This will cost us at the outset some trouble, but the effort will be well rewarded. For in the process we shall come upon all the important theoretical questions in their order, and, what is the chief point, we shall approach them from the side from which they appear in their most natural form, and from which we can most easily find a solution for them. I will attempt to

[2.] *Entwickelung der Gesetze des menschlichen Verkehrs.*
[3.] *Theory of Political Economy*, 1871, 2nd edition, 1879.
[4.] *Grundsätze der Volkswirtschaftslehre*, 1871. [English translation: *Principles of Economics*, The Free Press, Glencoe, Illinois, 1950.]
[5.] *Eléments d'économie politique pure*, 1874.
[6.] "Philosophy of Value," in the *New Englander*, July, 1881. Professor Clark was not then familiar, as he tells me, with the works of Jevons and Menger.

make this plain for a few of the most important cases, at least so far as it is possible to do so without entering into details of theory.

The law of final utility rests, as we have seen, upon a peculiar substitution of goods, due to sound prudential considerations. Those goods which can most easily be dispensed with must always stand ready to fill the breach which may at any time be made at a more important point. In the case of our peasant with the sacks of corn, the cause and the consequence of the substitution are very easy to understand. But in highly developed economic relations, important complications take place, since the substitution of goods will extend in various directions beyond the supply of goods of the same species.

The First Complication, Arising From Exchange

The first complication is that due to exchange. If the only winter coat I possess be stolen, I shall certainly not go shivering and endanger my health, but I shall simply buy another winter coat with twenty dollars which I should otherwise have spent for something else. Of course, then, I can buy only twenty dollars' worth less of other goods, and, of course, I shall make the retrenchment in goods which I think I can most easily dispense with; *i.e.*, whose utility, as in the foregoing example, is the least; in a word, I shall dispense with the final utility. Satisfactions, therefore, which are dependent upon whether or not I lose my winter coat are the satisfactions that are most easily dispensed with, the satisfactions which, in the given condition of my property and income I could have procured with twenty dollars more; and it is upon those other satisfactions, which may be very different in nature, that, through the workings of substitution by exchange, the loss, and with it the final utility dependent on it, is shifted.[7]

Escaping The "circulus vitiosus" Of The Expression, Supply And Demand, As Explanation For Price

If we carefully follow out this complication we shall come upon one of the most important of theoretical problems: namely, upon the relation between the market price of given goods, and the subjective estimate which individuals set upon those goods according to their very various wants and inclinations on the one hand, and their property and income on the other. I will merely remark in passing that the complete solution of this problem requires very subtle

7. Böhm-Bawerk, *Grundzüge*, pp. 38 and 49 [also, *Positive Theory of Capital*, p. 151f., Libertarian Press, South Holland, Illinois, 1959]; Wieser, *Der natürliche Wert*, 1889, p. 46ff. [English translation: *Natural Value*, Kelley and Millman, Inc., New York, 1956.]

investigation, which was first undertaken by the Austrian economists, and I will proceed to show the results which they have obtained. According to their conclusions, the price or "objective value" of goods is a sort of resultant of the different subjective estimates of the goods which the buyers and sellers make in accordance with the law of final utility; and indeed, the price coincides very nearly with the estimate of the "last buyer." It is well known that Jevons and Walras arrived at a similar law of price. Their statement, however, has considerable deficiencies, which were first supplied by the Austrians. It was the latter who first found the right way of escape from the *circulus vitiosus* in which the older theory of price as dependent upon supply and demand was involved. Since it was undeniable that, on the one hand, the price which can be asked in the market is influenced by the estimate which the buyer sets upon the goods, but, on the other hand, it is just as undeniable that in many cases the buyer's estimate is influenced by the state of the market (as, for instance, the final utility of my winter coat is materially less when I can replace it in the market for *ten* dollars than when it costs me twenty dollars); the theorists who found a more exact psychological explanation necessary for the law of supply and demand in general,[8] have usually allowed themselves to be beguiled into reasoning in a circle. They more or less openly explained the price by the estimate of the individual, and, vice versa, the estimate of the individual by the price. Of course, such a solution is not one upon which a science that wishes to deserve the name of a science can rest. An attempt to get to the bottom of the matter was first made by the Austrian economists by means of the subtle investigation of which I have spoken above.[9]

The Second Complication, Arising From "Production"

A second interesting and difficult complication of the substitution of goods is due to *production:* namely, given a

8. As, for example, in Germany, the highest authority on the theory of price, Hermann; cf. Böhm-Bawerk, *Grundzüge*, pp. 516, 527.

9. Austrian literature on the subject of price: Menger, *Grundsätze der Volkswirtschaftslehre*, p. 142ff. [*Principles*, 1950, 164ff.]; Böhm-Bawerk, "Grundzüge der Theorie des wirtschaftlichen Güterwerts," Part II, Conrad's *Jahrbuch*, N. F., Vol. XIII, p. 477ff., and on the point touched upon in the text, especially, p. 516; Wieser, *Der natürliche Wert*, p. 37ff. [*Natural Value*, 1956]; Sax, *Grundlegung der theoretischen Staatswirtschaft*, 1887, p. 276ff.; Zuckerkandl, *Zur Theorie des Preises*, 1889. I will not lose this opportunity to refer to the excellent account given by Dr. James Bonar, some years ago, of the Austrian economists and their view of value in the *Quarterly Journal of Economics*, October 1888.

sufficient time, the goods whose substitution is under consideration could be replaced by production. As in the former case the goods were replaced by the use of money, so in this case they can be replaced directly by the conversion of materials of production. But, of course, there will be less of these materials of production left for other purposes, and just as surely as before the necessary diminution of production will be shifted to that class of goods which can be most easily dispensed with, which is considered least valuable.

Take Wieser's example:[10] If a nation finds weapons necessary to the defense of its honor or its existence, it will produce them from the same iron which would otherwise have been used for other necessary, but more or less dispensable utensils. What, therefore, happens to the people through the necessity of procuring weapons is that they can have only somewhat less of the most dispensable utensils which they would have made of the iron; in other words, the loss falls upon the least utility, or the final utility, which could have been derived from the materials of production necessary to the manufacture of the weapons.

How The Foregoing Leads To The Determination Of Value Of Goods Producible At Will

From this point, again, the way leads to one of the most important theoretical principles, which under a certain form has long been familiar. This principle is that the value of those goods which can be reproduced at will without hindrance shows a tendency to coincide with the cost of production. This principle comes to light as a special case of the law of final utility, occurring under given actual conditions. The "cost of production" is nothing else than the sum of all the materials of production by means of which the goods or a substitute for the same can be reproduced. Since then, as pointed out in the foregoing, the value of the goods is determined by the final utility of their substitute, it follows that so far as that substitution can be made *ad libitum*, the value of the product must coincide with the final utility and value of the materials of production, or, as is usually said, with the cost of production.

"Cost" Is Not The Regulator Of Value, But The Value Of The Completed Product Determines The Value Of Factors Of Production Which Are Used

As to the final cause of this coincidence the Austrians have a theory quite different from the older one. The older theory explained the relation between cost and value to be

10.   *Der natürliche Wert*, p. 170 [*Natural Value*, 1956].

such that cost was cause, indeed the final cause, while the value of the product was the effect; it supposed the scientific problem of explaining the value of goods to be satisfactorily solved when it had appealed to cost as the "ultimate regulator of value." The Austrians, on the contrary, believe that herein only half, and by far the easier half, of the explanation is to be found. The cost is identical with the value of the materials of production necessary to the manufacture of the goods. Cost rises when and because the materials of production (fuel, machinery, rent, labor) rise; it falls when and because the value of the materials declines. Hence, it is evident that the value of materials of production must first be explained. And the interesting point is that when the explanation is carefully carried out it leads us to see that the value of the completed product is the cause. For without doubt we place a high estimate upon materials of production only when and because they are capable of furnishing valuable products. The relation of cause and effect is, therefore, exactly the reverse of what the older theory stated. The older theory explained the value of the product as the effect, and the cost — that is, the value of the materials of production — as the cause, and thought no further explanation necessary. The Austrian economists found: (1) that the value of the materials of production needs, first of all, to be explained; and (2) that after this explanation is made, and after the net of complicated relations is untangled, the value of the materials of production is seen in the end to be the effect, and the value of the product the cause.

The Correct Principle Has Long Been Recognized In Specific Cases, But The General Principle Has Not Been Appreciated

I know very well that this thesis will seem strange to many readers at the first glance. I cannot here attempt to demonstrate it or even to guard it against certain misapprehensions to which it is liable. I will call attention to only one circumstance. In the case of certain materials of production, whose true causal connection was for special reasons easy to see, the old theory recognized the principle; as, for instance, in regard to the value of the use of land, which is expressed in rent, Adam Smith observed that the price of the products of the soil is not high or low because rent is high or low; but, vice versa, rent is high or low according as the price of the product is high or low. Or again, no one supposes that copper is dear because the stock of the mining companies is high; but obviously the value of the mines and the stock is high when and because copper is dear. Now, just as well might the water of one river flow up hill while that of the river beside it flows down, as that in the case of different sorts of materials of production the causal connections should run in opposite directions. The law is one and the same for all materials of production. The difference is only that in case of certain materials the true relation of cause and effect is very easy to see, while in others, owing to manifold obscuring complications, it is very hard to see. The establishment of the law for those cases also, when deceptive appearances had led to the opposite explanation, is one of the most important contributions of the Austrian school.

Perhaps it is the most important of all. Every political economist knows what a vast part cost of production plays in the theory of political economy — in the theory of production no less than in that of value and price, and in this no less than in that of distribution, rent, wages, profit on capital, international trade, etc. It is safe to say that there is not one important phenomenon of economic life for the explanation of which we are not compelled either directly or indirectly to appeal to cost of production. And here rises the question which having once been thrown into the world is no more to be put out of it: What place does this much-appealed-to cost properly hold in the system of phenomena and their explanation? Does it play the part of a center about which as a fixed and absolute middle point all the other phenomena of value turn? Or is cost, the value of materials of production, in spite of all contradictory appearances, the variable part, determined by the value of the product?

Vacillation Is Not Justified; Either Costs Regulate Value, Or Value Regulates Costs

That is a question as fundamental for political economy as the question between the Ptolemaic and Copernican systems was for astronomy. The sun and earth turn, as every child knows, but one cannot be much of an astronomer today without knowing whether the earth turns about the sun or the sun about the earth. Between the value of the product and the value of the materials of production there exists a no less obvious and indubitable relation. But whoever wishes to understand this relation and the countless phenomena that depend upon it must know whether the value of the materials of production is derived from the value of the product or the reverse. From the first instant when this alternative comes into view in discussion everyone who wishes to be an economist must have an opinion, and a definite opinion. An eclectic vacillation, such as up to this time has been almost universal, will not do; in a scientific system we cannot have the earth turning about the sun and the sun turning about the earth alternately. Whoever, therefore, today wishes to contend that the cost of production is "the ultimate regulator of value" may continue to do so; but he will not find his task so easy as it has been heretofore. We shall justly expect him to attempt to explain to the bottom, without deficiency or contradiction, in accordance with his principle, the phenomena of value, and especially the value of materials of production. Probably, if he takes his task seriously, he will come upon difficulties. If he does not find them himself he must at least take account of those which others have met in the same path, by which they have finally been compelled to attempt the explanation of phenomena of value according to the opposite principle. At any rate, this part of economic theory will in future be treated with a considerably greater degree of care and scientific profundity than has before now been customary, unless our science wishes to deserve the reproach which has both in former and later days been so often cast upon it; that it is more a babbling over economic matters than a real, earnest science.[11]

The Problem Of The Valuation Of Complementary Goods

The question of the relation of cost to value is properly only a concrete form of a much more general question — the question of the regular relations between the values of such goods as in causal interdependence contribute to one and the same utility for our well-being. The utility furnished by a quantity of materials from which a coat can be produced is apparently identical with the utility which the completed coat will furnish. It is thus obvious that goods or groups of goods which derive their importance to our welfare through the medium of one and the same utility must also stand in some fixed, regular relation to one another in respect to their value. The question of this regular relation was first put into clear and comprehensive form by the Austrian economists; it had previously been treated only in a very unsatisfactory manner under the head of "cost of production." There is, however, a corollary to this general and important proposition which is not less important and interesting, but which has hitherto never received the modest degree of attention in economic theory which has been bestowed upon the problem of cost.

11. Austrian literature on the relation of cost and value: Menger, *Grundsätze*, p. 123ff. [*Principles*, 1950, p. 149ff.]; Wieser, *Über den Ursprung und die Hauptgesetze des wirtschaftlichen Wertes*, 1884, p. 139ff.; *Der natürliche Wert*, p. 164ff. [*Natural Value*, 1956]; Böhm-Bawerk, *Grundzüge*, p. 61ff., p. 534ff.; *Positive Theorie des Kapitals*, 1889, p. 189ff., p. 234ff. [*Positive Theory*, 1959, pp. 121-256].

Very commonly several goods combine simultaneously to the production of one common utility; for example, paper, pen, and ink serve together for writing; needle and thread for sewing; farming utensils, seed, land and labor for the production of grain. Menger has called goods that stand in such relation to one another "complementary goods." Here rises the question, as natural as it is difficult: How much of the common utility is in such cases to be attributed to each of the cooperative complementary factors? and what law determines the proportionate value and price of each?

The fate of this problem hitherto has been very remarkable. The older theory did not rank it as a general problem at all, but was nevertheless compelled to decide a series of concrete cases which depended *implicitè* upon that problem. The question of the distribution of goods especially gave occasion for such decisions. Since several factors of production — soil, capital, hired labor, and labor of the employer himself—cooperate in the production of a common product, the question as to what share of value shall be assigned to each of the factors, in compensation for its assistance, is obviously a special case of the general problem.

**The Old Bad Habit Of Circular Reasoning
On The Value Of Complementary Goods**

Now, how were these concrete cases decided? Each one was decided by itself without regard to the others, and hence, eventually, they formed a complete circle. The process was as follows: If rent was to be explained, it was decided that to the soil belonged the remainder of the product after the payment of cost of production, under which term was included the compensation of all the other factors — capital, labor, and profit of manager. Here the function of all the other factors was regarded as fixed or known and the soil was put off with a remainder varying according to the quantity of the product. If then it was necessary in another chapter to determine the profits of the entrepreneur, it was decided again that to him should be given the overplus left after all the other factors were compensated. In this case the share of the soil, the rent, was reckoned along with labor, capital, etc., as fixed, and the entrepreneur's profit was treated as the variable, rising and falling with the quantity of the product. In just the same manner the share of capital was treated in a third chapter. The capitalist, says Ricardo, receives what is left from the product after the payment of wages. And as if to satirize all these classical dogmas, last of all, Mr. F. A. Walker has completed the circle by stating that the laborer receives what is left over from all the other factors.

The Error Of Attempting To
Evade The General Problem

It is easy to see that these statements lead in a circle, and to see, also, why they so lead. The reasoners have simply neglected to state the problem in a general form. They had several unknown quantities to determine, and instead of taking the bull by the horns and straightway inquiring after the general principle, according to which a common economic result should be divided into its component factors, they tried to avoid the fundamental question — that of the general principle. They divided up the investigation, and in this partial investigation allowed themselves each time to treat as unknown that one of the unknown quantities which formed the special object of the investigation, but to treat the others, for the time being, as if known. They thus shut their eyes to the fact that a few pages earlier or later they had reversed the operation and had treated the supposed known quantity as unknown, the unknown as known.

After the Classical school came the Historical. As often happens, they took the attitude of sceptical superiority and declared altogether insoluble the problem which they were unable to solve. They thought it to be in general impossible to say, for example, what per cent of the value of a statue is due to the sculptor and what per cent to the marble.

Now if the problem be but rightly put, that is, if we wish to separate the economic and not the physical shares, the problem becomes soluble. It is actually solved in practice in all rational enterprises by every agriculturalist or manufacturer; and theory has nothing to do but rightly and carefully to hold up the mirror to practice in order in turn to find the theoretical solution. To this end the theory of final utility helps in the simplest way. It is the old song again. Only observe correctly what the final utility of each complementary factor is, or what utility the presence or absence of the complementary factor would add or substract, and the calm pursuit of such inquiry will of itself bring to light the solution of the supposed insoluble problem. The Austrians made the first earnest attempt in this direction. Menger and the author of this paper have treated the question under the heading, *Theorie der komplementären Güter* (Theory of Complementary Goods); Wieser has treated the same subject under the title, *Theorie der Zurechnung* (Theory of Contribution). The latter, especially, has in an admirable manner shown how the problem should be put, and that it *can* be solved; Menger has, in the happiest manner, as it seems to me, pointed out the method of solution.[12]

I have called the law of complementary goods the counterpart of the law of cost. As the former disentangles the relations of value which result from temporal and causal *juxtaposition,* from the simultaneous cooperation of several factors toward one common utility; so the law of cost explains the relations of value which result from temporal and causal *sequence,* from the causal interdependence of successive factors. "By means of the former the meshes of the complicated network represented by the mutual value relations of the cooperating factors are disentangled, so to speak, in their length and breadth; by the latter in their depth; but both processes occur within the all-embracing law of final utility, of which both laws are only special applications to special problems."[13]

Austrian Contributions To The Theories Of Distribution, Capital, Wages, Profits And Rent

Thus prepared, the Austrian economists finally proceed to the problems of distribution. These resolve themselves into a series of special applications of the general theoretical laws, the knowledge of which was obtained by a tedious, but scarcely unfruitful, work of preparation. Land, labor, and capital are complementary factors of production. Their price, or what is the same thing, rate of rent, wages, and interest, results simply from a combination of the laws which govern the value of the materials of production on the one hand with the laws of complementary goods on the other hand. The particular views of the Austrians on these subjects I will here omit. I could not, if I would, give in this paper any proper statement of their conclusions, still less a demonstration of them; I must content myself with giving a passing view of the matters with which they are busied, and, where it is possible, of the spirit in which they work. I only briefly remark, therefore, that they have set forth a new and comprehensive theory of capital[14] into

---

12. Menger, *Grundsätze,* p. 138ff. [*Principles,* 1950, 162ff.]; Böhm-Bawerk, *Grundzüge,* Part I, p. 56ff.; *Positive Theorie,* p. 178ff. [*Positive Theory,* 1959, pp. 161-168]; Wieser, *Der natürliche Wert,* p. 67ff. [*Natural Value,* 1956].

13. Böhm-Bawerk, *Positive Theorie,* p. 201 [*Positive Theory,* 1959, pp. 121-256, especially pp. 151-156, 161-168, 177, 248-256].

14. Böhm-Bawerk, KAPITAL UND KAPITALZINS: I *Geschichte und Kritik der Kapitalzinstheorien,* 1884; II *Positive Theorie des Kapitales,* 1889 [CAPITAL AND INTEREST, 1959, Libertarian Press, South Holland, Illinois: I *History and Critique of Interest Theories;* II *Positive Theory of Capital;* III *Further Essays on Capital and Interest*]; differing from the older teaching of Menger's *Grundsätze,* p. 143ff. [*Principles,* 1950, p. 165ff.].

which they have woven a new theory of wages,[15] besides repeatedly working out the problems of the entrepreneur's profits,[16] and of rent.[17] In the light of the theory of final utility, the last-named problem in particular finds an easy and simple solution, which confirms Ricardo's theory in its actual results and corroborates its reasoning in many details.

Of course, all the possible applications of the law of final utility have by no means been made. It is more nearly true that they are scarcely begun. I may mention in passing that certain Austrian economists have attempted a broad application of the law in the field of finance;[18] others to certain difficult and interesting questions of jurisprudence.[19]

The Hitherto-Neglected Doctrine Of Economic Goods

Finally, in connection with the foregoing efforts, much trouble has been taken to improve the implements, so to speak, with which the science has to work, to clear up the most important fundamental conceptions. And, as often happens, the Austrian economists find most to improve and correct in a department which has heretofore passed as so plain and simple that the literature of several nations — the English, for example — has scarcely a word to say about it. I refer to the doctrine of economic goods. Menger has put a logical implement into the hands of science in his conception, as simple as it is suggestive, of the subordination of goods (*Güterordnungen*),[20] a conception which will be useful in all future investigation. The writer of this paper has especially endeavored to analyze a conception which appears to be the simplest of all, but which is most

[15]. Böhm-Bawerk, *Positive Theorie, passim* and pp. 450-452 [*Positive Theory*, 1959, pp. 308-312].

[16]. Mataja, *Der Unternehmergewinn*, 1884; Gross, *Die Lehre vom Unternehmergewinn*, 1884.

[17]. Menger, *Grundsätze*, p. 133ff. [*Principles*, 1950, p. 157ff.]; Wieser, *Der natürliche Wert*, p. 112ff. [*Natural Value*, 1956]; Böhm-Bawerk, *Positive Theorie*, p. 380ff. [*Positive Theory*, 1959, pp. 334-337].

[18]. Robert Meyer, *Die Principien der gerechten Besteuerung*, 1884; Sax, *Grundlegung*, 1887; Wieser, *Der natürliche Wert*, p. 209ff. [*Natural Value*, 1956].

[19]. Mataja, *Das Recht des Schadenersatzes*, 1888; Seidler, "Die Geldstrafe vom volkswirtschaftlichen und sozialpolitischen Gesichtspunkt," Conrad's *Jahrbuch*, N. F. Vol. XX, 1890.

[20]. Menger, *Grundsätze*, p. 8ff. [*Principles*, 1950, p. 55ff.].

obscure and most misused: the conception of use of goods (*Gebrauch der Güter*).[21]

Increasing Attention To Practical Problems

Questions of practical political economy, on the contrary, have only just begun to be made the subjects of literary work by the Austrian economists.[22] This, however, by no means implies that they have no faculty for the practical needs of economic life, and still less, that they do not wish to connect their abstract theory with practice. The contrary is true. But we must build the house before we can set it in order, and so long as we have our hands full with simply raising the framework of our theory, there is little obligation to devote to numerous questions of practical detail that amount of time-absorbing care which their literary elaboration would require. We have our opinions upon them, we teach them from our chairs, but our literary activities have thus far been bestowed almost exclusively upon theoretical problems, for these are not only the fundamental ones, but are those whose long-continued neglect by the other side, the Historical School, must be repaired.

Purpose Of The Austrians; Renaissance Of Economic Theory; Character Of That Renaissance

What, now, is the short meaning of this long story? What is the significance to the science as a whole of the advent of a set of men who teach this and that in regard to goods, value, cost, capital, and a dozen other subjects? Has it any significance at all? In answering this question I feel the embarrassment of belonging to the group of men whose activity is under discussion. I must, therefore, confine myself to the statement of what the Austrian economists as a body are trying to effect; others may judge whether or not they are successful.

What they are striving for is a sort of *renaissance* of economic theory. The old classical theory, admirable as it was for its time, had the character of a collection of fragmentary acquisitions which had been brought into orderly relations neither with one another nor with the fundamental principles of human science. Our knowledge is only patchwork at best, and must always remain so. But of the classical theory this characterization was particularly

21. Böhm-Bawerk, *Rechte und Verhältnisse vom Standpunkt der volkswirtschaftlichen Güterlehre*, 1881, p. 57ff. [English translation: *Whether Legal Rights and Relationships Are Economic Goods*, p. 70ff. in this volume]; *Positive Theorie*, p. 361ff. [*Positive Theory*, 1959, p. 325ff.].

22. By Sax, for example, *Die Verkehrsmittel in Volks- und Staatswirtschaft*, 1878-79; Philippovich, *Die Bank von England*, 1885; *Der badische Staatshaushalt*, 1889.

and emphatically true. With the insight of genius it had discovered a mass of regularities in the whirlpool of economic phenomena, and with no less genius, though hindered by the difficulties that beset beginnings, it commenced the interpretation of these regularities. It usually succeeded, also, in following the thread of explanation to a greater or less distance from the surface toward the depths. But beyond a certain depth it always, without exception, lost the clue. To be sure, the classical economists well knew to what point all their explanations must be traced — to the care of mankind for its own well-being, which, undisturbed by the incursion of altruistic motives, is the ultimate motive-force of all economic action. But owing to a certain circumstance the middle term of the explanation, by means of which the actual conduct of men, in the establishment of prices of goods, of wages, rent, etc., ought to have been joined to the fundamental motive of regard for utility — this middle term was always wrong. That circumstance was the following: A Crusoe has to do only with goods; in modern economic life we have to do with goods and with human beings from whom we obtain the goods we use — by means of exchange, cooperation, and the like. The economy of a Crusoe is explained when we succeed in showing what relation exists between our well-being and material commodities, and what attitude the care for our well-being requires us to take toward such material commodities. To explain the modern economic order there is, apparently, need of two processes: (1) just as in Crusoe's economy, we must understand the relation of our interests to external goods; (2) we must seek to understand the laws, according to which we pursue our interests when they are entangled with the interests of others.

Two Distinct Problems: Relations Of Men To Things; Relations Of Men To Each Other

No one has ever been deluded into thinking that this second process is not difficult and involved — not even the classical economists. But, on the other hand, they fatally underrated the difficulties of the first process. They believed that as regards the relation of men to external goods, there was nothing at all to be explained, or, speaking more exactly, determined. Men need goods to supply their wants; men desire them and assign to them in respect of their utility a value in use. That is all the classical economists knew or taught in regard to the relation of men to goods. While value in exchange was discussed and explained in extensive chapters, from the time of Adam Smith to that of Mr. Macvane, value in use was commonly dismissed in two lines, and often with the added statement that value in use had nothing to do with value in exchange.

Past Underestimation Of Problems Of Relations Of Men To Things; The Yawning Defect Of Classical Economics

It is a fact, however, that the relation of men to goods is by no means so simple and uniform. The modern theory of final utility in its application to cost of production, complementary goods, etc., shows that the relation between our well-being and goods is capable of countless degrees, and all these degrees exert a force in our efforts to obtain goods by exchange with others. Here yawns the great and fatal chasm in the classical theory; it attempts to show how we pursue our interests in relation to goods in opposition to other men without thoroughly understanding the interest itself. Naturally the attempts at explanation are incoherent. The two processes of explanation must fit together like the two cogwheels of a machine. But as the classical economists had no idea what the shape and cogging of the first wheel should be, of course they could not give to the second wheel a proper constitution. Thus, beyond a certain depth, all their explanations degenerate into a few general commonplaces, and these are fallacious in their generalization.

This is the point at which the renaissance of theory must begin, and, thanks to the efforts of Jevons and his followers, as well as to the Austrian school, it has already begun. In that most general and elementary part of economic theory through which every complicated economic explanation must eventually lead, we must give up *dilettanti* phrases for real scientific inquiry. We must not weary of studying the microcosm if we wish rightly to understand the macrocosm of a developed economic order. This is the turning-point which is reached at one time or another in all sciences. We universally begin by taking account of the great and striking phenomena, passing unobservant over the world of little every-day phenomena. But there always comes a time when we discover with astonishment that the complications and riddles of the macrocosm occur in still more remarkable manner in the smallest, apparently simplest elements — when we apprehend that we must seek the key to an understanding of the phenomena of great things in the study of the world of small things. The physicists began with the motions and laws of the great heavenly bodies; today they are studying nothing more busily than the theory of the molecule and the atom, and from no part of natural science do we expect more important developments for the eventual understanding of the whole than from the minutiæ of chemistry. In the organic world the most highly developed and mightiest organisms once roused the greatest interest. Today that interest is given to the simplest microorganisms. We study the structure of cells and of amœbæ, and look everywhere for bacilli. I am convinced that it will not be otherwise in economic theory. The significance of the theory of final utility does not lie in the fact that it is a more correct theory of value than a dozen other older theories, but in fact that it marks the approach of that characteristic crisis in the science of economic phenomena. It shows for once that in an apparently simple thing, the relation of man to external goods, there is room for endless complications; that underneath these complications lie fixed laws, the discovery of which demands all the acumen of the investigator; but that in the discovery of those laws is accomplished the greater part of the investigation of the conduct of men in economic intercourse with one another. The candle lighted within sheds its light outside the house.

Discontent With The Necessity Of Rebuilding The Science Of Economics Is Not Apropos; We Must Build Better Than The Pioneers In Economics

It may, of course, be to many who call themselves political economists a very inconvenient and unpleasant surprise to find that to the field which they have heretofore ploughed with intellectual toil, another new field is added — a field by no means small, whose tillage is particularly laborious. How convenient it has been heretofore to conclude an explanation of phenomena of price with reference to the shibboleth of "supply and demand" or "cost"! And now, on a sudden, these supposed pillars tremble, and we are forced to build the foundations far deeper, at the cost of great and tedious labor.

Whether inconvenient or not, there is no other course left us than to do the work which past generations have neglected. The classical economists are excusable for having neglected it. In their time, when everything was yet new and undiscovered, investigation *per saltum*, scientific exploitation, so to speak, might bring rich results. But now it is otherwise. In the first place, we of later times, since we have not the merit of being pioneers of the science, should not lay claim to the privilege of pioneers: the requirements have become higher. If we do not wish to remain behind the other sciences, we too must bring into our science a strict order and discipline, which we are still far from having. Let us not be beguiled into vain self-satisfaction. Mistakes and omissions are, of course, to be expected at

any time, in every science; but our "systems" still swarm
with the commonplace, superficial faults, whose frequent
occurrence is a sure sign of the primitive state of a science.
That our expositions end in smoke before essentials are
reached; that they evaporate in empty phrases as soon as
they begin to be difficult; that the most important problems are not even stated; that we reason in the most undis-
guised circle; that not only within the same system, but
even within the same chapter, contradictory theories of
one and the same matter are upheld; that by a disorderly
and ambiguous terminology we are led into the most pal-
pable mistakes and misunderstandings — all these failings
are of so frequent occurrence in our science that they almost
seem to be characteristic of its style. I can easily understand how the representatives of other sciences, which have
become amenable to strict discipline, look down with a
sort of pity upon many a famous work of political economy,
and deny to the latter the character of a true science.

The German Historical School Has Not Contributed
Much To Solution Of The Problem Of Improving Economics

This state of affairs must and shall be changed. The
Historical School, which for the last forty years has given
the keynote to all Germany, has unfortunately done nothing
at all to this end. On the contrary, in its blind terror of
"abstract" reasoning and through the cheap scepticism with
which at almost every important point in the system it
declares the given problems "insoluble," and the struggles
to discover scientific laws hopeless, it has done its utmost
to discourage and obstruct the scanty efforts that have been
directed toward the desired end. I do not ignore the fact
that in another direction, in the provision of vast empirical
stores, they have conferred great benefit; but future time
will impartially show how much they have helped in this
direction and harmed in the other with their one-sided zeal.

But what both the classical and the historical schools
have neglected, the Austrian school is today trying to
accomplish. Nor are they alone in the struggle. In England,
since the days of Jevons, kindred efforts, to which the
great thinker gave the impulse, have been carried forward
by his worthy associates and followers; and incited partly
by Jevons, partly by the Austrian school, a surprisingly
great number of investigators, of all nations, have in recent
times turned to the new ideas. The great Dutch literature
is devoted almost entirely to them; in France, Denmark
and Sweden they have gained an entrance. In Italian and
American literature they are almost daily propagated; and
even in Germany, the stronghold of the Historical School,

against whose resistance the ground must be fought for almost inch by inch, the new tendency has taken a strong and influential position.

Can it be that the tendency which possesses so great a power of attraction is nothing but error? Does it not in reality spring from a need of our science, and supply a need which has long been repressed by one-sided methods, but which must eventually make itself felt — the need of real scientific depth?

EUGEN VON BÖHM-BAWERK

II

Whether Legal Rights And Relationships Are Economic Goods*

George D. Huncke Translation

*The title of the German original is *Rechte und Verhältnisse vom Standpunkte der volkswirtschaftlichen Güterlehre*, Verlag der Wagner'schen Universitäts-Buchhandlung, Innsbruck, Austria, 1881.

Contents

Publisher's Preface To English Translation

Böhm-Bawerk entitled this essay, *Rechte und Verhält-nisse vom Standpunkte der Volkswirtschaftlichen Güter-lehre,* and designated it a "critical study." If the title were transliterated into English, it would be *Legal Rights and Relationships from the Viewpoint of the Economic Doctrine of Goods.*

The subject matter of the essay is in the field of economic *theory,* a field which does not greatly interest some economists, in these times when statistics and economic history have come to the fore. Nevertheless, careful thinkers will realize that the meticulous and critical thought pattern manifested by Böhm-Bawerk is a requisite to laying a solid foundation under economics *as a science.* If the conclusions of this study *appear* limited, they are, in compensation to that, fundamental.

The *great* thinkers of the world have devoted major attention to definition of terms. Socrates comes to mind as a classic example. This essay attempts to purge an economic term, *good* or *goods,* of erroneous content and accretions.

Readers who will most appreciate this essay are those who are combination economists-logicians, or economists-philosophers. They will note that Böhm-Bawerk is a modern *nominalist* with an "approach" which is similar to that of William of Ockham (or Occam), the famous scholastic thinker, whose critique of the method of scholasticism tolled its death-knell and heralded the modern world. However valuable the *conclusions* of this essay may be, the Ockham-type *method* which it employs is even more valuable.

Ockham was critical of the content of general terms, and decried proliferating them, having become convinced by his exploration of terms that a delusory world was being created out of mere words. His famous formula was *Entia non sunt multiplicanda praeter necessitatem,* that is, terms should not be multiplied beyond necessity.

Böhm-Bawerk's essay is the unrivalled example, in economics, of Ockham's method.

Publisher's Note On Translator

Mr. George D. Huncke, translator of *Whether Legal Rights and Relationships Are Economic Goods* finished his work on this translation just prior to leaving the United States in March, 1960 in order to spend the summer or longer in Germany. His health had not been good. He hoped that a European trip would be beneficial. But he passed away in Kassel, Germany on May 11. It is a disappointment to us that Mr. Huncke did not live to see his translation in book form. To be a good translator of the works of an author as Eugen von Böhm-Bawerk requires the possession of extraordinary talents. In Mr. Huncke's memory, and in recognition of his excellent work as a translator, it is fitting that this mention of his last major labor before his death be recorded with appreciation.

Frederick Nymeyer

South Holland, Illinois
August, 1960

Author's Preface

In the pages presented here I have attempted to furnish a definitive and unambiguous solution of a question which, despite the simplicity of the subject with which it deals, has in the past furnished abundant grounds for error and misunderstanding and which, indeed, continues to furnish such grounds to this day. I am referring to the question of the true economic nature of those "rights and contractual relationships" which have come to occupy so anomalous a position beside the other constituents of that group of phenomena we call economic goods and which differ so markedly from those remaining members of that group to which they seek to gain entrance. That difference consists pre-eminently in the incorporeity which sets them apart from those members, namely, from concrete and objective material goods and from personal renditions of service.

In making this attempt, I was equally concerned to treat both of the two phases that this subject seemed to me to present. The first of these phases was a solution of the special and specific problem which appeared to me as, in and of itself, by no means unimportant and, furthermore, one that economic theory has, up to the present, been content to examine but cursorily and to regard as "taken care of" by mere approximations and generalizations rather than as worthy of a solution that is meticulous and exhaustive. The second phase of the question that caused me concern was the possibility that an examination into this special and specific problem might serve to shed more light upon some general, basic and fundamental tenet of economic theory and thus become a vantage point from which a revision of those fundamentals might be undertaken. I refer in particular to the basic *economic doctrine of the theory of goods*. I do not hesitate to make unblushing acknowledgment that our goods theory was in need of correction in several respects, or at least of such revision as to make it truly comprehensive and universally valid. And that it was incumbent upon us economists to strive for such comprehensiveness and universality struck me as increasingly imperative and, indeed, imperative in just such measure as I felt it to be essential that systematic soundness characterize an economic tenet embodying concepts and truths fundamental to every economic train of thought.

However highly one may, on other points, esteem enco- miums for originality, the author of these lines is anxious *in this very matter* to forgo praise on that score. Since it would seem to be true that, the more original a doctrine concerning such simple matters is, the more artificial it usually turns out to be, the author of these lines would prefer, by far, rather than appear as the originator of a new doctrine, to appear in the eyes of a large number of readers as a mere interpreter of well-known views — views which those readers have themselves long harbored, or which they have themselves uttered, though they may not yet have refined and distilled them to a degree of clarity that constitutes complete invulnerability to all possibility of contradiction or which they have, perhaps, not uttered or elaborated upon for the mere reason that they are thoroughly convinced of the completely axiomatic and self-evident na- ture of those views. Whatever loss, under such circum- stances, may be mine as an author is counterbalanced by the gain to the cause itself: and that should, after all, be a source of adequate satisfaction to any author. For he is, presumably, more concerned with convincing his readers than with astonishing them.

He need have no misgivings lest he may have expended his writing efforts on material that is all too obvious or self-evident, so long as the simplicity of his material be not patent by reason of the unanimity and incontrover- tibility of the general body of opinion that prevails with reference to that material.

It is my hope, therefore, that this small contribution to the subject will encounter friendly reception.

EUGEN VON BÖHM-BAWERK

Innsbruck, Austria
February 1881

Introduction

The science of economics presents several problems of unpretentious aspect which, at first blush, seem to lie outside the direct line of the development of that science and to be worthy only of secondary interest on the part of those who feel any concern for the minutiae of scientific detail. However, these problems, as soon as they are at all closely examined, reveal many connections with important questions that occupy a position in the very forefront of discussion—connections so numerous and important that not even the most captious critics will relegate consideration of these problems to the category of idle speculation.

One of these unpretentious problems is that of legal rights and contractual relationships and of the position they occupy as one category among those things into which are divided the "goods" which constitute the primary material with which economic science makes it its business to deal. The question arises: *Are legal rights and contractual relationships in sober fact genuine economic goods —that is to say, are they goods in the sense in which the science of economics uses and must use that term? Can they, by their nature, be such goods? And what, indeed, is that nature? And what is the economic significance of these abstract and nonmaterial things which play so important a part in economic life?*

This is not the first time that questions of this and similar content have engaged the attention of economic theorists. Altercations on the question of whether nonmaterial things could, in any event, be regarded as goods and as objects of wealth in the economic sense took up no inconsiderable amount of space in the textbooks on economic theory during the first half of the nineteenth century. And since that time at least one German economist has been moved to express himself in a highly significant monograph[1] on the subject. He was particularly concerned about the puzzling questions rising from such nonmaterial "goods" as are represented by rights and relationships. In short, there is evidence enough that questions of this kind are not, in and of themselves, unworthy of the attention that I claim for them.

There still remains the question of whether or not the treatment that has been accorded the subject does or does not exhaust it. Can it be said that the investigations hereto-fore devoted to the subject have so completely clarified it, that nothing more remains to be explained, and that whenever future questions on this matter arise, the economist

[1.] Schäffle, *Theorie der ausschliessenden Absatzverhältnisse,* Tübingen, 1864.

need but refer to the record where complete knowledge has been stored up for him? That question is so important to the justification of the existence of this present essay that I cannot escape the duty of devoting some words to it at this introductory juncture. That duty is the more compelling because for so long a time there has been complete silence in the field of polemical discussion on the subject of "nonmaterial goods." Indeed, the time has been so long that it might be all too easy to assume that the question has achieved the position of a *res adjudicata,* a place in our textbooks on economics which is definite, if not definitive, and hence all the more undisputed.

To be sure, my readers are unlikely to demand, at this point, any conclusive *proof* that the subject is still in need of discussion, and that such discussion is therefore not supererogatory. For, in the nature of such things, such proof is more appropriate at the end of a discussion than at its beginning. And the best proof of all would be furnished tacitly by the contents of such an essay itself. However, in order not to be completely remiss in the matter, I shall attempt to submit at this point a certain amount of what might be termed in juridical parlance testimony that is relevant and material.

I believe that two facts will qualify as such testimony. The first is the history of how these pages came to be written. The author has been impelled to write them down, not by a purely gratuitous penchant for theorizing, but rather by a conviction that he was meeting a completely practical need. For it was in the course of his research into a subject of highly practical import, namely, the doctrine of capital and interest, that he made the rather astonishing discovery that a whole series of economic concepts and images, which are of fundamental importance to that doctrine, and which economists generally have long supposed to be quite clear and incontestable, actually do not possess the clarity we are generally disposed to attribute to them, nor, indeed, that clarity which is indispensable in the case of concepts which are to serve as the foundation for continuing development and construction on the part of any science.

I discovered that the concepts and images employed in the field of the *doctrine of goods* were especially subject to ambiguity and lack of clarity.

It was this practical experience which moved me to institute an examination—by way of preparation, if you will—into certain phases of the theory of economic goods which were pertinent to the principal field of my research,

capital and interest. And I submit to the reader a portion
of that examination with the assurance that it was em-
barked upon with entirely practical rather than abstractly
theoretical interest.

However, since my testimony itself is based all too
emphatically upon the subjective experience of the author
himself, it becomes imperative to submit a second and
more objective bit of testimony. I can think of nothing
more appropriate, in that respect, than the fact that misguided or erroneous views concerning this topic have frequently, even in most recent times, given rise to erroneous
economic doctrines which have exerted widespread influence. And I am also convinced that the only road to successful and logical refutation of these erroneous doctrines
lies in the correction of certain of their basic concepts which
err, specifically, in the area of their theories of economic
goods. The erroneous doctrine that I have specifically in
mind right now is the view, well known and widely held,
that credit not only *conveys* goods, but actually *creates*
them; and the theorist's contribution to the theory of goods
which is adduced in support of that view is the idea that
a legal right to make a demand constitutes an independent
or an "intangible" good.

I need not go into minute detail to awaken in my reader
considerations which will bear sufficiently persuasive testimony to the essential inadequacy of that portion of the
economic goods theory which bears on the point of the
subject we are here dealing with.

It is a matter of common knowledge that in recent
times there has appeared in MacLeod a modern protagonist
of the doctrine of the power of credit to create goods. It
is a doctrine enunciated in the century preceding our own*
by John Law and one which it seemed had gone out with
Law himself. Now MacLeod is a scholar of originality and
acuity who lays at the door of economic theory the reproach that it has, in the past, overlooked one enormous
group of *goods,* namely, debts. A debt, says MacLeod, is
of itself an intangible good which has present value, and
the debtor himself has, for the time being, no power to
reduce its value, for, while he will at some future time be
obliged to meet the debt, he is not obligated to do so at the
present time. Therefore, MacLeod argues, it is a fallacy
to state, *Tout crédit n'est qu'un emprunt* [All credit is
merely a loan]. Credit, says MacLeod, creates debts and
thereby creates a number of "intangible goods." It is therefore not merely a means for the conveyance of existing
products but also for the "creation of wealth." MacLeod

* Translator's Note: Böhm-Bawerk was writing in the year 1881.

then predicts that the science of economics will be revolutionized by the adoption of those views which comprise, to put it briefly, the principle of the power of the act of incurring debts to double the quantity of goods in existence. That, for MacLeod, signifies the dawn of a new and significant era.[2]

It will doubtless be generally accepted today that the basic principle of that view is in error. It is all too patent that it involves an erroneous duplication in that it posits as a good not only the object which is conveyed on credit but also the right or legal claim which arises from the transaction. It makes both the debt and the right to demand payment of the debt into "goods." In spite of the complete self-assurance with which MacLeod's doctrine was advanced, it encountered virtually universal and unanimous rejection.[3] Now, the interesting feature of the whole matter is this: While it is true that prevailing economic theory unanimously condemned MacLeod's doctrine, it is also true that his doctrine was *an outgrowth of that same prevailing theory;* indeed, that it was, in very fact, a conclusion drawn therefrom by perfectly sound, though blind logic. It is that doctrine's quite legitimate though disowned offspring.

The matter may be put as follows: The premises on which MacLeod's syllogism is based can be expressed in two short sentences, viz: (a) when *A* lends *B* a dollar, then *B* possesses in that dollar a corporeal thing having the value of a dollar; (b) in his claim to the repayment of the dollar *A* possesses an intangible or nonmaterial good possessing a present value approximating one dollar which is not identical with the corporeal dollar itself.

Now it becomes inescapably necessary to establish (since the validity of these two premises is conceded) that there can be no objection to the conclusions that MacLeod proceeds to draw from these premises.

For, if we concede that before the loan only *A* possessed a good of the value of one dollar, but also concede that, after the loan is made, *B* possesses a tangible good, and that in addition, *A* possesses an intangible good *separate* and *distinct* from it, and that each of these goods has the value of one dollar, then it is in actual fact true that *credit has created new goods, not previously in existence,*

---

[2] MacLeod, *Elements of Political Economy*, London, 1858, page 12: "The present value of all the bills of exchange and promissory notes in Great Britain at this time is not less than £500,000,000 *and yet this is treated as nothing by political economists.*" Then, see further his page 265, Sections 40 to 42.

[3] Most emphatically and sweepingly in recent times by Knies in his *Der Credit*, Berlin, 1876, pp. 63-95.

and it thus becomes true that the power of credit to double the quantity of goods in existence is a fact—a miraculous fact—but nevertheless a fact.

No genuine refutation of this conclusion is achieved by the very popular but completely sophistical evasion which consists in recognizing in *B's* debt a *good that constitutes a minus quantity* and counterbalances his claim, thus reducing the total value of goods in existence to a total of one. For there simply is no such thing as a negative good, or a minus-quantity-good, any more than there are any negative or minus-quantity material things. If *X* owns an apple and *Y* owns an apple, different and distinct from *X's*, there is only one way to achieve the result that together *X* and *Y* possess only one apple. And that way is to deprive one of them of his apple. Now it is true that this deprivation may be expressed mathematically by stating that I record minus one apple. However, the apple that is physically present cannot be made to disappear by invoking a mathematical concept, but only by physically removing it.

In the same manner *B's* debt will eventually have the result that *his dollar will at some future time be taken away from him*. But during such time as it is not taken away, why, his dollar is still there. And the concept of his debt as a minus quantity is simply a symbol and a formula which is not in agreement with actual truth. And so, if we are to reject MacLeod's conclusions (and the world is unanimously agreed that they must be rejected), then we must begin with a rejection of his premises.

But his premises both contained a conclusion that a thing is a good, and therefore our judgment as to the soundness of the premises must be rendered in conformity with *the economic doctrine of goods*. The first premise, namely, that a dollar is a corporeal good is so manifestly correct that it affords no basis for refutation. Our refutation, therefore, must be directed against the second statement of the premise, which says that *A's* claim is a good which is not identical with the thing to which it lays claim.

Now what is the reaction of prevalent economic doctrine toward this premise? Frankness compels me to answer that the attitude is partly one of embarrassment, partly one of ambiguity, but not an unreserved denial. For ever since Say introduced into economics his *produits immateriels* economists have been almost unanimous in declaring that not only corporeal things, but also *intangible, nonmaterial* things may be goods, providing only that they are useful. And since rights, such as claims, are indubitably useful for him who possesses them, it would be difficult to deny them the possession of goods-quality, pure and simple. One single example would prove such a denial untenable. Let us consider the man whose sole wealth consists of his right to the income from his securities, that is to say, of "claims" or "rights." It would certainly be vain to deny that he is a man who possesses "goods." On the other hand, it is manifestly impossible to compute such claims as being something that exists *in addition* to the securities to which they pertain, when making an inventory of all existent goods as, for instance, in estimating the "amount of the national wealth."

Considerations like these which tend to deny goods-quality to rights and claims finally led to an ambiguous stand on the question and I hope I may say, without implication of reproach to its membership, that the brotherhood of economists simultaneously affirmed and denied such goods-quality. Or, if they did not do these two things simultaneously, then they at least alternately affirmed and denied the possession of goods-quality by incorporeal things.

I think it may be said, without casting any reflections on economists, that they adhered to the one or the other decision according to whether they pictured the "propertyless" man-of-independent-means or the duplicated national wealth as the more frightening conclusion to which their decision committed them.

It is not difficult to substantiate this charge of vacillation. I direct attention to one scholar of high repute who may be said to occupy a position of pre-eminence among economists, namely, Wilhelm Roscher. At one point in his *Grundlagen der Nationalökonomie* (10th ed., Section 90, Note 1) he clearly disagrees with MacLeod's assertion that a creditor's claim to payment is to be considered "intangible capital." At the same time Roscher himself, in another passage (Section 3), classifies useful "relationships to persons and things" as goods and, by citing the *res incorporales* of Roman Law and by specific reference (in his Note 7) to "evidences of debt," establishes that, as a matter of principle, he is in favor of classifying *rights* as intangible goods. We achieve, perhaps, maximum accuracy if we say of prevailing economic opinion that it unreservedly recognizes, *in principle*, the goods-quality of rights, but that it attempts to modify and partly to retract such recognition upon occasion—especially on those occasions which lead most clearly to the conclusions drawn by MacLeod from the principle; and that it does so modify and retract in order to protect itself from those very conclusions. And its modification and retraction take the form of maintaining that such rights are "naturally" to be regarded as goods only from the viewpoint of an individual's economy and not from that of the community's [see Roscher, *op. cit.*, Sec. 3, Note 7]. But the "naturalness" of this decision is left a matter for the decision itself to make manifest.

The purpose of the foregoing remarks is not even remotely intended to attribute to outstanding scholars statements that are irreconcilable. Rather is it my purpose to show how the whole MacLeod fallacy patently owes its origin to an obfuscated understanding of the economic nature of rights. And it is my further purpose to demonstrate how prevailing economic opinion, instead of correcting the MacLeod fallacy at its roots, betrays, on its own part, indecision and vacillation. The result is that economic science, by reason of the measure of recognition which, as a matter of principle, it accords to the claim to independent goods-value advanced on behalf of claims and rights, itself supplies the very basis for the fallacious conclusions of MacLeod which it thereupon rejects with more sound intuition than strictly logical reasoning.

A purely practical person might rest content with seeing that erroneous results have thus been eliminated. But the economic theorist cannot permit himself to do this. It remains his duty to demand that the rejection of error take place *for the correct reason.*

In the present concrete case what that amounts to is the following. The erroneous pronouncement which, by defining too many things as goods, violates the practical verities which underlie the theory of goods, must also be combated and disproven in accordance with the sound theoretical provisions of that same theory of goods. Only by such a procedure can we avoid the appearance of having rejected a fallacy through a purely fortuitous combination of circumstances; of owing this rejection, not to logic, but to our feelings and sensibilities and even more, perhaps, to the very crassness of the fallacy itself. It would then become necessary for us to make the further admission that this crassness is something we could not ordinarily count on if other, similar, related fallacies should turn up in subtler form. In that event they might remain unrecognizable for us.

And it is indeed true that fallacies of such subtler nature do haunt our science of economics, even today, in greater numbers than one might suppose.

And to that very end I do think that it is essential for us to have a clearer understanding of the economic nature of rights, claims and similar categories. That is to say, we ought to achieve greater clarity than characterizes the wavering decision of prevailing economic theory, as reflected in the somewhat dubious pronouncement that rights are goods from the viewpoint of an individual's economy, but that they are not goods from the viewpoint of a community's economy.

The pages that follow will constitute an effort to arrive at such greater clarity. The very nature of the subject and the occasion which motivates a discussion of it will make one point too obvious to mention. That is that our discussion will inevitably expand beyond the narrow confines of the subject itself and that it will therefore deal with many a point which belongs to the general theory of economic goods. Indeed, we are constrained to deal with one such general aspect at the very outset, in order to illuminate the theater of action of our specific topic. For, before we can understand clearly whether (and in what sense) rights and relationships are goods, we must understand what we mean by goods at all, in the economic sense of the word.

CHAPTER I
Historical And Doctrinal Comments On The Goods Concept And On Categories Of Goods

The Goods Concept

It is not in the least difficult to arrive at a clear understanding of the fundamental concept which is expressed by the economic term " a good." It may be said that writers on economics have never from the beginning been in any doubt — nor have they been divided — as to this basic concept. Every definition from Aristotle's day to our own sets forth, in one form or another, a single fundamental thought. It is that goods, in the economic sense of the word, are those things which *serve human beings as the means or tools for the attainment of their personal well-being*. This fundamental thought is then expressed in a variety of forms. The form may, in varying degree and at varying times, manifest the following characteristics:

1. It may be limited to factual description.

2. It may be casuistic in character.

3. It may involve other technical concepts which express general tendencies of the period or time at which it is presented, particularly ethical tendencies.

Thus, a good may at one time be defined simply as a "means to personal ends"; at another time as a "tool for well-being" or, again, as a "means to the satisfaction of human needs" or at still another, with the addition of an

ethical touch, as an "admittedly proper means to the satisfaction of *genuine* human needs," as a "thing subject to
our power of disposition which possesses the recognized
capacity to take its place in the chain of cause and effect
between human wants and the satisfaction of those wants."
All of these are, of course, merely numerous paraphrases
of one and the same clearly defined fundamental idea.

Economic theory encountered somewhat less difficulty
in the rigid definition and isolation of this fundamental
idea than in solving a few other problems which inevitably accompanied the further development of the concept
of an economic good. These problems included, primarily,
the detailed identification of the individual qualifications
implied by the apparently simple concept "instrument for
(or tool of) well-being"—qualifications which must serve
as the criteria of goods-quality in any given instance. A
second problem lay in the demarcation and differentiation
of the concept of a good in the field of economics as contrasted with that concept in other fields of human knowledge, especially the concept "good" in the field of ethics. The
third and final problem lay in the winnowing and investigating of everything that thereafter still remains under
the rubric of the economic concept, "good." In other words,
*the third problem lies in the establishment of the categories
of economic good.*

It is impossible to escape the conclusion that the foregoing problems are to some extent inter-related, and that
the accurate solution of the first would necessarily entail
the solution of the other two. However, economic theory
has chosen to proceed toward the solution of each of them
by an individual route. Of the three problems, the first certainly has met with the most definitive and the most un-
questioned solution and pre-eminently through the work
of German economists. For a time the process of solving
the problem was confined to the matter of defining a good;
at the outset economic science sought to explain what the
general concept of "good" included, as used in ordinary
speech, but gradually the explanation sought to make the
concept more significant and more detailed, and then to
embody, one after another, single criteria of "goods-quality."[1] So that at the present time the subject has under-

1. Jakob (*Grundsätze der Nationalökonomie*, 1805, Sec. 23) was
the first to recognize the existence of human need and the objective suitability of a thing to such need as conditions precedent of
goods-quality, when he wrote the definition: "That which serves for
the satisfaction of human needs is called a 'good'." That man's
"knowledge of usability" is a third such condition precedent is the
addition of such writers as Hufeland, Storch and Lotz (e.g., Lotz,

gone a treatment which may be said to have attained a form that is characterized by formal completeness and final definitiveness. That is to be found, most especially, in the work of Menger. His *Grundsätze der Volkswirtschaftslehre* (Vienna, 1871; see p. 3ff.) [English translation: Carl Menger, *Principles of Economics*, p. 55ff., The Free Press, Glencoe, Illinois, 1950] is a truly epoch-making work in its establishment of this specific concept and also of the supremely important basic concepts of economic science generally.

Since I adhere essentially to Menger, and feel that I am called upon to supplement his findings only in one minor respect, I shall set down the following as the attributes necessary to goods-quality, that is to say, the qualities which are required if a thing is to merit definition as a good for an economizing human individual. These qualities, be it noted, must be present simultaneously.

1. There must be a human *need* which the thing can serve. If there is no purpose to be achieved, there can be no means to the end; if there is no want, there can be no good.

2. The thing must be *objectively adapted* to bring about, directly or indirectly, the satisfaction of the want. Herein lies the criterion of goods-quality which most prominently attracts attention and which the layman frequently considers to be the only essential criterion. This may also be expressed by saying that a thing must possess properties which are, for man, *useful properties*. Bread must possess nutritiveness; steel must have hardness; glass must possess resistivity and transparency; ink must exhibit adhesion and color-fastness. These things must possess these qualities if they are to serve man's wants in the way of nutriment, shelter and the other respects in which his experience dictates that he relies on the things mentioned.

3. Man must *recognize and be aware of* this adaptability of the respective thing to the satisfaction of human wants. A "usefulness" that is unknown to man is of no use to him.

Before man discovered its medicinal qualities, the bark of the cinchona was to him a useless thing—it was not a "good." Even though man's knowledge be no more than theoretical or fragmentary, all that is required is that his knowledge be empirically adequate. Medicines were goods

Revision der Grundbegriffe der Nationalwirtschaftslehre, 1811, Sec. 3): "Things, as such, become goods as soon as the human mind recognizes them as means suitable for the promotion of human purposes." At the same time Roscher (*Grundsätze* 10, Note to Sec. 1) sets up the ethical provision that the need for the satisfaction of which a thing serves must be a "true" need, i.e., one that merits ethical approval.

from that moment on in which it was known that they could cure and heal, even though nothing was known as to the why and the wherefore of their effect upon the human organism.

4. Man must not only *be aware* of the capacity of the objectively useful thing for the satisfaction of his wants; he must also *have the power to utilize* that capacity. There must be no absence of what I should like to term "knowledge of use" or of "usability." It is, for instance, quite possible that a person may be quite conversant with the usefulness of a book or, say, a microscope. But for anyone lacking the technical knowledge of how to make use of them, both would be as completely unable to qualify as "goods" as was the bow of Odysseus for the suitors, none of whom had the strength necessary to bend it.[2]

5. Finally, it is necessary that the thing in question be disposable or available for us. We must possess the *power of disposal* over it if we are really to command its power to satisfy our wants. Any means to our ends which we are unable to put to actual use; because, let us say, of spatial considerations or because we lack the necessary power of disposal, is actually of no use to us and has no significance either for our well-being or for our economy. Gold mines on the moon, exceedingly attractive building lots situated on undiscovered South Sea Islands, or a house and lot belonging to someone else are *for me* not goods.

A review of the foregoing "conditions precedent" to goods-quality reveals that these conditions are inherent less in the things themselves than in the economic subjects for whom they are or are not goods. The existence of want, the awareness of usefulness and of "usability" are matters which are completely subjective, and availability and disposability are partly so (in that they exist or do not exist, according to the situation of the economic *subject*). The possession of useful qualities is the sole purely objective requirement to be fulfilled by the thing itself. That circumstance leads us to two observations regarding the nature of goods.

2. "Ability or knowledge of how to use" is lacking in Menger's enumeration of the conditions requisite for goods-quality. I felt that it was necessary to list it as a requirement independent of and different from the factor that Menger lists next under the name of "power of disposal." My reason for this is that the latter is a purely external factor while "ability to use" (or knowledge of how to use) is a purely subjective factor. Furthermore, if one were disposed to regard it as something that is included under power of disposal, the result would be, it seems to me, to assign to the latter factor too large an area to cover. And it seemed to me such an extension was excessive, in view of our understanding of the term in ordinary language usage.

The first of these—and it is something that has long been recognized—is that the goods-quality of a thing is never a purely objective matter, a quality inherent in the thing, such as the quality of being "wooden" or "iron," but that goods-quality depends on a *relationship* which must exist between the thing on the one hand, and an economic subject on the other hand. Furthermore, it may be true that the economic subject must possess completely peculiar individual qualifications.

The second of these observations—likewise something that has long been recognized—is that goods-quality can be caused and destroyed by the mere presence or absence of subjective relationships without the occurrence of any objective change whatsoever in the thing under consideration.

A further conclusion must be set down here—and this is one that is rather rarely emphasized though it is just as illuminating. That is that every good *can be a good only for those definite economic subjects* with respect to whom every one of the subjective economic "conditions precedent" is fulfilled. Only for those persons who feel or experience the particular want to the satisfaction of which a given thing is adapted; only those persons who are aware of the thing's adaptability; only those who possess the knowledge or skill necessary to use the given thing; and, finally, only those persons who possess the actual power of disposal over the thing—only for these persons is the given thing a good. But for all persons lacking the want, the required knowledge or the skill or awareness of the usability or the power of disposal (i.e., access to its availability) — for all such persons, the thing is *merely a thing*, not a good. Strictly speaking, then, one should never speak simply of goods as such, but always only of *goods for X or for Y or Z, or other specific economic subjects*. Hence determination of the goods-quality of a thing or the assignment of reasons for its possession of goods-quality will vary according to the degree to which the person making such determination or assigning such reasons succeeds in adopting the point of view of one or another economic subject. The most important difference that here comes into play is the difference between *the individual economic subject's point of view and the economic community's point of view*. The individual can recognize as goods only those things which are suitable for the satisfaction of the wants of that particular individual. And that is a circumstance which markedly restricts the area of things that are economic goods for the individual. On the other hand, the economic community's point of view embraces that of the sum total of all the natural economic subjects comprising the community (or nation) and treats them all as a single unified or collective economic subject. Since a community or a nation is not actually a natural entity and really consists of the totality of its members, it reacts, not as an entity, but as a collection of individual members. The community appears as an *active* economic subject to the extent that any one of its members is active; it appears as a *passive* subject to the extent that a member performs as a passive subject. With reference to the community-as-a-whole, therefore, all those things are goods which occupy the position of an economic good with reference to any single member of the community. That circumstance very considerably expands the area that lies open for a community's totality of goods as compared with the individual's.

If, in consequence, the totality of goods in an economic community is different from and larger than the totality of economic goods of a single individual, it does not by any means follow that, as a matter of economic principle, the things that are goods for the community are *different in kind* from those that are goods for the individual. It cannot, for instance, be said that certain categories of things are to be regarded as goods for one, but not for the other. It is, on the contrary, most patent that the great preponderance of those means to well-being which a community utilizes for the satisfaction of its wants must coincide exactly with the sum total of those things which constitute goods for the individual members of the community. There is a difference between goods from the point of view of the economizing community and goods from the point of view of the economizing individual only if one considers merely the point of view of a *single definite individual*, but not if one considers successively the viewpoint of all the individual members. Even then, whatever difference there may be is not a difference in kind, but only a *difference in volume*.[3]

Finally, it may be said that both ordinary usage and the economist's technical language make only tacit refer-

3. If the statements in the text above are in any need of proof at all, that proof may be found in the fact that the generally accepted use of the concept "political economy" presupposes that by "a nation's goods" we mean nothing more nor less than the things which the members of that nation find useful, even though it may be only isolated or individual members who do so; proof also lies in the fact that, accordingly, the term "goods" must necessarily mean all those things which are goods for any single member of the nation. This circumstance alone makes it clear just how dubious is the assumption, so general in the discussion of economics, (alluded to on a foregoing page) that there are things that constitute goods for an individual's economy but are not goods for a community's.

ence to a whole community or a whole nation as being an economic subject. When it does so, as when it mentions, "production of goods," "distribution of goods," "turnover of goods," it does so without the addition of any qualifying phrase which specifies any definite economic subject. This sort of use of the term "goods" is not to be regarded as a reduction of the goods-concept to objective terms (it would merit condemnation, if it were), but must be considered a perfectly legitimate ellipsis which tacitly assumes that the listener will supply, as the economic subject involved, that totality of that nation which the speaker has in mind. However, it is always a fact (and it is important for the solution of our problem not to lose sight of this fact) that every goods-quality takes for granted the existence of a definite economic subject in whose favor the goods-quality may be invoked. Just as every good must be good "for something," so also it must be a good "for somebody."

*　　*　　*

Exact determination of the specific criteria which must characterize the concept of an economic good will at the same time furnish us with the identifying particulars which will differentiate between the characteristics that warrant the use of the term "good" in ordinary language usage and those which warrant the use of the term "good" in the strictly economic sense. The former includes things which are, to be sure, "good" but not "good means to an end." The first of these consists of "goods" which are desired, not as means to an end, *but as an end in themselves.* Pre-eminent among such things are ethical, religious and many other kinds of "spiritual goods," such as virtue, happiness, contentment, peace of mind, and the like. The other group of goods which must be barred from inclusion in the concept of economic goods consists of those things that are termed "good" *by metaphorical speech usage.* Even at the colloquial level, our language abounds in figures of speech which attribute the quality of a good or of a means to well-being to things which are, by their very nature, incapable of functioning as a good and which can be clothed with the power so to function only by virtue of, let us say, personification or other metaphorical usage.

It goes without saying that purely metaphorical "goods" must be excluded from the economic concept of goods. Because of a strange concatenation of circumstances, that is an assignment which is by no means so easy to carry out in detail as the underlying principle would lead us to expect. Economic science is confronted with that assignment in the solution of what we have previously described as our "third problem," namely, the problem of "winnowing and investigating" the kinds of good still remaining in the properly delimited area of goods-in-the-economic-sense, that is to say, in *the establishment of categories of economic goods.*

And that is the portion of the entire field in which belongs the question of a decision with respect to our special topic—the matter of the goods-quality of rights and legal relationships. I hope to avoid the error of anticipation and of premature critique by setting down here a concise and condensed review of the course that the literature of economics has pursued in its treatment of this problem.

Categories Of Goods

From the very outset it appeared indisputable that there was just one group of things of which it could be said that there could be no doubt of its being entitled to inclusion within the concept of an economic good. That group comprised those tangible corporeal objects, the use of which served man for the satisfaction of his wants. Let us call them "material goods." But it must also be said that this is the *only group* to which there was, at all times and in all places, accorded the full right of citizenship in the realm of the goods-concept. The whole development of the economic goods-theory revolved about the question whether or not other things, besides material goods, could be genuine goods in the economic sense. That development of the theory reveals *three distinct phases.*

The *first* phase comprises all the literature of economics antedating Adam Smith. During that phase this question is not examined at all, but such reference as is made from one occasion to another permits us to recognize that whenever *economists* spoke of goods, they were thinking only of material goods. To be sure, even in those days the word "good" was used in a far broader sense; the economists spoke of a *bona coelesta* [heavenly goods]; the physiocrats of *biens moraux* [moral goods] in addition to *biens physiques* [physical goods] (for instance, Quesnay, in his *Droit Naturel,* ed. Daire, p. 54). At the same time it was considered a matter of course that the science of economics was dealing with no other *goods* than material useful objects. That thought was expressed most distinctly by Justi in his *Staatswirtschaft* (Leipzig, 1775, Section 421) where he said, after the preliminary statement that "in its ethical sense the word 'goods' is understood in an extremely broad sense"; that in the *science of economics,* however, it included only those things "which find application and use for the exigencies and conveniences of human life." In this connection he leaves no room for doubt that when he sets up this definition he has material goods in mind exclusively. In his Section 35 he lists as the materials of industry *"money and merchandise,* or everything that is understood under the name of goods."[4]

When we reach the *second* phase of the development of the economists' goods-theory, we find that the question has become the subject of deliberate inquiry, thoroughly oriented from the point of view of the economic theorist. But at the conclusion of the inquiry there was essentially nothing more than an adherence to the position occupied at the beginning, namely, a retention of the uncritical literalness which held that only concrete objective material goods could properly comprise that national wealth which was the proper subject of the economist's consideration.

This second phase is the phase of which Adam Smith is the pre-eminent and supremely typical example. While it must be conceded that Smith did not truly have a goods-theory nor, indeed, supply any development of the general goods-concept, nevertheless his discussion of the concept of wealth and more particularly his development of his views on the productivity and unproductivity of various lines of human endeavor make it most decidedly clear that he considered only tangible corporeal material goods as the things that man economized with or that the science of economics was properly concerned with.[5]

Then, finally, the *third* phase of the development of the theory of the economic good evolved from a polemic which began with protests against the Smithian concepts of pro-

4. This is similar to his statement in Section 419 where he states that by wealth in its narrower sense we understand movable and immovable goods. On the question of the purely objective concept of economic goods and of capital, as entertained by the canonists, compare Endemann, *Die nationalökonomischen Grundsätze der kanonistischen Lehre,* Jena, 1863, p. 109 ff.; also, pp. 134, 135, 138.

5. *Wealth of Nations,* Book II, Chapter 3, pp. 314-315: "There is one sort of labour which adds to the value of the subject upon which it is bestowed: there is another which has no such effect. The former, as it produces a value, may be called productive; the latter, unproductive labour. Thus the labour of an artisan adds, generally, to the value of the materials which he works upon, that of his own maintenance, and of his master's profit. The labour of a menial servant, on the contrary, adds to the value of nothing. . . . The labour of some of the most respectable orders in . . . society is, like that of menial servants, unproductive of any value, and does not fix or realize itself in any permanent subject, or vendible commodity, which endures after that labour is past, and for which an equal quantity of labour could afterwards be procured. The sovereign, for example, with all the officers both of justice and war who serve under him, the whole army and navy, are unproductive labourers. [First Modern Library Edition, 1937, Random House, Inc., New York.]

ductive and unproductive labor. But it was subsequently extended to the entire area of the goods-concept as a whole. Smith's distinction had, in and of itself, been a purely objective one and purely technical in its point of view with no direct meting out of either praise or censure, with no according of honor and no expressing of disparagement. Nor could anyone who was willing to recognize that Smith's differentiation was nothing but a technical economic distinction take offense. Nevertheless his differentiation did give offense and did cause bad feeling. It was only natural that the feeling should arise, that Smith's differentiation bestowed the accolade of productiveness on the humbler occupations and on common manual labor, while the more intellectual pursuits were largely branded as unproductive. Those engaged in the latter, therefore, found that this line of demarcation either placed them in the same category with some positively "anti-social" callings or at least classed them with some unwholesome occupations or with others that were held in scant regard, such as domestic servants, mountebanks and animal trainers. Possibly because the inclusion of these classes aroused resentment, or because the very appellations "productive" and "unproductive" conveyed, by implication, praise and dispraise, it was, at any rate, felt that the characterization of many estimable occupations as unproductive was an act of disparagement and that this called for every effort to disavow the imputation and to exonerate these callings from the reproach, as it was felt to be, of unproductiveness.

Now it is obvious that the concept of productivity is a correlative of the concept "product." And since the discussion revolved about the effect of activities on the state of the community's welfare as represented by an accumulation of goods, the term, productivity, also has some relation to the concepts of "wealth" (*richesse*) and of a "good." And so, willy-nilly, the altercation concerning productivity took on the form of an endeavor on the part of the champions of the nonmanual occupations to demonstrate that the latter, too, brought forth "products" and "goods." This was the outward cause for J. B. Say's introduction into economic theory of nonmaterial products and nonmaterial wealth (his *produits immatériels* and *richesse immatérielle*). Even the activity of a physician, said Say, or of a lawyer, or of an actor, led to "products" which, though not material, nevertheless quite as fully deserved to be termed "wealth" (*richesse*) as did material products.[6] And in no time at all scholars of economics gave

6. *Traité d'Economie Politique*, Chap. VII, Note 1; Chap. XIII.

their approval to this extension of the concept of the economic good. At first this approval was far short of unanimous, since it lacked the concurrence of a considerable number of English economists[7] who, making common cause with the few surviving physiocrats[8] and a few recent [at that time] French and German theorists,[9] continued to maintain the strict Smithian position. But opposition to Say's extension gradually dwindled. This is especially true of *German* economists. Indeed, it may almost be said that German economic literature alone can claim that it founded and developed a true economic doctrine of goods. The French[10] contributed only superficial treatment to the theory with their distinction between *bien* and *richesse* while the English ignored it. It would probably be fair to say that today the idea of the nonmaterial good has found universal acceptance and that the existence of nonmaterial economic goods side by side with material goods is universally recognized and approved by economic scientists.

If I have called the acceptance of intangibles as economic goods *a new principle*, I mean that only qualifiedly. It was, to be sure, something new for *writers on economics* to propound, as a matter of purely technical economic theory, and to make an affirmative reply to the question whether nonmaterial things could be goods and could constitute wealth, and to reply affirmatively. But in a limited sense this was a very old story. Even the law of classical antiquity had had its *res incorporales* [incorporeal things] and these included claims and other rights; and so it may be said that intangibles had for 2,000 years been recognized as independent constituents of wealth. And this long-established custom, as a matter of (Roman) law undoubtedly gave great impetus to the ready acceptance, as a matter of economics, of intangibles as goods.

7. Ricardo, Malthus, Torrens, Mill.

8. duPont de Nemours, "First Letter to Say" (ed. Daire, p. 399).

9. Sismondi; Rau, who rigidly restricts the concept of wealth to corporeal goods.

10. The earlier physiocrats, such as Mercier de la Rivière, the Abbé Bandeau and Le Trosne do, to be sure, offer definitions of the concept *bien*. However, it seems to be considered of so much less importance for the science of economics than the narrower concept of *richesse* that it was thereafter largely neglected and came to serve, at most, as a term of contrast for use in discussions, in order to lend all the greater emphasis to the term *richesse*, and came, finally, to fall into complete disuse. Even Say, who is admittedly so careful of his fundamentals, is so little disposed to consider the concept *bien* as fundamental that in his *Epitome des principes fondamentaux* it does not even appear under a rubric of its own. The English from the very outset merely define wealth as the equivalent of possessions, not as a commodity. For them, "goods" means the same as "wares."

The recognition, as a matter of principle, of the goods-character of intangibles brought about, as its consequence, that material goods could no longer be accounted the sole possible category of goods in the economic sense. But since the intangibles that might lay claim to the attribute of usefulness were infinite in number, the question arose whether, after all, it was not necessary to exercise some selection and to decide which of that infinite number were genuine goods. Some writers on economics plunged into the task with so little discrimination that some very strange things indeed were accorded recognition as "goods." But not even among those writers who did proceed more selectively was there discernible any established principle on the basis of which recognition was accorded to some goods and denied to others in respect of the possession or nonpossession of goods-quality. And thus the things that achieved varyingly general recognition as being worthy of classification as intangible goods included such things as *personal services, love, the organized state, the church, virtue, character* [as a means to the establishment of credit—MacLeod], *honor, investors' patents, the Iliad* [Rossi], *the security bestowed by the law, monopolies, the joy of demolition* [*De Augustinis;* quoted by Roscher in *Grundlagen,* p. 106], *counsel and advice, good health, strength, cleverness, "good sense," knowledge, good taste, companionability, freedom, ownership, morality, the relationship of a commanding officer to his soldiers* [Roscher], *credit* [MacLeod], *claims* [Hufeland and Roscher], *the "utilization of a good"* [Hermann] and, in general, *relationships* of whatever kind and many other such things.

The merest glance at this list will suffice to convince us that not everything on it deserves rating as a good in the economic sense. Some sifting is indubitably required. But what is to be the acid test that we must apply in our selection? We are anxious to give consideration to *all* goods but only to *genuine goods.* We must therefore exercise as much precaution against erring on the side of the "too little" as against erring on the side of the "too much." In order to avoid the sin of omission, we must take care that our categories of goods find a place for all genuine contributions to human well-being. Our care to avoid inclusion of too many things must be exercised with an eye to a twofold danger. The first is the danger of including among goods things which are not consonant with the economic goods-concept at all—things, let us say, which are admittedly useful but which while they are good as aims, goals or ends, do not serve as *means* to well-being. The second danger is lest our classification be open to the charge of *duplication,* of being pleonastic in character. That is to say, we must take care to avoid placing one and the same means to well-being in our classification under several rubrics. It is, for instance, obvious that it would be, in this sense, pleonastic to count as separate goods both

1. good fresh drinking water, and
2. its service in quenching human thirst.

It was quite clear that Smith has been guilty on the side of the "too little." Material goods fail by far to exhaust the number of means which exist for the promotion of the well-being of man. These means are comprised only in part of things belonging to the world of objective, impersonal and concrete objects. No less important and no less numerous are the means to well-being which belong to the *subjective world of the personal ego.* In this connection, the factors that need to be taken into account may be either, in the first place, the identity of the person or persons in the social group in which the "good" is being utilized or, in the second place, the *talents, powers and qualities* which capacitate the persons concerned for the services conducive to the well-being of themselves or others or, in the third place, the *renditions of service themselves.* I call particular attention to my expressions "either" and "or". For it would constitute a patent pleonasm or duplication to seek to list as goods not only the useful things and also their useful qualities but, *in addition,* their renditions of service. Strictly speaking, it is not within our province to investigate which of three conceivable bases of classification may be the most nearly correct. Hence I shall rest content to indicate very briefly that in my opinion the wisest procedure is to list among goods the *services* of persons. For under the social conditions that prevail in our society where slavery no longer exists, persons themselves can never again be regarded as economic objects. The same exclusion applies to personal qualities and powers. The only things that can have validity as economic commodities are the useful services which become available through those persons and those qualities and powers. It is these alone which can function as independent entities in economic life and become the object of consumption, of exchange, of rental, and thus in all essential respects play the rôle of goods.

At any rate, it is clear that the only category of things admitted by Smith to constitute economic goods must be so amplified as to include *personal services.* Is it also possible that it must be further extended to include other categories, too? At first blush that might appear questionable.

Several things in that long list of "goods" I quoted some four paragraphs previously may seem, on first scrutiny, to be inadmissible candidates for membership in the fellowship of goods. I cite as examples such "goods" as entertainment and the joy of demolition. For these represent not so much means of satisfying wants as a *state-of-satisfaction-attained*. Moreover, the "wants-quality" of these wants-that-have-been-satisfied does not appear to me to be unqualifiedly established. Likewise, it would appear that we can dispense with listing, under economic goods, *personal qualifications,* such as skill, talents, powers which capacitate persons for rendition of service on behalf of themselves or others, since such listing would duplicate or render pleonastic the listing of the renditions of service themselves. It would seem that, in addition to material goods and personal services the things that have the best right to advance a claim to membership among the things that have economic goods-quality are those *legal rights* and *relationships* of which it can be observed that they play an independent part in economic exchange and in legal transactions. Claims are conveyed, rental rights are bought at a price, namely, the rent that is paid. Goodwill often attains very real money value, no matter whether it depends on purely factual circumstances (such as the high repute of a firm's name) or on specific legal rights (such as patent rights or a granted monopoly). Phenomena such as these would seem to offer most persuasive evidence of the genuine goods-quality of nonmaterial things. As a matter of fact, even those authors on economic subjects who reduce to a minimum the list of intangible things to which goods-quality is to be accorded—even they make room in their lists for these legal rights and relationships. These regularly *constitute a third category of goods* to take a place beside material goods as one category and personal services[11] as a second.

Nevertheless there have been some doubts as to the propriety of these categories. It must be conceded that only rarely have such doubts found open expression as concretely worded charges or expressions of disapproval on the part of an author of a work on economics. Nevertheless, doubts of this ilk continue to buzz about in many a critical head and refuse to be laid completely at rest. Schäffle, who has gone into greater detail than anyone else in his treatment of this category of goods, supplies a dras-

11. E.g., Roscher, *Grundlagen*, Sec. 3; Schäffle, *Das gesellschaftliche System der menschlichen Wirtschaft*, Note 3 to Sec. 81, p. 143ff.

tic example on this score. He begins his *Theorie der aus-schliessenden Absatzverhältnisse* [Tübingen, 1864] with the words: "There are many teachers and not a few students of economics who become astonished and incredulous when they are told in their earliest and very fundamental discussions of economics that two categories of objects which are the object of economic exchange comprise (1) material, concrete things and (2) personal services; but that in addition to these two, and coordinate with them, there exists also that third category of economic goods which Hermann introduced into economic science under the name of 'relationships' and which, since his day, have maintained the position in which he placed them."

It need not constitute grounds for astonishment that hostility to this principle should still exist. For it will always be true that nothing can qualify as a genuine good unless it can be *used*, that is to say, can bring about a useful result. Now, no matter how completely one may disown an utterly and crassly uncompromising materialistic conception of our universe, no matter how amenable one may declare himself to the intrusion of ideational forces into our lives, still, logic will always demand that those forces be genuine forces, if we are to ascribe to them any power to exert actual influence on our lives. But the term "relationship" would seem to convey a concept that offers no slightest hope whatever of the possession of such genuine force and power for influence. When we consider such a thing as *2:3* or *x:y* — and all relationships really possess the same nature as these ratios or should we, rather, say, the same lack of nature? — when, I say, we consider such things, and are asked to accept them, not merely as representative of goods, but as actually *being* goods, that demand will doubtless always remain one of those things which, for lack of something better we accept as an expedient, "for the sake of argument," but toward which, to the very end, we retain ineradicable reservations.

Is the retention of such reservations testimony of the presence of a fallacy, or is it merely a confession that we refuse to give up our prejudices? It is my hope that the investigation set forth in the pages which follow will give a satisfactory reply to that query. For the problem which that investigation attacks is the determination of the economic nature of legal rights and relationships. And I propose to begin with an inquiry into the *nature of legal rights*.[12]

12. This, perhaps, is the proper point at which to observe one peculiarity of human behavior whenever it comes to a question of classifying, of placing in categories things which occupy a border-

line position between matter and spirit, between the real and the ideal, between matter and form, between reality and fancy, between essence and appearance. We are prone to "shy away" from committing ourselves to the rigid line of demarcation demanded by a crisp "either/or" and to seek, rather, to reserve to ourselves a slight margin, a species of neutral border territory on either side of the boundary line, within which zone we present judgment of a somewhat indefinite character under, as it were, an opalescent light. We thus establish, so to speak, a zone within which we feel at liberty to maintain a sort of dignified inconsistency.

The reader will doubtless be aware of many examples of this human propensity not only in the history of nearly every science, but also in the intellectual processes of nearly every individual. The latter concededly offer fewer occasions for sharp classification. I offer just one pertinent example culled from that classicist in our own science of economics, Adam Smith. In his definition of productive and unproductive labor he most emphatically restricts the concept of wealth to tangible corporeal goods. Yet, when he draws up a list of "kinds of capital" (in Chapter I of his Book II) he finds it impossible to resist the powerful force of analogy and under its spell he includes under "wealth" the acquired "useful capacities of the members of society." He says: "The acquisition of such *talents* always costs a real expense, which is a capital fixed and realized, as it were, in his person. The improved *dexterity* of a workman may be considered in the same light as a machine. The words "as it were" and "may be considered in the same light as" serve here as veritable boundary posts which signalize the fact that we stand on questionable ground. The whole phenomenon indubitably stands in close relationship to our involuntary and unfortunately not unjustified distrust of the infallibility of our judgment. The more lively is our impression (whether on the basis of our empirical k n o w l e d g e or on that of our theoretical study) that we are not truly capable of distinguishing essential verities, but that we merely postulate those verities and adorn them with the attribute of verity on the basis of the interpretations applied to phenomena by our minds—the livelier, I say, is our impression to that effect, the more distrustful do we become of the borderline phenomena that emanate from areas which we discriminate but faultily, as it is, and which we then, with some justification, look upon as something completely unknowable. Nevertheless, it is my conviction that considerations of this kind do not exempt economic science from the necessity of setting up a strict "either/or" in the matter of establishing categories.

If it be permissible for the skeptic who discredits the theoretical soundness of our economic knowledge in order to invoke his very awareness of our imperfect knowledge in order, by following logical and economically sound reasoning, to arrive at only relatively sound conclusions, then it becomes obligatory for economic science to establish some thoroughgoing system of organizing its phenomena and concepts even though that organization may turn out to be only one that is the relatively best available. It will then fare better than if, despairing of achieving absolute truth, it were to condone laxness in those respects in which, by exercising greater strictness, it would still achieve only admittedly relative truth but still a truth which would further our purposes and would be conclusive from the point of view of such capacity as we possess for the recognition of complete knowledge.

The pages which follow are set down in the spirit of such an attempt to further the truth.

CHAPTER II
The General Function Of Legal Rights In Man's Economy; More Specifically, The Function Of Property Rights And Their Position With Respect To Material Goods

General Function Of Legal Rights In Man's Economy

An infinitude has already been uttered and written on the significance of law and of legal rights. Some of these things have been set down from the juridical point of view, some from the ethical, some from the political, some from the economic point of view. There has been frequent and abundant discussion and dispute as well as eloquent description of the consequences that have arisen from the institution of property rights — that pillar of the law of property—consequences bearing on our whole lives, our well-being, our education and on the moral basis of all individual, family and community possession of property. If, then, we propose here to go into the question of the economic significance of law, it is not with the intention of limning a broad and abundant canvas. Our inquiry concerns a highly specialized topic, a very simple and prosaic question, an inquiry into the body of law as an economic structure. What, as a matter of economic functioning, does a legal right accomplish for the person who possesses it? And in what manner, and by what means does it accomplish it? What, in other words, does it mean, *economically speaking*, to possess a legal right?

Let us attempt to find some answers to these questions.

It is the most natural thing in the world that economizing subjects, if they are to derive any service or use from their goods, must establish themselves in *a position where they exercise control* over those goods. This is so indispensable a "condition precedent" that in the preceding chapter we observed that goods-quality is absolutely dependent on the occupation, on the part of the subject, of a position which enables him to exercise control over the good. We characterized and described this as having "power of disposal" over the good in question. It lies no less in the nature of things that this relationship of control must be one that is natural, that is to say, that it be *physical in character*. We are dealing with *utilization of goods*, and that always either consists in, or it involves, a physical act. Some *ideal* (as opposed to physical) relationship of control over a loaf of bread which I do not have in my physical possession or under my physical control would leave my hunger completely unsatisfied. On the other hand, it is not at all necessary that this natural or physical control be *absolute* and unlimited. It need extend only far enough to satisfy the requirements of the economic purpose which the good is to fulfill. That implies a degree of control which may vary widely according to the good in question. In the case of a penholder, I must be able to hold it in my hand and to manipulate it at will; in the case of the water in a millrace, it will suffice if I can control it momentarily—long enough to have it strike my mill wheel, even though immediately thereafter it be entirely free to follow its natural course. In order to attach a familiar name to a familiar fact, let us express this thought by saying that the accomplishment of man's economic purposes demands *possession* of his goods.

This possession is to be thought of as a material, a physical, matter and implies a relationship which conveys control of a thing; and, it may be added, it need go no further than that. For there is nothing in the economic relationship of man to goods that would require more than physical control over them. If I have a good under my physical control to such an extent that I can make use of it for my purpose, then my economic goal has been attained; any other sort of possession or control, if there be any, is superfluous.

In any situation in which man and nature confront each other as isolated entities there can, therefore, be no question of any kind of control-relationship other than a purely physical one. Man under these conditions seeks nothing more than mere physical possession of things and finds that quite sufficient for his purpose. But the situation is different where man has congregated in a legally organized society, in a politically organized state. Here there comes into being something different from purely physical possession, a new kind of thing, namely *legal possession*—a *legally sanctioned* power of control over goods— something which economizing human beings are equally ready to desire, acquire and esteem. If, in the light of this phenomenon, we reconsider our earlier statement that man's economic purpose demands no more than adequate physical control or possession of goods, then we are confronted, perforce, with the question, "Does the fact that man lives in politically organized states bring about a change in his relationship to goods (the relationship that formerly did not need to go beyond mere *physical possession*)? And if not, then what is the significance of the existence of legalized possession as something distinct from physical possession? Furthermore, what economic function can that kind of possession perform?

Let us consider these questions seriatim.

To begin with, it is clear that in a society characterized by the politically organized state, the matter of satisfying wants is dependent only on possessing those goods which are suitable for the satisfaction of wants and, furthermore, that such possession be accompanied by adequate physical control. I satisfy my hunger by means of the bread that *I possess,* regardless of the fact that it may be bread belonging to someone else and which is merely in my physical possession, no matter whether I exercise legitimate property rights over it or not. Accordingly, the first of the questions concluding the preceding paragraph must be answered in the negative. Thereupon the second question moves into the forefront of our attention, namely: Wherein does the economic function of legitimate possession consist? This legitimate possession is something apart from and in addition to physical possession. And yet, for the attainment of man's *economic* ends, only physical possession is, economically speaking, indispensable.

A modicum of attentiveness to the facts cannot fail to guide us toward the right path. The first fact to be noted is that legitimate possession of a thing coincides, as a rule, with physical possession. The person having the legitimate right to possess ordinarily, as a matter of actual fact, has physical possession, too. That is a phenomenon that is readily explicable. For in any well-organized powerful state the law usually has a compulsory power at its side —a power which is equipped and disposed to turn into a reality the condition which is recognized to be the legitimate one. Of course, the opposite is not seldom observed, that is to say, someone other than the person legitimately entitled to possession of a thing does, in actuality, have possession. Such a situation exists, for instance, when true legitimacy cannot be established before the state's instrumentality for justice. The cause may lie in a lack of adequate proof or in the "bearing of false witness" or in an error by "the bench" or in the complete concealment of illegitimate possession, such as complete failure to discover the thief or when (in states disintegrating with corruption) private power is stronger than the arm of the law.

These very exceptions to the basic principle are instructive in our study of the topic before us. For they lead us to the following important observation. *In economic exchange a legal claim is considered valuable and signif-*

icant only if it is either (1) *already combined with physical possession, or* (2) *accompanied by a good prospect that physical possession can be obtained by virtue of the legal claim. Conversely, it is observable that a legal claim is regarded as quite null and valueness if it is unaccompanied by physical possession and if there is no prospect that it will furnish the avenue to attainment of physical possession.*

How "good," for instance, is a claim against an absconding bankrupt, or how salable is the title to a watch which has been stolen by a thief who cannot be located?

If we may conclude from these observations that legal rights carry economic significance only if and to the extent that they embody physical control, or at least imply a means of acquiring such control, then we are safe in setting down the following conclusions: *in the first place*

1. Legitimate power of control, however clearly distinct it may be from ordinary physical control (based on possession and backed by the owner's brute strength), needs to be characterized by a quality akin to the power of physical control and indeed, needs, by its nature, to be convertible into physical force; and *in the second place*

2. This very characteristic (the absence of which reduces all law to impotence, to a desiccated form *sans* content) constitutes the essential quality which endows legitimate rights with economic value, or, indeed with economic character.

In actual fact, every legal claim partakes of this dependence on the factual and the physical. It is, in sober truth, dependence on *the state's physical powers of enforcement that lends to all law whatever cogency it may possess.*

We may summarize this point as follows: *wherever a good is to serve an economic purpose, there must, under all circumstances,* be present some factual possession, some physical controlling power adequate for the economic purpose concerned. In the case of an economic subject in isolation, it suffices if such physical power of control is based upon and is guaranteed by his own physical strength. And in such isolation there can be no question of any other kind of guarantee.

However, in an organized society and in a politically organized state the situation is different. Only in the rarest instances would the physical strength of any one individual suffice to preserve the physical control that is indispensable for the preservation of his economic requirements against the attacks of other individuals and especially against the wishes of the community. In this connection, therefore, the power of disposal and control which relies on individual physical strength must seek outside assistance. That assistance is forthcoming by virtue of certain presuppositions which determine objective right and the existence of which is responsible for our concept of subjective right. And that assistance is effected through the state's system for the administration of justice. That administration proceeds along the following lines: The first step consists in a ruling by the court as to whether or not the necessary presuppositions are in force, by virtue of which the instrumentalities of the community may be invoked; then the enforcement agencies of the state lend their physical support to the community-member entitled thereto, in order to place him or maintain him in the position of factual physical control of the thing in question.

The Function Of Property Rights In Relation To Material Goods

Hence a legal right or the legalized power of disposal over a thing is nothing more nor less than a necessary re-enforcement supplied by a politically organized state of the physical power which is needed by the owner of a good as a condition to its economic utilization. Such re-enforcement is provided because the physical power of the individual is inadequate to assure to the legal owner of a good the economic use thereof, and it is provided in order to supply that assurance through the state's facilities for the administration of justice. Under the economic conditions prevailing in our society, the desired complete and assured power of disposal over goods is, so to speak, divided between two agencies. The first is the strength of the individual, the second is the power of the state as represented by its agencies for the administration of justice. The natural power of disposal possessed by any individual economizing subject would be inadequate. For it would probably be at a disadvantage against the unlawful attacks of other individuals. And it would most certainly be unable to cope with the will of the community when that will is disposed to recognize the adverse legal claim of some other individual.

On the other hand, a legally based power of disposal alone without the natural, physical power would be inadequate because factual objective enjoyment of a good cannot be derived from that good without the natural physical control over it. Not until they are combined do legal and physical control constitute that fully assured power of disposal which is demanded by our economic interests and which, as we have already seen, bestows on the useful things in question their goods-character and makes them for us genuine *goods*.

Hence we sum up the economic significance of legal rights as follows: *The economic content of legal rights rests on the assistance furnished by the state's agencies for the administration of justice in the acquisition and preservation of physical control over goods.*[1] *And the law itself is a necessity that has evolved because mankind lives as an organized society and it is, at the same time, an integral feature of the entire structure of the economic power of disposal over goods.*

This feature of our laws makes it seem advisable to point out that, even though there is, in many ways, a difference between legal right and a purely factual power of control, nevertheless the economic function of legal rights very closely parallels that of objective control and physical possession of a good. Both express a species of power of disposal and, in combination with each other, they constitute the complementary constitutents of complete economic control.

Furthermore, the possession of this common feature enables us to recognize that if a right is to be elevated to the status of a *good*, it can achieve that status only by the same process and to the same extent as does physical possession. To whatever extent a right or claim has economic standing at all, it has it by reason of the fact that the state's agencies for administering justice issue in its behalf a covenant reading, "You will some day receive" or, "You shall not be deprived of . . . " And in the close vicinity there still hovers the ghost of physical possession.

Let us, then, begin by setting down the necessary preliminary question. *Is this a good, in the sense in which it is the duty of economic science to treat that concept?*

At first blush one might be inclined to answer this

1. Herein lies the reason for the effectiveness of the legality of claims. This is true even when the absence of any violation of legal rights makes unnecessary any appeal to the law. The very reason why there is no violation of the law is that those disposed toward wrongdoing stand in fear of the physical powers of the state. The latter, therefore, are the truly effective factors in administering justice. Nor is the point made in the text in any degree refuted by the following phenomenon: There exist certain combinations of circumstances in which legal control is advisedly and consciously separated from factual control. One example is the legal title to land which is occupied by a person or persons other than the owner, subject to a right of usufruct. For in such a case the economic content of the legal right of ownership lies not in the momentary but in the eventual physical power of control that is assured after expiration of the right of usufruct. That is clearly demonstrable by the fact that the value of the ownership of that land, the *nuda proprietas*, would be appraised as having a value of nil, if it were known with absolute certainty that before the expiration of the usufruct some disaster would destroy the land itself.

question affirmatively. One might suppose that a "good" which one does not have is not of any use, and that, accordingly, the *possession* of it is a "nonmaterial good" (since nonmaterial things, too, can be goods). However, it soon becomes apparent that this would be a very dangerous brand of logic. Pursuing that line of argumentation, one would be immediately led to other conclusions that could never be seriously entertained. Let us suppose that by arguing along that line I concluded that *possession* of good drinking water is a nonmaterial good. In that case I am immediately compelled to maintain that drinking water without its refreshing coolness and its thirst-quenching flavor does not constitute a desirable thirst-quenching beverage and hence is not a good. Continuation along that line of logic drives me to the further conclusion that "refreshing coolness" and "thirst-quenching flavor" are no less "nonmaterial goods" than the *possession* of the water. Indeed, it is possible to go still further! The best drinking water in the world would manifestly not serve for the satisfaction of any want at all, if it did not *exist*. Consequently, the existence of the water becomes still another useful circumstance and, by this brand of logic, a new good. By this time it is certainly clear what the logical error was by which we arrived at the creation of so many independent "goods." Quite simply, a number of circumstances which, when taken together, make up the goods-quality of drinking water, were considered separately, were personified and, finally, by way of metaphor, were honored with the appellation "good."

The only actual good that comes into question in this case is the *refreshing thirst-quenching water itself*. The fact that it exists, that it is refreshing, that it quenches thirst, that it is subject to the disposal of mankind in general or of a single economizing individual—all these things are nothing more than individual factors by virtue of which that water becomes a good in general, or a good for any one individual in particular. But they are by no means independent goods in addition to the drinking water. Anyone who called them so would be guilty of a flagrant error of duplication. It would be fully as bad as if an umbrella vender attempted to sell, in addition to his umbrellas, the cohesiveness of the fabric of which they are made, their power to cast shadow, their beauty, their luster, the possession of them and, finally, the existence of them—and tried to sell all of these separately.

The possession, then, of a good is simply one condition on which depends the fact that the particular good *is* a good for the person within whose sphere of control the good is located. But it is by no manner of means an independent good existent outside of and in addition to the good that is possessed.

Nor is the situation different, with respect to the *legal title to things*. Let us consider, first, the simplest case of the kind, the case of complete legal power of control, the case of complete ownership of property in fee simple. Let us think, finally, of a house—just any house at all. Then, second, let us modify the concept by thinking of this house as *my* house, that is to say, let us think of my right of ownership of the house as an additional concept. What is the difference between our "first" and our "second"? Does our first cover *one* good, and are there then subsequently two? By no means. Rather is it true that in the earlier instance there was *for me* no good in existence at all. The house did not become a good for me until it became my property. The thousands of other houses in the city to which I have no title, are just as certainly not goods for me as the millionaire's wealth is not a good for the beggar; or as certainly as it is impossible for me to satisfy my hunger with the bread that is on some other continent, or in some other country, or in some distant city, or under some other person's control. Legal title to a thing, like the physical possession of it, does not develop outside of, and in addition to the good to which it applies, so as to become a second, independent good. It simply helps to make the thing a good in the first place. And it does so because, in an organized state the physical power of control does not, of itself, confer adequate assurance of power of disposal; and it does so because it alone makes the thing *mine;* and because it complements factual and physical power of control with legal and legitimate power of control.

That is clear. Indeed, it is so clear that there could never have been any failure to recognize its truth, had it not been for two circumstances. One was that just the right of ownership (as something apart from other property rights) was singled out as a subject of inquiry; the other is that ownership rights, specifically, became the choice as the basis on which to raise — and settle — the question of whether rights can be independent goods. But such was not the actual course of events. For that inquiry one particular kind of legal right was used as the model. Yet that kind of right does not so manifestly coincide with the object to which it applies as does, for instance, a right of requisition, or as do servitude rights.* And herein lay the element which furnished the temptation to accord to "rights"—as

* Translator's Note: For such readers as find the phrase "servitude rights" puzzling or even contradictory, it may be helpful to

a matter of principle—independent standing in the hierarchy of goods.

I think it may be accepted as settled that it is erroneous to accord independent status, by implication, *to the right of ownership*. The only thing that would seem to remain open to question is whether other property rights might not furnish more tenable grounds for such a verdict in favor of independent goods-status.

There is one consideration that makes this, too, exceedingly unlikely. Economically speaking, *all* property rights have one fundamental feature in common. And that is true no matter how definite may be the differences between them (as, for instance, the difference between right of ownership and a servitude) or between both of these and a mortgage and/or a right of requisition or rights under a bequest. That one fundamental feature which they possess in common is that with the help of those state agencies which are devoted to the determination of and the execution of the law, these property rights are intended and are fashioned to obtain or secure for the possessor of the right the physical possession and control of the good in question. Within the framework of this common characteristic the differences among them are *quantitative* rather than qualitative. A right of ownership, for instance, confers more complete and more far-reaching power of control than does a servitude. But in comparison with purely personal rights, such as the right to repayment of a loan, or rights arising under a contract of sale, both right of ownership and a servitude are more apodictic (i.e., capable of clear demonstration) and subject to fewer vicissitudes in their enforcement. It can, for instance, be pointed out that, on behalf of the owner of a property, the provisions

point out that "servitude" is not only an abstract noun but may also denote a very concrete thing. *Webster's International Dictionary of the English Language* (Springfield, Mass., 1957) includes among its definitions one under the rubric "Law" which reads: "A right in respect of an object, usually land, owned by one person in virtue of which the object is subject to a certain use or enjoyment by another person or for the benefit of another thing, as in the case of the common-law easement (which is a species of servitude) . . . In Roman Law servitudes were classified as, (a) personal servitudes including usufruct, (mere) use . . . and habitation, right of residing in a house . . . (b) Praedial or real servitudes or rights over land vested in a person by virtue of his ownership of other land (called *praedium serviens)* and including rural or rustic servitudes affecting chiefly or only soil, urban servitudes, affecting a building or buildings on land . . . the more important *actus,* a right of way for a carriage or cattle . . . *via,* right of way in general . . ." In the foregoing and the subsequent (relatively infrequent) instances where Böhm-Bawerk speaks of "servitudes" the reader will presumably not go far astray if he thinks of them as "easements and the like."

of the law are operative no matter who may seek to deprive him of it or to alienate from him even a part of its usefulness.

On the other hand, the holder of a servitude can invoke the provisions of the law only to the extent that unwarranted action by a third party violates *some specific aspect of the good's usefulness*. And again, a person having contractual rights as a purchaser, when such person has not yet become a possessor, can seek redress for invasion of his rights only against one particular person, namely, the seller. But the purchaser of commodity A is entirely without defense against a third person such as, let us say, the legitimate owner of commodity A which has been sold to him by a seller not having title to commodity A, or even against another party to whom the seller has made a dishonest sale of that same commodity A. It goes without saying that legal procedure treats these shadings in the degree of recognized and legally protected power of control as *qualitative*, not quantitative differences. That is to say, the process of law does so for its own purposes, and those purposes demand minute and meticulous differentiation. But all that does not alter the fact that, *economically speaking*, one fundamental characteristic is present throughout. That characteristic is that the function of all legal rights is to afford to men the means of availing themselves of the provisions of the state's laws in order to procure for themselves physical control of the things they call goods. Now, if the right of ownership (which of all property rights is probably the most comprehensive and clearly defined) cannot be regarded as an independent good aside from and in addition to the thing to which it applies, then the conclusion must be obvious that other rights which perform the same economic function as the right of ownership, except that they do so less perfectly and in more limited degree, are equally incapable of meriting the status of independent goods.

At all times and in respect to all persons the right of ownership confers complete legal competency to guarantee to the possessor of title the physical possession and enjoyment of the thing to which he has title. The right to delivery possessed by a purchaser bestows equal legal competency, but only from that point in time forward at which delivery of the purchased commodity was contractually promised, and only as against the contractual seller. If the claim to the more comprehensive legal support is not, by nature, a good, how could it be possible for the less comprehensive one to be so, since the latter is fundamentally of the same nature as the former, but less far-reaching in scope? It is clear that the foregoing comparison or parallel constitutes an equally cogent refutation of the goods-quality of *all* property rights, without exception. However, I cannot deny that some of those rights possess, to a considerable degree, an appearance of independence—an appearance which has for centuries persuaded scholars to treat them as independent things, giving them the name of *res incorporales*. Since that is so, I do not feel I am entitled to deny that independence until and unless I have made a more thorough examination into the nature of these candidates for the status of a good. In the interests of such an examination I shall divide into two groups all property rights other than right of ownership since the latter represents *full and present* power of control over tangible goods. Of the two groups I shall treat, the first will include those rights which, though they apply to present goods, apply to them only in limited degree. They might be described as *"rights to partial utilization."* In this category belong such rights, applying to things, as most servitude rights, *emphyteusis** and *superficies**; they would also include rights, applying to persons, (as apart from things) such as relationships arising from land lease, rental, and *commodatum* loans. [A *commodatum* is a non-interest-bearing loan of a chattel—Trsl.] The second of my two groups will include rights which are, economically speaking, different in that they apply to *the future proceeds to be derived from goods*. In this group belong the preponderant majority of personal rights of requisition, such as *mutuum* loans, purchase contracts, exchange contracts; they would also include rights under pledge contracts[2] and also rights of inheritance and, finally, those rights (variously interpreted by lawyers) which are based on relationships that convey exclusive rights to proceeds of some kind. The most important representatives of rights of this kind include

* Translator's Note: These two terms are defined as follows: *emphyteusis*—a contract by which a grant was made of a right, either perpetual or for a long period, to the possession and enjoyment of land, originally agricultural, subject to keeping of the land in cultivation or from depreciation, (and subject to) payment of a fixed annual rent (or canon) and some other conditions; *superficies*—a real right of servitude consisting in a right in perpetuity to enjoy the superficies (i.e., everything on the surface of a piece of ground, such as a building and other things so closely connected as to constitute part of it, as houses, other structures, trees, vines, etc.) on payment of an annual or periodic rent.

2. The essential matter at issue under a pledge contract is control over the yield of the thing pledged. Control of the pledged thing itself rests only to an extremely limited degree with the creditor under the pledge contract, and can hardly be said to be of a positive nature at all.

patent rights, rights accruing by virtue of membership in an industrial organization, copyrights and authors' royalties. [3,4]

Let us turn our immediate attention to what I have called *"Rights to Partial Utilization."*

CHAPTER III

The Concept Of Material Renditions Of Service And Their Economic Status. Renditions Of Service As The Object Of Legal Rights To Partial Utilization. Economic Nature Of Such Rights.

The Concept Of Material Renditions Of Service And Their Economic Status

If I am to be completely clear in my investigation into the problem which constitutes the subject of this chapter, I shall once again be compelled to present some preliminary observations that are general in nature and which concern the economic nature of goods in general. And it will be more especially my obligation to develop a concept which is, to my mind, indispensable if we are to comprehend those numerous phenomena in the world of economics and of jurisprudence which reveal goods as being *partially* controlled through some relationship or other. I refer to the concept of the rendition of physical service or the concept of physical utilization. My going into this phase of the subject somewhat in detail may be justified on two counts. For one thing, it will serve to afford a firm basis for my theory which in many respects departs from orthodox theory. For a second, it will facilitate the presentation of subsequent portions of this work in that the way will have been better prepared.

[3.] I crave the pardon of the members of the bar if my tripartite classification into (a) property rights, (b) rights to partial utilization, and (c) rights to future proceeds of goods strikes them as unscientific from the legalistic viewpoint. I can only plead that a basis for classification which appears ill-chosen from the viewpoint of one science may be important and fruitful from the viewpoint of some other science.

[4.] I am here ignoring the purely negative* servitudes, concerning the economic nature of which clarification will be submitted in due course in Chapter VI.

* Translator's Note: A servitude may be affirmative or negative. It is "affirmative when it permits an otherwise unpermitted act by the owner of it; it is negative when it imposes forbearance of an otherwise permissible act."

All corporeal goods are useful to man by virtue of the activity of the peculiar natural forces inherent in those goods. Goods admittedly share this quality of being imbued with natural forces. That is to say, they share it with those things that are not useful, and even with things that are harmful. But experience shows us that, although all matter is imbued with natural forces, there must be some guidance, some "steering," if a useful purpose advantageous to man is to be achieved. And matter is capable of that guidance only if it has taken on a form which renders it amenable to such guidance. The natural force, for instance, which we call weight is inherent in all matter. But the weight of a mountain is a thing that man cannot turn to any account. However, man is thoroughly capable of utilizing the weight of a clock's pendulum or of the piece of metal placed in the pan of a balance-scale. The same applies to the natural forces that are inherent in carbon, but only if that carbon has assumed the form, let us say, of wood or coal but not, on the other hand, when it is a constituent part of the earth's atmosphere. On the strength of these facts it becomes possible to differentiate corporeal *goods* from nonuseful material things on the ground that *goods are such advantageous manifestations of matter that they permit man to guide the natural forces inherent in them into channels advantageous to him.*

If we consider in detail the manner in which it is possible for the multifarious goods that man avails himself of to become useful to him, we encounter an exceedingly wide variation and heterogeneity. A book is useful in a manner entirely different from that exhibited by a pair of shears; a house differs in its kind of usefulness from a pencil, a coat from a loaf of bread. But within the variegation in detail there nevertheless abides one common constant feature. And that is that goods are useful *by virtue of the forces of nature that reside in them or by virtue of the renditions of natural force which emanate from them.* This is a statement which, from the viewpoint of the science of physics, appears so axiomatic as to be a platitude. Nevertheless, from the viewpoint of economic discussion it may be regarded as something not at all unnecessary to state. This is particularly true if we are to lay a firm foundation for the concept of the utilization of corporeal goods —a matter that has often been forgone with resulting loss in both clarity and accuracy.

We must conceive of the *act of utilization of goods* as follows. Regardless of their form, all corporeal goods undergo utilization by virtue of the activation for the delivery of useful renditions of service of the forces of nature residing in them. This is no less true if the corporeal goods are persons or living creatures than it is if they are things. It applies with equal truth to the ditch-digger, the porter, the operator of a machine, to beasts of burden and other animals, such as a draft horse or a watchdog. In their case, just as in that of inanimate corporeal goods, it is the concrete activations of "harnessable" or "tractable" inherent forces of nature or renditions of power which yield to man the usefulness which he derives from these corporeal goods. The utilization of a good consists in man's evoking at the proper moment the renditions of power that are peculiar to the good he is dealing with, unless those renditions emanate spontaneously. It is then further necessary that man bring it about that the manifestation of power be applied to the object in connection with which he wants a useful result to be accomplished. Let us consider, as an example, the utilization of a locomotive to deliver motive power. By filling it with water and by applying heat, man causes the locomotive to deliver motive power. Then he brings it about that the motive power be applied to the railway carriages which contain the persons or things that need to be transported. Or, to observe another example, consider how man will effect a useful contact of, say, a book, a house, with his eye or with his entire person. These are examples of goods which are characterized by uninterrupted spontaneous emanations of their powers—light images in one case, protection in the other. It is a *sheer impossibility to conceive a utilization of corporeal goods which does not consist in either the reception of useful renditions of service or in the delivery of natural powers emanating from the corporeal goods undergoing utilization.* And any attempt to conjure up a concept at variance with that principle I consider (and with good reason) to be a gross violation of the physical laws of nature.

It is improbable that the foregoing pronouncement will encounter opposition in the form of any deliberate conclusion arrived at through a process of ratiocination. But it may conflict with conclusions based on impression or on a feeling that rises from a partiality to the belief that the whole matter of the utilization of corporeal goods represents a spontaneous interplay of the forces of nature. And it must be admitted that in the case of many objects which serve as goods the concept of them as bearers of forces of nature is utterly familiar. That would be true of draft animals, a locomotive, a millrace; but it is undeniable that it would be an unfamiliar concept in connection with a dwelling house, with a book of poems, and with a painting by Raphael to think of them as being useful only through activation of the forces of nature inherent in them. And yet it is a matter of sober truth that these things qualify as economic goods only by virtue of the natural forces which reside in them and do so in a manner peculiar to those things. The fact that a dwelling house affords protection and warmth is nothing more nor less than the effect of the forces of gravity, of cohesion, of resistivity, of impenetrability, of poor-heat-conductivity—forces which characterize building materials. The fact that the thoughts and feelings of a poet are reproduced in us is brought about through purely physical means—by means of light, color and written symbols; and this physical part of the communication of thought and feeling is the function of the book. Be it granted that the poet's soul must have originated thought and emotion, and be it further granted that only in another soul and through intellectual powers can those thoughts and emotions be reproduced, but the path from soul to soul leads through the physical world for one stretch of the journey and on that stretch the intellectual element must make use of the physical vehicle, that is to say, of the forces or powers of nature. The book is that physical material vehicle. So, too, is it with the painting or with the spoken word. In and of themselves they simply furnish the physical stimulus. Whatever intellectual element is added *we* supply out of our own "souls" when we react to the physical stimulus. But if we are not prepared for a fruitful reaction—if, that is to say, we cannot read or, even if we can read but are incapable of the necessary understanding or emotion, then nothing takes place beyond the physical stimulus. Our feeling that it is strange or unnatural to conceive of the utilization of certain goods as the manifestation of powers of nature can probably be attributed to the fact that in everyday life our concept of a "power" is far grosser and more limited than should be the case. We have a predilection for conceiving of a "power" as the producer of some movement or some change which is obviously and physically perceptible; and we like to think of clearly mobile objects as the bearers of such "powers." But the realization that where we see movement we may be seeing power *on the impelled side* as well as *on the impelling side,* that the *burden,* as well as the bearing of it represents power, that resistance is as much a manifestation of power as is the stimulation, that inertia, rest and the maintenance of a condition of rest are just as much the result of the exertion of power as is the most violent motion; in short, the realization that powers may be at work even when no physical motion on the part of bodies or of masses of matter may be visible—such a realization is one which enriches and rectifies our conception of the everyday world about us only when we apply to it scientific abstraction and scientific thinking. But ordinarily (and hence the feeling of strangeness and unfamiliarity) only certain manifestations of power gain our attention and arouse in us the concept that there is a "force," a "power," at work. And those "certain manifestations" are the ones which are most obvious, and which are most readily perceptible to our senses.

I should not have expended so many words in establishing so simple a matter if I did not believe that *impressions* are the very things that constitute more formidable antagonists than do reasoned counterarguments. For the former, as contrasted with the latter, have nothing in common with reason and hence, once entrenched, cannot be dislodged by an appeal to reason. For a similar reason I am impelled to add one brief observation. It may seem easy to draw the conclusion that, although it may be scientifically correct to attribute the manifestations of usefulness on the part of corporeal goods to the delivery of natural powers, it is, nevertheless, pedantic and absurd to set down and to elaborate with great emphasis this thought which is, in any event, quite obvious and self-evident. I should like to reply, quite briefly, that I admit there could be nothing more absurd than to compel myself, or the reader in *every* instance where the usefulness of a good is under discussion to envision, let us say, the use of a *painting* in terms of reflected undulations of the ether or the use of needle and thread as the operation of a physical wedge of such and such a degree of hardness plus the cohesive power possessed by the thread. But, however absurd it may be in an individual instance, to hound to death a thought that is basically correct, it is nevertheless fruitful to recognize and adhere to that thought as a *universal truth* when discussing the nature of *all* goods, especially if we thereby impart some firmness to several concepts which, being borrowed from colloquial usage, have hitherto even in their scientific application, failed to acquire true definitiveness, despite the fact that for our science they are of great—even fundamental—importance. Two such concepts are the *use* and the *yield* of goods.

After the foregoing deviation, let us resume the main thread of our discourse.

In order to gain a simple expression for a concept, one that we shall have to make use of frequently in the pages to come, let us use the term *renditions of service* to designate the individual useful activations to be derived from corporeal goods.[1]

From the nature of a good in the light of the concept "rendition of service" that I have just established, it is apparent that every object which would lay claim to being termed a good must have the capacity to deliver renditions of service and that when that capacity is exhausted, so is its claim to goods-quality. It thereupon drops from the category of goods and reverts to that of mere things. It is possible to conceive of the exhaustion of this capacity as something other than the exhaustion of the capacity to deliver manifestations of power at all. For just as matter is indestructible, so, too, are the powers inherent in it. These never cease to exist as emanations. But it is possible for the emanations to cease to be useful, i.e., to be renditions of *service* for the reason that the thing which was, at the outset, a good, in the course of delivering its renditions of service undergoes such a change, such a loss, transfer or combining of its parts with other bodies that, in its altered form, it can no longer be so guided or "harnessed" that its manifestations of power continue favorable to the purposes of man. For instance, after the carbon of wood which has been burned in the blast furnace has been combined with oxygen in the process of combustion, it is no longer capable of a second utilization of its permanent and naturally operative powers for the smelting of ore. A broken pendulum retains its weight, continues to exhibit its former gravitational qualities, but the loss of its pendulum-form renders it no longer favorable for guiding its natural power into the channel of regulating clockwork. This exhaustion of the capacity for the rendition of useful service brought about by the utilization of goods is customarily termed "using up" or consumption.

[1]. The concept I am here setting up is by no means an entirely new one, but was known long ago to economic science under the name "revenues" or "yields" of goods, using the word in a concrete sense. When one speaks of the "yield" that one can derive from a draft horse, a machine, a book, or a house, one means, obviously, only the renditions of service by those things that consist in the useful activations of the forces of nature that reside in them. However, I prefer to replace the traditional expression "yield" of goods with "renditions of service" because the latter expression seems to me to be more expressive of the actual nature of the thing under discussion, and seems to compel the imagination to a concept more nearly adequate to the desired purpose. This is in part because the expression "yield" has in economic science for a long time been of ambiguous significance and has been used to designate things quite different from the physical renditions of service afforded by corporeal goods. There is, for example, the "net yield" of capital. In fact, it has even come to be used with reference to consumptible goods, which is to say, of goods not by nature capable of long continued delivery of concrete renditions of service.

Now while it is true that all goods do and *must* possess in common this quality of having renditions of power to deliver, they differ very materially from each other in the *number* of such renditions of service that they have to deliver. On this fact is based the familiar division of goods into durable[2] and nondurable. Some goods are of such a nature that if they are to deliver at all the service of which they are capable they must deliver their entire serviceability at a single stroke, as it were, in one single more or less intensive rendition of service. The result is that in such case the first utilization completely exhausts their capacity for service and constitutes consumption. These may be termed consumptible goods, such as foodstuffs, gunpowder, fuels and the like. Other goods, again, are by nature capable of numerous renditions of service in such manner that in the course of a shorter or longer period of time they deliver these renditions *successively,* and thus, after the first or even after repeated utilization they retain their goods-quality. These are *durable goods,* such as clothing, houses, tools, jewels, land-parcels and so on. When a good delivers a long succession of renditions of service the manner of such delivery is twofold. In one case the successive renditions are recognizable as *distinctly separate occurrences,* so that they can be marked off and counted. An example would be the individual strokes of a trip hammer or the operation of the automatic printing press of a metropolitan newspaper. Conversely, emanations of the powers of nature may flow out from the good in an uninterrupted and uniform succession, such as the noiseless and continued furnishing of protection derived from a dwelling house. In this second case if, despite the continuity, we desire to segregate and apportion the renditions of service (and that often becomes a practical necessity), we take recourse to the loophole which is generally resorted to in the division of continuous magnitudes. When the thing to be subdivided does not, itself, exhibit any division into units, the dividing unit is borrowed from some extraneous circumstances—for instance, the expiration of a given time. Thus one grants to the tenant of a house the renditions of service that emanate from the house *over, say, a period of half a year.*

If we now turn from the external appearance of renditions of service by corporeal goods to the position they oc-

---

2. Even those goods which I should prefer to term "nonconsumptible" and which are commonly called "durable" do, in actual fact, get consumed, even though the process may be a slow one. The term "durable" I feel to be less expressive of the contrast between rapid consumption of goods in the course of utilization, on the one hand, and, on the other hand, their rapid deterioration without any reference to their utilization.

cupy in man's economizing, we find that the most interesting phase of their nature confronts us in their *independence.* However incomplete may be their physical independence, these goods, economically speaking, frequently
exhibit marked independence. Economic science has been
in the habit of registering this long familiar phenomenon
by the somewhat strange remark that under some circumstances the "yields" of goods are capable of *themselves be-
coming goods.*[3] An admission of this sort is no more than
a vague approximation of the highly important function
performed by the renditions of service on the part of corporeal goods amidst the workings of the various factors in
our economic activity. If we are to characterize that function fittingly, it is imperative that we go a step further
and make this additional observation. The only reason at
all *why men desire corporeal goods lies in the prospect they
afford of renditions of service. And these renditions of
service are capable of attaining economic independence
aside from the goods themselves. Furthermore, this characteristic is not something that is a purely incidental and
secondary matter. On the contrary, it is the renditions of
service rather than the goods themselves which, as a matter of principle, constitute the primary basic units of our
economic transactions. And it is only from the renditions
of service that the goods, secondarily, derive their own significance.*

It can hardly prove difficult to make clear this relationship between goods and renditions of service. But recognition of its existence has as yet been but inadequately exploited, and should still prove a fruitful point of departure
for an examination into the phenomena of the value of
goods. And it is probable that knowledge of this relationship has for a long time failed to be the subject of precise
formulation only for the reason that it seemed to be an axiomatic and self-evident truth. Nothing, it would seem, can
be clearer than that a house, a parcel of land, a loaf of bread,
a horse, is not an object of desire for its own sake, but
only because of the services which are promised to us by
reason of the forces of nature inherent in these things and
peculiar to them. It is equally obvious that if we should
be given objective control of a parcel of arable land, but
denied the enjoyment of its renditions of useful service,
we should be as scornful of that parcel as of the rind of an
orange from which the juice has been expressed. This indicates clearly enough that the economic significance which

---

[3.] E.g., Hermann, *Staatswirtschaftliche Untersuchungen,* 2nd
ed., page 109; Menger, *Principles of Economics,* page 156 *(Grundsätze der Volkswirtschaftslehre,* p. 132).

goods have for us lies in the economic significance which their *renditions of service* possess for us.

One further observation will make it clear that when we accord to these renditions of service (rather than to the goods themselves) the position of the veritable basic elements of our economy, we are not indulging in any mere figure of speech. That observation is as follows.

Whatever importance we accord to the corporeal objects of the world of economic goods derives from the importance which we attach to the satisfaction of our wants and the attainment of our purposes. The natural unit of means-of-satisfaction will be the one that corresponds to the means of satisfying one unit of our wants or to the attainment of one unit of our purposes. That unit, however, does not (unless merely fortuitously) consist in the good, but consists, rather, in the individual *rendition of service* which is necessary and adequate for the elicitation of one unit of concrete result. I do not completely consume a team of horses when I go for a pleasure drive, nor an "entire" hammer when I forge one nail, nor a piano when I play one sonata. In every activity some unit of useful purpose, in the form of a *concrete rendition of service*, is aligned, as it were, face to face with some corresponding unit of want and of consumption. To be sure, it frequently happens that a whole good comprises a single unit of want, such as one loaf of bread, one meal. This occurs only because, quite by chance, the good and the rendition of service coincide as a single unit and because the use content of such *consumptible goods* is exhausted by the single rendition of service.

Just as the renditions of service by goods, in accordance with the foregoing, constitute the most elementary units of means-for-the-satisfaction-of-wants, so also their economic significance or, in other words, their economic *value* is something that originates with them. It is not correct to say that renditions of service by a good enjoy a given estimation of value because a good has value, or high value. On the contrary, the value of the renditions of service is quite independently determined in accordance with the circumstances that are applicable to *them*. Indeed, the value of the goods themselves is established only derivatively in accordance with the value of the renditions of service. Now this pronouncement, which is completely characteristic for the position of objective renditions of service, has appeared repeatedly in the writings of economist authors, but merely in passing and only with respect to selected groups of corporeal goods. But it has not been recognized[4] as a principle possessing universal validity. For that reason I consider it incumbent on me to add a few words of demonstration. These, to be sure, cannot elevate the discussion above the level of mere suggestive remarks.

For no matter to what theory one subscribes concerning the origin and the measure of the value of goods, there is one point that must be admitted by both protagonists and opponents of any theory. That one point is that whatever importance and esteem we accord, in the form of *an estimation of value*, to the means to well-being is merely a reflection and a further development of the importance we accord to our *wants* and our *purposes*. Where there is no want and where, rightly or wrongly, there is no approved purpose, there is also no value. And even though one may be in agreement with numerous writers who contend that the measure of exchange value is, as a practical thing, regulated by *costs* or by the *expenditure of labor*, it is futile to deny that we discern behind the convolutions of that kind of cost-and-labor-theory the thing which Rau calls the "concrete use-value of goods" and which is nothing more nor less than their concrete significance for the purposes of our well-being. For the question of my willingness or unwillingness to expend costs or labor or of my willingness or unwillingness to compensate someone else for them

4. It has been indirectly recognized, e.g., in its application to land, by Roscher (*Grundlagen*, Sec. 154) when he says that the price of parcels of land depends on the amount of the income they bring, i.e., the price of the yield. But this opinion of his has not been adopted by Roscher as a principle that becomes an integral part of his economic principles. For this outstanding scholar immediately thereafter (Sec. 154, note 2) sharply criticizes the views of MacLeod which, basically, are founded on the same view, namely, that the purchase price of a piece of land represents the capitalized value of a given number of years' yield. There is no sign at all of any general recognition of the principle as valid for all goods. Nor is that a matter to cause astonishment. For, with respect to most goods produced in the regular course of production, this matter of valuation which, for land parcels, seems particularly obvious, is much beclouded by other conditions and hence made a matter of extreme doubt especially for those scholars who pay obeisance to the view that the value of goods, as a matter of principle, is determined by the cost of producing them. Since production, which exercises the most easily observable influence on supply and hence on price and exchange value, deals with physical units of completed goods, the situation begins to take on the appearance that the *development of value*, too, gets its initial impulse from completed goods. There is a failure to observe that an increase in the supply of completed goods can depress their price only indirectly because through that increase there arises also an increase in the supply of renditions of service by that particular kind of good. A careful and logical examination of the question will readily demonstrate the truth of this observation. I am obliged to forgo a more detailed discussion of this point, however interesting it may be in connection with the doctrine of value, because of the unavoidable extensiveness to which any logical treatment of the topic would necessarily commit me.

is in the last analysis decided by the "concrete use-value" of the things I must expend in comparison with that of those which I wish to acquire, either directly or indirectly.

It now becomes easy to reach the conviction that every decision as to the importance of means-to-our-well-being undergoes a transfer from a consideration of the *unit of purpose* to that of the corresponding unit of *means-for-ful-filling-the-purpose,* and that therefore the value of goods *first* comes into being in terms of the latter unit. For the whole make-up of the human mind and spirit is such that it is inevitable, whenever man appraises his emotions, his needs and his purposes (and these always furnish the basis for his appraisal of his goods), that he begin by establishing a *unit* of those emotions, needs, and purposes. It is utterly impossible for us to estimate the enjoyment we derive from three concerts or six dinners unless we first estimate the enjoyment we derive from one concert or one dinner and unless we then undertake some—admittedly not strictly mathematical—sort of multiplication.[5] Let us consider the opposite possibility, that man begins with a cumulative appraisal of a *plurality* of emotions, enjoyments, and purposes, and that he then proceeds to an estimation of the units by some process of division. That possibility not only finds no corroboration in human experience, but also, if it be maintained that such a procedure is *the rule,* it must at least be admitted that it proposes a psychological impossibility.

Now it is equally natural and obvious that an estimation of value which was *originally* based on the units-of-satisfaction or of useful purposes should immediately be transferred to the corresponding unit of the means-to-satisfaction. And that a complete multiplicity of means-to-satisfaction involves a complex judgment of value which can be arrived at only by applying to the appraisal of the units a process of derivation and a sort of summation. No farmer who wants to estimate the value of his herd of cattle and set a value for the individual beeves would dream of beginning by making an estimate of the whole herd in a lump sum and then apply a process of division to arrive at a value for the individual animals. And that is especially true if he is concerned, not with establishing an exchange-value, but a use-value. In such cases he will begin by estimating the use-value he can derive from one "cow" in order that from that point of departure he can set up

5. This does not exclude the possibility that at times, and when dealing with familiar things, we employ an abbreviated or short-cut process of estimation in order to avoid the necessity of estimating all the details *every time.*

an estimate of the total use-value that is to be derived from the entire herd.

There is no difference between the procedure that applies to a herd and a single beef and that which applies to appraising goods and their renditions of service. If I wish to arrive at a decision as to what value a draft animal has for me, or an axe, my only reasonable procedure is to begin by considering what renditions of service I can expect from these things, what value renditions of that kind have for me, and how numerous they will be, or how long they will last. Not until I have given consideration to the kind, the number and the individual value of the renditions of service can a secondary and composite estimate be made of the value of the animal or of the axe. The opposite procedure of first setting a value on the whole good, *a priori,* and then, by effecting a computation by means of division of the *a priori* amount, arriving at an estimation of the individual rendition—that is a method which is simply inconceivable as the initial step in forming an estimate of value. There is only one explanation of the fact that there may occasionally be instances where, on the surface, it might appear that we do form our estimates in that manner. That explanation is that we appear to substitute something else for the conscious reflection which weighs the proper grounds for an estimation of value. The reason for the substitution lies in the haste and pressure which characterize our economic transactions. And the substitution consists in taking recourse to habit, to our memory of precedent, to reliance on other persons' judgments, or to yielding to the influence of other *extraneous* factors. Of course, this latter method will come into play only after numerous appraisals of value, arrived at by the *natural* method, have provided the material which enables us to employ the substitution mentioned in the foregoing.

What may we conclude from all this? We conclude that, inasmuch as the concrete renditions of service are means for the satisfaction of wants in a more real sense than are goods themselves, these renditions of service are more keenly desired and more highly valued than goods. And we may conclude that, as I have previously stated, it is not goods, but it is in very truth the renditions of service which emanate from those goods which constitute the smallest independent units of our economy and that the former (i.e., goods) constitute only complexes of the latter, that goods are therefore a secondary category.[6]

6. This view indicates the path to the solution of another puzzle. I refer to the interesting and by no means simple phenomenon of devaluation, the so-called "wearing out" or exhaustion of goods.

This exhaustion has a physical but also an economic aspect. The former is apparent in the deterioration in physical condition of the "worn out" good; the latter becomes apparent in the diminution in number (and often simultaneous deterioration in quality) of the renditions of service procurable from the good. This economic deterioration parallels and goes hand-in-hand with the physical. This characteristic of exhaustion becomes the cause of devaluation or loss of value because the value of a good is comprised, at any given time, of the totality of the values of the renditions of service derivable from it; and because the magnitude of that totality diminishes in the same measure as the process of exhaustion progresses. But this basically simple explanation encounters the following complicating feature. Why is it true (as experience proves it to be) that in the case of durable goods the degree of exhaustion does not equal the total of the renditions of service which have been derived from the good? A dwelling, for instance, worth $50,000 yields renditions of service in the form of housing for a year, worth $5,000. But it does not decrease in value by $5,000 but, at the most, by only a few hundred, if it is solidly constructed. And in the case of goods that are perpetual, such as parcels of land, why is there no depreciation or devaluation, despite the fact that here, too, a yearly quota of renditions of service is withdrawn? This ought to mean that the residual total of renditions of service has been reduced. The answer which I can only hint at here is, briefly, as follows: While it is true that the residual renditions still inherent in the good have suffered some *quantitative* diminution, they have also experienced some *increase* in value or (qualitative) appreciation, caused by the fact that they have approached closer to the status of having *present value*. What was, at the beginning of the year "next year's" rendition of service is now "this year's"; what was the rendition that was "two years away" is now "only one year away"; what lay three years in the future now lies but two years in the future, and so on. And, by the general principle of discounting, all undergo a higher valuation of their present worth. Now, when the series of annual renditions residing in a good is a very long one, the total of the increases in value can virtually counterbalance the depreciation caused by withdrawal of the annual quota of renditions. And where, as in the case of land, the total for all practical purposes is equal to infinity, the sum of the increases does, actually, completely counterbalance the devaluation.

These meager hints may suffice to permit us to recognize that the hitherto largely disregarded phenomenon of the exhaustion of goods nevertheless does present a very interesting aspect and that it is impossible to gain a complete understanding of it without a detailed examination of the useful content of goods and without giving recognition to the principle that renditions of service are, in truth, the independent factors in the estimation of value and the independent economic entities that I have claimed for them in the foregoing text. But I should like to anticipate and forestall possible misunderstanding by making clear that it is not my contention that renditions of service are the natural units *in all economic relationships*. They certainly are not, for instance, in the area of production. Production, for obvious reasons, is oriented to the good as its natural unit (which, for the most part, contains a multiplicity of renditions of service). And in other areas, too, such as transportation, appraisal of value, etc., the good is frequently the natural unit. But in *consumption* which, for the existence of goods, is the most important economic activity, because it represents the area in which goods fulfill their destiny—in consumption the rendition of service is the natural unit, and that is the reason why it can also be the unit in other economic relations, such as in economic exchange and in the estimation of value. At any rate, this will suffice to justify that the measure of economic independence which I have claimed in the foregoing text is properly attributable to renditions of service.

In sober fact, the independent status of renditions of service, as I have set it forth in such detail, is not and has not remained a mere theoretical abstraction. It is, on the contrary, clearly recognizable in a number of the phenomena of practical economic life. And these serve both to corroborate and to explain that independence. And just as it is true that the law, in general, accommodates itself to economic activity and adapts legal forms to the phenomena and interests of economizing man, so also is it true that these peculiar manifestations of concrete renditions of service, now recognized to be independent economic entities, are duly reflected in jurisprudential procedure. And thus we arrive at the point where we may return to the discussion of the subject before us, namely, the analysis of the economic aspects of *rights*.

Renditions Of Service As The Object Of Legal Rights To Partial Utilization

There are cases by the thousand arising in everyday practical economic life in which someone needs, for his particular purpose, the control or power of disposal over only a single rendition of service by an objective good while, at the same time, he has no interest whatsoever in any control over its remaining renditions of service; or he may, in fact, be in a position where those might merely be burdensome to him, which is another way of saying that outright possession of the whole good would be quite unwelcome. Let us say a traveler wants to get from the railroad station to the hotel. For this purpose it would be very desirable for him to command some gasoline, an automobile and a taxi-driver to get him to his destination. But because he is scheduled to stay in that particular city only a very short time, any command of subsequent renditions of service by the things and the person mentioned is a matter of complete indifference to him. Indeed, it would be quite burdensome for him since he would have to be responsible for their continued maintenance and storage, etc. Another example might be that of a farmer whose arable land lies on the far side of a parcel owned by someone else. He would find it desirable to make use—extremely limited use, to be sure, of the intervening parcel as a means of access to his own. But it would be exceedingly awkward and entirely unnecessary for him to be compelled for that purpose to acquire *all* the renditions of service of the intervening parcel, or, in other words, to buy that land.

Man's practical good sense has brought it about that in cases of this kind he acquires economic power of disposal, *not* of the entire goods, but of their individual renditions of service. Thereupon, practical *de facto* occurrences of that kind inevitably had to find *legal* sanction. Just as it was necessary, in the case of outright ownership rights to provide legal sanction for complete and unlimited power of disposal over entire goods, just so did it become necessary to provide that less-than-entire powers of disposal should also find legal sanction and to confer upon these independent economic entities the character of economic legal entities as well. Thus there arose a number of rights to which we may, perhaps, apply an inclusive name by calling them *rights to renditions of service* or *rights to partial utilization*. In the field of property rights these include, pre-eminently, the various types of servitude and such things as hereditary leases and hereditary rentals (*emphyteusis* and *superficies*) (see definition of these terms on p. 65) ; in the field of personal rights, rights under rental contracts and rights of the borrower (of a *commodatum* loan).[7]

The distinguishing feature of all these rights is as follows. The person possessing the right has control, not of the *total number* of renditions of service of which the object of his legal relationship is capable, but is limited by some line of demarcation setting apart some portions of the renditions which alone are subject to the control and disposal of the possessor of the right. There is a variety of ways in which that line of demarcation may be drawn. In some cases single renditions of service are set aside and *individually* delimited and determined, such as a single trip of a conveyance from point A to point B. In other cases a whole class of renditions of service is set aside and conveyed, such as the rights to pasturage within a given tract of forest land. (In such a case the person possessing the right has no claim to the renditions of service residing in the wood of the forest, either as lumber or as fuel.) Then, again, in other cases the right applies to the totality of the renditions of service, *but only for a limited time*. Then all renditions procurable from the good after expiration of the stipulated time revert to the owner. This latter kind of case (which includes usufruct and land rental over long periods) naturally always entails a presupposition that the good is capable of delivering renditions of service over an extended period of time; and there is an implied proviso that the possessor of the right is to avoid any manner of utilization which will result in immediate exhaustion of the

---

7. This is not the same, in my opinion, as the rights of the debtor under a contract covering the loan of fungible goods (a *mutuum*). I shall reserve the details of my reasons for this distinction of presentation at a more appropriate point. In this matter I am not in agreement with Knies (see his *Geld*, Berlin, 1873, p. 72ff.).

entire capacity of the good for rendition of service. Now, no matter what the manner in which the line of demarcation may be drawn, these rights always manifest one common feature which distinguishes them from the right of ownership. The latter confers complete control and disposal[8] over the totality of renditions of service procurable from a good; legal claims and rights, on the contrary, confer legally sanctioned control and disposal over only a portion of the procurable renditions of service; and control over the good only to whatever degree is indispensable to enjoyment of those renditions covered by the right. I now find it incumbent upon me to propound the following query. *Is it proper, from the economist's viewpoint, or is it not proper to regard legal claims and rights, as they have been described in the foregoing, as entitled to be ranked as goods in their own right—goods possessed by the beneficiary under the right?*

It is my belief that an insight into the economic nature of these claims and rights, as we have just attempted to gain such insight, and as it is afforded by our understanding of the nature of the thing to which the rights apply, namely, the renditions of service as independent economic entities—that insight, I say, necessarily leads me to the conclusion that the answer to the question propounded at the close of the preceding paragraph must be *in the negative.* Indeed, I shall go so much further as to say that the thought process that we must follow to arrive at the answer bears close similarity to the line of reasoning which we followed earlier when we reached the conviction that *property rights* are in no sense genuine goods.

Economic Nature Of Such Rights

Let us take as our starting point the fact, already established in detail, that renditions of service do possess the character of independent economic entities. As such they are no less subject than are concrete goods themselves to the requirement that they must possess certain qualifications if they are to have the status of *goods.* But even the one vital qualification (that they constitute the economic means of satisfying economic wants) is itself subject to certain qualifications. It is obvious that those must be the same ones by which manifestations of power by a mere thing qualify as renditions of *service.* A want must exist, which the rendition satisfies; the latter must be objectively suitable to meet the want; man must be aware of that suit-

8. With the exception of such cases as concern property that is expressly encumbered by servitudes and similar legal rights of third parties.

ability; he must possess the knowledge of how to utilize that suitability; finally—and this is a "last, not least"—the rendition must be available to man and *subject to his power of disposal.* All that brings us to such a point that we need but draw a parallel to the reasoning previously followed when we reached our earlier conviction that *property rights are in no sense genuine goods.*

Let us return to the rental rights of the passenger in the taxicab and his right to the renditions of service on the part of the gasoline, etc. Just as it is impossible to speak of that rendition of service as a separate good, as something aside from and in addition to the engine's ability to pull a load, aside from and in addition to the auto's speed, so also is it impossible to speak of the factual or legal power of disposal on the part of the taxi passenger as anything more than or other than a *circumstance* by virtue of which the rendition of service acquires *for him* the economic character of a rendition of service: it is impossible, therefore, to speak of his power of disposal over the rendition of service as an independent good beside and in addition to the rendition of service itself. This legal right is just a right of partial utilization which the passenger possesses. It is quite obvious (and this makes the parallelism of the present line of reasoning to the earlier one regarding property rights all the closer) that this right stands in the same relationship to the rendition of service as that in which the right of ownership stands to the object to which it applies. The right of utilization means the legally assured right of possession with respect to the rendition of service in the same way as that in which the right of ownership means the legally assured possession with respect to the concrete good to which it applies, that is to say, with respect to the totality of its renditions of service. Whenever a "right to utilization" is appraised, purchased or conveyed, there is just one thing which constitutes the true economic object or thing we are dealing with, just one object which is expected to, and which does, satisfy a want. That is the rendition of service or the group of renditions of service to which the right applies. This is no different from the situation which exists when it is a matter of acquiring or conveying right of ownership. For in this latter case what is actually being acquired or conveyed is the *things* to which the right of ownership applies.

And so, even the phenomenon of independent legal rights to partial utilization does not, in the slightest, compel us to take recourse to the artificial hypothesis of the existence of a separate category of intangibles called rights. Quite on the contrary, even if we limit our categories of goods to (1) material objective goods, and (2) renditions of service, we have adequate room to take care of rights, provided we give proper recognition to the appearance, as independent entities, of objective renditions of service, both in economic and in juridical transactions.[9]

CHAPTER IV

Rights To Future Yield Of Goods. Their Position With Relation To The Computation Of Wealth, As Well As The Position Of All Rights In This Regard. Basic Principles Concerning Computation Of Wealth. The Distinction Between Materials Of Wealth And Forms Of Wealth.

Rights To Future Yield Of Goods

One step still further ahead will lead us to a consideration of that group of rights of which the essential characteristic is that they apply to *the future proceeds of goods*. Among these the most prominent and the ones possessing

9. It is possible that to an occasional reader it may seem that I myself have been guilty of pleonasm or duplication when I speak of the renditions of service on the part of goods as independent economic entities in addition to the material goods themselves. To avert the possibility of misunderstanding, I wish to submit the following observation. I think of the relationship between objective goods and their renditions of service as being like that between an ear of grain (such as wheat or maize) and the individual kernels contained in the ear. The ear embraces the totality of the kernels in one single physical unit. This does not preclude the possibility of removing the individual kernels from the ear, nor, for that matter, of making previous independent disposition of them. That is to say, it does not preclude the existence of the kernels as independent entities. And in any event the ear derives its entire significance from the kernels it contains. In the same manner the good is for me the physical unit that contains a collection of renditions of service. The latter, maturing successively, can be withdrawn and independently disposed of. They constitute the economic content of the good which, once divested of them, is no better than would be an empty ear. However, we must take into account one circumstance. There are no constituent component parts of the substance of the good, to be "shelled out" like kernels, and so our nomenclature must be revised. And thus I take recourse to "renditions". I am not here attempting to extend the metaphor — nor should I approve of doing so for the sake of my theory. For, since I have only *postulated* material goods as bearers of functioning powers and have further *postulated* those powers as sources of the known manifestations of natural power possessed by the good, the substance of the good is not to be termed a source of utility in any more truly objective sense than are the manifestations of natural power emanating from the material good.

greatest theoretical importance are *payment-claims*.* It is these which particularly effect a shifting of *relationships of wealth*, as opposed to relationships of ownership which, that is to say, make it possible that wealth can be present even in a quarter where there is no direct possession of property and of goods. It is these which, more than other rights, play the part of independent objects of wealth and which must especially be distinguished from material concrete goods, and which constitute the strongest motive for economist authors to recognize rights as independent nonmaterial, intangible goods. And it is these which, when they are present in a community, cannot be said to increase the material wealth as a whole, but which do increase the wealth of those individual members of that nation who possess these rights.

Even in the case of this class of rights I think I can furnish a much simpler and more natural explanation than is afforded by the creation of a special class of "intangible goods" which, despite its apparent simplicity is, after all, an artificial explanation.

In my opinion the only true goods that come into play when a "payment-claim" is bought, exchanged or appraised, etc., are the *objects themselves which constitute the matter of the debt* and to which, knowingly or unknowingly, the creditors look as the material underlying the loan. But the payment-claim is merely the expression of the relationship of *"being-about-to-receive"* just as ownership is the expression of the relationship of the *assured possession* of real goods. Now, just as surely as it is impossible for the possession of a good, by its nature, to be a separate and distinct good, just so surely is it impossible for the still unrealized possession, or the "being-about-to-have-possession," to be such a good. Rather is it true that it is no more than the condition precedent *for some particular person* of the *coming-into-existence of* a good, just as possession is *one condition precedent* for the *possession of goods-quality* on the part of the thing.

Alternatively, we may express this by saying that, since the payment-claim is an expression of the circumstance that the thing which constitutes the matter of the debt will, *at some time in the future*, become a good for the person possessing the right to advance the claim, it therefore merely constitutes the condition precedent of

* Translator's Note: Böhm-Bawerk is speaking of rights to demand repayment of a loan or, more generally, rights to demand payment of any debt. This translator takes the liberty of coining the expression "payment-claims" signifying right(s) to make claim that an obligation be paid (or repaid, as the case may be). Böhm-Bawerk's German word is *Darlehensforderung* or *Forderungsrecht*.

future goods-quality, just as the right of ownership constituted the condition precedent of an already present goods-quality.

Relation Of Payment-Claims To Wealth

This explanation, patent though it be, nevertheless leaves one point obscure. The right to demand payment is claimed to be merely the condition precedent of a *future* goods-quality. For the time being, the goods in question are not the goods of the possessor of the right, but of someone else. The possessor of the right does not yet possess the goods that are to be delivered some time in the future. And even the right-to-demand, which he does have, is stated not to be a good. All this amounts to saying that at the moment he possesses *no good at all*. How, then, does it come to pass that he nevertheless at the present moment does possess an undeniable present wealth, the value of which is measured by the value of his right-to-demand-payment? And, more especially, how can this be so, when he who possesses the objective goods which constitute the material of the debt—possesses them as his own peculiar goods—does not possess in them any wealth? In other words, how is it possible that a payment-claim, without being a good, is nevertheless an undeniable object of wealth?

Not until we have solved that problem can we hope to attain full clarity with respect to the economic nature of such payment-claims and, indeed, of all those less definitive rights which apply to the *future* proceeds of goods. Furthermore, this problem itself leads us into a new field, a field we simply cannot leave out of consideration. That is the field of *the computation of wealth,* or of the manner and the rules in accordance with which men form their judgments and make their computation of what constitutes their *wealth.*

The origin and the concept of wealth is very simple. The natural interest which all of us take in the satisfaction of our wants will necessarily arouse in every human being who takes thought for his well-being the wish to make provision for and to gain control over the problem of satisfying his needs, so far as he can recognize them and foresee them. The natural way to this end lies in his striving to draw into his sphere of influence and to retain there an abundance of those things which he knows to be suitable means to such satisfaction and which are not, by nature, at his command in ample measure. The result of this striving is that individual economizing human beings gather about them accumulations of goods (some larger, some smaller) belonging to them exclusively. And it is these accumulations which we are in the habit of calling "wealth."

According to that, wealth is nothing more nor less than the totality of the economic goods that stand at the disposal of an economizing subject.

This definition contains such simple and clear provisions that it can afford no difficult or involved problem to determine, even in applying the definition to a given individual, what constitutes his wealth and how great it is. There would seem to be nothing more required than a simple inventorying, a mechanical counting up, in order to determine the goods which are under a person's power of economic disposal or, in other words, to determine his wealth.

Basic Principles Concerning Computation Of Wealth

And yet the matter is not entirely without its difficulties. The reason is, in part, that when we compute wealth we are not content merely to know *the things comprising that wealth*, but we also want to have some estimation of their significance, their economic importance—that is to say, their *value*, in order that we may add them up and compare them with other accumulations of wealth. But, in further part and more particularly, the reason is that men will not restrict their computation to a bare inventorying of goods, a dry cataloguing of the factual amount of goods on hand at a given moment, but indulge in certain liberties and modifications which they apply in interpreting the dry facts. And there are profound and well-justified reasons for these liberties. These liberties and the manner in which, consciously or unconsciously, they are exercised bear interesting witness to a fact that is often observable in economic matters, namely, that men exercise "good sense" more through habit than through deliberation and that they act from motives (without themselves taking account of them) which are so exceedingly delicate and subtle that any investigator who seeks to unearth those motives can scarcely untangle the subtle and artful convolutions by which the most ordinary of men are wont to arrive at their everyday economic decisions.[1]

There are, ordinarily, three liberties taken by way of modifying the "naked truth" of the factual situation of the moment:

1. *Anticipation of future utility;*
2. *Interpolation of hypothetical goods and of hypothetical estimations of value into the computation of wealth;*

[1] The most striking example, perhaps, is the assurance with which your "man in the street" will arrive at an estimation of the objective value of goods whereas men of science, before puzzling out his truly admirable conquest of the intricate subtleties of his problem, believe themselves to be confronted by an incomprehensible contradiction, a *contradiction économique.*

3. *Discriminatory treatment of goods expected to materialize in the future, according to the source from which they are expected to arise.*

I wish to remark, incidentally, that my use of the term "liberties" is not intended to indicate that men, in making their computation of wealth, act arbitrarily or loosely. On the contrary (and as the observations which follow will demonstrate), they are virtually constrained to exercise these liberties and make these modifications under the stress of all sorts of practical considerations. They look like "liberties" only to the theorist, since it is the business of theory to display concern about a thing which practice very rightly simply "takes in stride." That thing is the meticulous accuracy which forbids allowing imagination to draw a picture that varies by a hair's breadth from the actual state of affairs.

Let us examine these liberties more closely. To begin with, economic science is not concerned only with *today* and it cannot permit itself to be concerned with today alone. Man knows that he will just as surely experience wants that demand satisfaction tomorrow and one year hence as was the case yesterday; and as soon as this consciousness of the time that lies before, this thought for his future situation has once been awakened, his practical striving for well-being can no longer limit itself to concern for the moment. As soon as economic reflection is so extended as to become *economic foresight,* then those active measures to provide the objective means to well-being which constitute the essential activity man calls economizing must perforce be extended to active provision for the future. And that is a step which we see all races and nations taking as soon as they begin to rise above the level of mere animal existence. Once that step has been taken, the future has gained a sure and important place in our economizing. The providential or "forward looking" manner of considering our economizing soon leads us to acquire that habit of looking upon the future situation side by side with the present one and of considering, measuring, and estimating the former exactly as we do the latter. More particularly, we acquire the habit of considering our *future needs* in advance, of weighing them and of allowing our economic behavior in the present already to be governed by the prospective presence of future needs just as if they were already upon us in the present. Nobody would do his sowing in the spring if he did not look ahead to the needs of the autumn. But we cannot limit ourselves to a unilateral anticipation of only the needs of the future. In consistent fashion we also acquire the habit of giving due consideration, even in the present, *to the advantageous events* that the future holds in store for us and so, even in the present we enter in our economizing account the debits of our future needs against the credits of our future advantages. We do not take the position that things which are not already of use to us must, for that reason alone, be a matter of indifference to us. This feeling that they are not a matter of indifference finds expression in the fact that we are quite prone to record in the catalogue of our "available goods" any future gains that we regard as more or less assured, much as we look upon next year's crop from our land or future payments by our debtors. And we are as certain to include among our "available goods" and to record as part of our present wealth our future emoluments as we are the goods that already stand at our disposal for the meeting of the needs of the present moment. There thus results a transfer of the anticipatory consideration of the future (without which successful economizing would, in any event, be quite inconceivable). That transfer quite naturally brings it about that our taking into account of the future is extended to our computation of the results of our economizing and to the computation of our (present) wealth. It is nothing more than anticipation of the future if, even today, we place an estimate of value on a young forest which will provide fellable timber forty years hence and if we enter it, even now, as part of our wealth. And it is nothing more than anticipation of the future if we place our arable land or our house on our balance sheet at a value in excess of that of this year's crop or the annual rental we are collecting this year. And it is likewise nothing more than anticipation of the future if we enter as part of our *present wealth* the sum of money which a debtor owes us but which is not due to be paid until one or two years hence. However natural may be the way in which we have arrived at the anticipatory method of computation and however expedient it may be for all practical economic purposes, we must, nevertheless, not overlook the fact that this way does not, strictly speaking, *correspond to* the facts but that, on the contrary, it *conflicts with the facts*, that it contains a *fiction*, albeit an expedient one. For this anticipatory way of computing includes, among the things available for the satisfaction of our wants, things and renditions of service which at the present time are *not* available for the satisfaction of our wants. And it is quite possible that under untoward circumstances we may be painfully reminded of the fictive character of this manner of computation. The farmer who has placed a high appraisal value on his fertile lands discovers after one or two crop failures that, despite the high computation he made of his wealth, he is, in actual fact, stripped of his wealth and in danger of starving to death. And in the throes of a panic a merchant, whose debtors are actively in business but, at the moment insolvent and, because of their inability to realize on their own assets, involved in the general collapse —such a merchant becomes only too conscious that, despite the soundness of his claims against his debtors, he possesses at the moment no real goods, but only fictive goods, and that the inventory of his wealth was a fictitious one.

The fiction that always resides in anticipation of the future may come into being along two lines. One may occur when a good in actual fact stands available at the present time. In this case the fiction consists in ascribing to the good a value which it can and will attain only in the future. That is to say, by this method of anticipatory computation a value is placed upon a present good which depends on conditions to be fulfilled in the future. This occurs, for instance, when an estimate of value is placed today on a stand of timber which will not be fellable until ten years hence. The second possibility is that the very existence of *the goods themselves* is anticipated—goods that at this moment are not on hand at all, or at least not on hand for the possessor of the wealth in question. This kind of anticipation includes the listing, as a component of present wealth, of claims due to be paid in the future; it may lead, under certain circumstances to the anomalous phenomenon of *wealth without goods*. Let us assume, for instance, the following situation. There are two colonists, A and B, both devoid of wealth, but both industrious and able-bodied; they live at a point remote from the rest of their community. A, in consideration of a service done him by B, promises B a sum of money "when his ship comes in." Now this promise has a sound basis in the economic soundness of the debtor; it could as justifiably be accounted by B a part of B's wealth as could the bond of a solvent government or private individual by a European, a man-of-independent-means living on the income from his securities. And thus in that small colonists' "circle" an amount of wealth will have come into existence where there is a complete absence of any factual supply of goods. In this manner, by the method of anticipation of the future, goods and values are taken up into a computation of wealth before they have even begun to exist.

In some respects it may be said that we permit ourselves even greater liberties along the line of the second of these two possible methods of anticipatory computation. Such is the case when we take up into our account *hypothetical values and goods.*

Even this liberty is by no means devoid of sound reason. For the first requirement imposed by the nature and the purpose of our wealth on anything that would lay claim to being part of that wealth is that all goods must be *economically subject to our power of disposal.* Indeed, this power of disposal must be such that it is possible to "summon up" those goods for the satisfaction of our wants. It is obvious that, to that end, it must be possible that those goods can be brought under physical control, to whatever extent may be necessary. It is further self-evident that in the case of *future* goods and renditions of service physical control in the present is *an impossibility* and that we must consequently content ourselves with a reduced degree of power of control, if we are to include them at all in our computation of wealth. This reduced degree of power of control will consist in the circumstance that either

1. their complete availability is, for the time being, *assured* only *for the future;* or

2. their future factual addition to the sum total of our wealth is at the present time assured by some already existent relationship.

It is evident that we cannot, in principle, permit any relaxing of the demand for an assurance of future utility. For if that, too, were forgone, everyone would be in a position to enter in the accounting of his wealth all the future treasures of the earth, if he so pleased—which would be a manifest absurdity. Nevertheless the application of even this principle is in actual practice subject to a peculiar modification. For nothing that is future is for us *absolutely certain.* It is therefore never possible to say with complete and demonstrable certainty that *assurance,* in the strict sense of the word, of a future advantage is provided by any existent relationship. This applies even to such things as the ownership of a parcel of land assuring receipt of next year's crop, the possession of a claim to payment of a debt assuring that a sum of money will be paid, and the ownership of a house assuring the utilization of that house as a dwelling during some subsequent year. Rather are we everlastingly dealing with *probabilities* of an infinite number of degrees of probability which will range from something bordering on complete certainty—such as, for instance, the expectation that the ground on which my house stands will continue to support it next year, or that a check or a bill of exchange drawn on the house of Rothschild and endorsed by a dozen or so of the most prominent banking houses will be honored. From these the degree of probability will decrease to mere doubtfulness and from there on to an almost disappearing possibility, such as that the ownership of a single one out of a total of 100,000 lottery tickets will bring an assured future return.

Herein lies the source of a certain amount of embarrassment for us in our computation of wealth. On the one hand, it will not do to limit our anticipation of future advantage, if we elect to indulge in any of it at all, to those cases in which the materialization of the future advantage is so highly probable that it may, for practical purposes, be considered to be a virtual certainty, and to ignore all lesser degrees of probability. For we have the distinct feeling that possession of 500 or 900 out of a total of 1,000 lottery tickets, while it confers no certainty of gain, does nevertheless entail so considerable a likelihood thereof that we cannot be completely indifferent to it. And we also have the feeling that we should fare badly if we denied all estimation of value to things which promise future gain with anything *less than complete certainty*, and if we blindly excluded them from any consideration whatever in our computation of wealth. And so, as a practical matter, we are constrained to content ourselves in the matter of the computation of a prospective future advantage with the mere probability of its materializing.

On the other hand we have a feeling, no less distinct, that it is impossible to place a merely possible future advantage on an absolute par with a certainty. It is, for instance, impossible to consider as equally entitled to inclusion in our computation of wealth (1) a single lottery ticket out of a thousand where the prize is $1,000, and (2) a well-vouched-for promissory note for that amount.

There exists but one avenue of escape from the dilemma that here confronts us. That escape consists in accepting, to be sure, a merely possible future advantage as something to be included in our computation while we express the unreliability of its materialization in accordance with whatever may be the degree of probability that obtains in a given instance. That involves a further difficulty in that we cannot differentiate "sure dollars" from "probable dollars" and again from "possible dollars" and in that, if we could, we should not arrive at a final uniform total, any more than we can arrive at a sum resulting from adding apples, pears and plums. Consequently we can do no more than transfer the gradation in degree of probability from the area where it exists but cannot be expressed, *the degree of probability*, to an area where it does not exist but where it can be expressed, namely, the magnitude of the prospective advantage. That is to say, we modify *the magnitude of the prospective advantage* or modify the estimation of value that we place upon it. The result is that we place a greater but less probable advantage on a par with a smaller but more probable one and the latter, again, on a par with a still smaller but certain advantage. Briefly, we reduce all possibilities of advantage to *terms of certainty* and compensate for it by the following process. Whatever had to be added in the way of probability of the prospective advantage, in order to raise it to the level of a certainty is deducted from the *magnitude* of the prospective advantage or from its *value*. Thus, if we are computing our wealth, a draft on the international house of Rothschild would be entered at its face value (except for the discount which belongs to an entirely different area of phenomena and originates from an entirely different circumstance); at the same time we should list one of a total issue of ten tickets in a lottery paying a prize of $1,000 at, say, $100 —but if there were 100 tickets issued, one could be entered at $10, and if 1,000 tickets, then one could be entered at $1.[2]

Objectively considered, this manner of computing wealth (except for the case of complete certainty) *always* leads to a result that is wrong. For (adhering to our example of the lottery ticket) the real result is going to be either a prize or a blank. In the former event the value will subsequently turn out to have been $1,000; in the latter, the value will have been nil. But in no case will its value ever turn out to have been either $100, $10, or $1.

Hence we may say that if we put the lottery ticket on our balance sheet at any of the foregoing figures, we are indulging not only in a hypothesis, but in a very free or loose hypothesis of which it can only be said that we are convinced in advance that it can never convey the exact truth and that, handicapped by the inadequacy of our foresight, we have taken recourse, under compulsion, to an expedient in order to rescue at least a sort of *on-the-average* correctness for our computation of wealth. In any single case, to be sure, this average can be a far cry from the truth. If, for instance, the ticket valued at $100 wins the $1,000 prize, the error comprises one amounting to ten times the entered value, or 1,000%.

---

2. In actual practice, as Adam Smith observes, an estimation of value of this kind is usually somewhat higher. This arises from a widely prevalent over-estimation of the favorableness of the laws of chance or from a mathematically quite unjustifiable overconfidence in our own "good luck."

The Distinction Between Materials Of
Wealth And Forms Of Wealth

If it be conceded that the very anticipation of future advantage, in general, constitutes a first step in the matter of taking liberties with our statement of the amount of actual goods underlying our computation of wealth, then it must be further conceded that a second step is taken when we enter hypothetical magnitudes in our computation. But even that is not all. For a third step in the same direction is taken when, out of purely subjective personal considerations, we exclude from our listing of objects of wealth a whole class of well-assured future gains. That class comprises the future personal earnings of the economic subject.

The economic subject's own person is one of the most effective present instruments for the creation of future advantage. Innumerable human beings who live by their labor have the expectation that all of what they can dare to hope for in the way of future economic advantage will accrue to them from the utilization of that instrument. And for most of the rest of mankind, that is also true of at least a part of such future economic advantage. And that instrument assures us such future advantage in effective and reliable fashion. Concededly, it gives no assurance of accurately determinable future advantage. But the quality of the assurance is at least equal to, if not superior to, that which applies in the case of many indubitably measurable material goods. It is at least equal, for instance, to the expectancy of advantage to be gained from ownership of a beast of burden; it is certainly superior to that which applies to the possession of a lottery ticket. Nevertheless we exclude from our computation of wealth any consideration of the future advantage guaranteed by *our intellectual or physical labors*. On the contrary, we set up a sharp and conscious contrast as between the concept of "personal earnings" and that of "wealth." The artisan or the artist who has not yet amassed any of "this world's goods" we regard as one *who possesses no wealth*. And yet if such a person were to promise to leave to a third person the future proceeds of his labor, we should recognize them as wealth, *in respect to that third person*, regardless of the fact that those proceeds still occupy the status of an augmentation of goods that is merely hoped for.

This is a phenomenon which, in the eyes of anyone who thinks that a balance sheet is a cataloguing of goods which coincides exactly with the facts, would present the appearance of an inconsistency. Nor does it constitute an adequate refutation of that charge to contend that, because the totality of an individual's labors can never under modern circumstances furnish a unified object of economic exchange, there can therefore be no reason for going through the process of making a unified estimate of their value, for an intended sale is by no means the sole purpose of a computation of an economic subject's wealth. Quite often it is undertaken with no thought at all of making a sale but merely with the purpose of making a survey of what we have and what it is worth. And such a reason for an estimation of wealth would certainly be equally valid with respect to our future earnings. In actual fact we do often enough make an estimate of our future personal earnings, only we do do so, not in the form of a *statement of an accumulation of wealth,* but in the form of a *statement of our income.* When a man by his personal labors has assured earnings of, say $10,000 annually, we speak of him as a "man with an income of $10,000."

It is an equally poor argument against undertaking this kind of statement or estimation of wealth (i.e., the kind that includes future earnings—Trsl.) to urge the indefiniteness of the amount. The indefiniteness is far greater in the case of many items which are nevertheless included in estimations of wealth. One example is furnished by questionable accounts receivable. The true reason for the exclusion of future earnings from a statement giving a computation of an economic subject's wealth might perhaps be found in the psychological circumstance that personal earnings, if they are to become a reality, involve *personal labor* that is still to be performed. And because of the burden and the exertion that are involved, most persons look upon that labor in the light of an evil, the endurance of which still stands as an obstacle in the path of the acquisition of the hoped for gain. While man is ready to contemplate the good that is to be hoped for, he cannot ignore the evil that confronts him; and since the latter, as it were, counterbalances the former, there is nothing left over out of the whole matter which man could or would reckon as *a net gain* to be placed on a par with the otherwise already assured economic gains which he is able to register.

Whatever the correct explanation may be, it remains a fact that men do make a difference in their treatment of those prospective future economic gains which depend on their personal economic activity. And that difference constitutes an interesting nuance, which offers a simple though only a partial explanation of a widely discussed circumstance.[3] I refer to the circumstance that the constituent

3. See, especially, Lauderdale's *Inquiry into the Nature and Origin of Public Wealth.*

elements of *a nation's wealth* do not coincide with the constituent elements comprising the *individual accumulations of wealth* of the persons comprising that nation.

When we speak of national wealth, the nation appears as the economic subject, that is to say, the unified possessor of that wealth and is thought of as an entity comprising all the individual members of that nation. Now, while for any individual the fruits of the future exertions of some other individual may, according to the prevailing method of computation, very well count as an object of wealth; the individual who is in debt, on the other hand, becomes absorbed in the economic subject—the possessor nation—and the fruit of *his* labor appears as something which depends on a sacrifice still to be made by him and hence it is excluded from computation. Therefore, whatever one member of the nation owes another will, although it appears as a part of an individual's accumulation of wealth, be eliminated in computing the wealth of the nation.

But the fact that the computation of individual accumulations of wealth can differ at all, as to the objects of wealth it lists, from a computation listing those objects which comprise the national wealth as a whole, can stem from only one cause. That cause is that the method of computation elected by mankind simply does not mirror the facts with objective fidelity, but is, rather, an operation replete with subjective interpretations and insinuations. For it is self-evident that, objectively speaking, there ought to be complete indentity as between those things which serve the individual members of the nation for the satisfaction of wants and those which serve the nation, consisting of those individual members, in the same capacity.[4]

All the foregoing observations consistently point to the conclusion that our customary method of computation is one that takes extreme liberties with the facts and one that interprets facts according to the dictates of practical expediency. And I have advisedly and with due emphasis expounded and pointed out everything that will support that conclusion. For I feel it is necessary to do just that in order to avert the drawing of a conclusion which *seems as natural as it is erroneous* and which, in ninety-nine cases out of a hundred, is arrived at with utmost confidence and utter conviction, and the fallacy of which can be revealed only by affording an insight into the falsity—or, if that word seems too harsh—the inexactness of our whole method of computing wealth. The conclusion I have in mind is the following. Because a thing has been labelled an object of

4. Cf. p. 43 f. above.

wealth, it is therefore an independent good. Now this conclusion is premature despite the plausibility of its premises
which are as follows: An accumulation of wealth is, by
its nature, a collection of goods. A given thing—let us say
a payment-claim, or a relationship that commands patronage is, according to the thousand-tongued verdict of all
reasonable people, an object of wealth; hence, people say,
it must really be a good. That is the conclusion; and the
very common application of this conclusion is the following: whenever the thing which is labelled a good fails to
fit into any of the existing and recognized categories of
goods, people consider themselves justified in creating a
new category of goods for the thing. That, obviously, is
how economists came to cling to their aversion to denying
goods-quality, for purposes of the individual's economizing,
to payment-claims, despite their clear recognition of the
fact that, for purposes of a nation's economizing, they are
not true goods. A payment-claim—thus ran the argument
—is an object of wealth and consequently a good of some
kind; it is neither a material good nor a personal rendition of service; consequently there must exist, in addition
to material goods and personal renditions of service at
least one additional category of good—a third category, that
is to say, in which rights, legal relationships and intangibles
of that sort find their place. This line of argument would
be incontrovertible if the thousand-tongued verdict of all
reasonable people to the effect that claims are objects of
wealth could summon up the good sense and the logical
consistency to demonstrate that those claims are goods
which are truly objective, genuinely existent, and that they
are entered as goods on an inventory of objects of wealth
on the strength of their apparent goods-character. But
that line of argument loses all its cogency as soon as we
recognize that those sponsoring such a method of computation are governed by such motives and following such
methods that it is impossible to regard their dicta as well
considered and reliable verdicts concerning objective goods-
quality. This becomes the more conspicuously true as soon
as we recognize that their method of computation is entirely at variance with the objective state of things on at least
two counts. The first of these is that their method indulges
in fictive anticipation of that which is *not yet in existence*
in that it sets up hypothetical values which do not and
perhaps never will exist, and which, though they may,
on the average be correct, are nevertheless, in any individual case almost always wrong. The other count is that it
leaves completely out of account goods and renditions of
service which have every reasonable prospect of being

realized. Once we realize this, we shall certainly decline to accept, without considered investigation, the argument that we can, on the basis of the labelling of a thing as an object of wealth, conclude that in the form in which it is labelled it possesses goods-quality. But if we make that investigation, the probable result will be that we arrive at a point where we must set up a distinction which I consider fundamental to the whole understanding of the phenomena of wealth. To put it in two terms, we must distinguish between *the materials of wealth* and *the forms of wealth*.

Now, at the basis of every accumulation of wealth there is an underlying collection of real, genuine goods which stand in such a relationship to the economic subject that he is impelled to regard them as, in some way, shape or manner, belonging to him. These genuine goods are the actual, proper *materials of wealth*. But the verdict concerning the relationship is not, as we have just convinced ourselves, always rendered in purely objective terms which describe the things and the kind of relationship in a form that is scrupulously in accord with the objective and factual state of affairs. On the contrary, the person making the computation considers the question from a subjective viewpoint, influenced by certain secondary motives and certain practical considerations which contribute their influence or which may even be the only factors to exert any influence at all.

The result is that, responding to whatever subjective influence and considerations may be operative, he will look at one and the same thing, now in one light, now in another. The situation is comparable to that which obtains when an observer regards a building. Subjectively, its aspect varies, according to which of its four sides the observer is looking at, even though objectively it remains the same. In like manner there come into existence *forms of wealth* as the multifarious aspects under which one and the same *material of wealth* presents itself subjectively to our imagination—an imagination, I would add, which is prone to indulge in subjecting the factual situation to subjective coloration, to biased interpretation, and even to downright distortion.

By the terms of this description, the materials of wealth are patently identical with the genuine goods which in actual fact lend support to our life and our well-being. The forms of wealth, as mere creatures of our subjective interpretation, on the contrary, are manifestly not so. Only to the core which underlies them does goods-quality attach.

And, both in essence and in name, that core can be something quite different from what appears under the label in question, as it is presented in the statement of the computation of wealth.

If the wealth of modern economic life appears under a multitude of names, to a number far exceeding the substantial goods which comprised the simple catalogues of goods of our ancestors, such as house and farm, crops, beasts of burden, house furnishings and clothing—if, I say, in addition to these, our lists include things of such subtle nature as shares of stock, warrants, servitudes, checks, inventors' patents, goodwill, trade secrets, copyrights and the like, the reason for listing these as objects of wealth lies not, in my opinion, in the circumstance that the categories of *materials of wealth are more numerous*, but that the *forms of wealth have become more multifarious*. I believe that the great bulk of the materials of wealth is completely taken care of by the few categories we have of material goods, of objective goods and of personal renditions of service. I think that all the remaining "objects of wealth" which we cite in ordinary speech are really mere forms under which we are in the habit of picturing for ourselves the justification for classifying goods of the kinds that go under these names as objects of wealth; that is to say, I consider them peculiar *computation-forms* which under certain presuppositions we are accustomed to apply to goods of the common kinds. But the presuppositions which supply a reason for the origination of special computation-forms are as a rule mere peculiarities or, rather, *elaborations of the inner-relationships* which are responsible for allying certain goods or complexes of goods with what we term "wealth."

If the actual object of wealth is still remote, even to the extent of being not yet definitely determined—nay, nor even definitely determinable—but if only its relationship to wealth is close and distinct, then our imagination readily occupies itself with the characteristic which merely relates the object to wealth, and so imbues it with a quality of independence which renders it an "object of wealth." *Special peculiar qualities of the true good* constitute factors that tend to work along toward the same end, and these peculiarities cause us, by reason of some consideration or other, to disapprove the direct naming of the true good as the object of wealth.

*   *   *

It now devolves upon me to furnish some support for all the foregoing statements and to exemplify them with concrete instances. I believe the most expedient course for me to follow toward that end is to survey, one after the other, the most important "forms of wealth" in which goods can be allied with what we call wealth. In that way I shall attain not only the goal of thoroughness in general, but the further desirable goal, in particular, of preparing a step-by-step development of an analysis of the "rights" and "relationships" which constitute the chief object of our interest.

CHAPTER V
Continued Discussion Of The Various Forms Of The Assurance Of Future Economic Advantage. Legal Rights As Computation Forms.

The more completely an economic means-to-an-end and the advantage expected from it belong *to the present,* the less opportunity is offered for the introduction of complicating relationships. It is then merely a question of *possession* or *nonpossession.* Hence little opportunity remains for the introduction of variegated computation-forms. The coat that I am wearing on my back, the loaf of bread that stands on my table, the book that is lying on my library table, are simply shown on my "list of assets" as one coat, one loaf of bread, one book.

Forms Of The Assurance Of Future Economic Advantage

The outstanding possibility for complication has to do with the manner in which disposal over a *future* economic advantage is assured us. And for that reason it behooves us to pay special attention to this possible avenue for the introduction of complicating factors. Now the following are the chief forms in which future economic advantage can be assured in the present. And I am using the word "assured" with all the reservations applicable thereto as I noted them previously, on pages 90 and 91.

1. One such form consists in the *existence and possession of some material good of direct, though deferred utility* —things, for instance which will be useful only at a later season, or on some future occasion, such as winter clothing or ice skates in the summer, travel equipment, the prospective bride's "hope chest," future reserves of all sorts of goods. In such cases the computation of wealth proceeds with utmost simplicity. The future advantage attaches to the present good, and we simply list the latter as an object of wealth, at the same time assigning to it the value of its future utility.

2. A second form consists in *the possession of a good of direct utility which extends over the present and into the future as well*, that is to say, possession of a durable consumptible good, such as, for instance, a house, furniture, paintings, musical instruments. Goods of that kind unite with the present utility which they afford the assurance of a utility which will run on into a more or less remote future. The computation of wealth in such cases, too, proceeds along the simple line that the value of the future utility is ascribed to the bearer of that utility itself, and appears in the computation of wealth merely as *an augmentation of the value* of the good. To the latter is assigned the *capitalized* value of its total utility.

3. A third form consists in the *possession of a good* of *indirect utility*, as I should like to term it. I wish here to make use of a very fruitful concept introduced by Menger into our economic terminology. But I should like to modify the term he uses and say this third form consists in the possession of goods of more remote orders.[1]

It will be worth while to devote somewhat detailed attention to the manner in which goods of this kind attain significance in our computation of wealth. This class of goods is of paramount importance, and to it belongs the entire mass of goods which constitute the *capital* of our economy.

To begin with, I should like to say a few words about the distinction itself, which constitutes the underlying basis for the concept of *orders of goods*. All goods, by the very terms of the concept "good" itself have one feature in common. That feature is that they are capable of constituting a link in the chain of cause and effect—the causal chain, if you will, between human needs and the satisfaction of those needs. Now this causal relationship may be direct or remote; it may be immediate or it may function by way of one or more intermediate links of the chain. In the nature of things these intermediate links of the chain are themselves goods, and the transmission of their utility takes place in such manner that from goods of remote utility there are first produced other goods which are closer by one stage to the (final) stage of direct utilization; then through these goods there is effected either the direct satisfaction of the want, or the production of still another good which, in its turn, occupies a place that is one stage closer to that which represents the satisfaction of the human want.

Thus the totality of our goods presents the appearance of a serial structure, or a *succession of orders of goods*, the

1. In place of the expression selected by me, Menger uses the term "higher order," which might easily give rise to a misconception.

first and nearest of which serves directly to satisfy human needs, while the remoter orders serve, by a system of gradation, for the production of goods which in every case constitute the order from which the next succeeding order will arise.[2]

Let us consider, for instance, bread, houses and clothes. These furnish direct satisfaction of the human needs for nutriment, for shelter, for clothing. *They are therefore goods of the first order.* But flour, ovens and the baker's labor serve to produce the *bread;* cloth, needles and thread serve to produce the *clothing;* bricks, lumber, lime, nails, and the labor of the builder serve to produce *dwelling houses.* Hence these things occupy a place that is one stage removed, and are goods of *second order.* Then, again, there is another group of goods which serves to produce the goods of second order, such as flour mills, wool, lime pits, tree trunks, sawmills, limestone quarries, etc. These are goods of *third order.* Further behind these are still other goods which produce goods of third order, such as arable land, farming implements, barns, the building materials used to construct the flour mill, timberland, sheep, cotton plantations, and various kinds of labor. All these will find their place among goods of *fourth order.* And even these are produced by means of goods that function even more indirectly, and thus constitute goods of *fifth, sixth* and *still remoter* orders.

This successive inter-relationship of goods is a matter of great theoretical importance because it is the source of important logical relationships which exist between goods

2. Naturally, these "orders of goods" are not hermetically sealed off from each other, because on account of the multiple utilization of which they are capable, many goods may belong simultaneously to both a nearer and a more remote order; see also Note 3 following. It must be noted, in particular, that the widely extended system of exchange which is characteristic of our modern economy embodies the possibility sometimes of abbreviating and of lengthening at other times the causal chain between the good and its satisfying of the wants of the individual economic subject, and thus likewise the possibility of disrupting the allocation of goods to orders and thus of effecting a modification or shift in the designation of the order to which, from the viewpoint of the consuming economic subject, a given good is to be allocated. The strange phenomenon of "utilization by way of exchange" simply reveals here a feature which is apparent in many other aspects of the nature of goods, the vexatious power of causing supposedly well-defined characteristics to fade and become obliterated — a power which has so often caused economists in general to surrender to what Robinson calls "the role of the inevitable supernumerary." How frequently, for instance, in a society which engages extensively in "utilization by way of exchange" do we find there is a "watering down" in the subjective requirements that I postulated on page 41f.! This applies pre-eminently to the requirements of adaptability of the thing to the need it is to serve and, secondly, to the knowledge that must be possessed by the economic subject, of how to use the good.

that occupy a sequential position with respect to each other. One thing is certainly patent with respect to a whole succession of goods which belong to various orders and which are successively transformed into the remaining members of that succession until they finally become goods of first order. That one thing is that, in the case of such things as arable land, grain, flour, bread, all these things derive their economic significance from *one and the same source, namely, the want* which is finally served by the ultimately produced good of first order. If we imagine our need of nutriment as nonexistent, or satisfied by some substitute for food, then flour, bread, grain, and arable grain fields which are now of transcendant importance in our economy would then immediately have no significance for us at all.

This basic relationship, then, gives rise to two laws, of which one applies to *goods-qualtiy* and the other to the value of goods belonging to the remoter orders in the succession of goods. The first law reads: *The goods-quality of every good of remoter order is conditioned by the goods-quality of the totality of goods belonging to the successively less remote orders, to the production of which it contributes.*

The truth of this pronouncement is obvious. For, since the goods-quality of a thing is based on its causal connection with human well-being, and since that connection, in the case of goods of remote order, is always transmitted through intermediary links, it is clear that there must be no interruption of that connection with the successive links-of-the-chain, if the connection is to be preserved until the ultimate member of the succession is reached. A weaver's loom obviously could not be a good if the cloth which is woven on it, and for the production of which it serves, were not also a good.[3]

The second law, affecting *value*, provides that *the value of goods of remoter order is conditioned as to its existence and as to its magnitude by the value of the goods of less remote order for the production of which they serve.* Hence

---

3. Since, however, many goods permit of varied methods of utilization, it often happens that one and the same good (when subject to one certain manner of utilization) may belong to a different or more remote order than if utilized in some other manner. For instance, building materials can be devoted to the construction of a dwelling and so be a good of second order, or they may be used to construct a flour mill and so become a good of fourth order (the succeeding orders consisting of mill, flour, bread). In practice this circumstance often obscures the strict conditioning of the goods-quality of these things by reason of the goods-quality of the intermediate goods of less remote order. But though it may obscure it, it does not remove it. In place of a single condition *sine qua non* there simply appears an alternative condition. The goods-quality itself abides, even if the causal connection is interrupted in the case of just *one* out of several possible methods of final utilization for the satisfaction of wants.

no good of remote order can possess economic value unless the corresponding goods of less remote order possess such value. And hence, likewise, the magnitude of its value is also dependent on the magnitude of the value of the goods of less remote order.[4]

The correctness of this statement, which is as simple as it is significant, I need not defend beyond setting down one incontrovertible deduction based on it. It is impossible to deny that in the last analysis the value of all goods arises from the *importance of the wants* which owe their satisfaction to those goods. Now, goods of remoter order cannot satisfy needs that are different from and—more especially—more numerous than are satisfied by the goods of less remote order which they (i.e., the goods of remote order) produce. And it is also true that the degree of the immediacy of the value of any individual stage of goods varies directly with the proximity of the order to the original source of value, namely, the wants-to-be-satisfied. From these two preceding statements it follows that the value of goods of remote order is derived from and is determined by that of goods of less remote order, *and not vice versa.* A loom could not possibly possess value if the cloth woven on it did not. But the cloth could have value, even if the loom had none.[5]

4. This law, as well as the one preceding it, was first developed by Menger (*Grundsätze,* p. 11 ff. and also p. 123 ff.) [*Principles of Economics,* p. 58 ff. and also p. 149 ff.]

5. It would lead us too far astray from our immediate problem if I were to go into detailed proof of this statement which is of fundamental importance for the whole theory of the value of goods. Therefore I must restrict myself to making reference to the excellent treatment of this topic to be found in Menger *(op. cit.).* Just a few observations may, however, not be amiss at this point. There is a widespread — nay, almost general — adherence to the opinion that the value of goods is determined by their cost-of-production. Since those costs comprise nothing more nor less than the goods of remoter order which have been expended to produce them, that opinion expresses a doctrine diametrically the opposite of what I have set down in the text above. It states that the value of goods of *less remote* order is conditioned and determined by that of goods of *remoter* order. That opinion, expressed as an underlying principle cannot but be erroneous for the very reason that goods of remoter order can most patently acquire economic significance only through the mediation of the goods of less remote order which stand closer to the source of value. If the "cost theories" have nevertheless been able to win so many adherents, the explanation must lie in the following circumstance. While Menger's law of value is irrefutable in the eyes of the abstract theorist who considers the problem in the light of pure logic, it does not, from the pragmatic viewpoint present itself as obviously and convincingly inescapable. Nor is it by any means easy so to present it as to make it demonstrably and palpably valid, because many goods of remoter order permit of a multiplicity of ways of utilization and for that reason draw upon a multiplicity of sources of value. A further reason why it is difficult to demonstrate Menger's law lies in the fact that in most instances the production of a good

The value of goods of remote order is, accordingly, a *derived value*. But at the same time it is a value that is *prospective in nature* and that *anticipates the facts*. This brings us back to our narrower problem of the computation of wealth. It is anticipatory for the following reason. Since the attainment of ultimate utility by way of consumption, which is what we look for in goods of remoter order, demands a transmutation of those goods of remoter order into goods of less remote order, and since it therefore calls for processes which can take place only *in the course of time*, those goods of remote order represent, in our computation of wealth, a *future utility;* and the value that is placed upon them (a value which is only a derived value, accruing to them only through the mediation of goods of less remote order and hence a value that is derived from the final common utility) is nothing but the *form* (the *third* form according to my enumeration) in which an indirect future advantage enters into the computation.

There is one conclusion to be drawn from the foregoing statement which is so significant that I must not fail

of first order is contributed to by *such a very large number* of goods of rather remote order and that therefore its value is "pulverized" as it were and very thinly spread out. Finally, there is the further circumstance that, for a number of reasons, it is practically never feasible to gather the evidence to show that the sum total of the value of all these contributing participants taken together is exactly equal to the value of the good of first order — which would constitute the one piece of conclusive evidence that would establish the validity of Menger's law. Possibly the following analogy may cast some light on the problem. If six oarsmen are rowing a boat, admittedly the progress of the oarsmen will, in a certain sense, follow the progress of the boat that is conveying them. And it is true, in a sense, that one may regard the progress of an individual oarsman as conditioned and caused by the progress of the boat. And the greater the number of oarsmen, and hence the more nearly negligible the cooperation of that individual oarsman, the more readily might one accept, as a generalization, the statement that the progress of the individual is conditioned by the progress of the boat. But despite all this it would be obviously absurd to maintain that the oarsman's progress was caused by the progress of the boat instead of stating the case the other way around and saying that the progress of the boat is caused by the oarsman. The situation is the same with respect to the question of which is cause and which is effect in the matter of the value of goods of remoter order, and goods of less remote order. If a good of remote order, such as human labor, because of the multiplicity of the possible avenues of application attains an estimation of value via a large number of channels, then its value with respect to one single object to which it has been applied, and which is considered separately by itself, will appear to be something definitely established and firmly determinable. And in that event, since we are inclined to use goods of definite value for the production of other goods only if the product can attain at least equal or perhaps greater value, then it is easily possible that that labor, regarded from a biased viewpoint, can appear as *causing* the value of the product. And yet it would remain an absurdity to enunciate, as a principle, that the value of the costs of production are the cause, and the value of the product is the effect instead of stating the case the other way around.

to comment on it. And I do so even though I am thereby carried outside the narrower area of our topic to which, however, this conclusion is related by a number of "internal" connections. As I have already stated, the whole sum of our *capital possessions* comes under the form, just described, of the assurance of future advantage. There are many meanings which have in the course of time been attached to the word, capital.[6] Of all of them I believe the one that deserves preference is the one that embraces the concept of capital as a *complex of the means for the production of earnings* in contrast with the concept of capital as a complex of consumptible goods. I believe this because that meaning of "capital" calls up a concept of transcendant importance for all economic theory. It becomes a matter of minor importance and a mere question of terminology, whether our definition should restrict capital to *movable* means for the production of earnings or whether it should include land as well. Incidentally, that question seems, generally, to have been resolved in favor of the former alternative.

Every capital, in this sense, is then a collection of goods of remoter order. As such, with respect to goods-quality and to value, it is completely subject to the laws that I have just declared to be in force with respect to goods of remote order in general. All capital value is an *anticipation* of the value of the prospective consumptible end-product. Production, of which capital is the tool and the material (e.g., machines and raw materials) is the condition, the justification and the materialization of the value which has temporarily been ascribed to capital goods; it is the process by virtue of which the *future* value of a capital good is transmuted into the present worth of the matured consumptible end-product, the process which leads to capital's fulfillment and justification.

From this we draw another conclusion. And it is one that hints at a very serious difficulty—a difficulty that encumbers the explanation of the phenomenon of interest and of the so-called *productivity of capital* and which, up to this time has been almost completely disregarded by economic theory and hence, naturally enough, not solved by it. That conclusion is that production, with its transformation of capital goods into consumptible goods, is not a process of creating values, at least not on the part of capital[7], but

6. Cf. Knies, *Das Geld*, Berlin, 1873, p. 6ff.

7. The situation is different in the case of just one good of remoter order, namely, labor. But that, as we have seen earlier is one good that is *not* entered in our computation of wealth at its anticipated future value.

merely one of confirming values that have already been borrowed, as it were, by virtue of presuppositions made in advance. And that still leaves us facing the question of how we can reconcile the statements I have just set down with the *productivity of capital* that is so generally ascribed to capital.

If the prospective value of the product has already been ascribed to the producing capital *in advance*, how is capital, in the course of production to produce a "surplus value"? The greater is the value of the product, the greater, also, was the anticipated value of the means of production—let us say, for example, of the ore and of the mine when iron and steel have a high value. And if the former is only a reflection of the ultimate value of the product, how can that ultimate value exceed the proportions of what it reflects, in other words, how can it outgrow itself? It would be easier to comprehend the attainment of a surplus value in those cases and at those times which are marked by some surprisingly favorable development in production which caused the attainment of an *unexpectedly* high value which, just because it had *not* been anticipated, had not in advance been ascribed in its full measure to the (capital) means of production. Under these circumstances a true augmentation would represent a natural occurrence.

But that is not what really happens in the case of the regular "productivity of capital." Rather would such an extraordinary augmentation be ascribed to the cleverness of the producer and looked upon as a product of the entrepreneurial labor or activity that is associated with capital.

But the productivity of capital, it is claimed, finds expression quite generally in the average and *regular attainment* of surplus value by the end product, over and above the expended capital value (and without regard to the result arising from labor).

Whence this phenomenon of capital's outgrowing itself?

What I am setting down here is merely a slight indication of the existence of a problem which, in my opinion, has received far too little attention on the part of economic science.[8] I hope to be able to offer a solution at some future time in an independent work toward the preparation of which the present work constitutes a preliminary labor. In

8. Even excellent writers on economics rarely make any attempt to *explain* the productivity of capital as an elucidation of the phenomenon of interest; they merely *name* it as such, without furnishing any real explanation of it. As I have pointed out in the foregoing

fact, the present writing is an outgrowth of work already performed in preparing that future work.*

* * *

The possession of goods of remoter order concludes the series of those forms in which the acquisition of a future economic advantage is brought about and assured by a *material good* which in the present is already under the complete control of an economic subject—a good concerning which not only the relationship to the economic subject possessing power of disposal is a matter clearly recognized and under no cloud of doubt—a good which can in all respects appropriately be recognized as the bearer of utility and which can properly be regarded as an object of wealth. Indeed, in the three types of cases just considered the material good which was to yield the future economic advantage replaced that advantage itself in the computation of wealth.

Legal Rights As Computation Forms

That series of three kinds of material good is now followed by a series of what might be termed "forms of association" with future economic advantage. These do not

text, there is a truly crying need of such an explanation. Among the earlier essayists I might make mention of Turgot and especially Lauderdale; the more recent ones include Rösler (*Grundsätze der Volkswirtschaftslehre*, Rostock, 1864, p. 448ff.), Strassburger ("Kritik der Lehre vom Arbeitslohn," appearing in Hildebrand's *Jahrbücher*, Volume for 1871, p. 325ff.) and, above all, that genius among modern economists, Menger (*Grundsätze der Volkswirtschaftslehre*, pp. 123-136) [*Principles of Economics*, pp. 149-159] whose name it is impossible to extol too often or beyond his deserts whenever there is any discussion of the problems affecting the unshakable fundaments of economic science. The socialists, on the other hand, recognize quite clearly that the treatment of the question of productivity, as it is undertaken by prevailing economic theory (as represented, let us say, by Roscher) leaves many a question unanswered. But their behaviour represents action that can well be described as throwing out the good with the bad. For they simply denounce the whole producing of surplus value on the part of capital as an injustice. While it must be admitted that prevailing economic theory does not adequately explain surplus value and hence admittedly does not justify it, yet the socialists merely denounce it instead of correctly elucidating its causes. The importance of the whole problem is readily understandable on the basis of the following circumstance. The question of the justness or injustice of interest on capital is one about which revolves much of the social problem of our time, and it is one that is impossible to solve without previously determining the causes from which the whole phenomenon of interest on capital arises. And it is a question concerning which, in its present stage of development, economic science leaves us very much in the dark.

* Note: Böhm-Bawerk refers to his major work, *Kapital und Kapitalzins* (in three volumes) published in 1884, 1889 and 1909-1912; English translation, *Capital and Interest*, Libertarian Press, South Holland, Illinois, U.S.A., 1959.

adapt themselves to that very simple form of computation which was so feasible for the three kinds of material good discussed in the foregoing pages. The reason for this lack of adaptability is not any absence of a presently existent factual source of future advantage (for in the absence of *some* assuring factor of future advantage, there simply could be no question of an *assured* future advantage). No, the reason lies rather in the fact that for some special reason this presently existent source of advantage cannot appropriately be listed as an object of wealth.

To this class belong the cases cited below, to which I will assign the numbers 4, 5 and 6 in order to coordinate them with the first part of our enumeration.*

(4) *Some person is obligated (in adequately assured fashion) to perform a future labor-service or other personal rendition of service.* For example, a troupe of players, having received its fee in advance, has engaged with the owner of a theater building to give a series of performances. The object of future utility which is assured the owner consists in this case in the promised *services* of the actors. These services themselves are future goods but they are already assured in the present and, indeed, the assuring element is the *very persons of the actors* who are obligated to render the services that are "owed"; the assurance lies, further, in their capability to render those services (possibly not without the cooperation of a threat of legal compulsion). The assurance consists, furthermore, in the existence of the actors, in their capability, and in their willingness to perform. These things assure the theater owner his performances in a manner analogous to that in which

---

* Translator's Note: The reader may well have lost sight of the fact that the present chapter (V) opened with the promise of an enumeration of the *forms* of wealth which constitute alternatives to *materials* of wealth in computation of wealth. Böhm-Bawerk limited himself to the discussion of forms of wealth constituting "assured" future economic advantage. The first three of these were of a material, concrete nature and comprised

    (1) existence and possession of a material good of direct but deferred utility (ice skates in summertime, "hope chests")
    (2) existence and possession of goods of lasting utility ("durable goods" - e.g., house, furniture, paintings)
    (3) existence and possession of material "producers' goods" (goods of remoter order)

After his lengthy divagation to explain "orders" of goods he now returns to three further kinds of goods "assuring" future advantage. These, it will be noted, are not material, concrete goods, but constitute "forms" under which the assurance of a future advantage may warrant their being regarded as what, in today's ordinary business parlance, we term "assets."

the existence, the qualities and the availability of a pear tree give assurance to the owner of the tree of the garnering of a crop of pears. But whereas that owner sets down the designation of the material bearer of his assurance of future economic advantage in his computation of wealth (viz., one pear tree) the theater-owner cannot do likewise with the factual source of his advantage, the persons of the actors. He does, to be sure, possess a species of power of disposal over them, and by recourse to legal compulsion such power of disposal might take on physical form. But in the modern organized state this power of disposal can at best be only a partial one, very strictly limited to the specific matter of the obligation[9]; and in view of this less-than-complete power of disposal, and in view of our conception in modern times of human dignity, anyhow, it would be unfitting to designate the obligated persons who are, in actual fact, the bearers of the future advantage as objects of wealth to be listed in a computation. Hence some other form must be resorted to if there is to be any recognition of the situation in a computation of wealth. The situation is closely similar in the matter of the other two kinds of cases which follow.

(5) *Individual future renditions of service on the part of a thing (which is otherwise the property of a third person) are assigned to an interested party other than the owner by virtue of some special right that obtains in the premises.* An example would be a temporary right of usufruct applying to a house or a tract of arable land. In this instance the right of ownership residing in another person is the obstacle which prevents the holder of the partial right from listing the present existent bearer of the utility (the house or the land) as an object of wealth in *his* computation.

(6) *There is an expectation of the future receipt of material goods or material renditions of service to be delivered by some person.* An example would be the following. Some definite obligated person is expected to make a payment, at some future time, of a definite sum of money. This type of case is of very widespread importance. In this category belong all payment-claims and all credit relationships. The present existent bearer of the future economic advantage is, as in the case of type (4), the actual person[10] of the debtor—"ready, willing, and able." But for

9. Under the laws of classical antiquity it was quite possible for the existence of a debt to lead to the literal enslavement of the debtor. Such a slave did then truly become an "object of wealth."

10. The law of classical antiquity emphasized far more clearly than is the case today that payment of material goods based on pay-

the same reasons as those that were applicable before, his person cannot suitably be listed as an object of wealth. Hence in this case, as in the other two, some other form must be resorted to under which the expected future entity can be computed in a different, independent form. *What shall that form be?*

* * *

It would be possible and, indeed, closest to a true description of the facts for us, in all cases where, for good and sufficient reasons, it is impossible or undesirable to name the factual present bearer of the future advantage, *simply to list the future good under its own designation*, with the possible additional designation of "future." For instance, someone might possess one claim to a payment of $20,000 net and already due, and another claim to $10,000 payable one year hence. Such a person might compute his wealth as consisting of *20,000 present dollars and 10,000 future dollars;* or the possessor of a usufruct applying to a rentable house could list as part of his computation of wealth *ten,* let us say *of the future installments of rent* he is entitled to receive. However, we do not use this most direct way of designating our wealth. And there are various reasons for that. To begin with, the amount of the future fruit of a relationship that is presently established is not always definitely determinable. For example, I own a lottery ticket. If it is drawn, it may win me $100,000 or $20,000, or $10,000, or $100, or $20, or $10. Which of these possible future amounts am I to list in my computation of wealth? Furthermore, it is difficult and sometimes downright impossible, when designating these future advantages, to give proper expression to the various *differences in the degree of probability* attaching to the future advantage. Finally, there is no inconsiderable burden imposed on our powers of imagination, and we feel ourselves under compul-

ment-claims is made as the fulfillment of a personal obligation. Under the oldest form of Roman Law the person of the debtor could not be eliminated from the transaction, either for the benefit of the debtor or that of the creditor. The latter, if the debtor was able but not willing to make payment, could not ignore the debtor's person and take direct recourse to his property. He had to carry out his rights (and these did, to be sure, enjoy effective compulsive sanctions) against the person of the debtor in order to compel him to make the inescapable *rendition* of payment that his indebtedness implied. Conversely, the idea that the debtor owed personal performance of an act found expression in the fact that the debtor was not permitted to force his creditor to take direct recourse to his possessions and thus exempt his person. The *cessio bonorum* (surrender of goods - Trsl.) came into Roman Law only at a late date.

Quite in contrast with this, modern jurisprudence is lenient in permitting substitutes for personal rendition by the debtor, and even provides for total elimination thereof by substituting for it the activity of the bailiff.

sion to resort to the inconvenient, even though technically correct making of deductions, even though we adopt some wording that preserves awareness that the things to which we ascribe values are really not yet existent and that, for the present, they exist only in our imagination, even though we treat them like present factual things for purposes of acquisition and of transfer.

And then, our highly developed system of exchange affords an opportunity at all times to exchange future goods and renditions of service for present ones.[11] That tends to obliterate the consciousness that we are dealing only with future goods. Hence we are prone to allow our imagination, which in any event is fond of resorting to simple symbolic representation, even at the cost of accuracy, to disregard all limitation in the matter of anticipation of the future and, in the matter of inventorying wealth, to list future advantage under the name of *a present something*.

Now if, for all sorts of reasons, we are not in a position to name the actual bearer of the future advantage, our first recourse is to the device of verbal circumlocution. And instead of giving the name of the thing itself, we mention some circumstance that is prominent in the matter—we mention the relationship we occupy toward the thing. Our strongest preference is for naming a relationship that touches very closely the advantage which we shall derive from the thing. A prominent attendant circumstance of this sort exists when we possess a *right* to the future personal service of another person or to the utilization, say, of a house or a land-parcel, or to this or that object or complex of goods which constitutes the matter of his indebtedness. Hence in the case of all three of the last mentioned "association-forms" of a future advantage we are in the habit of naming our *right* to the future utility as our object of wealth.[12]

[11]. Trading in "futures" is today exceedingly extensive. All loans fall into this category. (The repayment of principal plus interest represents the repayment of what was a "present value" in what was at that time "future goods".) This category also embraces purchases of payment-claims and of rights of all kinds, of government obligations, of bills of exchange and many other securities, as well as, in a certain sense, even of houses and land parcels, for in these latter cases we are dealing with a utility that is still to be derived in the future.

[12]. We observe a phenomenon akin to this in the fact that many authors on economic subjects are not content to apply the name of "goods" to individual useful services rendered by persons. No, these authors devise a comprehensive expression for the totality of economic advantage emanating from human beings. But they still decline to designate human beings themselves as goods, so they take recourse to naming personal qualities as goods. Thus, the "skill" of an

Now such rights are pre-eminently fitted to assume and to play the part of a "substitute" in this manner, because the exigencies of jurisprudential transactions have since time immemorial fostered the device of representing rights as independent entities. By sharply differentiating rights from the material things to which they applied, by designating them as *"incorporeal things,"* by speaking of the origin, the transfer, the encumbrance, the destruction of rights in a "tone of voice" as if a right were an entity, a sort of being, the law brought it about that gradually in their conception of the conduct of practical affairs men became oblivious of the fact that rights do not belong in the category of *things* at all, but in that of *relationships.* And hence it became and still remains possible, in the field of the computation of wealth, for rights to slip rather inconspicuously into the role of representatives of the things to which they pertain. However—and this is something on which I most emphatically insist—we are merely indulging in a bit of verbal substitution when we declare a right to be "a good" or an "object of wealth." One who speaks thus is never speaking the literal truth. A right can be only a variant of a *computation form;* it can never be the name of an independent *material of wealth.*

* * *

Perhaps I can, in conclusion, clarify this thought still more sharply by means of an example of the manner in which we vary the computation form we employ for one and the same material of wealth, according to whatever attendant circumstances may be present.

Here are five possibilities—all *shadings* of the manner in which I can convey the single economic fact that three months hence I shall have at my disposal a hundredweight of hay.

1. As of today I already possess and am the regular owner of and exercise full physical control over, one hundredweight of hay.

2. As of today I have title to a hundredweight of hay which the manager of my landed estate will ship to me within three months.

3. I own a tract of meadowland which affords me the opportunity to harvest a hundredweight of hay within the next three months.

4. I possess a servitude that applies to a tract of meadowland belonging to someone else, which will permit me

artisan, the "vocal talent" of the diva is to them a "personal good." Quite obviously, this is nothing but a verbal circumlocution which serves to rescue them from an embarrassing difficulty. It is comparable to listing among one's assets not the penknife one owns, but the penknife's "sharpness."

to garner a crop of that kind and amount within three months.

5. I possess a payment-claim (a right) covering the return to me within the next three months of a hundredweight of hay which I loaned out some time ago.

In all five cases there is involved a *hundredweight of hay which will be at my disposal in three months' time.* That is the one single good to which I am looking and to which I must look, if I am to justify at all the inclusion of this item of wealth in my balance sheet as of today.[13]

Now let us observe in what varying manner it is possible for our computation to present this single set of facts. Everyone will agree that where possibility (1) obtains the economic subject can justly describe it by saying that his wealth includes one hundredweight of hay. The same is true of possibility (2). Possibility (3) he will describe by placing on his balance sheet one tract of meadowland. In the case of possibility (4) his balance sheet will list a servitude (a right) as his object of wealth. In the case of possibility (5) the balance sheet will list as the object of wealth the *right to enforce a claim.* Here, then, are four different computation forms under which one and the same good is listed!

At this point I submit, in addition, two brief comparisons—one involving possibilities (3) and (4), and the other involving possibilities (2) and (5).

In possibility (3) the role of substitute for the future hundredweight of hay is assumed by the tract of meadowland—an undeniable good and just as undeniably an independent material of wealth which, by way of anticipation of the future, needed merely to borrow its value from its future yield. But in possibility (4), too, the tract of meadowland is most patently the good which is on hand in the present and which assures the future hundredweight of hay. But if, in possibility (4) it is *not the meadowland* which is listed as the present object of wealth, but rather a *right,* then the reason cannot lie in the fact that some different present good constituted a *medium or means* of acquiring the hundredweight of hay. No, the reason must lie in the fact that, for some reason or other, one declines to name as one's object of wealth the meadowland (which functions as a medium just as truly in possibility (4) as it does in possibility (3), and that one chooses, rather, to employ a verbal replacement. Now this enables us to draw an entirely unambiguous in-

13. In cases 3 and 4, in addition to the crop that will be **gathered** in three months, additional future crops also come in for consideration.

ference, namely, that the right is here a mere computation form. If the right were really an independent object of wealth, then in possibility (3) there would also have had to be a listing of a right (for there was a right involved there, too, namely, the right of ownership). And if a right were an independent good, it would have been inconceivable that in possibility (3) the *right* of ownership should have been completely suppressed and passed over in silence!

Possibilities (2) and (5) may be similarly compared. They possess one feature in common. That feature is that the economic subject temporarily forgoes his hundredweight of hay and merely has a right applicable to the hay —a right which is going to place the hay under his physical control within three months. Now, if a right of that kind is a good at all and an independent material of wealth, it would have to be so in both the cases we are comparing. And the fact that it certainly is *not* so in the earlier case is proof enough that it cannot possibly be so in the latter case, either.   *   *   *

Now that we have gained some insight into the nature and the treatment of computation-forms, including what we have learned concerning the *third* group of rights as we previously differentiated them—we can now say with reference to that third group of rights (i.e., rights that pertain to the future acquisition of goods) that our evidence here points in the same direction as I hope I have demonstrated it did in the case of ownership rights and rights of partial utilization.

I believe, then, that I have demonstrated for all three classes of rights that all our evidence is to the effect that rights—however much they may in our language, in our commercial exchange, in our practical life, take on the appearance of independent things—do not, in sober truth, deserve a place among independent goods. Appearances to the contrary notwithstanding, they belong at best *among conditions precedent of goods-quality,* and they constitute at best *computation-forms* under which true goods may on occasion be listed in our computations of wealth.

I should not have devoted to this thought, which is neither complicated nor farfetched, a treatment so extended —and one that may strike many readers as wearisome—had I not been aware that it would earn for me the united opposition of both jurists and economic theorists. I knew it was inevitable that I should encounter the opposition of the former who so very long ago proceeded along this line of thought only to arrive at a point where *rights* and *things* came to be looked upon as coordinate entities and where

the former were elevated to the rank of *res incorporales*. I
knew, too, that I must expect the opposition of the economic
theorists who followed suit and registered acceptance of
the jurists' stand in the matter of classifying rights as
intangible goods.

I think this opposition, however widely it may be sub-
scribed to, is nevertheless based on a strange misunderstanding which cropped up long, long ago and has never since
been rectified. For, when the two categories were set up,
namely, the categories of real goods and of rights, that is to
say, of *res corporales* and *res incorporales* as classes of objects of wealth which had to be kept asunder, it simply
escaped general attention that a contrast was being set up
which in actual truth was utterly nonexistent. There was
a failure to observe that where *rights* were observed to exist, there, of necessity, *goods* had to exist, too—goods which,
by virtue of the rights, were also bound up with wealth; and
there was a similar failure to observe that where only *things*
were observed to exist and were designated as objects of
wealth, there were also *rights* as well—rights applying to
those very things—rights of the most complete and effective
kind which, in turn, were bound up with those same things
—that is to say, were bound up with wealth. If it be true
that rights were seriously considered to be things (and by
"seriously" I mean without any awareness that men were
indulging in a figure of speech) then it can only be said that
men were allowing themselves to be deceived by shadows,
as it were. In a sense, rights *are* shadows—the juridical
shadows which real corporeal goods cast upon the image
of our wealth. For where there is no corporeal object to
which a right pertains, there can be *no right*. The more
substantial and the more distinct these shadows are (and
they can be so only because the corporeal thing that casts
the shadow stands, substantial and distinct, in close proximity) the more indubitably are they recognizable *as shadows*. The more vague, the more indistinct and the more
unrecognizable the corporeal thing is which casts the shadow, the weaker, the more nebulous the shadow consequently
is, the more easily is it possible for us to fail to recognize
it as a shadow, and the easier it is to consider the shadow
to be an independent entity. That is how it has come about
that, where there is a corporeal good, tangible and visible,
it has never occurred to anyone to proclaim that the right
to the good constituted the good's double, its *alter ego*. And
that is how most people, at least from the economic viewpoint, have always recognized that payment-claims depend
for their essential soundness upon the corporeal goods to

which they apply, and that their appearance of being goods is merely something borrowed. And again, that is how it happens that, the more complicated certain legal relationships are, and the more indefinite, the more difficult to perceive and the more subject to indirection in their acquisition are the true goods which a "right" promises to deliver to us, the more general and the more pronounced is the disposition on the part of the economic theorists to declare the rights to be independent goods and, finally, that is how it is that just where those conditions are present in the highest degree (the field of patent rights and copyrights) the recognition of the independent goods-character of rights is accepted without exception.[14] Nevertheless that recognition ought not to be unanimous, as it is. For the economic nature of property rights is always one and the same throughout all the possible gradations of genuineness and directness with which they confirm the status of goods as part of our wealth. Beginning with the right of ownership and proceeding thenceforward through the weaker kinds of property rights, including limited rights such as rights to partial utilization, rights to enforce claims, and from there on to the most indirect rights and the most tenuously defined, such as copyrights, monopoly rights, rights based on speculative purchase and rights *to* rights, such as hereditary rights to payment-claims or rights to patent-rights—throughout all the gradations, I say, rights are never goods in and of themselves, *but only conditions of the subjective goods-quality of the things to which they pertain.* To put it more concretely, they are the form that is habitually assumed or necessitated, in a legally constituted society, by that general requirement of all goods-quality, the "power of disposal" over a thing.

In view of this description of the nature of rights, which I think I have sufficiently established, I believe we may abide by the conviction that wherever we encounter rights purporting to be objects of wealth, they can never signify an augmentation of the materials of wealth or of true goods, but at all times signify only a *form* under the guise of which men have a predilection for thinking of and representing other goods, other things and other renditions of service, especially for purposes of a computation of wealth.[15]

14. Even Menger, who displays the strongest disposition to reduce the totality of economic goods-material to the two categories of material goods and "useful personal actions and forbearances" expresses the opinion (English Translation: *Principles of Economics*, page 54) that goods-quality cannot well be denied to such things as "firm names, monopolies, publication rights, patronage and goodwill."

15. This principle is habitually and duly recognized by those writers of the old school who, going to excess in the other direction,

CHAPTER VI

An Analysis Of "Relationships" As "Goods"

In "rights," then, we have eliminated from the categories of goods one group of nonmaterial goods—a group which is as extensive in number as it is suspect in nature. The many kinds of *"relationships"* constitute a group which is of kindred nature but is to an even higher degree only vaguely definable. To this group it formerly seemed necessary to accord a place among intangible goods. I refuse to concede that relationships of any kind whatever can ever possibly be true, independent goods. Even when they are called goods and given a name as such, they are, in truth, nothing *but metaphorical personifications or comprehensive names* for the genuine goods that are concealed beneath them. These genuine goods may be either *material goods* or personal and real *renditions of service.*

In order to submit proof of my thesis, I wish first to set down a few preliminary observations of a general nature for the benefit of those readers who still place any value at all on inferences which belong to that puzzling domain concerning which we possess only names and words rather than true knowledge—a domain to which belong the concepts of *substance,* of *essential nature,* of *power,* of *quality,* of *relationship* and the like. Thereafter I shall, in the course of a "test-and-scrutiny" procedure, select a few of the most important and most frequently cited relationships which are widely recognized as intangible goods, and, by making an analysis of them, show that they really belong in the goods categories that I do recognize, namely, material goods and renditions of service. I shall prove that they are dispensable, and shall thus establish their pleonastic or supererogatory nature.

To begin with, we can be certain that we cannot recognize as a good in the economic sense anything which is incapable of *bringing about a useful effect.* My question is,

insisted there are no such objects of wealth as nonmaterial things, or even personal services, but who are outvoted on this point by the writers of the newer school. I cite as an example Rau's *Volkswirtschaftslehre,* 8th ed., Sec. 49, Note a: "To this extent wealth also includes noncorporeal objects but only by reason of the different *forms of power of disposal,* while certainly only material goods constitute the object toward which the power of disposal is directed." Here, as on many another occasion, the sober theory of the ancients hits upon the truth more accurately than does the "progressiveness" ·of the younger school which is prone to "test its wings" all too freely!

"Can a relationship bring about any effect at all?" Perhaps I shall receive the answer, "Why not?" "Why should a 'useful relationship' not just as well be of use as any other useful thing?" To that question I reply with my second question, viz., "Are we not allowing ourselves to be deceived by a mere liberty of speech when we put any faith in a useful effect on the part of *relationships* and, if a relationship ever seems to be useful, is it not rather the *things* that are concerned in the relationship which bring about the useful effect?" In order to bring about an effect, powers are required, be they material powers or be they intellectual powers. But a "relationship" has neither the one nor the other and hence cannot possibly function as the cause of any sort of effect at all, that is to say, cannot function as a good. The situation with respect to relationships is, in my opinion, no different from the situation with respect to the *qualities* of things. They themselves are nothing; they are merely ascribed by us to things. The proof that a quality cannot be a good is easy to furnish. For it is obvious that whenever any useful quality of a thing plays a part in the accomplishment of a useful effect, it is, in truth, the thing which is endowed with the quality that really brings about the effect. It is, for instance, obvious that in the case of a cold drink of water it is not the abstract "coldness" which slakes thirst, but really the "cold water." Once that is established, it becomes impossible to maintain, with economic seriousness, that the quality of coldness can be termed a good which exists *in addition to*, or more especially *instead of* the cold water, except by indulgence in a pleonasm or a totally impermissible metaphor.

So much for qualities. And relationships are hardly to be described as anything but a sort of quality of things and they cannot be temporarily (or at all) represented *as entities* or as things. Quite often, indeed, in our imagination and in our speech they are transformed into a quality whenever, due to a shift in viewpoint, we choose to regard as unified entities disparate things which our imagination had until then been dealing with. Thus the "relationship" that consists in the fact that the component parts of a house or a set of furniture are arranged at uniform or well-proportioned intervals is transformed, as we speak of the house or the furniture as a single entity, into the *quality of symmetry*. The unevenness of a surface, the sharpness of a knife, the roundness of a bullet are likewise nothing but a declaration of the *relationship* between the whole and its parts. Whatever may be the true situation in this regard, it still remains impossible to escape the conviction that, in view of the utter characterlessness of both qualities and relationships, we cannot ascribe to either of them any power to effect a result except by a species of *borrowing*, nor can we escape the conviction that whatever power to effect a result does exist emanates from the *things* which possess the quality, or which occupy the relationship in question. But as soon as the possibility of the ability to effect a result vanishes, so does the possibility of being a genuine tool for the promotion of human well-being, that is to say, of being a good. And that applies to the entire category of things that may be called relationships.

I would not be remiss in the exercise of that care and caution to which this subject is entitled—a subject so important for jurisprudence as well as for economic theory and at the same time so pregnant with opportunities for going astray. In order to avoid such remissness, I will proceed to the analysis of a few "relationship-goods" which may serve as typical of the entire group. For the purpose of testing such sample cases let us choose the relationships that go under the names of *"good will"* [Schäffle], *"the state"* [Roscher], and *"friendship and love"* [Hermann].

Good Will As An Economic Good

The most important and most difficult of these test subjects, and probably of all relationships, as a class, is the "good" called *good will*. It is a phenomenon which in more than one respect exhibits characteristics that render it both strange and worthy of observation. And the manifestation of those characteristics has for a long time served to draw to it the attention of economic theorists who concern themselves with our question of goods. Indeed, its nature impelled an outstanding economist[1] not very long ago to devote to it a special monograph in which he subjected it to searching examination and did not deny that it possessed genuine goods-quality. *   *   *

The phenomenon of good will is so well known that it hardly needs to be described in detail. It consists in the fact that many persons are in the habit of satisfying their needs along the line of certain kinds of material goods or renditions of service by regularly making their purchases at one particular source of supply. This habit may be based on all sorts of different circumstances. It may be that the desired goods can be procured from only one particular vendor because, either by chance or because of the existence of some exclusive right (such as a patent right) that particular vendor has no competitors. Or, again, it may be that the shop of that particular vendor is situated in a

---

1. Schäffle, *Theorie der ausschliessenden Absatzverhältnisse.*

location that makes patronizing him especially convenient and favorable; or it may be that the buying public through long experience has come to have especial confidence that just from that vendor it can secure merchandise that is outstandingly reliable or priceworthy. Regardless of the particular circumstances that may be responsible for this habitual patronage on the part of the buying public, the fact remains that this habit becomes a *source of profit* for the favored vendor, since the latter registers a larger or smaller profit on every one of these multitudinous transactions. Now if the factual or legal relationships underlying this habitual influx of custom happen at the same time to be of such a nature that they contain a promise of any likelihood that the situation will continue to exist for some time on into the future, then the vendor seems to be assured not only of a current profit but of a series of future profits as well; and in that case the situation will comply with the laws developed earlier as applying to the computation of wealth, in that an economic advantage that is anticipated in the future finds expression in the *computation of the present wealth*. A practical reason for such a computation arises when the vendor "sells his good will" to someone else, some person who wants to take over the vendor's business under conditions which assure the former patronage as, for instance, under a continuance of the previous exclusive right of sale, or on condition that permission be granted to do business under the name of the previous vendor— the name that inspired the buying public's confidence, that is to say, permission to use the former "firm name." It is an everyday experience that in such cases a price is placed, not only on the merchandise inventory, on the accounts receivable, etc., but also on the "good will." And the price of that good will represents the capitalized value of the future profits which the good will relationship appears to assure, due consideration being given, of course, to the degree of probability which characterizes that assurance.

Such is the outward appearance of the thing called "good will" and such is the manner in which good will customarily functions in our economic life. Now let us attempt to analyze this phenomenon somewhat more closely.

In the first place, there can be no doubt that whatever present value is placed upon good will is based on an *anticipation of a future economic advantage*. Whenever a previous proprietor of a business has sold his "good will" or his "firm name" to a successor and purchaser, it is obviously the *hoped-for future profits*, arising out of exchange transactions (i.e., sales), arising by reason of the existence of the relationship of good will which both parties to the contract are dealing in—one deliberately parting with them, the other deliberately acquiring them.

A further feature which is conspicuously observable in such a transaction is that the form of assurance which applies to the anticipated future economic advantage differs from the forms of assurance that we have considered in all previous cases. In the first three principal instances of the computation of wealth* it was a *material good* which gave assurance in the present of a future economic advantage. This material good was in all except the fifth possibility under the complete power of control of the economic subject; in the fifth possibility the control was only partial. In possibilities (4) and (6) the medium was a person *bound by a legal obligation*. In the case of good will, on the contrary, although there are assuring elements which are already operative in the present (without such there could be nothing even approaching an assurance of future economic advantage), nevertheless the form of assurance is far less strict, the assuring elements are far less closely knit, but are far more complicated and far more dispersive.

Let us make an attempt to gather together these dispersive elements.

We must not lose sight of the fact that the future economic advantage, the assuring of which we are talking about consists in future *profits on sales*. And these, if we examine them closely, are revealed as being those material goods which, in the course of sales transactions, are acquired as the consideration (the *quid* that is acquired *pro quo*) and they are, furthermore, revealed as that part of the consideration which, after subtraction of costs and expenses *will be left over as profits*. As soon as we search out the elements which furnish the medium through which those things are acquired which constitute the consideration in the aforementioned sales transactions, we discover the following exemplifying elements:

1. The merchandise that has to be surrendered in order to acquire the things that constitute the consideration.

2. The location of the business plus its furnishings.

3. The rendition of labor by the vendor and his employees.

4. The helpful activity of business friends, commission salesmen and others who promote sales.

5. Advertising, and the like.

6. And, finally, that element without which all the foregoing are pointless, the *patronage of the buying public*.

All the elements listed in the foregoing, in addition to

* See page 108f.

many others, the exact enumeration of which is of no interest to us, engage in a sort of cooperative competition to promote and increase *gross receipts*.

If we continue our analysis by attempting to segregate the individual contributions by the competing elements, we shall find that here this case is like all cases where surplus proceeds are effected through the competing activities of several factors. Under such circumstances our first step is to compute that contribution which stems from elements, the value of which is definitely determined because of our familiarity with them in some other connection, such, for instance, as their having a regular market price. What is finally left over is then ascribed to that factor the value of which is least determinable and the value of which can be established only by reason of this concrete utilization of it. In our case, the case of good will, that factor is *"patronage of the buying public."* The situation here is analogous to that which obtains in agricultural computations. In agricultural computation what remains after deducting from the total agricultural proceeds all costs of production constitutes the surplus proceeds attributable to land or, more accurately expressed, it constitutes that portion of the surplus proceeds which still remains after deduction of the quotas attributable to all competing factors having independently determinable value. Just so in our case (that of good will) the corresponding final element is the "patronage of the buying public" which must be regarded as the element which constitutes the source of all *net profit* which remains after meeting all "costs" including an appropriate entrepreneurial wage.

This explains why among all competing factors it is just this patronage that must be acclaimed as the source of *profit*, although the other factors contributed no less to its emergence.

The patronage of the public which we accordingly must regard as the specific source of the future profits on sales is patently a comprehensive term. If we proceed with our examination in greater detail to determine what elements are concealed under that patronage, the first thing that we observe is the *customers' acts of purchasing*. These acts, inasmuch as they constitute the medium which enables the vendor to obtain the profit-bringing revenue from sales he makes, must be regarded as having for him the character of *useful renditions of service*.

To characterize them thus may seem strange to many a reader who is aware that in everyday life nothing is further from our thoughts than to consider that the vendor who hands over a purchased article is thereby rendering us a particular service. Or that same reader is equally unlikely to entertain the thought that the action of a customer who hands over the consideration to the vendor can be regarded as rendering a service. But economic theory is under obligation to take a view of the situation which is more discerning than that of practice which examines less minutely, though as closely as is expedient for its immediate purpose. For, from the theoretical viewpoint, it must be maintained with conscientious consistency that *every* thing and *every* rendition which has a place in the chain that leads to the satisfaction of a need (even though it merely promotes an intermediate stage) must be regarded as a good, or as a useful rendition of service. To the customer, for instance, who needs the baker's bread, the act of the baker who *hands* it over the counter or of the errand boy who delivers it at his door, is just one of a series of indispensable things and services including the arable land, the farmer's labor, the grain-crop, the miller's labor, the flour, the baker's labor, the loaf itself, the labor of the freighter transporting the flour or the loaf to the city and a host of similar things which everybody recognizes as useful renditions of service. *Everyday practice* does not bring such minutiae to mind as useful renditions of service. These minutiae are analogous to the acts of the customer which redound to the benefit of the vendor. They, too, do not come in mind as renditions of service. That is partly because they seem too minute, too transitory and too inconsequential. In further part it is because they are acts which we, intent on the material good itself, regard *as too self-evident*, too much a matter of course for us to accord to them significance as acts worthy of individual attention. But theory, which cannot regard even the smallest thing as nonexistent, merely because it is small, must be exact in this point, too, and must lay claim to the character of useful renditions of service on behalf of these mere acts of "handing over," just as surely as it does for more comprehensive and laborious services. And it becomes the special duty of theory to do so when, as in the present case, services like these, because of their large number, do really constitute a practical factor of perceptible import. And even though practice *as a general rule* tends to overlook them, these acts of "handing over" *do* occasionally become perceptible, as a practical matter, when, fortuitously, circumstances render them conspicuous. If, for instance, I have bought something and have paid the purchase price, but the vendor, for some inconsequential reason or other, refuses to hand over the purchased article, it might well happen that, rather than inaugurate an unpleasant lawsuit, I would make a direct payment to the recalcitrant vendor as a direct inducement to "hand over" the purchased article. That would certainly be an act which would make it clearly recognizable that the handing over is a useful and, indeed, an indispensable service. But the goods-character of these acts of handing over and of similar minute actions does become clearly recognizable when one considers them *in large numbers;* shop employees, for instance, and "sales personnel," whose duties consist entirely or at least in large part in merely handing things over, are regularly paid a salary for performing such acts.

It may be difficult to accept the statement that the acts by which customers consummate purchases are to be regarded as so many renditions of service. And yet that statement, as a matter of theory, is indubitably absolutely correct. But those renditions of service are not, by far, the ultimate link of sources of utility revealed by an analysis of good will. For these actions on the part of customers still lie in the future, and if they are to perform the function of an element assuring profits from sales, they must themselves be assured, and must therefore have their roots in some element that already exists in the present. A search for *such elements* leads us to a discovery of the following: *the persons predisposed to make their purchases at the particular source of supply;* further, *the persons who confirm and spread that predisposition in and to other persons (such as satisfied customers who are also commenders and "boosters")* ; in addition, other such elements consist in *material goods* in *such amount and of such a nature that they encourage and promote the patronage of the buying public.* They might include such things as famous buildings, or even art galleries which attract travelers to visit the city in question, or even railroads which facilitate travel to that city and *all sorts of other secondary factors that work toward the same end.*

Useful services upon which one may count to some extent may fairly be said to be, to that extent, *economically available.* In that sense we may safely say that all those persons and things which facilitate custom do, to a certain degree, stand subject to the vendor's power of disposal. Hence there would be a certain degree of justification for counting the useful renditions of service by those persons and things among the vendor's objects of wealth, on the ground that they are, in that sense, subject to his power of disposal.

This power of disposal is admittedly far from complete

or absolute but it does, after all, exist. And it is based upon factually present and existent factors. The occurrence of the latter is, indeed, often subject to circumstances which favor their "utilization" by a business man for his own advantage. Thus people become tributary to the physician because of their sicknesses, to the quack because of their superstitions, to the bucket-shop operator because of their passion for gambling, to the dispensers of fashionable attire in foreign metropolises because of their predilection for imported merchandise. Thus needs, caprices, follies are the weaknesses by reason of which even the freest among human beings become subservient to the interests of another. And if we would prove that these weaknesses and also the force of circumstances along other lines make it possible for a *real power of disposal* to be built up, we need search no further than these very "transfers of good will" that take place by physicians, lawyers, agents, and the like.

The fact that this power of disposal rests on so tenuous a foundation and that it is absolute to so small a degree, could not, of itself, constitute a hindrance to inclusion in a computation of wealth of those objects to which this power of disposal pertains. For even bees are regarded as goods and as component elements of an accumulation of wealth, even though the power of disposal over them is based merely on their established trait of returning honey to the hive, and even though the economic subject would be powerless in the face of a suspension by the bees of their habitual behavior. Nevertheless, in the case of good will it is *not* the usual procedure to count as part of one's wealth the factual elements which have just been stated to be what brings about the economic advantage derived from good will. The reason for that is, in part, that they are individually too indefinite, too difficult to observe and, above all, because their contact with any relationship to the vendor's advantage is all too tenuous and incomplete.[2] *Minima non curat praetor** is a maxim which we will do well to apply constantly in our deliberations and computations in the field of economics.

---

2. In the case of the useful *persons* the failure to count them as elements is, quite simply, ascribable to the very same reason that applies in the case of payment-claims and which is responsible for the fact that the right (to claim payment) is listed in the computation rather than the person of the debtor. Cf. p. 108.

* Translator's Note: Literally, this Latin phrase means, "The magistrate has no regard for trifles." It is strongly reminiscent of the similar phrase so frequently cited in the course of the practice of law in the English language, namely, *De minimis non curat lex*, meaning, "The law does not concern itself with trifles." This citation as well as its kinship with the language of jurisprudence should convey its own implications to the reader.

It is customary for us to bring the major portion or aspect of an economic advantage, so far as its nature will permit, under our economic power of disposal and that portion or phase then always finds direct expression in our computation of wealth. We count as an object of wealth belonging to *us* that thing the chief utility of which is guaranteed by physical possession and ownership, and we do the same with respect to a personal service which is similarly guaranteed to us by reason of our having a right to enforce a claim.

But in addition to that chief portion or aspect of the advantage there arise all sorts of incidental renditions of service and useful effects (constituting, as it were, a sort of overflow). With respect to these it is either impossible or not the usual practice to effect any physical or legal segregation for our individual advantage. Thus the utilization of firewood and of pasture opportunities are incidental aspects of the advantages derivable from forest land, and such utilization is for the most part an object of private property rights. But other incidental aspects, such as utilization of the forest land for pleasure walks and for the aesthetic pleasure of looking at it and for the satisfaction derived from admiring it as one element contributing to the beauty of the landscape—these are all incidental advantages which for natural reasons are free for everyone. Such partial and incidental renditions of service emanating from things which, with respect to the chief portion of their economic advantage, are in the economic service of some other person we habitually ignore completely as a practical matter. No one would ever dream of including as part of his wealth a rosebush (or the renditions of service of that rosebush) because he has a daily opportunity to breathe its perfume into his nostrils as he walks past it; nor would anyone be in the least inclined to include in the computation of his wealth a forest and a mountain, the view of which from his window is something he constantly enjoys.[3]

Nor is there any greater disposition on the part of a merchant to enter as a component part of his wealth the rendition of service on the part of the railroad train which brings a customer to his city, nor so to enter the action of a customer who, by his recommendation, wins another customer for the merchant.

However it is only the *isolated* incidental "splinter" of

[3]. That such things and opportunities for such utilization *can* by their nature be objects of wealth is apparent from the fact that at times and under certain circumstances they are made the object of *rights* that pertain to them. For instance, there are servitudes which are concerned with a view out upon other parcels of land.

economic advantage that is deliberately ignored in this way. When on the contrary a large number, nay, even a multitudinous number, of these "splinters" join together, people begin to count on them and to realize that their existence and their value signify an important object of wealth. But that recognition and realization does not apply to the individual particles of advantage (since these, for the most part, escape attention anyway) but attention is directed to the combined mass of them, *all "lumped together"* and it is, by preference, treated as a *unified and conglomerate concept*. And when, as in the case we are considering, that conglomerate concept is one that covers, say, *"custom"* or the *"relationship of patronage"* and the concept is listed as an object of wealth, that listing appears under some special appellation. And that appellation in this case is "good will."

I call it an appellation. And after our analysis of what its actually useful elements are, and of the manner in which they are useful, there can be no doubt that we are dealing here with nothing more than an appellation. It is an abstract and collective term for a number of very concrete useful elements. All of them belong in the categories of material goods or of personal and/or material renditions of service; they most distinctly constitute the "patronage of the buying public" and they comprise, and prepare the way to the desired result of that patronage, namely, profits on sales. And the only reason they do not make their appearance in any listing of wealth under their own proper names is that they are gathered up into the "sphere of influence" of the economic subject in too fragmentary form and in a guise characterized by only partial power of disposal. They *are* the true objects of wealth, but are *not named* as such for reasons that lie less in themselves than in our conception of them. But if "good will" (the "relationship of patronage") is only an appellation covering other objects of wealth, and not a peculiarly constituted *material* of wealth in its own right, then we may without misgivings of any kind rule it out of the list of genuine goods, as being something that does not enrich that list but merely constitutes a pleonastic addition to it. Let it find its true place among those things which are but *forms* of computing wealth.

Patents And Copyrights As Economic Goods

These last observations of mine have applied most particularly to such relationships of patronage as are based only *upon factual circumstances*. In order to avoid leaving an obvious gap in my treatment I wish to add here a few words by way of mention of the *legally compulsive re-*

lationships of patronage which are based on a vendor's exclusive right of sale. This group includes, besides others, such rights as *patent rights and authors' copyrights*. Of these the latter have been a source of especial embarrassment to jurists who have been unable satisfactorily[4] to classify them with either objective or personal rights.

From the economist's viewpoint these compulsive patronage relationships, these exclusive sales rights (name them as you will) can be analyzed and broken down into a series of successive goods-elements in the same manner that I employed for the purely factual patronage-relationships. The goods-elements would, in this case, too, all fit into the categories of material goods and or material renditions of service. The one difference is that now that series would be augmented by the addition of those things and conditions which constitute the basis of the legal protection furnished by the state. A brief analysis of authors' copyrights will yield the following picture.

The legal protection afforded by such rights (apparently reducible to the activity and services of those agencies of the state which promulgate and execute the law) consists of the prevention of any competitive selling. This protection against interference affords an opportunity for the entrepreneurial activity of an author (or his authorized publisher) to engage unimpeded in the lucrative reproduction and distribution-in-quantity of his intellectual product— assuming, of course, the assistance of the commercially necessary material goods. His economic advantage is initially achieved by means of public patronage consisting of a large number of individual renditions and comprising, in the last analysis, the totality of the purchase prices amassed through all the "acts of purchase," or, rather, the profits derived therefrom. The things, then, that are truly useful in this instance are, successively,

1. *Material goods* resulting from *buyers' actions* which constitute a response to the *entrepreneur's efforts;* and

2. Entrepreneurial activities, promoted and fostered by the *activities* (operating in the background) *of those agencies of law enforcement* which prohibit all competitive activity. Now all these things are real, concrete, factual; they are all material goods or material services and they leave no room anywhere for any independent intangible "relationship-good."

4. The conception of authors' copyrights as *intellectual property* (the word, property, being used in a strictly legalistic sense and designating an objective right) bears so plainly the stamp of a fiction, resorted to in order to evade the burden of explanation, that it could not possibly prove satisfactory.

Helpful Forbearances And Nonperformances Are Not Economic Goods

I cannot conclude my discussion of patronage-relationships without making mention of the treatment accorded by one pre-eminent research scholar to a kindred question of undeniable theoretical importance. Menger[5] (*Principles*, p. 54f.) was, to my personal knowledge, the first to express (though not in apodictically definitive form) the opinion I have just set forth, namely, that relationships in general and patronage-relationships in particular, despite their appearance of possessing goods-character, nevertheless are not, in and of themselves goods but only a complex of material goods and personal services. Now in the course of his efforts to remove the shell and present the genuine kernel of goods-character that does reside in relationships, this pre-eminent thinker also touches upon another question of undeniable interest. That is the question whether it is not possible for us to derive use-benefit not only from positively *useful acts* on the part of other persons, but also from *useful forbearances* on their part. He seems inclined to answer this question in the affirmative. In this connection I would say that it seems he was moved to that decision by the fact that we often *pay a price to secure* forbearances just as we do to secure goods and *positive* services. For example, a physician, Dr. *D*, who settles in a certain town, will enter into an agreement with his predecessor in that town who is retiring, and pursuant to that agreement will pay him a consideration representing a purchase price for which he buys from Dr. *A* the latter's *ceasing to practice*. In this case a forbearing to practice or, in other words, a pure nonperformance is something that is obviously useful to the new physician and is something that he purchases for money, and it therefore appears to meet all the criteria which enable it to qualify as possessing goods-quality.

However it nevertheless remains my opinion that pure forbearances can never find an equal place beside true goods and positive renditions of service in an inventory of things that promote human well-being. For a so-called useful forbearance is, strictly speaking, not the cause of an economic advantage, but only *the cause of the absence of any economic disadvantage*. If we wanted to count as an economic good every absence of any cause of an economic disadvantage, we could easily go too far in this respect. For instance, it is clear that for our young physician not only his predecessor's (Dr. *A's*) forbearing to practice is economically important, but it would also be of equal or at

[5.] Cf. Note 14 to foregoing Chapter 5.

least similar importance for him if Dr. *B* in a neighboring town also forbore to practice in Dr. *D's* town, and also if Professor *C* in the capital city and, indeed, if all other capable and qualified physicians forbore to practice there. Now it certainly will not do to register the forbearance of all the thousands of physicians who *do not* practice in Dr. *D's* town as so many "goods" possessed by Dr. *D!*

To my mind the true picture of the situation can be drawn as follows. Every economic advantage, if it is to eventuate, requires, on the one hand, *a positive causative* element that will *effect the advantage,* but it also requires, on the other hand, a host of negative presuppositions, presuppositions that there will be an *absence of elements which would prevent or vitiate the positively useful progress* of events. If, let us say, I wish to grow grapes, I must have, as the positive causative element a vineyard, grapevines, warmth, moisture, etc., but at the same time I need negative presuppositions such as "no flood waters" "no unseasonable frost," "no insect pests," "no grape blight" and the absence of another 100 or 1,000 untoward happenings which are capable of destroying a grape harvest. Or let us put it this way: if an economic advantage is to eventuate, one or several things must function in a positively useful manner and all other things must function negatively —either in a nonvitiating or at least in an indifferent manner. Clearly, we cannot apply the term "good" to the factors that are merely indifferent or nonvitiating, but can apply that term only to the factors that *function on the positive side.* The numberless negatives that are required for the eventuation of every economic advantage are simply *in toto* tacitly understood presuppositions for the goods-quality of the positive factors. If we knew concerning a thing that the advantage of which, in and of itself, that thing is capable would definitely be vitiated, then that thing simply would not be a good. That would be true, for instance, of a vineyard in a climate that is regularly subject to the incidence of unseasonable frost. Thus it may be said that when we count as goods and compute as objects of wealth any positive factors we are at the same time tacitly including in the computation the totality of necessary negative presuppositions. That makes it impermissible for us to make any special computation for some selected individual instance out of the entire class of negative factors simply because for some special reason our attention is specially and conspicuously directed to that single factor. It is that sort of selected individual negative factor which, in the example of young Dr. *D,* is represented by Dr. *A's* forbearing to practice.

The fact that a price is paid, or that costs are incurred to bring about a forbearance, by no means makes the latter a *good*. On the contrary, the payment merely represents the rendering indifferent of a factor which would otherwise be disadvantageous. If, for instance, a ring of pitch is applied around the trunk of a fruit tree to protect the fruit from ants and caterpillars, that ring of pitch is admittedly a good but the caterpillars and ants, now rendered innocuous, do not become goods. The same can be said of dikes, which are goods, but the prevented floods are not goods. In the same manner we may say that the agreed sum of money which Dr. *D* pays Dr. *A is* a good, but Dr. *A's* forbearance is not. In my opinion there is no place among goods for pure forbearances, for simple nonperformances. The concept of a good must be limited to positive factors for the attainment of an economic advantage.[6]

The State As An Economic Good

The second of the "relationship goods" that I announced my intention of analyzing is the *state*.

Any thinking person must be deeply aware that the joining together of human beings as members of an organized state is a highly productive source of human well-being. And that fact must have furnished a strong incentive to regard the state as a "good" and, indeed, as an extremely valuable good.

Upon close examination, however, it becomes apparent that every economic advantage which we can ascribe to that imaginary entity, "the state," can in reality be traced back to the following two sources:

1. *The renditions of service on the part of those per-*

---

[6]. These observations will explain why in Note 4 on page 66 I could not assign to *negative servitudes* a place either among the rights to partial utilization or among the rights to future proceeds from goods. I understand true negative servitudes to be such as are directed, not to the retention of some positive useful quality of the thing that is rendering service, but rather to the warding off of positively harmful influences. Such true negative servitudes have as their object some forbearance which cannot be recognized as either a good or a rendition of service. It goes without saying that neither the servitude itself nor the forbearance can be a "good" any more than can other rights concerning which that point has already been made abundantly clear. Accurate analysis reveals a similarity between the situation which obtains in (a) the case of these negative servitudes, and (b) the case of exclusive sales rights. That analysis reveals the presence in (a) of the activities of the agencies which afford legal protection by preventing injurious action, thereby enhancing the usefulness of positive goods belonging to the possessor of the right; and it reveals in (b) the utility derivable from the goods required for the conduct of the sales enterprise, including the activity of the entrepreneur; it reveals also in (a) the presence of an advantage derivable from the thing to which the servitude applies. However, the positive indirect advantage naturally cannot count as the object to which the servitude pertains.

sons who have made it their vocational or professional duty or have otherwise taken it upon themselves to solve "problems of state." That is to say, this source comprises the useful services of judges, teachers, soldiers, police and sanitation officials, members of the central administration, jurymen, and the like.

2. *The renditions of service on the part of material goods* which are placed by the "state" at the disposal of the general public for purposes of the general welfare. This includes such material goods as streets, harbors, bridges, public buildings (e.g., courthouses), canals and the like.

It would probably be impossible to think up any economic advantage emanating from the "state" which could not be allocated to one or the other of the foregoing two sources or to some interaction of either with the other.

The person who derives some positive economic advantage traceable to one or the other of these sources will have a peculiarly vivid consciousness of the fact that a definite person or thing has been useful to him. He will know clearly that an individual policeman rescued him from the hands of a homicidal criminal; he will be aware that the government-operated postal service made prompt delivery to him of a particular, crucially important message. But only a very tiny fraction of the total advantage derived from the state's institutions impresses itself upon any individual as a direct and positive rendition of service. The individuals comprising the community are the recipients of far greater advantages *partly in the form of a far-flung system of distribution; and partly in the negative form of protection from harmful disturbances.*

Persons for whom wrongs are righted by a judge in a court of law are not the only participants in the benefits of the state's activities on behalf of right and justice which are performed by civil and criminal court judges. All others, including those who never see a court of law, share in these benefits too (and perhaps in even more beneficial manner), because of the respect for law which prevails throughout the land by reason of the activities of those same judges. Every resident of any metropolitan center shares indirectly in the benefits emanating from the activities of the quarantine and sanitation or public health forces that operate at the national borders to prevent the introduction of epidemic diseases; he also shares in the benefits derived from the activities of all teachers and educators who, by giving intellectual and moral training to the entire body of our youth, train all persons to become his useful fellow citizens, just as he benefits from the activities of all private and public promoters of industry and from those of public or private individuals who contribute to the smooth functioning of traffic and trade—in short, he shares in the benefits arising from the activity of all the individuals in the community who make any direct or indirect contribution to the general welfare. When the general recognition that this particular quarter (the state) is the source of a tremendous impetus to our well-being combines with an awareness of the fact that we are totally unacquainted with the individual persons, things, actions and services that contribute so heavily to the promotion of our well-being, there ensues a highly natural propensity *to lump together* all the beneficent factors which we are unable to observe in detail and to *gather them under a single concept.* That is undoubtedly the source from which arises the concept that the *"state"* is a *"good."* The "state" (the word being used as a name for the source of economic advantages) is, like the patronage-relationship, *a comprehensive appellation—* an inclusive title *for a totality of concrete causative factors of economic advantage. And all these factors are amenable to classification* in the *categories of material goods and renditions of service on the part of things and persons.*

Love And Friendship As Economic Goods

The same thing is true of the relationships of *love and friendship,* of *family* and of other kindred "relationship-goods." And with those I wish to conclude my "testing by sample." In this field, too, we can easily convince ourselves that every useful promotion of well-being which we derive from these sources consists, in actual truth, of nothing but beneficial renditions of service, predominantly personal ones but also of a material nature, renditions that are given and received and that may often, to be sure, be of a highly intellectual and delicate nature but that are, nevertheless, *genuine renditions of service in the economic sense.* Of course, we feel a certain reluctance to think of the influences of such tender relationships in terms *of economic acts.* But if we undertake a theoretical examination of the sources of our well-being, we cannot but recognize the truly useful element when it is present, even in this area, in personal and material renditions of service, nor can we do aught but recognize that, from the economic viewpoint, such "goods" as family, church, love and the like are merely linguistic disguises for a totality of concretely useful renditions of service.

Conclusions

It would be wearisome to demonstrate by still more individual examples an idea that is not, in itself, difficult to comprehend. I presume, therefore, that I may now conclude. If we pause and glance about to determine what result our investigations have attained, that result may be briefly stated in the following words: *We have disencumbered the economic goods concept of a whole category of pseudo-goods.* It was a mistake to regard rights and relationships as goods in and of themselves, or as goods which existed beside and in addition to the categories of material goods and services. For the whole category we are dealing with concerns not the *existence* of goods but only the *connection* of goods with individuals, or it concerns the assignment of reasons for subjective goods-qualities.

We will therefore, as economists, speak of rights and relationships only where we are dealing with the form of the connection between persons and goods, but when, on the contrary, we are dealing with goods themselves, we shall speak only of the elements *underlying* rights and relationships, of their *substratum,* as it were.

That substratum or those substrata, be it noted, are at all times amenable to allocation to the categories of material goods and/or material renditions of service. And, be it further noted, these categories exhaust the number of categories into which genuine economic goods are classifiable at all.

What will be the direct and immediate effect of the result we have attained on economic theory and economic practice?

I expect *no* direct and immediate effect *at all* in the field of *economic practice.* No matter how clearly I may have proved that payment-claims and good-will relationships are not genuine goods, no matter how clearly I have therefore proved that, whenever, in practical economic life rights and relationships are bought and sold, it is not, in truth, those intangibles that are meant and are valued and transferred, but that actually it is material goods and renditions of service that are so dealt in; no matter, I say, how clear my proof, I am not going to pretend to believe that economic practice will submit to any slavish accuracy in the matter. It will in the future continue to be the custom, and rightly so, to say that *A's* wealth consists in payment-claims, that *B* sold his good will for $50,000 to *C*, and that the state, the church and the family are valuable "goods." Yes, I believe even *economic theory* will, quite properly, continue talking that same language because it is the language that all the world talks and understands. For it would be an absurd undertaking to banish from the language of *economic theory* every manner of speaking that is not literally correct; it would be sheer pedantry to proscribe every figure of speech, particularly since we could not say the hundredth part of what we have to say, if we refused ever to take recourse to a metaphor.

One requirement is essential, that economic theory avoid the error of confusing a practical habit, indulged in for the sake of expediency, with scientific truth. I do make the request that economic theory, *when it speaks* ex cathedra *about goods and categories of goods, substitute the two underlying associates, material goods and renditions of service, for the figurative appellations,* "intangible rights" and "relationship-goods." *And I make the further request that, whenever it does employ figures of speech in mentioning these things as goods, it remain at least tacitly conscious of the figurative nature of its expressions. To put it briefly, I think that economic theory should always retain the exact truth in its armory and bring it forth at all times when there is any real necessity for doing so.* If it does that, it may be permissible to retain the accustomed terminology of an outmoded error, just as we do in other fields. For do we not still speak of the sun "rising" and "setting," of its "coming up" and "going down"?

There, as I see it, lies the *whole* importance (and no slight importance, either) of the "purification" or "cleansing" of the categories of goods. The important thing is not the correcting of a classification of goods which has been pleonastic in character by reason of duplicating one and the same good and listing it under several names. No, the important thing is that we be preserved from self-deception through involuntary fictions which, because they are not true to life can never give rise to aught but erroneous concepts, but which, *because they are thought to be true to life* prevent a search for the full truth which is therefore never missed; and which thus become a storehouse of misconceptions for the whole domain of the goods-concept and for the functioning of goods; and which lull us into a false feeling of contentment with the specious solutions of our problems at which we have arrived. And I request, finally, *that having once broken the comfortably illusory crutch of an erroneous concept, we now recognize the compulsion we are under to get to the very bottom of the truth whenever we are face to face with a truly important problem.*

Nor will there be any lack of such occasions. One of

the most important of them is offered by the phenomenon of *credit*.

We can truly say that it is the mission of a sound goods theory to be the foundation and the test of every theory of credit. And with such a sound theory, all the misconceptions concerning the nature of credit as they appear in the theories of Law and MacLeod would have been avoided. And so, too, would the difficulties have been avoided that become apparent in the following situation. Prevailing economic theory experienced embarrassment and was forced to take recourse to devious subterfuges because of its recognition of the following paradoxical situation. It knew it was *obliged to disown* the conclusions concerning credit reached by MacLeod, but it knew also that it *could not disown* his premises, for those premises it was in agreement with and had, indeed, itself established. All this, I say, would have been avoided if, from the outset, economic theorists had clarified the issue as to what things are truly useful, and as to what things are genuine goods and what things are merely labels and appellations of goods or of groups of goods.

For the matter is really very simple. If *A* lends *B* a good, then neither from the viewpoint of the economizing nation, nor from that of the economizing individual can there ensue any creation of a new good called a "demand." The fact of the matter stands as follows: the one and only good (the good loaned) that comes into play either before or after the loan is *B's* good *today* but it is scheduled to become *A's* good again *after the expiration of the term of the loan.* (Either the good itself will revert, as such, to *A* or it will revert as represented by a similar good of the same kind and value.)

Now this state of affairs which obviously involves just one single good then becomes subjected to two treatments. *On the one hand it is the basis of the creation of a right, on the other hand it becomes the basis of a computation of wealth.* Since the law and the right assume the defense of the present situation, *the situation "as of now," the right becomes transformed into a property title which B has to the loaned object;* but since the right also makes provision for the future (the time-after-expiration-of-the-term), it becomes a right-to-make-a-demand possessed by *A*, affecting the return of the loaned object. The law was capable of creating two claims to one and the same object, because it was not forced to make the things it created apply to a single point in time. Thus, despite the unitary character of the object of the loan, it was possible for this duality of rights to arise. *But the situation is altogether different with respect to the computation of wealth. That is forced to depict the position of both interested parties as of one and the same time.* The computation therefore cannot allocate the good to one party "as of now" and to the other "as of then." It must make a choice as to which party the good is to be allocated to. For sufficiently profound reasons it elects to look to the future and to the ultimate result. Hence it allocates the value to the creditor who is ultimately scheduled to receive back the good. In doing so it *sets up a fiction.* The fiction it sets up is that the future has already arrived. (The fact that it does in truth set up a fiction is doubly attested.) In the first place, it allocates the value of the good to the creditor *who does not have it yet,* and in the second place it allocates *nothing* to the debtor who does have the good, not only in his indubitable physical possession, but also in his completely confirmed legal possession. (He has both title and possession.)

Now it is that fiction which turned out to be a trap for many a writer who has written on the subject of credit. He perceived that a value was being attributed "as of now" to the creditor and so was persuaded that "as of now" there had to be some good in existence, the value of which was being allocated to the creditor. He overlooked the fact that the computation of wealth could allocate something to him only because it adopted the viewpoint of the future; and he overlooked that he himself (i.e., the writer) would be entitled to infer, on the basis of the result of the computation, only the existence of future goods (or, to put it more accurately, the future existence of goods). It is to be assumed that the drawing of such erroneous inferences in the future will be forestalled if it is recognized (it now can be) that a computation of wealth is not a catalogue *of facts,* but only a catalogue of *interpretations of the facts,* and since it can further be recognized that when we are dealing with rights and relationships we are, in any event, not dealing with genuine goods, but only with *forms of concepts* that are substituted for goods.

*   *   *

In addition to this topic of credit, I think that in the matter of an investigation into the phenomenon of *capital and interest* we have a second area in which it becomes of supreme importance to avoid a mystically hazy ideational image and to achieve an essentially accurate and true-to-life conception of what goods are and of how they effectuate their usefulness, and of how they function *usefully.* Capital and interest are phenomena which in the course

of modern times* have attained ever increasing importance
no less because of their bearing on the economic progress
of human society as a whole, than because of their bearing
on the manner in which *this world's goods* are distributed
within human society; furthermore, in these phenomena
there is contained a goodly portion of the material with
which today's "social question" is concerned. Concerning
these phenomena there is a veritable plethora of opinions
hovering in the atmosphere—opinions as to whether "capital" is a boon or an evil, whether possession of capital is
just or unjust, and whether interest represents the well-
earned compensation of the capitalist or an iniquitous bit
of extortion. But in respect to any investigation into the
why and wherefore (which is something that should in all
justice precede any formation of opinion, if that opinion
is not to be mere prejudice)—in that respect, I say there
not only is no plethora, but far, far too little of the sort
has been attempted at all. I consider both the theory of
the productivity of capital, as it has been presented by representative economic writers of our country, and also the
theoretical polemics of the well-schooled chieftains of socialism which inveigh against the former, to be alike of
immature development and to belong to the most beclouded
sections of the entire field of economic science. In the field
of these phenomena many a question has been left unanswered and many a riddle has not even been formulated as a
question.

I hope at some later time to present the foundation for
a considered judgment on those questions and those phenomena. Indeed, it is my hope that this present essay will
serve as a preparatory and preliminary (if still remote)
presentation of some of the material that will contribute to
the later treatment of the problem of capital and interest.**

* Translator's Note: *Rechte und Verhältnisse* was published
in 1881.

** Böhm-Bawerk, *Capital and Interest* (in three volumes),
Libertarian Press, South Holland, Illinois, U.S.A., 1959.

EUGEN VON BÖHM-BAWERK

III

Control Or Economic Law?*

John Richard Mez Translation

*The title of the German original is "Macht oder ökonom-
isches Gesetz?". This essay first appeared in *Zeitschrift
für Volkswirtschaft, Sozialpolitik und Verwaltung*, Vienna,
Austria, Volume XXIII, December 1914, pp. 205-271. Also
reprinted in Volume I (1924) of *Gesammelte Schriften* by
the same author, (Hölder-Pichler-Tempsky A. G., Vienna).
A translation was made in 1931 by John Richard Mez
whose address was given at that time as Eugene, Oregon.
It had an Introduction by Frank William Taussig of Harvard University. No copyright of this article is recorded
in the United States copyright office. Efforts to commu-
nicate with the translator have been unavailing.

Contents

Present Publisher's Preface To "Control Or Economic Law?"

In this essay, not published until after Böhm-Bawerk's death, he considers the problem: *Can human laws or human coercion of any kind permanently and successfully neutralize or overwhelm "economic law"?*

The original German title by Böhm-Bawerk is *Macht oder öconomisches Gesetz?* which can be translated *Coercion or Economic Law?*. The question mark is important in these titles. Böhm-Bawerk is contrasting "Power" or "Coercion" exercised by anyone (by governments, businessmen, labor unions) on the one hand, over against what he calls "economic law." If the question mark were not in the title, then it probably should read, in elaborated form: *Control (Power or Coercion of any kind) versus the Indestructible Operation of Economic Law.*

Böhm-Bawerk rejects the theses: (1) that there is *only* a historico-socio-legal aspect to economic problems; or alternatively, (2) that there is *only* an economic aspect. He declares that both aspects exist and remain operative. His answer is therefore not that of the Classicists who considered only (or very primarily) the economic aspect; nor that of the Socialists who considered only the historico-socio-legal, and especially the *power* aspects of the question. Böhm-Bawerk's position is, in a sense, in the "middle-of-the -road." By an illuminating analysis he comes to the conclusion that the economic aspects cannot be negated, and that they are ineluctable.

Specifically this essay shows that the power of monopolists — whether employers in cartels, or employes in labor unions — cannot prevail. The "power" of such groups cannot annul "economic law." Rather economic law triumphs eventually.

The reason why Böhm-Bawerk comes to that conclusion is because, in this situation, he identifies economic law with the ineradicable and imprescriptible human motivation to self-preservation and to the pursuit of the self-regarding interests. In other words, Böhm-Bawerk is arguing from what might be called "the nature of things," from the facts of creation and existence, as substantiated by universal human observation.

In his *Introduction* to the original Mez translation, the late Frank William Taussig, professor at Harvard University, wrote:

> Böhm-Bawerk was distinguished among the economists of the generation now passing from the stage by an unusual combination of qualities — learning, accuracy, independence of judgment, originality and incisiveness of thought, dialectical skill, mastery of exposition. His learning was extraordinary.

> The first volume, *History and Critique of Interest Theories,* of his great [three volume] treatise, CAPITAL AND INTEREST, gives a history of the theories of interest from ancient times to the date of its publication; this book is a model scholarly performance. Not only does it show wide-ranging command of the literature, but what is too often lacking in histories of doctrine, real grappling with the reasoning of the several thinkers and schools, and penetrating criticism of its validity.

> He followed the writings of his contemporaries in all the modern languages no less exhaustively and critically, and the numerous reviews and papers which he published from time to time in subsequent years, among which the very last is here presented in an English version, were marked by a quality too rare among critics — they always went to the core of the subject in hand.

> The second volume of the treatise, *Positive Theory of Capital,* is too well known as a landmark in the development of economic thought to need characterization. As an intellectual performance, there are few books on economics in any language that can be ranked with it. One may not agree with all that is said, but the book bears the unmistakable impress of a great mind.

> The paper here presented in translation is noteworthy in two ways. It restates the main conclusions of the author on the distribution of wealth, and in some ways amplifies them. It also points out the manner in which social conditions and currents may modify them, while yet the reasoning on which they are based is not impugned. In this respect

there is shown a clear understanding of the realities of life, and of the manner in which the underlying dominant forces may be deflected, concealed, sometimes even permanently altered in their working, by those on the surface. The whole is to be commended to the serious student of economics as a model of systematic exposition, of thoroughness in method and treatment, and of noble spirit.

This essay can be read with especial profit by those who are representing employers or employes in wage rate discussion; or by those who believe that statutes passed by legislatures or decisions delivered by judges in courts are the *last* word in economic problems.

The contents of this essay reveal that Böhm-Bawerk assumes that his readers are familiar with his earlier three-volume work, CAPITAL AND INTEREST, especially Volume II, *Positive Theory of Capital*, Book III, with the title, "Value and Price." Wherever the text seems difficult or obscure, the trouble will probably be that the reader does not know what Böhm-Bawerk had written previously.

In general, the Mez translation has been followed; but there are a few changes.

Translator's Preface

A theoretical inquiry into the relative limitations of all attempts at price control (owing to the inevitable triumphant emergence of the law of supply and demand) is a contribution to economic science as fascinating as it is timely. Again and again efforts are being made in various parts of the world, to regulate prices both of commodities, and of services of labor, and, indeed, of gold itself!

The masterly manner in which Böhm-Bawerk approaches so complex a problem made it appear an inviting task to render more accessible his analysis to the student of political economy in the English-speaking countries.

The original of this essay was written in fulfillment of a promise made by the author in 1898, in the introduction to the third edition of his famous *Positive Theory of Capital,* in which he indicated his intention to inquire in an independent investigation into "the great problem before us, and *to trace the exact nature and extent of the influences emanating from two different sources, from the social and from the purely economic categories.* This phase of economic theory," he wrote at that time, "has never been adequately presented, not even by the marginal-utility school." It was published in December 1914, several months after the author's death, in the economic quarterly *Zeitschrift für Volkswirtschaft, Sozialpolitik und Verwaltung,* published in Vienna, which, incidentally, he himself, had founded twenty-two years before.

The translation follows the original text as closely as possible; a few sentences of a controversial and no longer relevant nature have purposely been omitted. Where illustrations of prices were given in the pre-war currency of Austria, the American dollar standard has been used instead.

JOHN RICHARD MEZ

Eugene, Oregon
Summer 1931

CONTROL OR ECONOMIC LAW?

CHAPTER I
The Extent And Nature Of The Influence Of Institutional Controls Versus The Natural Course Of Economic Phenomena

Are Economic Laws Immutable?

Economic theory, from its very beginnings, has endeavored to discover and formulate the *laws* governing economic behavior. In the early period, which was under the influence of Rousseau and his doctrines of the laws of nature, it was customary to apply to these economic laws the name and character of *physical laws*. In a literal sense, this characterization was, of course, open to objection, but possibly the term "physical" or "natural" laws was intended merely to give expression to the fact that, just as natural phenomena are governed by immutable eternal laws, quite independent of human will and human laws, so in the sphere of economics, there exist certain laws against which the will of man, and even the powerful will of the state, remain impotent; and that the flow of economic forces cannot, by artificial interference of social control, be driven out of certain channels into which it is inevitably pressed by the force of economic laws.

Such a law, among others, was considered to be that of *supply and demand*, which again and again had been observed to triumph over the attempts of powerful governments to render bread cheap in lean years by means of "unnatural" price regulations, or to confer upon bad money the purchasing power of good money. And inasmuch as in the last analysis, the remuneration of the great factors of production—land, labor and capital—in other words, the distribution of wealth among the various classes of society, represents merely one case, although the most important practical case of the general laws of price, the entire, all-important problem of distribution of wealth became dependent upon the question whether it was regulated and dominated by natural economic laws, or by the arbitrary influence of social control.

British Classical Economists Accepted
Idea That There Are Economic Laws

The early economists did not hesitate to decide this question with fearless consistency in favor of the exclusive predominance of "natural laws." The most famous, or rather notorious, illustration of this interpretation was the "wages-fund theory" of the classic and post-classic school of economists, according to which the amount of wages was determined by a natural relationship of almost mathematical accuracy thought to exist between the amount of capital available in a country for the payment of wages, the so-called "wages-fund," and the number of workers. All workers jointly were considered incapable of ever receiving more than the existing "wages-fund," and the average was thought to result with mathematical accuracy from the division of the wages-fund by the number of workers. No artificial outside interference, including strikes, could change the operation of this law. For if, through a successful strike, the wages of one group of workers were to have been raised artificially, a correspondingly smaller portion of the wages-fund would be available for the remaining workers, whose wages would then have to come down accordingly. A general, or average increase of wages above the total of the "wages-fund" was held to be out of the question.

Socialist Distinction Of Economic Categories
Versus Historico-Legal Categories

Later generations have adopted a different view of this matter and of economic "laws" in general, and have developed different new formulas in accordance with their changed views. Following the example of Rodbertus and Adolf Wagner, a distinction was drawn between "purely economic categories" and "historico-legal categories." The former were to include all that was permanent, generally valid and recurrent in economic phenomena under any conceivable social order; the latter were to represent the historically varying types, brought about by changed legal systems, laws, or social institutions. Henceforth, a determining, or at any rate far-reaching influence upon the laws of distribution was ascribed to this latter or "social" category, a term used frequently ever since, especially by Stolzmann.[1]

This may have been right or wrong, but it was certainly not without some justification. But how far-reaching was the influence of control to be, and how and where was it to be delimited against the influences emanating from

---

[1]. *Die Soziale Kategorie in der Volkswirtschaftslehre*, Berlin 1896; *Der Zweck in der Volkswirtschaft*, Berlin 1909.

the other "categories?" These questions were not, and have never been, definitely settled to this day. A few years ago, at another occasion, I wrote: "Nowadays it would be idiotic to try to deny the influence of institutions and regulations of social origin on the distribution of goods." It is obvious that distribution under a communistic order would have to be materially different from that in an individualistic society, based on the principle of private property. Nor could any sensible person deny that the existence of labor organizations with their weapon of strikes has been of pronounced influence on the determination of wages and labor.

But, on the other hand, no intelligent person would claim social "price regulation" as being omnipotent and decisive in itself alone. Often enough one has seen governmental price regulations to be incapable of providing cheap bread in lean years. Every day we may see strikes failing, when they are directed towards the attainment of wages "not justified in the economic situation," as it is commonly expressed. The question, therefore, is not whether the "natural" or "purely economic" categories on the one hand, and the "social" categories on the other, *do* exert any appreciable influence on the terms of distribution; that both *do*, no intelligent person will deny. The sole question is this: *how much* influence do they exert? Or, as I have expressed myself several years ago, in reviewing an older work by Stolzmann, entitled *Die Soziale Kategorie*, when I said: "The great problem, not adequately settled so far, is to determine the exact extent and nature of the influence of both factors, to show how much one factor may accomplish apart from, or perhaps in opposition to, the other. This chapter of economic theory has not yet been written satisfactorily."

I should like to go almost so far as to say that, until quite recently, not even a serious attempt has been made to elaborate this problem by either one of the two great schools which compete with each other in the perfecting of our science: the theoretical school, represented primarily by the well-known "marginal utility theory," and the historical or sociological school which, in its struggle against both the old classicists and the modern marginal value theorists, likes to place the influence of control (*Macht*) into the very heart of its theory of distribution.

Marginal Utility School's Interpretation That, On The Basis Of Economic Law, Each Factor Of Production Is Rewarded According To The Public's Evaluation Of That Factor's Contribution To Value

The "marginal-value" school has not ignored the problem confronting us here, but, so far, it has not elaborated it extensively; it has conducted its investigations up to the confines of the whole problem, so to speak, but so far has stopped at these confines. So far, it has principally occupied itself with the developing of the laws of distribution under the assumption of free and perfect competition, perfect both in theory and in practice, thus precluding the predominance of one party, as would be implied in the term "influence of control." Under this, and the other modifying assumption of the exclusive prevalence of purely economic motives, the marginal-value theory has come to the conclusion that, in the process of distribution, each separate factor of production receives approximately that amount in payment for its contribution to the total production which, according to the rules of imputation, is due to its cooperation in the process of production. The shortest formulation of this idea is contained in the familiar concept of the "marginal productivity" of each factor.

But in making this contribution, the marginal-value school had furnished only an incomplete skeleton of the theory of distribution as whole, and it was well aware of this shortcoming. It never pretended fully to have covered the complex reality with that concept; on the contrary, it never failed to emphasize, again and again, that its past findings had to be supplemented by a second series of investigations, whose task it would be to inquire into the changes that would be produced in this fundamental concept by the advent of changed conditions, particularly those of "social" origin.[2] The reason why the marginal value school took up that part of its investigation first, was only that it seemed to require priority in methodical treatment, that primarily one should know and understand how the process of distribution, or, more generally, that of price formation took place in the absence of all outside social interference.[3]

Value And Price Studies Should Begin With Economic Factors

First of all, a starting point, or point of comparison, had to be ascertained from which the changes might be measured that would be produced by the advent of special outside factors of a "social" origin. The marginal-value theory, thus, as a whole, first laid down a general theoret-

2. I may refer, for instance, to my statement in regard to two complementary parts of the price theory, published as early as 1886.
    See my "Foundations of the Theory of Economic Value" in Conrad's *Jahrbücher*, N.F. 1886, Bd. XIII, pp. 486; and my *Positive Theory of Capital*, Book III, A and B.

3. Of course, there must always exist a certain minimum of outside interference, as shown in detail further on, because there always must exist a social order of some kind.

ical frame for the problem in formulating its general value and price theories, and, within that frame, it elaborated in detail only the theory of free competition, while until now it has left a gap where the influence of social "control" should have been studied and described.

Increasing Importance Of Non-Economic Factors In Determining Prices

This imperfection has always been felt as such; with every new decade it is being sensed more because in our modern economic progress, the intervention of social means of control is continuously gaining in importance. Everywhere trusts, pools and monopolies of all kinds interfere with the formation of prices and with distribution. On the other hand, there are the labor organizations with their strikes and boycotts, not to mention the equally rapid growth of artificial interference emanating from the economic policies of governments. In the eyes of the classical economists, the theory of free competition could claim to be the systematic foundation of the entire problem, as well as the theory of the most important normal case. But at present, the number and importance of those phenomena which no longer find an adequate explanation in the theory of free competition probably already exceed the number of those cases which may still be explained by that one formula.

Historical School Of Economics Has Not Developed Adequate Explanations Of Prices

Nor has this gap left open by the marginal-value theory ever been filled by that other school of economists, those who place the influence of the "social" category in the foreground.[4] The reason for this is that they again overestimated the explanatory power of their favorite formulas. When, with an air of conviction, they proclaimed that under this or that condition, for instance, in determination of wages, it was "power" that ultimately decided matters, they thought to have given a content to their explanation, which, if applying at all, was to supplant or exclude explanations on purely economic grounds. Where power, or "control," entered into the price, there was no economic law, they thought, and thus the mere mention of "control" was both the beginning and the end of the explanation to be given. It was accompanied more often by a fierce denunciation of the "economic laws" developed by other theoretical schools,

4. A few gratifying attempts to fill this gap have begun to appear in recent English and American literature, particularly in the form of a careful study of the theory of monopoly prices. But these attempts do not suffice to render superfluous the presentation offered in these pages.

than by a careful investigation of the question where and
how the two "categories" relate to each other. Moreover,
the term "two categories" was merely a phrase of a rather
vague and ill-defined meaning, and thus by no means very
suitable to the conducting of clear and penetrating investigations.

At the present time it is probably Stolzmann who may
be considered as the typical representative of that school of
thought. Other authors of a similar type, like Stammler
or Simmel, may have become more widely known and influential, but Stolzmann has the merit of having tried to
follow up, one by one, and to elaborate systematically the
suggestions made by older economists, since Rodbertus and
Wagner, and then he has the additional asset of having
shown himself more familiar with economic theory than
many authors starting from different approaches. He is
thus, I think, the one representative of his school best qualified to discuss these basic principles.

The Thesis That Power Alone Controls The Distribution Of Proceeds To The Various Factors Of Production

Now, Stolzmann declares as the fundamental idea in
his theory of distribution that it is not, as taught by the
marginal-utility theory, the purely economic conditions of
imputation, i.e. not the contribution of each factor of production to the total, that determines the distribution of the
produce among landowner, capitalist, and laborer, but
rather that it is social control. It is "power alone that determines the size of each factor's share." What determines
its distribution is not what each factor of production contributes to the total produce, but what the men standing
behind the factors of production are able, by virtue of
their control, to command for themselves as remuneration
according to the social power exerted by each. These and
similar statements are coupled with an incessant attack on
the marginal-value theory based on this very same consideration, that in its theory of distribution it had failed
to give any place to the decisive factor of "power," and instead had reverted to the old "naturalistic" interpretation,
the theory of the eternal and unchanging laws of nature.

One-sidedness Of An Approach Considering Only Power Or Control

But obviously this was not a correct method of penetrating into the intricacies of the problem before us. To
have "power" alone determine the manner of distribution
was just as one-sided. It was all too obvious that power
could not determine everything in distribution, and that

the purely economic factors meant something too. Nor could this dilemma be solved by a compromise in assigning determining and decisive influence to control, and only a vague and restricted influence to natural forces. A true solution, it seems to me, is still to be sought, in spite of Stolzmann's 800 pages, and by other means than evasive dialectics.

Power As A Factor In The Valuation And Pricing Processes Should Be Considered Only After Natural Economic Laws Are First Known

Let us then first state what is really before us in this controversy much neglected in economic science: neither more nor less than the *scientific foundation of a rational economic policy*. For it is obvious that any artificial outside interference in the economic sphere will be without sense, unless the preliminary question whether anything *can* be accomplished through the influence of "power" in opposition to the "natural economic laws" can be answered in the affirmative. The problem is to gain a clear and correct insight into the extent and nature of the influence of "control" against the natural course of economic phenomena.

That is what we must *see*, or we shall *grope* in the dark! I do not think that this seeing can be facilitated or replaced by simply interchanging two terms for the different causal influences, or by ascribing a merely conditional influence to the former and a determining one to the other.

In the following I shall therefore try to raise a few questions and suggest their answers through which I think the way to understanding must lead. What I am offering here are nothing but humble suggestions, for I am well aware of the fact that a full systematic treatment would require much more than what is presented here. And moreover, in making these suggestions, I shall have to mention things most of which have not the least claim to novelty or originality. For the most part, I shall have to start with self-evident trivialities which are close at hand. I shall merely present them in a certain connection and lead them into certain conclusions, equally so manifest that they merely need to be formulated with full clarity and purpose.

CHAPTER II

The Question Whether "Control" Asserts Itself In Conformity With Or In Contradiction To Economic Laws

As I do not wish to repeat obvious things, I do not stop to inquire *whether* "control" *is* an influential factor in the determination of prices, generally speaking, and more particularly in distribution. This I consider to be an accepted fact, settled long ago among all modern economists. My first question, therefore, is whether this influence of control asserts itself in conformity with, or in contradiction to, the economic laws of price, whether it counteracts and invalidates the theoretical laws of price, or whether it harmonizes with these. This question is analogous to one that had to be asked, once upon a time, in the field of production of economic goods: "Is the admitted ability of man artificially to increase the production of goods a power that asserts itself apart from and in contradiction to the natural laws, or something that can take effect only within and in compliance with the natural laws of production?"

Extension of "Control" Does Not Suspend The Independent Economic Laws Of Price

As is known, everybody agrees, in regard to this question, that the "power of man over nature" can be exerted only in harmony with the laws of nature and in strict conformity to them. And I am convinced that once the question before us is explicitly and clearly stated, an analogous consensus of opinion will be easily arrived at: namely, in the problems of price and distribution, "power" (*Macht*) is evidently not asserted apart from or in contradiction to, but within and in conformity with the economic laws of price. Let us first elucidate this with a few familiar illustrations in which the element of power is particularly patent.

Example of Usury

There is first the case of *usury*: What is it that gives to the usurer that "control" over his victims which is at the bottom of the familiar "extortionate" usury prices? Nothing else than those very same factors which the allegedly "pure economic" theory of marginal utility furnishes us in its price formula: it is the urgent want of the borrower which, but for the usurer, would go unsatisfied; it is the satisfaction of most pressing wants which depend on the services obtained from the usurer.

As a result of that, moreover, the subjective value, determined by the corresponding utility, and therewith the upper limits of the possible prices are being moved up. And since the borrower finds no aid from any competition among the suppliers of money who would have to underbid each other, there are equally absent all those more subtle price-restricting elements which, in the case of free competition, determine the valuation of the competitors to be contended with on the supply side.[5]

The usurer, through his inflexibility, thus obtains the power to raise his price to almost the extreme upper limit, which corresponds to the high subjective valuation of the hard-pressed borrower.

Example Of Monopolies

Or there is the typical case of *monopolies*. Each owner of a complete monopoly has the "power" to fix the price of his product at any point he pleases. He again owes that "power" to the existence of certain classes of demand of a high and highest intensity on the part of people whose urgent wants and high purchasing power combine toward creating a correspondingly high intensity of demand, together with the factor just explained, that the absence of competitors does not establish any lower limits likely to interfere with their taking advantage of the most intense demand among the buyers.

But the fact that the monopolist's "power" is rooted in these very *economic* factors will also determine certain familiar and oft-explained limitations: the monopolist can, after all, never fix the price at a point higher than that close to the valuation of the highest, most intense class of demand, and, moreover, what is still more important, he must always reckon with the restriction of the quantity that can be sold at the higher price. He can, in other words, never escape the economic law according to which the price is fixed at the intersection of supply and demand, at that point where equal quantities are offered and taken.

Since he can arbitrarily determine amount and intensity of the supply which he may wish to offer, he may select that point of intersection at a low or at a high point on the scale of possible prices; but the higher that point is, the smaller will become the number of those remaining on the demand-side, and the smaller will be the quantity to be disposed of at that point.

5. See *Positive Theory*, Book III, pages 121-256, especially pages 135ff. and 219ff.

The monopolist thus never has unlimited control; he merely has the choice within the laws of price of different "economically possible" price levels. He can select that price at which the combination of profit for each article, and the number of articles to be sold at that price, are likely to promise the greatest total profit, but he cannot exert his "power" in any other way than in conformity with the laws of price, for it is his behavior that establishes the "price-law", namely the conditions of the amount offered at a given price level—but never can he counteract the laws of price.

Individual Force — Robbery, Extortion And Slavery— Are Here Excluded

The same as shown in these typical illustrations will probably always be true, whenever any kind of so-called "economic power" is applied, for it is this kind of power only that concerns our problem, not physical force or direct compulsion. Highway-robbery or extortion, force of arms or enslavement would, of course, belong to an entirely different category. But the exertion of economic control never introduces any new element into the determination of price that had not previously found a place in the purely theoretical laws of prices.

What conclusions are to be drawn from these facts in regard to our problem, I shall discuss later. For the present, let me refer to an important distinction which should be made in this connection between the influence of "economic control" and "non-economic motives."

Necessary Distinction Between "Economic Control" And "Non-Economic Motives"

For, while the effects of the latter may be contrary to, or conflicting with the economic laws of price, the exertion of control must always be in conformity with them. Where non-economic motives, such as generosity, philanthropy, class or race-hatred, national sympathies and antipathies, vanity, pride, and so forth play their part in the fixing of prices and distribution, they may lead to prices at variance with, or contradictory to those to be expected according to the price-law formula. Whoever is moved by non-economic, outside considerations like friendship or humanitarian impulses to make a gift to the other party of the bargain, may as a buyer consent to a price which will exceed his subjective valuation and as a seller be content with a price far below his own valuation of the goods; or who, from patriotism or national prejudice, wishes to buy only from his compatriots, may consent to prices higher than those offered by their competitors in foreign countries.

Non-Economic Motives Are "Independent" Factors Influencing Price, But "Controls" Are Not

This disturbing effect of non-economic motives conflicting with the price-laws is based on the familiar fact that the economic laws of price apply and claim validity only so long as the conditions on which they are based really prevail by themselves alone, without outside interference; analogous to the physical law of gravitation which holds true only under the assumption of the exclusive effect of gravitation, as exists for instance in a vacuum, while any interfering disturbances, such as friction or buoyancy as exercised by a balloon loaded with gas, would cause phenomena of motion contradictory to the law of gravitation. As distinct therefrom, the price-determining influences emanating from economic "control," or preponderance of "power," always remain within and in conformity with the formula laid down by economic theory: they never form an exception to, but always an application of the economic law of price.

Economic Laws Should Not Be Appraised As Suspendable

From this there follow two things which are of significance to our problem:

(1) First that we neither should nor even can accept the idea of suspension of the validity of the economic laws of price and distribution, when the influence of power comes into play. We need not, in regard to them or the non-economic motives, resign ourselves to the view that our economic laws are valid only so long as no such influence intervenes, as in the case of non-economic motives, that they hold good only in an imaginary world in which such influences are absent, but not in the world of realities in which social power plays a role more pronounced day by day. Nor should we take that resigned view, which would greatly diminish the usefulness of our theoretical laws and reduce their general validity, that our economic laws need not explain this or that case at all.

Economic Laws Should Be Developed

(2) And then, this leads to the second conclusion: whoever wishes adequately to set forth the influences of social control in the explanation of price-determination should not cast aside those laws operating with so-called "purely economic" factors, but he should accept and develop them. He must not accuse them, as does Stolzmann in regard to the laws of price and distribution developed by the marginal-utility theory, of considering the effects of "natural factors" only, so that these theories would have to be discarded or rejected before one could adequately pre-

sent the effects of social influences; no indeed not, we should accept these laws and develop them through a careful analysis in those directions in which social forces actually become operative, when we try to formulate their effects on price determination and distribution.

Our task is not to discard but to develop these allegedly "purely economic" laws of distribution. The fact that economic control cannot affect the conditions of distribution in any other way than through the medium of the categories of "marginal utility" and "subjective value" is indeed not a remote conclusion, and has been explicitly stated here and there in the past, thus for instance, not so long ago by Schumpeter, who attacked a vague statement by Professor Lexis in his theory of distribution, referring to the influence of power, with these words: "The reference to the relative strength of economic power in itself does not explain anything. For if one asks what constitutes economic power the answer can only be: the control over certain goods. And it is only from the economic function of these goods and the subsequent formation of value that a real explanation can be derived."[6]*

[Is not Lexis's argument like the allegation] that the speed of a steamship depends not upon the power of her engines in relation to the resistance to be overcome, or the weight to be propelled, etc., but on the number of rotations of the propellers, which, in turn, of course, depends exclusively upon the power of the engines?

Control Does Not Determine Prices; It At Most Constrains Them

Nor does that explanation do justice to what Stolzmann has stated at several other places in his writings to be the relation between the natural and the social "category"; namely, that natural factors operate as "conditions" or "premises," merely determining the possible limits, whereas within these limits and premises it is the social factors which really "determine" and "decide" matters. Now it is quite true that, at first, the effect of economic factors is essentially that of delimiting the margins of the price; the subjective valuations of buyers and sellers merely determine the upper and lower price limit. But even this "setting" of "limits" may stiffen into actual "fixing" of prices, whenever and wherever the limits from above and below become so numerous and so closely placed that they reduce the interval to a small zone or even to one distinct point, as is generally

6. Review in Vol. 21 of *Zeitschrift für Volkswirtschaft, Sozialpolitik und Verwaltung*, 1912, p. 284; similarly also "Oswald versus Liefmann" in *Zeitschrift für Sozialwissenschaften*, N.F.
*Present Publisher's Note: Mez translation here omits one page.

the case with intense and at the same time perfect competition among many individuals. Nor does "control," on the other hand, ever "determine" anything. It can at best exercise a "constraining" influence, where economic delimitations establish the margin.

Diverse Factors Influence Prices Within Limits Set By Subjective Valuations

He who deals with a needy purchaser, in the absence of competition, has the "power" to fix the price at any point of the probably wide range located between the value of the urgently needed goods to the anxious buyer as the upper limit, and the value of the same article to the not anxious seller as the lower limit. But at what exact point of this extensive range the price will ultimately be fixed is not determined by the relative "power" alone, for with equal "power" the philanthropist will make an entirely different price to the poor man than the usurer. Or there may be different degrees of skill in bargaining, or in sizing up the position of the other side, of perseverance, of patience, of disregard for public opinion, of defiance or fear, even in case of equal objective "power," which will move the price to a very different point of the scale.

Power Does Not Possess Price Fixing Capability Or Ultimate Control

But when the "relative power" of the two parties seems to fix the price at a quite definite point of the scale, it certainly has again been nothing else than the coincidence of a majority of "restrictive influences" which narrow down the limits from both sides to such an extent that the price level itself appears to be "determined" thereby. Nor is any other outcome to be expected, for since, as shown before, "economic power" can become effective only through the intermediary determinants of the theoretical price formula, and since these determinants can again fix the price only through a consecutive *delimitation*, it is obvious that "power" can equally determine prices in no other way than through the fixation of limits; it does not possess any independent "price-fixing capacity," as distinct from this "restricting" or "limiting" ability.*

Rodbertus And Others Overemphasize Historico-Legal Category

From this it will become clear why, in the discussion of these questions, the old terms of "purely economic" or

*Publisher's Note: This will be clear especially to readers familiar with *Positive Theory of Capital*, Book III, on "Value and Price," pp. 217-235.

"historico-legal" categories, as Rodbertus called them, or of "natural" and "social" categories, as applied by Stolzmann, are not sufficient. These terms may have served a purpose in their time. At least they have, roughly speaking, indicated certain distinctions which should also be kept in mind, and they have been particularly helpful towards the elimination of the old, one-sided view that there are only "natural laws" operative in our economic life. But in the theoretical explanation of the phenomena of price and distribution they do not play that role which their authors ascribe to them. They fail to draw a straight and clear line of demarcation between social phenomena, because these are always permeated by both factors. A certain amount of the "historico-legal" or "social" element is sure to be present in all economic phenomena. There is no room left for an opposite, "purely natural" category. There literally exists no price nor any form of "distribution" (except perhaps highway-robbery and the like) without containing at least some legalistic-historical aspect. For, in every civilized community, there must always exist some social order which will apply when two members of that society get into contact with each other, and thus determine the nature of that contact.

It is, therefore, either saying too little or too much, when anyone claims the phenomena of distribution for the "social," as distinct from the "natural," category; or it is but an empty truism, which, in its very concept, applies to every singly economic or social phenomenon, for obviously a Robinson Crusoe could not even so much as "barter" with himself. One member of a society can only trade with another if both can acquire ownership of the goods to be exchanged under the existing social order. Any statement attempting to express more than that truism is too far-reaching.

Thus Rodbertus shoots way beyond the mark, when with that peculiar emphasis he defines interest on capital as being the typical fruit of the existing social order, and denies its "purely economic" justification. And Stolzmann equally shoots beyond the mark, when he holds that the "social category" alone "determines" distribution, and when he falsely accuses our theory of distribution of teaching purely natural laws of distribution, because it also does justice to the economic foundations of social power.

A closer analysis of social power, however, must inevitably lead straight across the line of demarcation between the "social" and "natural" categories; power is present on both sides of the line.

The Category "Social Control" Is Not A "Pure Category"

Social "control" is not an abstraction or a distilled product in which the influence of the purely social category is reflected as such. Nor are the explanations given by the marginal value theory, which Stolzmann calls extremely "naturalistic," an unmixed distillation of only the natural and purely economic influences. Instead they always take into consideration certain characteristics of the existing, or an assumed economic order. With proper elaboration they will be found capable of expressing the entire influence of social power, but even so, it remains true that prices are determined more or less accurately by the subjective valuations based on the marginal utility. And it remains equally true that the value of productive goods depends on nothing else except the value of the products to be obtained from them. In the last analysis, therefore, the value of the factors of production depends on the share of the product attributable to each factor in the productive process.

"Social control" and "social category" are thus not synonymous. The latter term, like its antithesis "natural" or "purely economic" category, has been so confused and misconstrued that I would prefer to dispense with its use altogether in the interest of a clear presentation. Where I did use these terms in this or in previous writings, I did so, not because they form part of my own vocabulary, but rather because I could not well avoid altogether the use of a generally accepted term. In order to make myself understood, I had above all to use the language of those whose opinion I was discussing. Nor have I failed at earlier occasions to make reservations in this respect.

And now I shall try to submit a few thoughts concerning the direction in which the old economic theory will have to be developed so as to embrace systematically in its teachings the influence of "control" (*Macht,* or "outside power").

CHAPTER III

Price Determination Through "Control" In The Settlement Of Wage Disputes Involving (1) Monopoly And (2) A Strike

What I have to say may, I think, best be developed by looking at a typical instance which illustrates price-determination through social control in a particularly noticeable manner: the case of the settlement of wage disputes by means of a *strike.*

A. In Free And Perfect Competition Wages Are Determined By Marginal Productivity Of Labor

According to the accepted formula of the modern wages-theory, based on the marginal-utility theory, the amount of wages in case of free and perfect competition would be determined by the "marginal productivity of labor," i.e., by the value of the product which the last, most easily dispensable laborer of a particular type produces for his employer.

His wages cannot go higher, for if they did, his employer would no longer gain any advantage from employing this "last" laborer; he would lose, and consequently would prefer to reduce the number of his workers by one.

Nor could the wages be substantially lower, in the case of effective competition on both sides, because the employment of the last worker would still produce a substantial surplus gain. As long as that is true, there would be an incentive to the further expansion of the enterprise, and to the employment of still more workers. Under an effective competition among employers this incentive would obviously be acted upon, and could not fail to eliminate the existing margin between the value of the marginal product and the wages in two ways: by the rise of wages, caused by the demand for *more* workers; and by a slight diminution of the value of the additional produce, caused by the increased supply of goods.

If those two factors are allowed to operate without outside interference, they would not only delimit wages, but actually fix them at a definite point, owing to the nearness of these limits, let us say for instance at $5.50 for a day's labor.

B. The Case Of Wage Determination Under Employer's Control (Or Monopoly)

But let us now assume competition to be not quite free on both sides, but that it be restricted, or eliminated, on the side of the employers; either because there exists only one enterprise of that particular branch of industry over a large territory, thus giving it natural monopoly over the workers seeking employment, or because there is a coalition of entrepreneurs within that industry, who mutually agree not to pay their workers a wage higher than, let us say, $4.50. In either case, this coming into play of "control," a superior power of the employers, will certainly suffice to lead the wages to be fixed at a point below $5.50, say at $4.50, other conditions remaining equal.

Factors Affecting Limits Of Wages Under
Employers' Monopoly; (1) The Upper Limit

How would this correspond with the standard explanation offered by the marginal-value theory? The answer is not difficult. In fact, the solution has been repeatedly stated in the fairly well-developed theory of monopoly prices. I shall merely try to restate the familiar arguments in a clear and systematic manner.

We have before us a case of "buyers' monopoly." The widest margin within which the monopoly-price can be fixed is limited, from above, by the value of the labor to be purchased by the entrepreneur exercising that monopoly, and from below, by the value of unsold labor to the laborer himself. The upper limit is determined by the value of the produce of the *last* worker, for the reason that the entrepreneur will not assume any loss from the last worker he employs and that the same amount of labor cannot be paid for in unequal amounts. This upper limit of the possible wage would, in our illustration, be $5.50.

(2) The Lower Limit; The Use Value To The
Worker Of His Own Labor

More is to be said in regard to the lower limit. The very lowest limit is determined by the utility which would be left to the worker if he were not to sell his labor at all. It is thus, primarily, the use-value to the worker of his own labor, provided he can make some use of his labor for himself alone.

In thinly populated new countries, with an abundance of unoccupied land, where everybody may become a farmer at will, this labor-value might represent quite a considerable amount. In the densely populated "old" countries, however, this limit is extremely low, because most of the workers lack capital, and can hardly ever profitably utilize their own labor as independent producers.

A worker who has accumulated some savings may find some compensation for not selling his labor in the escape from discomfort and hard work, or in the enjoyment of rest and leisure. Those who have any such means of subsistence will figure out just what minimum of wages would compensate them for the effort of working. To those who have nothing to fall back on, the marginal utility of a money-income to be gained by working is so extremely high that even a very low wage will be preferred over the enjoyment of leisure. In order to illustrate this with actual sums of money, let us assume this lowest limit, the use-value of labor and the enjoyment of leisure, to be very low, say $1.50.

This amount may be even far below the minimum of subsistence which, for well-known reasons, determines the lower limit of the possible *permanent* wages without, of course, determining temporary wages or those of each individual case.

(3) Intermediate Wage Points

But there may also arise other, intermediate wage levels. In the foregoing illustration we have excluded all competition among the employers in that one particular branch of industry. If such competition were existing, it would inevitably force up the wages to the upper limit of $5.50; but even in its absence, there would still remain a certain amount of outside competition, namely with employers in all the other branches of industry.

That means that the worker in our particular industry still has the alternative of escaping the very low wage offered to him in his own line, by switching over into other branches of production, although a number of circumstances may greatly reduce the gains to be expected from this expedient. To change from one occupation, for which one has been trained and adapted, into another, is likely to result in less productivity, and the maximum wage level attainable in the new occupation will be likely to remain far *below* $5.50.

The curtailment in wages will vary for each worker entering into a new branch of production according to his adaptability, or his ability to perform a different kind of skilled labor. The most painful cuts in wages will be suffered by that probably largest portion of the workers, who are not adequately trained to perform any other kind of skilled labor, and who will have to switch over from "skilled" into "unskilled" trades, and accept a poorer position in some type of common labor. Still another slight lowering of the wage level may result from the fact that the influx of new workers into that occupation may force down slightly the marginal productivity of the last worker, and thus lower the wage level for all.

(4) Minimum Wage Necessary For Existence

Under the influence of all these circumstances we would now have to assume that the various workers set for themselves a series of individual minimum limits, below which no one would allow his wages to be reduced by the monopolistic pressure of the entrepreneurs. To illustrate these various gradations of minimum wages, let us assume the minimum of existence to be $3.00, which, as has been said, would represent not the temporary, but the lowest wage level permanently possible. The wages obtained by the most common type of labor would thus be very near to $3, say $3.10. A smaller and smaller number of workers could find employment in other occupations, as the wage rate increased in the following ascending sequence: $3.50, $3.80, $4, $4.20, $4.50, $4.80, $5. Note, however, that the upper limit of this wage-scale would still remain below the marginal product of the original occupation, thus below $5.50.

Wage Determination Within Widest Limits Of $1.50 And $5.50

What effects and limitations will result from this state of affairs in regard to the monopolistic fixation of wages within the original widest zone of $1.50 to $5.50?

Let us assume, to begin with, that the monopolistic entrepreneurs use their power in an unrestricted, purely selfish policy, unaffected by any considerations of altruism, or consideration of public opinion, uninfluenced by any apprehension that the workers might fight back through means of a labor-union or strike, and convinced that they are absolutely assured of an atomized, effective competition among the individual workers.

Under such premises, the rate of wages would be fixed according to the general formula applying to a purely selfish monopoly, already mentioned before in another connection: they would be fixed at that point which promises the largest returns, after a careful consideration of all circumstances, and with due regard to the inevitable fact that with changing prices, the amount of goods to be disposed of profitably will change, only that in the case of a buyers' monopoly the results are exactly opposite to that of a sellers' monopoly.

Or stated concretely: the *lower* that the wage rate is fixed by the monopolist, the smaller will be the number of workers available, and from a correspondingly smaller number of workers will the entrepreneurs be able to collect that increased return which might accrue from pushing the wage-scale down below the value of the product of the marginal laborer, i.e., below $5.50; in fact, this value might even increase through a reduction in the output, which would cause a rise in the price of the finished goods.

Of course, there may again enter certain counteracting tendencies, such as increasing costs, with the restricted expansion of the enterprise, the growth of overhead expenses, etc. With an increase in wages, which, however, we always assume to remain below the marginal product of $5.50, the gain per laborer would decrease; but, to offset this, the number of workers from which that gain can be made will increase, or even be brought back to normal.

From these considerations, it would be most unlikely that the monopolists could fix the wage-rate at $1.80 or $2.00 or at any point below the minimum of existence of $3, both because this rate would not be likely to remain in force, and because it would be lower than the wage paid outside for common labor, and therefore would at once cause the majority of the workers to withdraw into those unskilled occupations which, in our illustration, receive $3.10.

This danger will diminish gradually with each increase in the wage rate, and disappear almost entirely at some point, say at $4.50, at which only a few exceptional workers might find it possible to obtain higher wages in other skilled occupations, if such be open to them at all. Under the assumed circumstances, the danger of men withdrawing would have almost disappeared, and a successful attempt might be made by the monopolistic employers to fix the rate of wages at this point, without running the risk of any considerable restriction of output caused through a shortage of workers.

Two other considerations might influence an intelligent monopolist to exercise his power "with restraint." First, a wage rate remaining far below that of other skilled occupations may, if only in the long run, lead to a shortage of workers, for while the laborers accustomed to their occupation might hesitate to change their job owing to the difficulties of transition, the new supply would fall off. Secondly, too high a rate of profit per worker would exert too powerful a strain on the employers' combination, and is likely to lead to the dissolution of the coalition by those members wishing to expand their business, or to the formation of new enterprises outside of the coalition, thus creating new competition, likely to cut down prices and to raise wages. Generally speaking, the fear of outside competition forms perhaps the greatest safeguard against too unscrupulous a use of monopolies preying on the general public.

Despite "Control" (In This Case An Employers' Monopoly) Wage Price Is Nevertheless Determined In Conformity With Marginal Utility Theory

I hardly need to re-emphasize the fact that if, under such conditions, through the "control" of the monopolists the wage level were to be reduced from $5.50 to $4.50, this would, from first to last, happen by virtue of and in conformity with the elements of the price-law, as formulated by the marginal-value theory.

It is in consideration of these elements that both contending parties would fix the price at that level, by "delimiting" it from above and from below. By such action, no "fixed" price would be determined, but merely a wider price-range, as distinct from the case of perfect competition on both sides. The monopolists might just as well decide upon $4.20 or $4.80 than upon $4.50. This situation is explained by the fact that several factors entering into the calculation, such as the number of workers likely to drop out at a certain wage level, or the probability of outside competition, are not definitely known, but only to be conjectured.

The monopolists would naturally try to select the most favorable point of the wage scale; but, owing to the uncertainty of so many elements entering into the formation of this optimum point, there results a certain more or less elastic zone for its approximate location, just as in ordinary market competition for prices, when negotiations are carried on with covered cards, traders less experienced or less shrewd commit errors in sizing up inside market situations, so that actual prices are caused to fluctuate over a wide range around the "ideal" market price.

C. The Case Of Wage Determination Under Labor Union "Control" (Or Monopoly)

Let us now turn to the other case, equally interesting and complicated, the influence of "control" exerted by labor unions, through the use of their instrument of power, the strike.

Let us retain all previous assumptions with the same figures as above: $5.50 for the value of the product of the "last" worker, $1.50 as the personal valuation to the working man of his unsold labor, $3 as the minimum of existence, etc., and introduce into our assumed case only one novel element, namely that the workers of the industry under discussion do not compete against each other, but that they be unionized, and thus be in a position to enforce their joint demand for higher wages by means of a strike.

Now I do not for a moment deny that this coming into play of "power" on the part of the workers may profoundly influence the price of labor. It might even raise it not only above the level of $4.50, reached in the case of reduced competition among the monopolists, but even beyond the level of $5.50, which would have been attainable under perfect competition.

This last fact is particularly noteworthy and striking, for hitherto we had regarded the value of the marginal product of labor, *precisely those* $5.50, as the upper limit of the economically possible wage, and at first sight it might look as if "power" could actually accomplish something in contradiction to the price-formula of the marginal-value theory, something that did *not* conform to this law, but disproved it.

Distinction Between Marginal Utility And Total Utility

Here now enters into our explanation the distinction between marginal utility and total utility, i.e., the fact that the value of a total aggregate of goods is higher than the marginal utility of each unit multiplied by the number of units contained in the total.*

The fundamental question in the evaluation of a commodity or an aggregate of goods is always how much utility may be derived from the command over the good to be valued. Under the assumption of competition among all the workers, the thing to be evaluated by the employer is always the labor-unit of each worker. If the employer had in his employ, for instance, 100 workers, his negotiations with each one of the 100 workers over his wages would merely hinge upon the question of how much additional profits the employers would make by employing that one additional worker, or how much he would lose by not employing this one "last" worker. In that case we were fully justified in arriving at the marginal utility of each unit of labor, that is, the increase in output which the labor of the last one of the 100 workers adds to the total output of the enterprise, or $5.50.

But now this is different: in the case of a joint strike of all the 100 workers, the point in question for the employer is no longer whether he is going to run his enterprise with 100 or 99 workers, which to him would mean a difference in the output of $5.50, but whether he is to keep his enterprise going with 100 workers, or not at all. On this depends not 100 times $5.50, but obviously much more than that, if for no other reason, that that labor is what is called a "complementary" good, a good which cannot be utilized by itself alone, without the necessary other "complementary" goods, such as raw materials, equipment, machinery, etc.

If only one man out of a hundred withdraws from the enterprise, the utilization of the complementary factors

* Publisher's Note: For further information on Total Utility, see Böhm-Bawerk's *Positive Theory of Capital*, pages 135ff., especially 146-150.

will, as a rule, be little disturbed. One single operation, the one which can be dispensed with most easily, will be omitted, or replaced, as far as possible, through a slight change in the division of labor, so that with the deduction of *one* man, not more is lost than the marginal product of one day's labor, namely $5.50.

The withdrawal of ten men would cause a more serious disturbance. But a changed disposition in the use of the remaining ninety workers would probably make it possible to find some way for at least the most important functions to continue unhampered, and the loss again to be shifted to that place where it is least felt. A continued depletion of the complementary good, "labor," would make itself felt more and more severely.

While the withdrawal of the first worker would have caused a decrease in the daily production of only $5.50, that of the second might amount to a diminution of the output by $5.55, that of the third by $5.60, and that of the tenth by as much as $6. If, as would be the case in a strike, all the one hundred men walked out, there would be caused a loss, not only of the specific labor product of those 100 men, but additional productive goods would cease to be utilized. The machinery would have to stand still, the raw materials would lie idle and depreciate, etc. The loss in the value of the product would increase out of all proportion, far beyond a hundred times the last laborer's marginal product.

This loss, of course, would be subject to great modifications, according to the actual conditions existing in each case. If the idle machinery and capital do not suffer any other damage by being idle, the additional loss would merely consist in a postponement of the completion of the respective products from the capital goods, temporarily not utilized on account of the lack of the complementary factor of labor. Their produce will be obtained in an undiminished amount only at a later period, after the resumption of production. This loss must at least equal the interest on the dead capital for the period of idleness. It may amount to more, if the delay should involve added losses, such as the inability to take advantage of favorable business opportunities, whereby indirect depreciations may be incurred.

But the damage would be still further increased if the specific character of the idle capital-goods should not only cause a temporary delay, but a definite curtailment in the profits, as for example in the case of perishable raw materials, such as beets in an idle sugar refinery, or agricultural products that cannot be harvested owing to the worker's strike, unused animal power—such as horses—or the water-power of an electric power plant. The enforced shut-down may also threaten the fixed capital investments, as in mines, where ventilation and water pumps must not stop, lest the entire plant be destroyed.

How does all this affect the determination of wages in the case of a strike?

Let us realize, first of all, that although wage disputes are formally concerned with the *per capita* wages for *each individual worker*, to the manufacturer it is always a question of obtaining, or not obtaining, the *total* labor of these one hundred workers. He will either get all of the workers, or none, according to whether the negotiations lead to an agreement, or to a break. The decision as to how much wages he can pay at most will thus hinge on the value which the hundred workers represent to him jointly. The per capita wage is a secondary item, and is determined by dividing the total value by the number of workers. To him, this quota represents only an arithmetical concept, not a value; to him it does not represent the value of a unit of labor.

The Theory Of Imputation

But how high is the total value? This is explained by the theory of imputation. The value of that aggregate of labor is derived from the value of that amount of products which may be ascribed to the availability of that particular total of labor, and this again is identical with the amount of the product of labor.

Here comes into play a remarkable phase of the theory of imputation, which I recently had to defend in detail against differing opinions.[7]

For if the withdrawal of that amount of labor, whose value we are trying to ascertain, not only prevented the use of that labor itself, but also stopped the use of other, complementary goods, the utility of these goods would have to be added to that of labor, regardless of the fact that under certain circumstances the use of labor might have to be imputed to its corresponding complementary good, without which the products could not be obtained.

I shall merely recapitulate here without detailed discussion the various steps of the argument leading to this conclusion. Fundamentally, the total value of a whole group of complementary goods is dependent upon the amount of

7. *Further Essays On Capital And Interest*, Essay VII, "On The Theory of Value of Complementary Goods and the Theory of Imputation."

the (marginal) utility which they possess jointly, and thus, in case of complementary productive goods, upon the value of their common product.[8]

The distribution of this total value among the various units of the complementary group may take different directions, according to the different causation. If none of the units admits of any other use than joint use, and if, at the same time, no one member contributing toward the joint use is replaceable, then every single member has the full total value of the entire group, while the other members are valueless. Each complementary unit is equally capable of holding either one of the two valuations, and it is solely the outside circumstances that determine which one of them shall be worth "everything," by being absolutely essential in the ultimate completion of the group, or which one is worth "nothing" through its isolation.

When Total Joint Utility Must Be Attributed To Labor

In our case of an impending strike of all the hundred workers, the employer is threatened with the total loss of the joint gain arising from the use of the two complementary groups, labor and capital, to the extent stated above, and this is why in that case he would have to attribute to labor that *total* joint utility, including that part which under other conditions might have to be attributed to the complementary capital goods. His subjective valuation of labor must be based upon all these things.[9]

A New Upper Limit

Consequently, the upper limit for the highest rate of wages will advance. For all the hundred workers jointly it will rise beyond the hundred-fold amount of the single value of each day's labor, that is, beyond 100 times $5.50, at least by the amount of the interest of the capital left idle and perhaps even above this, by the amount of the actual loss from perishing or deteriorating complementary capital goods. Thus, for instance, in case there be merely a postponement or loss of interest, it would rise above $550, up to, say, $700 for each day. In case of a direct loss in the utilization of the complementary goods, it would rise in proportion to the extent to which an actual loss takes place,

8. *Positive Theory*, Book III, Chapter VI and *Further Essays*, Essay VII.

9. Naturally, I cannot, in passing, review the entire difficult and complicated theory of distribution with all its details, and have to ask the readers who are interested in the complete discussion of the foregoing conclusions to read the fuller explanation given in my *Positive Theory of Capital* and *Further Essays On Capital and Interest*.

perhaps to $1000, perhaps even to $2000 per day. And the maximum of the economically possible wage level for each individual worker would thereby rise from $5.50 to $7 or even to $10 or $20.

This means that with any wage level remaining below this maximum, the entrepreneur would, at least for the time being, fare better than if he were to cease employing all the hundred men. This "faring better" need, however, not imply actual profits to the entrepreneur, but merely a smaller loss than he would incur in the other alternative, the "lesser evil" which is, of course, to be preferred to the greater one.

This rise of the last possible per-capita wage to $7 or to $20, on the other hand, does *not* represent the subjective valuation of one day's labor to the entrepreneur. This has already been stated in the foregoing and it can hardly be sufficiently emphasized. The employer would never pay that wage, if it were a question of employing *one* laborer only. It represents the hundredth part of the total value of 100 laborers, which is a very different unit from the individual value of each unit of labor.

In the wage negotiations between an employer and a labor-union the range would thus be limited by the value to the laborer of his unsold labor, (i.e., the amount of $1.50 as his lowest limit), and by the per-capita quota of the total value of all 100 laborers at the rate of $10 as upper limit—to take one of the three figures as an illustration.

A Theoretical Range
From $1.50 To $10.00

In our imagined case, direct competition being absent on both sides, entrepreneur and workers would meet each other within their limits on similar grounds, just as the two parties of buyers and sellers meet in the case of isolated exchange.[10]

In theory, it would not be unthinkable nor impossible for the rates to be fixed at any single point within the wide range between $1.50 and $10. We have, of course, come to know some circumstances which make it appear rather unlikely, though not altogether economically impossible, that the wages be fixed within the lowest section of the zone lying between the absolutely lowest limit and the minimum of existence of unskilled labor; and for reasons of similar nature, it is not very likely that the wage rate would be raised up to a point near the upper limit of $10.

10. *Positive Theory*, Book III, Part B, pp. 207-256.

That it could not be kept at such a point for any length of time I shall try to demonstrate in a future investigation which I consider of special theoretical import. But not even temporarily will it readily be pushed so high. For any wage level substantially exceeding the output of the "last worker" would meet with a strong and increasing opposition on the part of the employers as involving a loss to them. Before granting such a wage rate, they would probably prefer to risk the decision of the supreme trial, consisting in fighting matters out in a lockout or strike; although an intermediate wage, approximating the actual services of the last worker, might conceivably be granted by the employers, anxious to avoid the risk of the certain losses involved in a strike, and the added uncertainty of its outcome. Nor would workers find it to their advantage to push the wages up to a level actually causing losses to the entrepreneur, for this again might threaten them with a restriction, or suspension of work, and force them out of their jobs. Thus there enters the question about the permanency of wages, which will be investigated later.

Strike Problems Of Employes

On the other hand, the workers' difficulties will become all the greater by the strike, the more excessive wage demands they make. The threat from strike-breakers or "scabs" from other branches of industry will increase with the more favorable terms which the entrepreneur can still grant below the refused rate of wages. If the striking workers should insist on a wage rate of $9, a wage of $7 may perhaps already contain a very tempting premium to scabs and substitutes, who in other occupations requiring similar qualifications may obtain only a wage of $5.50, corresponding to the output of the last worker. And once substitutes are employed, the cause of the strike is usually lost, whereas, in the other alternative, the outcome is by no means certain.

In a strike that party wins, as a rule, which, popularly speaking, can "hold its breath" for the longest time. To the worker, the strike means unemployment. For the time being the worker may meet this loss by means of savings accumulated for this purpose, by aid from strike-funds, by consuming his property, by selling or pawning dispensable goods, or by incurring debts as far as his credit will permit. With the longer duration of the strike, these savings will become smaller and smaller until they are used up. During the period of gradual diminution of savings, the marginal utility of the rapidly decreasing means of subsistence goes up, more and more of essential wants go unsatisfied, and more and more of the vital necessaries are neglected, with the increasing shortage of funds.

Finally the point is reached at which the very maintenance of life depends on a renewal of income through work, if only at a modest wage: at this point even the most obstinate resistance of the strikers is broken—provided, of course, that the resistance of the opposite party, the employer, is not crushed beforehand.

Strike Problems Of Employers

In the ranks of the employers there are the same phenomena. With the increasing duration of the strike, the desire for a settlement becomes more and 'more intense. The idle plant produces no income. Some of the costs of production and at least the personal living expenses of the manufacturer continue, and have to be met. If the entrepreneur has a large fortune, these expenses may be covered therefrom. If not, then the pressure of the strike will be felt much more rapidly and intensely. In any case, there are here two very distinct phases of the effects of the strikes which should be distinguished. The successive and increasing lack in the means of subsistence may first threaten the business of the entrepreneur, and then, if there are no funds left for the most urgent living expenses, his *personal* existence.

This latter, more intense effect of strikes, will normally arise only in the most exceptional cases. Nor is it likely, for these and similar reasons stated before, that in a strike wages will be fixed at the most extreme—neither at the very lowest nor at the very highest—marginal areas of the wide range "economically possible," at least for the time being. In our illustration this zone was assumed to extend from $1.50 to $10, and a wage rate below $3 would be just as unlikely as one above $8, although, as I want specially to emphasize, such extreme wage-rates are not unthinkable, nor altogether economically out of question for a *short period* of time.

Power Must Operate According To Marginal Utility Principles

Most of what has been said so far is based on obvious and almost trivial facts and observations which have become sufficiently familiar through common experiences with strikes. I have merely restated these matters, so to speak, in the terms of the marginal utility theory, in order to make plain the essential point of the theoretical principle under discussion, namely, that the "influence of power" in the case of strikes, so familiar to all engaged in industry, is not altogether distinct from, or opposed to, the forces and laws of the marginal utility theory, but wholly *in conformity* and *in harmony* with these, and that every deeper analysis of the question, through what intermediate agencies and to what marginal points "power" may control the course of events at all, must lead into the more specific exposition of marginal utility, in the theory of imputation, where the ultimate explanation is to be sought and found.[11]

The Real Question Is, How Permanent Are The Effects Of "Power"?

There is another far more interesting question: When will the terms of distribution, obtained through means of power, be of lasting effect? This question is all the more interesting, in that it is by far the most important one. Even the most ephemeral fixing of prices or wages may have considerable importance to that group of individuals or for that short span of time which happens to be affected by it. On the other hand, these temporary fixations mean little or nothing for the permanent economic welfare of the various social classes; just as the classical economists have held long-trend prices to be far more important and challenging than momentary fluctuations; thus Ricardo hardly touched upon the latter, and found it worth while only to elaborate the theory of long-trend prices. Similarly, in the theory of distribution, paramount importance is attached to the *permanent* trends according to which the shares of the various factors of production tend to be distributed, as distinct from all ephemeral and temporary fluctuations. Even the most ephemeral phenomena must also be understood and explained, if for no other reason than that the laws controlling them are, in the last resort, not different from those determining their permanent effects, but it goes without saying, that that phase of our theory which covers those cases outlasting the others in time and space will be far more important to us than the explanation of rapidly passing exceptions.

But there is a second reason why it seems to me that the consideration of the influences of "power" deserves greater attention from the viewpoint of their permanency, for, as far as my knowledge of economic literature goes,

---

[11]. I need not call the attention of those familiar with the theory to the fact that all of what I have said here is absolutely in conformity with the so-called "theory of marginal utility", even in parts where I had to deal with the concept of total utility. For this is merely a term introduced into the modern theory of value, chiefly by the Austrian School, as one of its particularly characteristic traits. This same theory, of course, covers and explains those cases in which valuation is based on total utility as well as those far more frequent cases in which valuation takes place literally from a "marginal utility." (See my *Positive Theory of Capital*, Book III, Part A.)

this most important phase of the subject has never been investigated.

While the problem of the influence of power on prices as such has hitherto been only scantily treated, and never in a systematic manner, in economic theory, fundamental investigations into the permanent effects of such influences of power seem to be totally lacking, so that here we enter, in a certain sense, upon virgin land.

CHAPTER IV

Examination Of The Permanence Of Gains Obtained By The Exercise Of Power Or Control

Let me again start from our concrete illustration, and discuss, one by one, the various alternatives. What is typical and generally true in each individual case will thus easily become clear, and, moreover, specially stressed and summarized at the end.

Consideration Of Wage Determination Alternatives

Temporarily, as we have seen in our assumed conflict between the power of entrepreneurs and workers, any wage rate between $1.50 and $10 was economically possible, although it was not likely to be fixed, not even for a short period, near the extreme upper or lower limit possible, but rather somewhere near the middle of the total range of wages. In order to make our discussion theoretically exhaustive, we shall have to consider both extremes, as well as each one of the possible rate levels within the total range of wages.

1.

I need not waste any words about the fact that a wage-rate *below the minimum of existence*—thus in our example below $3—cannot possibly be permanent. This follows from the familiar reasons stated often and in detail elsewhere, pointing to the diminution of the labor supply as the inevitable consequence of a wage-level no longer sufficient for the support of the workers' families, and to the subsequent increase of wages, necessitated by the law of supply and demand; allowing, of course, for familiar exceptions in favor, or rather in disfavor, of those exceptional types of occupations which are being followed merely as a side-line by people who draw their real means of subsistence from other sources.

2.

Nor can wages be fixed permanently *below the rate of the most common type of labor*—in our illustration, below $3.10. This hardly needs any further explanation, for the reason that all the causes applying to point 3 which follows, will evidently apply here too, even to a greater degree. The exceptions, familiar since Adam Smith, for occupations connected with special attractiveness or privileges and in which, therefore, many people are satisfied with a smaller remuneration than that available in other less attractive or less respected occupations, will, of course, also apply here, without, however, affecting the general theory of distribution.

3.

Wages higher than those of common labor, but *below the "marginal product of the last laborer"* (in our illustration, wages between $3.10 and $5.50), will hardly be able to remain in force, if imposed through temporary preponderance of power, certainly not when the use of that power was limited to one particular group, such as to the workers of a single factory, or to a single branch of production, while in other occupations, requiring the same or a similar amount of skill, wages prevail commensurate with the natural amount of the marginal product (in our case, of $5.50). For although the personal discomfort connected with a change of occupation may prevent a large-scale exodus of an entire generation of skilled workers from a less remunerative branch of production into other, better-paid occupations, the gradual effect upon the selection of occupation among the younger generation of workers will be all the greater. They will naturally seek the better-paid occupations, and shun those with exceptionally poor wages. Normal deficiencies in the original supply of workers will no longer be met, and the gradual depletion of employees will ultimately force the employers to offer their workers a wage rate equal to that obtainable in other industries of a similar type.

Course Of Events When There Is A Monopolistic Coalition Of Employers

A more complex analysis would have to be made in the case of a universal reduction of wages through artificial forces affecting all lines of production. Such a contingency is, however, far less likely ever to occur, for the reason that a universal coalition of entrepreneurs of all branches of industry which alone could exert such control would be extremely hard to organize, and still harder to hold together. But let us assume such a case, at least for a certain period of time, for our theoretical analysis. Obviously, the worker would then no longer find it possible to escape into another, more remunerative branch of production, and thus there would cease to exist that most influential factor, which, in the case of a partial reduction of wages, would sooner or later insure the restoration of the original wage-rate. Instead, there would now appear some new, although slow-working, factors within the ranks of the entrepreneurs.

A wage-level fixed below the marginal productivity of labor results in a special gain which goes to the employer, first, in the form of an increased profit, which, however, in case of a prolonged continuance of this condition, will have to be surrendered in part to the capitalist in the form of higher interest, for the reason that pending on, and owing to this condition, other equally profitable types of investment will be open to capital. The very fact of an increased entrepreneur's profit will in itself alone work as an incentive to the expansion of existing enterprises (this incentive might perhaps be temporarily curbed by binding the old entrepreneurs to coalition agreements) and also to the formation of new enterprises founded by outsiders, not belonging to the coalition, who, of course, can attract the needed number of workers only by offering somewhat higher wages. The increased interest rate, moreover, will shift the margin of profit among the various more or less capitalistic methods of production toward those with less machinery, labor-saving devices, and so forth.

An increased interest on capital and a cheaper supply of labor will transform the smaller profits into losses among those producers near the margin of profitability, especially in those enterprises where a low interest charge prevails coupled with higher wages, so that where previously a slight advantage had been found to exist in a more capitalistic, or machine production, at the expense of manual labor, it now becomes more profitable to reverse the methods of production through increase in the use of manpower, and a less intense use of capital equipment.[12]

Naturally this incentive will not lead to quick results. Capital invested in such a manner in instruments of production will not suddenly be abandoned, but rather tend to be used up first, or at least not be replaced, because human labor, having become cheaper, will be preferred in its place. This again will lead to an increased demand for labor which can only be met by granting somewhat higher wages. These, of course, must not completely neutralize the advantages of the less capitalistic method of

12. That, and how a low interest charge and high wages tend to make for the lengthening, and a high interest charge and low wages for a shortening of the average period of production, I have shown in my *Positive Theory of Capital*, p. 353 ff.; and *Further Essays on Capital and Interest*, p. 19ff.

production. This motive may be operative both within and without the employers' coalition, and to a very different degree among the various types of producers. It will be hardly at all operative among those who had employed very little fixed capital and much physical labor; very little among those with whom capital predominates to such great technical advantage that even considerable changes in the level of wages or interest will not bring about any transition towards a less capitalistic method; but far more among a third group of producers, whose technical equipment is such as to divide their methods of production just equally between machinery and labor. These great individual differences will not remain without profound influence on the probable course of events.

Factors Contributing To Dissolution Of Coalitions Of Employers

Industrial coalitions comprising the producers of one and the same line of industry, or of similar industries, will as a rule be based on a harmony of interest, sufficient to favor a continuation of the coalition which benefits all members equally. But if the coalition should include certain groups whose interest makes them disagree in regard to the desirability of a continuance of the coalition, then in all human experience, harmony cannot be maintained, particularly not when the inevitable appearance of outsiders pierces a hole through the dominant phalanx of entrepreneurs.

All employers, of course, stand to gain to some extent by keeping the wages down, but these gains will differ widely in the various industries, according to the physical distribution of capital and labor. In those branches of production in which this gain is comparatively small, it may be neutralized by the enforced inability to expand or to introduce more profitable methods of production.

Now, if an industrialist sees that the benefits he has sacrificed in favor of the coalition are unscrupulously reaped by outsiders and feels their competition more and more keenly, then the psychological moment has come for his withdrawal from the ranks of the coalition; for those industrialists whose particular situation would enable them to profit most from an expansion and a change in their methods in violation of the rules of the coalition, will prefer to reap these advantages for themselves, before their last chance has been destroyed by outsiders.

And that is the beginning of the end of the coalition: the re-appearance of a steadily widening stream of competitors with the final effect that the wage level will again be raised from that dictated by superior control to the level of free competition, i.e., to the level of the marginal product!

Reasoning In These Cases Is Necessarily Deductive

This kind of deductive reasoning may perhaps be found to be convincing only in part. But it should be remembered that in problems of this nature there are no other than deductive methods at our disposal. We shall never be so fortunate as to assemble reliable direct observations, or to make experimental tests. The assumed employers' coalition embracing all industries has never actually existed, and if it should ever come into being, it would soon disappear again, like all social groupings, and it could not even be considered as an empirical proof of my deductions. The question might still be, whether its dissolution was caused by the factors cited in my deduction, or by some other, new factors. The reasons given in my argument can, by their very nature, operate gradually only.

And conditions would hardly remain unchanged for so long a period as might be necessary to produce these effects. One would never be able to determine beyond a question through purely empirical methods, whether the ultimate result was due to the gradual undermining influence brought about by these alone *within* the original state of affairs, or whether, and to what extent, it might be ascribed to the advent of new factors. But precisely because we are dependent in these questions upon deduction as the sole source of our knowledge, and because they cannot be verified through direct observation, as is possible in other cases, we have no choice other than to elaborate such deductions; and these, of course, must be made on the basis and according to the methods of economic theory, which alone after all, as we have seen, will explain the influences of outside power.

At the same time, we must observe that supreme caution and precaution which the use of the deductive method always requires, particularly where the lines of deductive reasoning are long and complex, and where it is not possible to check them up, step by step, through empirical observations.[13]

It is from these considerations that I wish to submit here and in the following pages a few suggestions which, I realize, constitute only a rough, unfinished sketch of such deductive thoughts as may lead to a more detailed investigation later on, and in a general way at least, may indi-

13. See preface to my *Positive Theory of Capital*, p. 387-394.

cate the direction in which, in my opinion, the attainable amount of knowledge and understanding may be found.

Course Of Events When There Is
Monopolistic Control By Employes (Unions)

Let us then continue our inquiry into the wage-rates located above the level of the marginal product (within the range of possible wages), and beginning from above, start with the highest conceivable rates.

4.

It is obvious without any further discussion that such extremely high wages cannot endure, because they would cause such great capital losses to the entrepreneur that their perpetuation would lead to bankruptcy, although temporarily they might represent the minor evil as against a prolonged shutdown. (See foregoing.)

5.

Nor can the wage level following next, as is equally obvious, remain in force permanently because though not threatening the entrepreneur with immediate financial ruin, it would still cause him actual losses, although of a smaller extent. If continued over a long period of time, even small losses must also lead ultimately to financial ruin, so that case 5 would flow over into case 4; and without doubt, in such cases the entrepreneurs would prefer to liquidate their unprofitable business, or at least give up the unprofitable branches.

6.

The greatest theoretical interest attaches to the next-following level of wages: can that wage rate endure which, though not causing any actual loss of capital to the entrepreneur, absorbs or reduces the interest on his capital investment?

Let us first answer a preliminary question. Would it be possible for the entrepreneur's profits proper to disappear or to be permanently reduced, while in other branches of business, such as in the loan market or nonproductive investments like real estate (apartment houses), the rate of interest remained unchanged?

The answer is emphatically, No! Entrepreneurs working with borrowed capital would suffer an actual loss from the difference between the higher rates of interest which they would have to pay to their creditors, and the lower rate which that capital would bring them in their business, and thus the matter would lead back into the situation presented under point 5 foregoing. Nor would those entrepreneurs who work wholly or in part with their own capital be able to stay in business under such a state of affairs. Once capital is invested in an enterprise, it may have to content itself with a lower rate of interest, when and because its withdrawal would not be feasible nor possible without a great depreciation of the capital-stock itself. There would be little inducement to replace used-up capital funds, if the investment should promise a smaller return to its owners than the same capital could produce in other kinds of investments, such as in real estate or in the loan market. And the familiar and often discussed causes which, generally speaking, tend to equalize the interest rate in the various markets of capital (not artificially isolated) would surely also tend to prevent a one-sided diminution or elimination of the entrepreneur's original capital return. Its reduction would thus either have to extend all over the other fields of capital employment, or they could not occur at all.

Can Labor Unions Ever Permanently Deprive Businesses Of The Customary Return On Capital?

The question under investigation thus assumes the following form: "Can that wage-rate remain in force permanently which, though not affecting the entrepreneurs' capital-stock, takes away capital-interest* from business, or at least reduces the 'natural' rate of interest prevailing under free competition?" In other words, can a wage-increase obtained by the use of power permanently absorb interest on capital, or reduce it below its natural level?

The rather difficult answer to this question will be somewhat facilitated if we investigate separately the two stages involved, namely, one as to the *total*, and the other as to the *partial* absorption of interest on capital.

Case 1 — Total Elimination Of Return On Capital

I consider it impossible that interest could disappear completely from a nation's economic life, with the exception of the almost unthinkable case, hardly applying here, of capital accumulation far exceeding all demand. The disappearance of the "incentive to thrift," contained in interest, would eliminate that most important portion of capital which is formed through savings made only for the sake of interest. It might happen, of course, that that other type of savings, intended as a "rainy-day-penny," might then be somewhat increased, if people were to provide for their future by accumulating capital alone, without the support of interest. But it is generally believed

---

*Publisher's Note: *Capital-interest*, here and when used elsewhere, refers to originary interest, or profit. See *History and Critique of Interest Theories*, pp. 5-7.

that on the whole there would result a substantial diminution of capital stock, and the subsequent shortage of capital supply would probably exert a strong pressure in the opposite direction, i.e., in the direction of a renewed increase, rather than in that of a permanent disappearance of interest.

But even though the supply of capital were to be reduced, the thing that would be of decisive importance is the demand side of capital. Let us assume for a moment that interest had actually disappeared from economic life, i.e., that present and future goods could be exchanged for each other on the same level without discount, and that loans could be obtained without interest. The inevitable consequence of this would be an increase exceeding all bounds in the demand for present goods. The empirical law of the larger productivity of time-consuming, more highly capitalistic, roundabout methods of production, could not fail to make itself felt, in the sense that industrialists would compete with each other in lengthening the periods of production, and would adapt their enterprises to the technically most economical, but at the same time, most extended and time-consuming methods of production.*

The automatic check which counteracts such a tremendous lengthening of the productive process at present would have ceased to exist; that check is the interest payment which automatically places a progressive tax on lengthened methods of production. But once the lengthened methods of production were freed from the burden of interest, and did not cost more than the shorter one, and at the same time, produced more than the latter, a general incentive to an enormous prolongation of the productive process would be called forth.

It would, however, find its existing limitation in the subsistence fund (maybe reduced by less saving) during the increased period of waiting, imposed by the lengthened period of production. From the existing, and possibly reduced, subsistence fund, it would be impossible to support the same number of workers for an indefinitely prolonged period of waiting. Instead, the trend of wages will necessarily be held down from two sides within the margins of the possible price range.[14]

* See *Positive Theory Of Capital*, Book IV.

[14.] I do not wish to take into account that the assumed increase in wages would also increase the standard of living at which the workers would have to be maintained; this, however, may be offset by the lower rate of interest with which the "propertied classes" would have to content themselves after the elimination of interest on capital.

First, the duration of the periods of production, although somewhat longer, will be restricted to the shortest possible time through a process of selection which will be made under free competition in favor of the most profitable among the various possible extensions of the productive process; and as this selection can only be effected in regard to the most effective part of demand by granting higher prices, which means, in this case, by granting a correspondingly higher premium on the demanded subsistence fund, then, at least in regard to this phase of the inevitable development, interest will be restored to business—as I have described more fully in my *Positive Theory of Capital.*[15]

But at the same time something else will happen. The just-described process of selection leads to a restoration of interest and the periods of production will be no longer indefinitely lengthened, although they will still continue to be somewhat longer. The entrepreneurs who profit by paying the highest premium on present goods, will under normal circumstances be forced to resort to longer periods of production than they employed originally. For while before the advent of wage increases, the permanency of which we are investigating, they had to pay only as much for interest and wages jointly as they now have to pay for the increased wages alone, now moreover, they have to pay for the restored interest. This condition can only be met through larger profits than before, and these increased profits can be made only through a corresponding lengthening of the period of production, unless we should invoke the advent of new inventions with a subsequent increase in the output, like a *deus ex machina,* instead of concluding our argument by sticking to the original assumptions.

But then it would be impossible for the same number of workers as before to be provided for, throughout this prolonged period of production, out of the existing reduced, rather than increased, subsistence fund. There must therefore be a limitation in another direction, a restriction in the number of employed workers, in approximately the same proportion in which the consumption of the subsistence fund has been extended. This physical necessity will be met economically through the motive of self-interest, with high wages and a low interest rate under a more capitalistic method of production, that is, the employment of

---

[15]. Book IV in *Positive Theory Of Capital* and Essay XII in *Further Essays on Capital and Interest.*

fewer workers in lengthened periods of production is more profitable.[16]

As long, therefore, as the enforced wages prevail at that high level, there will come about a provisional state of equilibrium of approximately this description: The general adoption of the lengthened period of production will tend to increase the workers' per capita output. The "marginal product of labor" will thus be increased; as also by a reduction in the number of workers—and it will now correspond with the enforced higher wage-level which had risen beyond the "marginal product" of the previous stage. Interest on capital which has been restored is now lower than previously. The entrepreneurs manage to survive because, with the increased "marginal productivity of labor," even the last worker in their employment will still produce to them the higher wage to be paid, and also because the surplus productivity of the entire lengthened process of production will leave them a sufficient amount above the wage increase to compensate them for the interest on capital. But this new equilibrium is possible only at the expense of employing a smaller number of workers. And it is for this reason that, in all probability, this temporary equilibrium will again be disturbed.

For now, the labor union will be split in two, one group employed at a high wage, and another group not employed at all. The greater an increase in wages has been enforced and the more the new methods of production are protracted, the bigger will be the number of unemployed. Two developments are possible. Both groups of workers may stay together within the union, which implies that the unemployed members would have to be supported by contributions from their employed fellow-workers.* If these contributions are large, they will absorb the surplus accruing to the workers from the wage increase—for it should not be overlooked that the total output that can be produced by a reduced number of workers with the same capital, must, even with improved methods of production, remain below that obtainable from a full employment of capital and labor. Thus nobody would be benefited from the new artificially created order of things, as against the previous "natural" order;

16. See on this subject my detailed discussion in *Positive Theory of Capital*, particularly the comparison in the table on p. 356, to which I merely wish to add that the assumption of a totally perfect competition has in this case been eliminated by our present assumption, at least on the side of the workers who have eliminated underbidding by strictly cooperating with each other.

* Publisher's Note: Böhm-Bawerk did not consider tax funds being made available for this.

many would indeed be at a disadvantage—which fact would again be distinctly unfavorable to the prolonged maintenance of a situation created through a strong combined pressure of power. But if the standard of living of the unemployed workers were to be substantially reduced, these latter again would not allow such a condition to persist; there would be discontent, discord, and ultimately dissolution of the union. The malcontents would sooner or later become outsiders, and compete by offering their services to the entrepreneurs; the revived competition, with its underselling, would put an end to the monopolistic dictation of wages by the labor union, and would force wages back to the level economically justified under the full employment of all workers, i.e., to the "marginal product" of the last worker employed in an again reduced period of production.[17]

If, ultimately, the employed workers should fail to provide for their unemployed fellow-workers, then the same process would take place, even more rapidly. The mass of the unemployed would enter into competition and even more violently underbid wages.

Consequence Of Ending Of Union Monopoly

One might perhaps think of an alternative in another direction; namely, that the unionized workers might enforce not only higher wages, but also the full employment of all workers at that higher wage rate. But even though the workers might have the power temporarily to enforce these conditions, they could not be permanent. For this would necessarily lead over into one of the two alternatives considered above, under numbers 4 and 5. By being forced to pay the workers not only a wage which in itself is higher than the entire amount of the originary interest on capital, and in addition to this a restored interest on capital (although somewhat smaller in the aggregate), the entrepreneur will find that his costs have increased, and

17. I fully realize that a lengthening and shortening of the process of production cannot be carried out at a moment's notice, without trouble, in that it always affects the entire structure of fixed capital. But, on the other hand, it is hardly probable that the pendulum would swing to the full extreme of a complete disappearance of interest and back toward the original starting-point. It would be far more likely for those economic forces which swing the pendulum back from the extreme towards the starting-point to intervene long before that point had been reached, and to keep the swing of the pendulum within much narrower limits, thus restricting the technical changes in production necessary in adaptation to the respective prices of the factors of production. But as I did not wish to make any omission in the method of presentation, I was anxious to consider also the extreme cases, with their counter-effects, just as if they actually occurred in practical life.

he will suffer losses and sooner or later abandon the enterprise, or go into bankruptcy.

Moreover, it is almost unthinkable that any employer could ever be compelled to employ all workers available at a given time. At best, the labor union may, through violence, prevent dismissals from the former supply of workers. But any attempt to enforce the employment of additional workers, in proportion to the natural attrition in their ranks, or even that of an increasing number of workers, corresponding to the natural growth of population, would be well-nigh impossible.

From all these considerations, which could and probably ought to be elaborated in far more detail, I believe that a complete absorption of interest and capital through artificial, enforced wage-increase is out of the question in the economic life of a nation.

Case 2 — Reduction In Return On Capital

But would, perhaps, even the partial elimination of originary interest on capital be permanently possible?

I do not see any reason for assuming a course of events differing from the one assumed above. A smaller increase in wages at the expense of interest on capital will cause exactly the same reactions and effects, only in a correspondingly smaller degree. A mere reduction in the interest rate will at first not destroy the premium for saving contained in interest, but merely diminish it; the effect of this on the amount of future savings cannot be predicted with certainty.[18]

Possibly the amount of savings would decrease, and possibly not. But this would not alter the general trend of events, as shown in the preceding chapter of this inquiry, where I have purposely mentioned incidentally only, the probable reduction in the supply of capital, without ascribing to it any decisive influence. The determining factor is to be found in the demand for capital, and in this phase of the problem it is inevitable that each increase in wages beyond the actual marginal product, followed by a reduction in the interest-rate, will tend to cause a lengthening of the methods of production and thus a diminution in the number of workers.

If the entrepreneur is not to suffer any actual loss, which he could not take for any length of time, the wage-increase must be covered by an increased marginal productivity of labor, which can best be brought about through an extension of time for the various stages of production.

18. Compare this problem with the interesting discussion in Cassel's *Nature and Necessity of Interest*, p. 144ff.

This again, under otherwise equal circumstances, can be accomplished only by a simultaneous reduction in the number of workers, unless improvement through inventions, etc., should happen to be introduced, or other developments of an accidental nature should take place, contingencies which can be left out of account.

Enforced unemployment of a portion of the workers would also tend to lead toward the dissolution of the labor union, only in a less intense degree, in accordance with the smaller extent of wage-increases attained by the labor union, under this assumption. The weakening of the forces counteracting the continuance of such a temporary condition does not mean a different result, but merely the postponement of effect. It cannot mean that an adjustment exceeding the natural limits, if only by very little, could last, nor can it mean that the suspension of a smaller number of workers would not cause them to compete for employment. But it *does* mean that such a condition will continue to exist for a longer period against the pressure of minor influences, so that, for instance, trifling losses caused by this temporary situation could be borne for a considerably longer time by the employers, before they would go into bankruptcy or go out of business; or else a small number of the unemployed might be supported from union funds for a longer period, or through moral pressure be prevented from underbidding the union members.

And this again may imply something else. As I have already shown above, protracted periods of time are likely to bring in their wake changes in other directions. If a process of economic change is spread over a certain length of time, its general progress will, in most cases, be affected by other incidental or independent, outside causes, which almost spontaneously will affect the general situation. Over a period of several years, methods of production, or the business-cycle, never remain unchanged. The latter may move up or down, the former will most likely progress, and if the interval is very long, there may even occur considerable changes in the general economic structure, such as the number of population, and their relation to the capital stock.

Besides this, another alternative is possible. Those very impulses, whose normal effects I am trying to observe and investigate, may themselves contain certain additional, almost accidental effects on other external factors. For example, they need not necessarily, but may, affect the technique of production. These chances should thus not be left altogether out of consideration, but should not be inserted as a factor in the series of deductions, as they cannot be foretold with absolute certainty.

In our case, for instance, the entrepreneurs may find themselves pressed by the enforced wage increase, and this may form a powerful and effective incentive for the adoption of technical improvements in the methods of production, just as free competition is generally credited with forming a powerful incentive to industrial progress.

Or it may happen that the permanent improvement in the standard of living attained by the workers by way of an enforced wage increase may retard the growth of population, as is commonly the case among wealthier classes, etc.

Now, should some such accidental or incidental development occur which would directly or indirectly increase the marginal productivity of labor, then it may also happen that the initial wage-increase, exceeding that marginal productivity, might subsequently counterbalance the unexpected increase in the marginal productivity, and thus remain in force permanently. This would be all the more frequent, the less excessive the original enforced wage increase had been, i.e., the less it had gone beyond the marginal productivity of labor existing at that time. But of course, in the case of small wage-increases, it is impossible to expect this with any degree of certainty, because such accidental events as these may fail to take place, or even have opposite effects. Business cycles may show a downward trend, population may increase more rapidly than capital-supply, etc., in which case wages would be reduced all the more rapidly.

Hallucination Regarding Permanence Of Wage Increases Being Result Of Dictate Of Power

Those cases, however, in which a subsequent change of economic environment may render permanent an originally excessive wage increase obtained through force, might tend to confuse the theoretical analysis. They appear to give empirical proof of the fact that, through the dictate of power, wages can be raised above the limits laid down by marginal productivity, not only for the time being, but with a lasting effect. On close observation, however, they do not furnish this proof. The original wage-increase was the effect of a dictate of power. Its permanent duration, however, is not the result of power, but of outside influences of a third order, which have increased the marginal productivity of labor, and therewith increased the possible permanent higher wage level, quite independently from the dictate of power, or at least without necessary connection with it. I shall have to return to this point further on, in summarizing the results of this investigation.

Before that, however, for the sake of completeness, I shall have to consider a seventh possibility, so small, however, in practical importance, as to be out of all proportion to its theoretical complexity.

7.

In the scale of possible wage-rates, there enters, between that wage which already absorbs a part of the interest and that wage-level which coincides with the marginal product of labor, another rate of wages which, though exceeding the marginal productivity of labor, does not cut into the reward of capital with this excess amount, but remains within the total produce of labor. For when an increasing number of workers cooperate with a given capital stock, each additional worker entering the field will contribute only a decreasing addition to the joint product.[19]

The last worker employed at a given time adds the "marginal product"; each one previously hired adds a little more to the total produce. That is why the entrepreneur gains nothing from the last worker employed provided his wages just equal the marginal product, and successively more and more from each previous worker, leaving out of consideration the share to be attributed to the contribution of capital. Now, if the wages increase above the marginal product, the entrepreneur will suffer a loss from the employment of the last worker, or workers. This loss may, however, be offset to some extent by the gain from the workers employed previously. So long as this is the case, so long as the total sum of wages does not consume more than is covered by the joint output of all workers together, the share of the capital need not be reduced.[20] The share of wages exceeding the marginal product will then be paid at the expense of the real, pure profits which previously had gone to the entrepreneur.

For the purposes of this investigation we must now ask whether such a wage increase, affecting or absorbing, as it would, only the entrepreneur's profits, if achieved temporarily through a dictate of power, could possibly remain in force permanently. This question is, it seems, even harder to answer through methods of deductive rea-

19. According to a not entirely uncontested variation of the law of "diminishing returns".

20. I wish to state that, in reasoning thus, I purposely omit all such losses as may be caused by the partial elimination of workers through interference with the existing organization; I assume, as it were, an enterprise that can be reorganized without difficulty, as indicated above, when I said that the capital employed was to be constant in its amount, although not in its physical composition.

soning than was the case in previous parts of this inquiry, and it is altogether unsuited for an empirical test. There would be no lack of forces counteracting the continuance of the new wage level, but they would be weak, and only gradual.

The entrepreneurs suffering losses from the last worker employed will endeavor to reorganize their enterprise at an early opportunity, so as to reduce the number of workers by eliminating those causing losses. There may be some opposition made to such a reorganization on the part of the workers who will not tolerate any dismissals; this may postpone the elimination of the excessive number, until natural vacancies occur which are no longer filled. Moreover, the best possible organization of the enterprise with a reduced number of workers will require a change in technical equipment.

If extra losses through the sudden elimination of capital equipment are to be avoided, this can also be effected only gradually, by using up the old equipment. During these protracted periods, however, which thus would counteract the effectiveness of the other influences, weak in themselves, all sorts of changes in the general situation may arise which will affect the upward and downward trend of wages far more violently, and either absorb those insignificant tendencies, or counteract them altogether; the small waves emanating from these influences will melt away unnoticed and imperceptible under the much higher waves of new economic factors.

To test this in practice would be practically impossible; all the more since changes in wages affecting merely profits, without affecting the other factors of production, must of necessity be of very limited nature. A general wage-increase enforced over the entire nation would affect both great and small, strong and weak enterprises, and a wage-increase which is to be fully met out of the net profits of entrepreneurs, even in the weakest types of enterprises with the lowest profits, can hardly extend very far. For as soon as it became appreciable, it would cut into the capital-gain of at least some of the entrepreneurs, or into capital itself, whereby the matter would lead over into one of the cases discussed above.

A conclusive theoretical investigation, therefore, should not pass by this seventh case without at least an attempt at a more detailed investigation, which would meet even greater difficulties than those indicated here. However, the greatest practical and theoretical interest does not attach to this, but to the previous case, number six, which is concerned with the question as to whether any artificial influence of power *may* or *may not* be able permanently to increase the share of labor at the expense of that of capital.

As the reader has seen, I was not able to answer this question affirmatively.

Labor CANNOT Increase Its Share At The Expense Of Capital

I know quite well that this part of my belief will probably meet with very strong opposition, and (1) that I will be accused of relapsing into the old, outgrown theory of "pure natural laws" in economics; (2) I also know that many will find a strong empirical contradiction of my views in the undeniable fact that during the last decades countless strikes have led to an improvement in the workers' economic status never abrogated afterwards, and that almost universally and everywhere the standard of living of organized labor, which is able to apply the lever of power, is higher than that of unorganized workers. But I believe I am able to meet both these objections.

Universal Influence Of Self-Interest

It would certainly never occur to me to attempt a revival of the old concept of "pure natural laws" in our economic science and therewith to oppose the belief in the effectiveness of the influence of control. On the contrary, I *do* believe in the effectiveness, in fact in a considerable and far-reaching effectiveness, of power, but I do *not* believe in its omnipotence; and since a careful analysis has shown me that these economic influences of power are in themselves based on motives of economic self-interest, I cannot close my eyes to the fact that any situation brought about by means of "power" may in itself again bring into play motives of self-interest, tending to oppose its continuance.

If an entrepreneur is induced, through the motive of self-interest, to select the "minor evil," and permits a wage increase exacted from him, then an analogous motive of self-interest will urge him to reorganize the various factors of production by means of which he produces his goods. If the factor of production called "labor" has become more expensive than before, in comparison with the other factors of production, through an extorted wage-increase, then it is almost unthinkable that the same relative apportionment of the various factors of production would remain the most rational in an economic sense.

If the entrepreneur finds his hands tied by the price of labor, but not in regard to the physical equipment of his factory, and he desires to adopt the presently cheapest combination of factors of production, he will prefer a combination different from the one used before, one that will enable him to make savings in the now more costly factor of labor, just as, for example, an increase in the cost of land may cause the transition from extensive to intensive methods of cultivation.

If, ultimately, this saving in the now more expensive factor of labor continues to lead to the reduction in the demand for labor described before, which will ultimately render the enforced wage-rate untenable, then it is no longer nature that has won a victory over power, but it is merely a new motive of self-interest, produced by changed conditions, that has prevailed over another motive of self-interest operative at another, no longer existing condition; or, stated more correctly, the same motive of self-interest which has led to the selection of the relatively most favorable combination of means of production, will, under changed conditions, have made itself felt in a different direction.

This is not a belief in "natural economic laws," but merely the rebuttal of the short-sighted idea that if, after a profound change in the costs of the various factors of production the trend of economic self-interest continued to work in the same direction as before, and that therefore, one had to submit to the dictates of power, as if they were imposed by providence, and to cease to defend one's self-interest.

Summary Of Exceptions

I emphatically repeat that I *do* recognize the effectiveness of the influence of outside power in distribution, both in theory, and to a considerable extent, in practice. And I might also mention the fact that it makes no difference whether these artificial influences of outside control emanate from monopoly, such as employers' coalitions or labor unions, or from a direct intervention by government authority.

The reason why I have not specially mentioned or discussed this latter case is merely that it seems to me to differ in motive rather than in method of application from the far more frequent case of control exerted by contending parties. I believe, for instance, that the legal fixation of a minimum-wage will have to be interpreted in its effects in the same way as the dictate of wages by a well-organized labor union.

But in order not to leave any room for misunderstandings, I shall once more summarize the results of my investigations: Temporarily at least, the influence of outside control may produce intense and far-reaching, in fact very profound, effects. Under certain conditions these effects may become permanent, particularly when they are merely applied to neutralize an opposite influence of control which previously had deflected the dividing line away from its natural position. Thus, for instance, a strike may achieve an increase of wages up to the point of the marginal product, whenever the entrepreneurs had previously held the wages down *below* the marginal product by force of *their* monopoly-power.

Furthermore, when a subsequent economic development suddenly transforms the original, artificial dividing line into a natural one, then the advent of power simply means a temporary anticipation of a development which would equally have taken place without such intervention, only later.

Finally, control may temporarily be equally successful when it leads to certain lasting effects, and to efforts among the defeated party to improve its economic status, so that this improved condition may again become the "natural" condition. This contingency, however, will always occur only as an exception to the general rule, and can never be expected with certainty to take place, but it does represent the most favorable and outstanding combination for effective dictates of power: For in this case, and probably in this case alone, can we claim with a certain amount of justification that not only the advent, but also the continuance of a rate of distribution elevated beyond the natural rate has, even though only indirectly, been caused through the influence of power.

*   *   *

But apart from these special cases stated before, there is, in my opinion, not a single instance when the influence of control could be lasting as against the gently and slowly, but incessantly and therefore successfully, working counter-influences of a "purely economic" order, called forth through that artificial interference and the new situation created thereby.

And, I hope to have made clear, there is one more thing that not even the most imposing dictate of power will accomplish: *It can never effect anything in contradiction to the economic laws of value, price and distribution; it must always be in conformity with these; it cannot invalidate them; it can merely confirm and fulfill them.* And this, I think, is the most important, and the most certain conclusion of the foregoing inquiry.

**There Is No Empirical Evidence That
Union Power Raises Wages**

But how about the second objection which I anticipate, namely the alleged empirical counterproof which the practical experiences with strikes and wage struggles seem to have supplied during the past generations?

Well, if these are interpreted correctly, they do not supply such a counterproof. For whenever a strike has led to an enduring success, there always appears to have prevailed one or the other additional circumstance by which, in my opinion, the permanency of this result can be explained.

(1)   Above all, I believe that the ensuing efforts by labor unions found a general situation in which the competition among employers had been restrained to the detriment of workers. Situations existed in which employer coalitions or individual employees enjoying superior strength had created a monopoly or a quasi-monopolistic position towards the atomistic workers. In all such situations force merely could offset or present the effects of an opposite artificial force. This is probably *one* plausible reason for the apparently better conditions of organized labor over unorganized labor.

A second reason for this may be found in the fact that, wherever an increase of wages in the economic world is about to take place, organized labor may accelerate its advent by using its power, and thus always keep a step ahead of unorganized labor.

And, finally, one should not overlook the fact that sometimes it only appears as if conditions among organized labor had been improved. For as the skillful or more highly qualified types of workers are more often and more generally in the advantageous position of organizing than are the common or unskilled workers, the contrast between organized and unorganized labor may often coincide with that between skilled and unskilled labor. The former, by virtue of general economic laws, have in themselves a claim to higher wages than the common workers. The higher wage level of labor unions as compared to unorganized labor must not, or at least must not unreservedly and exclusively, be ascribed to the influence of power exerted by their unions.

(2) Moreover, our generation has passed, and is passing, through a period when, omitting ephemeral fluctu-

ations, the general trend of economic progress was and is continuously highly favorable to a wage increase. Therefore, it has never been really possible to test by way of experiment or actual observation whether an enforced increase in wages, achieved by means of a strike, might not perhaps have been gradually demolished again by those gently and slowly working counterforces, the undermining effects of which I have referred to above. In every case there always is a great amount of counteracting and modifying outside influences which, in the majority of cases, in their net results were favorable to the elevation of the productivity of labor and the increase of its marginal product, which alone ultimately determines the wage rate.

And thus the great part of the considerable and lasting wage-increases of the past generation may easily be explained by the combined factors referred to in my analysis: At first, these wage increases were caused by the labor-unions and strikes. But the reason why they could be maintained without being rescinded was that the stupendous progress of our times continuously produced such great techincal improvements, improved methods of utilizing human labor, and coincided with a substantial increase of population, and an even larger increase of capital.

But we have no way of showing how things would have turned out, or what they would be at present, if those successful strikes had led into a period of depression, or of moderate, slow progress, instead of coinciding with a period of the most stupendous progress, so impetuous that many a blind enthusiast has seriously begun to question the iron foundations of Malthus' "law of population."

(3) And finally there is here too a sense in which merely the impression of a lasting wage increase is being created, where in reality no increase has taken place at all. Many a wage increase obtained through strikes has been neutralized, not through any formal wage reduction, but through the increase in the cost of living. To what extent a subsequent rise in prices of certain important means of subsistence, together with a general indirect increase in the cost of living through depreciation of money, has deprived wage increases of their reality, and transformed them into quite immaterial nominal money increases at best, is a much contested question. Personally I do not by any means agree with the contention often made by socialists that the wage increases obtained during the past pre-war decade have altogether disappeared in this manner. I rather believe that a considerable part of them have been genuine and permanent in character; but this is true

only in part, and as regards the other part, that process of absorption through quiet and imperceptible counterforces, to which I have referred already, has actually taken place; it is the same story in a different form.

Concluding Remarks

It may be that my analysis, which I personally do not consider exhaustive by any means, may have to be amplified, elaborated, and corrected in many points. To me, the essential thing is that in the problems discussed here we need, in any event, a new method of approach, free from the preconceived notion that this entire question has been decided long ago. The struggle between the natural and the social categories has been fought over twice already in economic science, and in both instances decided by an error of judgment: the first time by the classicists in a one-sided manner in favor of the natural laws; the second time in the modern theories of social distribution, with a similar partiality in favor of social control. What is needed is to undertake the whole procedure again, and to finish it, without prejudice, on the basis of the [seemingly] unimportant truth, not sufficiently acknowledged so far, that the influence of social control does, and must operate through the formulas and laws of pure economic theory.

Functional versus Personal Distribution

In order finally to avoid new misunderstandings, let me add a last word which should not remain unsaid at this place. John Bates Clark, whom I had to oppose polemically on several occasions in important questions, and whom I look upon as one of the most original and deepest authorities of our science, has, on a certain occasion, set up a very important and distinctive line of demarcation, with the felicitous and characteristic terms of "functional" and "personal" distribution.[21]

"Functional" distribution determines the rate according to which the individual factors of production are to be recompensed for their share in production, irrespective of the person who has made that contribution, and without regard to the question whether any single person has contributed much or little. Functional distribution thus explains the division of the total national dividend into the great categories of wages, rent, interest and profits.

"Personal" distribution, however, explains the size of the share which each individual obtains for himself from the national dividend without regard to the function from which he obtains it, and particularly regardless whether

21. *Distribution of Wealth,* page 5.

he receives his share for one single, or for several, functions contributed simultaneously.

Functional distribution explains high and low wages, high and low rates of interest, etc.; personal distribution explains large and small incomes, indicating how one and the same income of $100,000 may just as well result from wages of a well-paid bank president or from rent, or from high or low interest, or from a mixture of several functional types of income, or how a modest income of $1000 may just as well be that of a worker without capital or that of a small capitalist or landowner.

Functional distribution explains relatively few and simple facts of a general nature; personal distribution gives us highly colored, mosaic-like pictures, resulting from the application of those simple and general laws of distribution to a vast variety of data, and explains the function, amounts, and qualities that have been contributed by each individual to the total production. The primary object of all scientific theory of distribution, and thus also the object around which have centered the old disputes referred to above, is *functional* distribution.[22]

These statements which I have made regarding the limitations of outside control of distribution apply only to functional distribution. As to the influence of control on personal distribution, the limits are infinitely more elastic, both as to intensity and as to the lasting effectiveness of that influence.

Since outside control may also permanently change the other factors to which the laws of functional distribution apply, it may happen that certain effects in the sphere of personal distribution may be brought about without temporal limitation; when the government of a country turns proletarians into landlords through distribution of land, they and their descendants may, for all time, find their income increased by rent from land, quite regardless of how the line of division between rent from land and wages of labor may be drawn in functional distribution.

And if a socialist state should introduce common ownership of all means of production and transform all capital and all land into social property, in the produce of which each member of society shares in one way or the other, then for all future, or at least as long as such a so-

---

22. " . . . The science of distribution does not directly determine what each person shall get. Personal sharing results from another kind of sharing; only the resolving of the total income of society into wages, interest and profits, as distinct kinds of income, falls directly and entirely within the field of economics". Clark, *Distribution of Wealth*, page 5.

cialistic order may continue, all personal shares would, in the same or similar way, be composed of the produce of each one's own labor, and a similar contribution from the produce of the social property, in a manner widely and permanently differing from our present system of personal distribution.

Eugen von Böhm-Bawerk

IV

Unresolved Contradiction in The Marxian Economic System*

Alice Macdonald Translation

---

*The title of the German original is "Zum Abschluss des Marxschen Systems." This essay first appeared in *Staatswissenschaftliche Arbeiten - Festgaben für Karl Knies zur Fünfundsiebzigsten Wiederkehr*, Berlin, Haering, 1896, pp. 85-205. Translation by Alice Macdonald, *Karl Marx and the Close of His System*, T. Fisher Unwin, London, 1898 (The Macmillan Company, New York, 1898) and Augustus M. Kelley, New York, 1949. The word *Close* in the English title is ambiguous and confusing. Probably a better word would have been *Completion*. In this edition the title has been changed radically.

Contents

Present Publisher's Preface To "Unresolved Contradiction In The Marxian Economic System"

When in 1898 Alice Macdonald translated Böhm-Bawerk's essay, *Zum Abschluss des Marxschen Systems* she gave it a nondescriptive title, *Karl Marx and the Close of His System.* Confident that a better title is needed in the English-speaking world, the present edition has a new title, *Unresolved Contradiction in the Marxian Economic System.*

The positive formulation of his Exploitation Theory by Marx in Volume I of his *Das Kapital,* published in 1867, contained a gross improbability which could not be glossed over, but which Marx procrastinated in solving by promising the solution later. Marx died in 1883 without in his lifetime "completing" his system or relieving it of an exceptionally obvious, logical defect. His friend and collaborator, Friedrich Engels, published Volume II of *Das Kapital* in 1885. The "problem" was not solved in Volume II either, and it became necessary to wait for Volume III. In 1894 (eleven years after Marx's death) Engels published Volume III, which was to contain the grand solution. That "solution" by Marx turned out to be no solution whatever, but is worthy of derision.

But eschewing derision, Böhm-Bawerk analyzed painstakingly the fallacies, inconsistencies, and absurdities of the final, *completed* Marxian system. To that analytical critique upon the "completion" of the Marxian system (something not accomplishable until Engels published Volume III of Marx's *Das Kapital*), Böhm-Bawerk gave the title, "On the Completion of the Marxian System." It is confusing to have had an English title referring to the "Close" of the Marxian system. "Close" in this case can only be understood figuratively as, say, the keystone closing (or completing) an arch. The deficiency of the title consisted in the fact that the "keystone" turned out to be no real keystone. And so, we have selected the title, *Unresolved Contradiction in the Marxian Economic System.*

In a brief "Introduction" Böhm-Bawerk explains the essential features of the self-created problem of Marx.

In Chapter I, "The Theory of Value and Surplus Value," Böhm-Bawerk summarizes Marx's allegation regarding the source of profit for the capitalist.

In Chapter II, "The Theory of the Average Rate of Profit and the Price of Production," Böhm-Bawerk elucidates the Marxian scheme of things further.

In Chapter III, "The Question of the Contradiction," Böhm-Bawerk engages in a detailed, destructive critique of Marx's argument; Böhm-Bawerk removes the Marxian structure from the terrain of credibility. In the process, Böhm-Bawerk's argument appears to become a little tedious, but the cause lies in Marx, not in Böhm-Bawerk.

The climax of the argument comes in Chapter IV, "The Error in the Marxian System — Its Origin and Ramifications." This shows Böhm-Bawerk at his best. It will be read with lively interest.

In Chapter V, "Werner Sombart's Apology," Böhm-Bawerk dissects the deficiencies of Sombart's attempted salvaging of Marx's system.

The Marxian system has always been contrary to common observation and common sense. It could only be accepted as a religion (spurious, of course), or as a lame justification for envy, hatred, covetousness, and rebellion against the realities of the world, the actual world in which finite men find themselves. Unattractive emotions lie at the root of acceptance of the Marxian system: or if an emotion is not involved, then there is an intellectual infirmity of some sort.

An attempt was made in 1904 by Hilferding (a Marxian who was subsequently unsuccessful as Finance Minister in the ill-fated, socialist Weimar Republic in Germany) to rebutt the critique of Böhm-Bawerk. Hilferding's "argument" is not respectable logically. He finally climaxes what he believes is his case by declaring, in a manner as if it explained something, that after all Böhm-Bawerk was basing his critique on the premises of the so-called school of thought in economics, which is generally described as being founded on the *subjective theory of value*. But merely declaring that a man belongs to a particular school of thought does not substantiate that his ideas are invalid. Neither Hilferding nor any other socialist has been able to shake the findings of the neoclassical school which developed the doctrine of subjective value.

One idea, profitably to be learned from this essay of Böhm-Bawerk, is especially worthy of note, namely, Marx's dependence and reliance on the economics of Adam Smith and David Ricardo, or more accurately expressed, Marx's reliance on certain parts (internally inconsistent and erroneous) of the economics of Smith and Ricardo. The significant conclusion to come to, on the basis of that fact, is that Smith and Ricardo were not adequate on many economic subjects. Their ideas are in part invalidated by their own ambiguities and errors, which were the parts ostentatiously taken over by the socialists; hence a more modern economics is needed than what Smith and Ricardo left to mankind. This the Neoclassical school (to which Böhm-Bawerk belonged) provided.

INTRODUCTION

Marx's Good Fortune
As An Author

As an author Karl Marx was enviably fortunate. No one will affirm that his work can be classed among the books which are easy to read or easy to understand. Most other books would have found their way to popularity hopelessly barred if they had labored under an even lighter ballast of hard dialectic and wearisome mathematical deduction. But Marx, in spite of this, has become the apostle of wide circles of readers, including many who are not as a rule given to the reading of difficult books. Moreover, the force and clearness of his reasoning were not such as to compel assent. On the contrary, men who are classed among the most earnest and most valued thinkers of our science, like Karl Knies, had contended from the first, by arguments that it was impossible to ignore, that the Marxian teaching was charged from top to bottom with every kind of contradiction both of logic and of fact. It could easily have happened, therefore, that Marx's work might have found no favor with any part of the public—not with the general public because it could not understand his difficult dialectic, and not with the specialists because they understood it and its weaknesses only too well. As a matter of fact, however, it has happened otherwise.

Nor has the fact that Marx's work remained a torso during the lifetime of its author been prejudicial to its influence. We are usually, and rightly, apt to mistrust such isolated first volumes of new systems. General principles can be very prettily put forward in the "General Sections" of a book, but whether they really possess the convincing power ascribed to them by their author, can only be ascertained when in the construction of the system they are brought face to face with all the facts in detail. And in the history of science it has not seldom happened that a promising and imposing first volume has never been followed by a second, just because, under the author's own more searching scrutiny, the new principles had not been able to stand the test of concrete facts. But the work of Karl Marx has not suffered in this way. The great mass of his followers, on the strength of his first volume, had unbounded faith in the yet unwritten volumes.

Circumstances Which Contributed
To Marx's Good Fortune

This faith was, moreover, in one case put to an unusually severe test. Marx had taught in his first volume,
that the whole value of commodities was based on the labor embodied in them, and that by virtue of this "law of
value" they must exchange in proportion to the quantity
of labor which they contain; that, further, the profit or
surplus value falling to the capitalist was the fruit of extortion practiced on the worker; that, nevertheless, the
amount of surplus value was not in proportion to the whole
amount of the capital employed by the capitalist, but only
to the amount of the "variable" part—that is, to that part
of capital paid in wages—while the "constant capital," the
capital employed in the purchase of the means of produc-
iton, added no surplus value. In daily life, however, the
profit of capital is in proportion to the *total* capital invested;
and, largely on this account, the commodities do not as a
fact exchange in proportion to the amount of work incorporated in them. Here, therefore, there was a contradiction
between system and fact which hardly seemed to admit of
a satisfactory explanation. Nor did the obvious contradiction escape Marx himself. He says with reference to it,
"This law" (the law, namely, that surplus value is in proportion only to the variable part of capital) "clearly contradicts all *primâ facie* experience."[1] But at the same time
he declares the contradiction to be only a seeming one, the
solution of which requires many missing links, and will be
postponed to later volumes of his work.[2] Expert criticism
thought it might venture to prophesy with certainty that
Marx would never redeem this promise, because, as it sought
elaborately to prove, the contradiction was insoluble. Its
reasoning, however, made no impression at all on the mass
of Marx's followers. His simple promise outweighed all
logical refutations.

Long Delay Of Marx In Fulfilling Promise
Of Solving Paradox

The suspense grew more trying when it was seen that
in the second volume of Marx's work, which appeared after
the master's death, no attempt had been made towards the
announced solution (which, according to the plan of the
whole work, was reserved for the third volume), nor even
was the slightest intimation given of the direction in which
Marx proposed to seek for the solution. But the preface
of the editor, Friedrich Engels, not only contained the re-

[1] *Das Kapital*, Vol. I, 1st edition, p. 285; 2nd edition, p. 312.
[2] *Das Kapital*, Vol. I, 1st edition, pp. 285, 286, and 508 note;
2nd edition, pp. 312 and 542 note.

iterated positive assertion that the solution was given in the manuscript left by Marx, but contained also an open challenge, directed chiefly to the followers of Rodbertus, that, in the interval before the appearance of the third volume, they should from their own resources attempt to solve the problem "how, not only without contradicting the law of value but even by virtue of it, an equal average rate of profit can and must be created."

Unusual Response To Engel's Program Enlisting Contestants To Pre-Solve The Marxian Paradox

I consider it one of the most striking tributes which could have been paid to Marx as a thinker that this challenge was taken up by so many persons, and in circles so much wider than the one to which it was chiefly directed. Not only followers of Rodbertus, but men from Marx's own camp, and even economists who did not give their adherence to either of these heads of the socialist school, but who would probably have been called by Marx "vulgar economists," vied with each other in the attempt to penetrate into the probable nexus of Marx's lines of thought, which were still shrouded in mystery. There grew up between 1885 (the year when the second volume of Marx's *Kapital* appeared) and 1894 (when the third volume came out) a regular prize essay competition on the "average rate of profit," and its relation to the "law of value."[3] According to the view of Friedrich Engels—now, like Marx, no longer living—as stated in his criticism of these prize essays in the preface to the third volume, no one succeeded in carrying off the prize.

Marx's "Solution" Published Finally In 1894 After 27-Year Delay

Now at last, however, with the long-delayed appearance of the conclusion of Marx's system, the subject has

[3] From an enumeration of Loria's, I draw up the following list ("L'opera postuma di Carlo Marx," *Nuova Antologia*, Vol. I, February 1895, p. 18), which contains some essays not known to me: Lexis, *Jahrbücher für Nationalökonomie*, 1885, new series, Vol. XI, pp. 452-465; Schmidt, *Die Durchschnittsprofitrate auf Grund des Marxschen Wertgesetzes*, Stuttgart, 1889; a discussion of the latter work by myself in the *Tübinger Zeitschrift für die gesamte Staatswissenschaft*, 1890, p. 590ff.; by Loria in the *Jahrbücher für Nationalökonomie*, new series, Vol. XX (1890), p. 272ff.; Stiebling, *Das Wertgesetz und die Profitrate*, New York, 1890; Wolf, "Das Rätsel der Durchschnittsprofitrate bei Marx," *Jahrbücher für Nationalökonomie*, third series, Vol. II (1891), p. 352ff.; Schmidt again, *Neue Zeit*, 1892-3, Nos. 4 and 5; Landé, *ibid.*, Nos. 19 and 20; Fireman, "Kritik der Marxschen Werttheorie," *Jahrbücher für Nationalökonomie*, third series, Vol. III (1892), p. 793ff.; finally, Lafargue, Soldi, Coletti, and Graziadei in the *Critica Sociale* from July to November, 1894.

reached a stage when a definite decision is possible. For of the mere promise of a solution each one could think as much or as little as he liked. Promises on the one side and arguments on the other were, in a sense, incommensurable. Even successful refutations of attempted solutions by others, though these attempts were held by their authors to have been conceived and carried out in the spirit of the Marxian theory, did not need to be acknowleged by the adherents of Marx, for they could always appeal from the faulty likeness to the promised original. But now at last this latter has come to light, and has procured for the thirty years' struggle a firm, narrow, and clearly defined battleground within which both parties can take their stand in order and fight the matter out, instead of on the one side contenting themselves with the hope of future revelations, or on the other passing, Proteus-like, from one shifting, unauthentic interpretation to another.

Has Marx himself solved his own problem? Has his completed system remained true to itself and to facts, or not? To inquire into this question is the task of the following pages.

CHAPTER I
The Theory Of Value And Surplus Value

The pillars of the system of Marx are his conception of value and his law of value. Without them, as Marx repeatedly asserts, all scientific knowledge of economic facts would be impossible. The mode in which he arrives at his views with reference to both has been described and discussed times without number. For the sake of connection I must recapitulate briefly the most essential points of his argument.

Marx's Definition Of Value Limited To "Commodities," And Arbitrarily Restricted Further To "Products Of Labor"

The field of research which Marx undertakes to explore in order "to come upon the track of value" (I, 23)[4] he limits from the beginning to *commodities*, by which, according to him, we are not to understand all economic goods, but only those *products of labor* which are made for the market.[5] He begins with the "Analysis of a Commodity" (I, 9).

[4] I quote from the second edition (1872) of the first volume of *Das Kapital*, from the 1885 edition of the second volume, and from the 1894 edition of the third volume; and unless I otherwise indicate, I always mean by III the first section of the third volume.
[5] I, pp. 15, 17, 49, 87, and often. Compare also Adler, *Grundlagen der Karl Marxschen Kritik der bestehenden Volkswirtschaft*, Tübingen, 1887, pp. 210 and 213.

A commodity is, on one side, a useful thing, which by its properties satisfies human wants of some kind; and, on the other, it forms the material medium of exchange value. He then passes to an analysis of this latter.

> Exchange value presents itself in the first instance as the quantitative relation, the proportion, in which values in use of one kind are exchanged for values in use of another kind, a relation which constantly changes with time and place.

Exchange value, therefore, appears to be something accidental. And yet there must be in this changing relation something that is stable and unchanging, and this Marx undertakes to bring to light. He does it in his well-known dialectical manner.

> Let us take two commodities, wheat and iron, for example. Whatever may be their relative rate of exchange it may always be represented by an equation in which a given quantity of wheat is equal to a given quantity of iron: for example, 8 bushels of wheat = 1 cwt. iron. What does this equation tell us? It tells us that there exists a common factor of the same magnitude in two different things, in 8 bushels of wheat and in a cwt. of iron. The two things are therefore equal to a third which is in itself neither the one nor the other. Each of the two, so far as it is an exchange value, must therefore be reducible to that third.

> This common factor [Marx goes on], cannot be a geometrical, physical, chemical or other natural property of the commodities. Their physical properties come into consideration for the most part only in so far as they make the commodities useful, and so make them values in use. But, on the other hand, the exchange relation of commodities is obviously determined without reference to their value in use. Within this relation one value in use is worth just as much as any other, if only it is present in proper proportion. Or, as old Barbon says, "One sort of wares are as good as another, if the value be equal. There is no difference or distinction in things of equal value." As values in use commodities are above everything of different qualities; as exchange values they can only be of different quantities, and they can, therefore, contain no atom of value in use.

> If then we abstract from the value in use of commodities, there remains to them only one common

property, that of being products of labor. But even as products of labor they have already, by the very process of abstraction, undergone a change under our hands. For if we abstract from the value in use of a commodity, we, at the same time, abstract from the material constituents and forms which give it a value in use. It is no longer a table, or a house, or yarn, or any other useful thing. All its physical qualities have disappeared. Nor is it any longer the product of the labor of the carpenter, or the mason, or the spinner, or of any other particular productive industry. With the useful character of the labor products there disappears the useful character of the labors embodied in them, and there vanish also the different concrete forms of these labors. They are no longer distinguished from each other, but are reduced to identical human labor—abstract human labor.

Let us examine now the residuum. There is nothing but this ghostly objectivity, the mere cellular tissue of undistinguishable human labor, that is, of the output of human labor without regard to the form of the output. All that these things have now to show for themselves is that human labor has been expended in their production—that human labor has been stored up in them; and as crystals of this common social substance they are — values.

With this, then, we have the conception of value discovered and determined. It is in dialectical form not identical with exchange value, but it stands, as I would now make plain, in the most intimate and inseparable relation to it. It is a kind of logical distillation from it. It is, to speak in Marx's own words, "the common element that manifests itself in the exchange relation, or exchange value, of commodities"; or again conversely, "the exchange value is the only form in which the value of commodities can manifest itself or be expressed" (I, 13).

Marx's Idea Of The Measurement Of Value By Amount Of Socially Necessary Labor

After establishing the conception of value Marx proceeds to describe its measure and its amount. As labor is the substance of value so the amount of the value of all goods is measured by the quantity of labor contained in them, which is, in its turn, measured by its duration—but not by that particular duration, or working time, which the individual who made the commodity has happened to need, but by the working time that is socially necessary. Marx defines this last as the working time required to produce a value in use under the normal conditions of production, and with the degree of skill and intensity of labor prevalent in a given society (I, 14). It is only the quantity of socially necessary labor, or the working time socially necessary for the production of a value in use, which determines the amount of the value. The single commodity is here to be regarded as an average specimen of its class. Commodities, therefore, in which equal quantities of labor are embodied, or which can be produced in the same working time, have the same value. The value of one commodity is related to the value of any other commodity as the working time necessary for the production of the one is to that necessary for the production of the other. As values, all commodities are only specific quantities of crystallized working time.

From all this is derived the subject matter of the imposing "law of value," which is "immanent in the exchange of commodities" (I, 141, 150) and governs exchange relations. It states, and must state, after what has gone before, that commodities are exchanged in proportion to the socially necessary working time incorporated in them (I, 52). Other modes of expressing the same law are that "commodities exchange according to their values" (see I, 142, 183; III, 167), or that "equivalent exchanges with equivalent" (I, 150, 183). It is true that in isolated cases according to momentary fluctuations of supply and demand prices occur which are over or under the values. But these "constant oscillations of market prices . . . compensate and cancel each other, and reduce themselves to the average price as their inner law" (I, 151, note 37). In the long run "the socially necessary working time always asserts itself by main force, like an overruling natural law, in the accidental and ever fluctuating exchange relations" (I, 52). Marx declares this law to be the "eternal law of the exchange of commodities" (I, 182), and "the rational element" and "the natural law of equilibrium" (III, 167). The inevitably occurring cases already mentioned in which commodities are exchanged for prices which deviate from their values are to be looked upon, in regard to this rule, as "accidental" (I, 150, note 37), and he even calls the deviation "a breach of the law of the exchange of commodities" (I, 142).

Marx's Doctrine Of Surplus Value, From Which Capitalists Are Alleged To Get Their Gain

On these principles of the theory of value Marx founds the second part of the structure of his teaching, his re-

nowned doctrine of surplus value. In this part he traces
the source of the gain which capitalists obtain from their
capital. Capitalists lay down a certain sum of money, convert it into commodities, and then—with or without an intermediate process of production—convert these back again
into more money. Whence comes this increment, this increase in the sum drawn out as compared with the sum
originally advanced? or whence comes "the surplus value"
as Marx calls it?[6]

Marx proceeds to mark off the conditions of the problem in his own peculiar way of dialectical exclusion. He
first declares that the surplus value cannot originate either
in the fact that the capitalist, as buyer, buys commodities
regularly under their value, nor in the fact that the capitalist, as seller, sells them regularly over their value. So the
problem presents itself in the following way:

> The owner of money must buy the commodities at
> their value, then sell them at their value, and yet
> at the end of the process must draw out more
> money than he put in. Such are the conditions of
> the problem. *Hic Rhodus, hic salta!* (I, 150ff.)

"Labor Power" As The Alleged
Source Of Exchange Value

The solution Marx finds herein is that there is one commodity whose value in use possesses the peculiar property
of being a source of exchange value. This commodity is
the capacity of labor, labor power. It is offered for sale
in the market under the twofold condition that the laborer
is personally free, for otherwise it would not be his labor
power only that would be for sale, but his whole person as
a slave; and that the laborer is destitute of "all the means
necessary for benefiting from his labor power," for otherwise he would prefer to produce on his own account and
to offer for sale his products rather than his labor power.
It is by trading in this commodity that the capitalist obtains the surplus value; and he does so in the following
way: The value of the commodity, "labor power," is regulated like any other commodity by the working time necessary for its reproduction; that is, in this case, by the
working time which is needed to create so much means of
subsistence as is required for the maintenance of the work-

---

[6] I gave at the time in another place (*History and Critique of
Interest Theories* [Volume I of Capital and Interest], p. 284ff.,
English translation by Libertarian Press, South Holland, Illinois,
U.S.A., 1959) an exhaustive account of this part of his doctrine. I
make use of this account now, with numerous abridgements, such as
the present purpose demands.

er. If, for example, a working time of six hours is required in a given society for the production of the necessary means of subsistence for one day, and, at the same time, as we will suppose, this working time is embodied in three shillings of money, then the labor power of one day can be bought for three shillings. If the capitalist has concluded this purchase, the value in use of the labor power belongs to him and he realizes it by causing the laborer to work for him. But if he made him work only so many hours a day as are embodied in the labor power itself, and as must have been paid for in the buying of the same, no surplus value would arise. For, according to the assumption, six hours of labor could not put into the products in which they are embodied a greater value than three shillings, and so much the capitalist has paid as wages. But this is not the way in which capitalists act. Even if they have bought the labor power for a price which only corresponds to six hours' working time, they yet make the laborer work the whole day for them. And now in the product made during this day there are incorporated more hours of labor than the capitalist was obliged to pay for. He has, therefore, a greater value than the wages he has paid, and the difference is "surplus value," which falls to the capitalist.

Marx's Example Of Alleged Exploitation Of Labor Power To Get Surplus Value

Let us take an example: Suppose that a worker can spin ten pounds of cotton into yarn in six hours; and suppose this cotton has required twenty hours of labor for its own production and possesses accordingly a value of ten shillings; and suppose, further, that during the six hours of spinning the spinner uses up so much of his tools as corresponds to the the labor of four hours and represents consequently a value of two shillings; then the total value of the means of production consumed in the spinning will amount to twelve shillings, corresponding to twenty-four hours' labor. In the spinning process the cotton "absorbs" another six hours of labor. Therefore the yarn that has been spun is, as a whole, the product of thirty hours of labor, and will have accordingly a value of fifteen shillings. On the supposition that the capitalist has made the hired laborer work only six hours in the day, the production of the yarn has cost him at least fifteen shillings: ten shillings for cotton, two shillings for wear and tear of tools, three shillings for wages of labor. Here there is no surplus value.

It is quite a different thing, however, if the capitalist makes the laborer work twelve hours a day. In twelve hours the laborer works up twenty pounds of cotton in which forty hours of labor have been previously embodied, and which are, therefore, worth twenty shillings. He further uses up in tools the product of eight hours' labor, of the value of four shillings. But during a day he adds to the raw material twelve hours' labor, that is, a new value of six shillings. And now the balance sheet stands as follows: The yarn produced during a day has cost in all sixty hours' labor, and has, therefore, a value of thirty shillings. The outlay of the capitalist amounted to twenty shillings for cotton, four shillings for wear and tear of tools, and three shillings for wages; in all, therefore, only twenty-seven shillings. There remains now a "surplus value" of three shillings.

Surplus value, therefore, according to Marx, is due to the fact that the capitalist makes the laborer work for him a part of the day without paying him for it. In the laborer's working day two portions may be distinguished. In the first part—the "necessary working time"—the worker produces the means necessary for his own support, or the value of those means; and for this part of his labor he receives an equivalent in wages. During the second part —the "surplus working time"—he is exploited, he produces "surplus value" without receiving any equivalent for it (I, 205ff.). "All surplus value is in substance the embodiment of unpaid working time" (I, 554).

Characteristic Marxian
Definitions Of Surplus Value

The following definitions of the amount of surplus value are very important and very characteristic of the Marxian system. The amount of surplus value may be brought into relation with various other amounts. The different proportions and proportionate numbers which arise out of this must be clearly distinguished.

Definitions Of Constant Capital
And Variable Capital; And Rate Of Surplus Value

First of all there are two elements to be distinguished in the capital which enables the capitalist to appropriate surplus values, each of which elements in relation to the origin of surplus value plays an entirely different rôle from the other. Really new surplus value can only be created by the living work which the capitalist gets the worker to perform. The value of the means of production which are used is maintained, and it reappears in a different form in the value of the product, but adds no surplus value. "That part of the capital, therefore, which is converted into the means of production, that is, into raw material, supplies, and equipment, does not alter the amount of its value in the process of production," for which reason Marx calls it "constant capital." "On the other hand, that part of capital which is converted into labor power does alter its value in the process of production. It reproduces its own equivalent and a surplus in addition," the surplus value. Therefore Marx calls it the "variable part of capital" or "variable capital" (I, 199). Now the proportion in which the surplus value stands to the variable part of capital provided (in which alone the surplus value "makes good its value"), Marx calls the *rate of surplus value*. It is identical with the proportion in which the surplus working time stands to the necessary working time, or the unpaid labor to the paid, and serves Marx, therefore, as the exact expression for the extent of exploitation for another's benefit (I, 207ff.). If, for instance, the working time necessary for the worker to produce the value of his day's wages of three shillings amounts to six hours, while the actual number of hours he works in the day amounts to twelve, so that during the second six hours, which is surplus working time, he produces another value of three shillings, which is surplus value, then the surplus value is exactly equal to the amount of variable capital paid in wages, and the rate of the surplus value is reckoned at 100%.

Definition Of Rate Of Profit

Totally different from this is the rate of profit. The capitalist calculates the surplus value, which he appropriates, not only upon the variable capital but upon the total amount of capital employed. For instance, if the constant capital be £410, the variable capital £90, and the surplus value also £90, the rate of surplus value will be, as in the case just given, 100%, but the rate of profit only 18%, that is, £90 profit on an invested capital of £500.

It is evident, further, that one and the same rate of surplus value can and must present itself in very different rates of profit according to the composition of the capital concerned: the greater the variable and the less the constant capital employed (which latter does not contribute to the formation of surplus value, but increases the fund in relation to which the surplus value, determined only by the variable part of capital, is reckoned as profit), the higher will be the rate of profit. For example, if (although this is almost a practical impossibility) the constant capital is nothing and the variable capital is £50, and if the surplus value, on the assumption just made, amounts to 100%, the surplus value acquired amounts also to £50; and as this is reckoned on a total capital of only £50, the rate of profit would in this case also be 100%. If, on the other hand, the total capital is composed of constant and variable capital in the proportion of 4 to 1; or, in other words, if to a variable capital of £50 is added a constant capital of £200, the surplus value of £50, formed by the surplus value rate of 100%, has to be distributed on a capital of £250, and on this it represents only a profit rate of 20%. Finally, if the capital were composed in the proportions of 9 to 1, that is, £450 of constant to £50 of variable capital, a surplus value of £50 would be calculated on a total capital of £500, and the rate of profit would be only 10%.

Now this leads to an extremely interesting and important result, in pursuing which we are led to an entirely new stage of the Marxian system, the most important new feature which the third volume contains.

CHAPTER II
The Theory Of The Average Rate Of Profit And Of The Price Of Production

"Organic Composition" Of Capital Differs By Industries; Rate Of Profit, Therefore, Should Vary

That result is as follows: The "organic composition" (III, 124) of the capital is for technical reasons necessarily different in the different "spheres of production." In various industries which demand very different technical manipulations, the quantity of raw material worked up on one working day is very different; or, even, when the manipulations are the same and the quantity of raw material worked up is nearly equal, the value of that material may differ very much; as, for instance, in the case of copper and iron as raw materials of the metal industry; or finally the amount and value of the whole industrial apparatus, tools, and machinery, which are available to each worker employed, may be different. All these elements of difference when they do not exactly balance each other, as they seldom do, create in the different branches of production a different proportion between the constant capital invested in the means of production and the variable capital expended in the purchase of labor. Every branch of economic production needs consequently a special, a peculiar, "organic composition" for the capital invested in it. According to the preceding argument, therefore, given an equal rate of surplus value, every branch of production must show a different, a special rate of profit, on the condition certainly, which Marx has hitherto always assumed, that commodities exchange with each other "according to their values," or in proportion to the work embodied in them.

The Marxian Contradiction
Of The Facts, Or The Paradox

And here Marx arrives at the famous rock of offense in his theory, so hard to steer past that it has formed the most important point of dispute in the Marxian literature of the last ten years. His theory demands that capitals of equal amount, but of dissimilar organic composition, should exhibit different profits. The real world, however, most plainly shows that it is governed by the law that capitals of equal amount, without regard to possible differences of organic composition, yield equal profits. We will let Marx explain this contradiction in his own words.

> We have thus shown that in different branches of industry varying rates of profit are obtained according to the differences in the organic composition of the capitals, and also, within given limits, according to their periods of turnover; and that, therefore, even with equal rates of surplus value, there is a law (or general tendency), *although only for capitals possessing the same organic composition*—the same periods of turnover being assumed—that the profits are in proportion to the amounts of the capitals, and that therefore equal amounts of capital yield in equal periods of time equal amounts of profit. The argument rests on the basis which has hitherto generally been the basis of our reasoning, *that commodities are sold according to their values.* On the other hand, there is no doubt that, in reality, not reckoning unessential, accidental, and self-compensating differences, the difference in the average rate of profit for different branches of industry *does not exist* and could not exist without upsetting the whole system of capitalist production. *It appears therefore that here the theory of value is irreconcilable with the actual movement of things,* irreconcilable with the actual phenomena of production, and that, on this account, the attempt to understand the latter must be given up (III, 131).

How does Marx himself try to solve this contradiction?

To speak plainly, his solution is obtained at the cost of the assumption from which Marx has hitherto started, namely, *that commodities exchange according to their values.* This assumption Marx now simply drops. Later on we shall form our critical judgment of the effect of this abandonment on the Marxian system. Meanwhile I resume my summary of the Marxian argument, and give one of the tabular examples which Marx brings forward in support of his view.

Marxian Examples Of Rates Of Profit

In this example he compares five different spheres of production, in each of which the capital employed is of different organic composition, and in making his comparison he keeps at first to the assumption which has been hitherto made, that commodities exchange according to their values. For the clear understanding of the following table, which gives the results of this assumption, it must be remarked that C denotes constant capital and V variable, and in order to do justice to the actual diversities of daily life, let us assume (with Marx) that the constant capitals employed are "worn out" in different lengths of time, so that only a portion, and that an unequal portion, of the constant capital in the different spheres of production, is used up in the year. Naturally only the used-up portion of constant capital—*the "used-up C"*—goes into the value of the product, while the whole *"employed C"* is taken into account in reckoning the rate of profit.

	Capitals	Surplus Value Rate	Surplus Value	Profit Rate	Used-up C	Value of the Commodities
I.	80C + 20V	100%	20	20%	50	90
II.	70C + 30V	100	30	30	51	111
III.	60C + 40V	100	40	40	51	131
IV.	85C + 15V	100	15	15	40	70
V.	95C + 5V	100	5	5	10	20

We see that this table shows in the different spheres of production where the exploitation of labor has been the same, very different rates of profit, corresponding to the different organic composition of the capitals. But we can also look at the same facts and data from another point of view.

The aggregate sum of the capital employed in the five spheres is = 500; the aggregate sum of the surplus value produced = 110; and the aggregate value of the commodities produced = 610.* If we

*Present Publisher's Note: In this quotation Böhm-Bawerk used data from a table appearing on page 133 in Marx's *Das Kapital* (Volume III, Hamburg, 1894) which assumed that the whole of C would be consumed. Marx then went on to write that that was hardly realistic, and in a new table on page 135 he assumed varying percentages of consumption for C. His purpose was to show that that difference in the calculation would not change his conclusion. Böhm-Bawerk, therefore, combined part of Marx's first table with that part of Marx's second table which was more realistic in regard to the consumption of C. In Marx's second table (which Böhm-Bawerk used in part), the aggregate value of commodities is 422, which would be the appropriate figure in the table and text shown here; but Böhm-Bawerk did not change the *text* figure from 610 to 422.

consider the 500 as a single capital of which I to V form only different parts (just as in a cotton factory in the different departments, in carding-room, roving-room, spinning-room, and weaving-room, a different proportion of variable and constant capital exists and the average proportion must be calculated for the whole factory), then in the first place the average composition of the capital of 500 would be $500 = 390C + 110V$, or 78% C + 22% V. Taking each of the capitals of 100 as being one-fifth of the aggregate capital, its composition would be this average one of 78% C + 22% V; and likewise to every 100 would accrue as average surplus value 22%; therefore the average rate of profit would be 22% (III, 133-4).

Now at what price must the separate commodities be sold in order that each of the five portions of capital should actually obtain this average rate of profit? The following table shows this. In it has been inserted the heading "Cost Price," by which Marx understands that part of the value of commodities which makes good to the capitalists the price of the consumed means of production and the price of the labor power employed, but yet does not contain any surplus value or profit, so that its amount is equal to V + used-up C.

Capitals	Surplus value	Used-up C	Value of the Commodities	Cost Price of the Commodities	Price of the Commodities	Profit rate	Deviation of the price from the value
1. $80C + 20V$	20	50	90	70	92	22%	+ 2
II. $70C + 30V$	30	51	111	81	103	22	− 8
III. $60C + 40V$	40	51	131	91	113	22	−18
IV. $85C + 15V$	15	40	70	55	77	22	+ 7
V. $95C + 5V$	5	10	20	15	37	22	+17

Taken together [comments Marx on the results of this table], the commodities are sold $2 + 7 + 17 = 26$ over their value, and $8 + 18$ under their value, so that the variations in price mutually cancel each other, either through an equal division of the surplus value or by cutting down the average profit of 22% on the invested capital to the respective cost prices of the commodities, I to V; in the same proportion *in which one part of the commodities is sold over its value another part will be sold under its value. And now their sale at such prices makes it possible that the rate of profit for I to V be equal,* 22%, without regard to the different organic composition of the capital I to V (III, 135).

Marx goes on to say that all this is not a mere hypothetical assumption, but absolute fact. The operating agent is *competition.* It is true that owing to the different organic composition of the capitals invested in various branches of production

> the rates of profit which obtain in these different branches *are originally very different.*
>
> [But] these different rates of profit are reduced by competition to a common rate which is the average of all these different rates. The profit corresponding to this common rate, which falls to a given amount of capital, whatever its organic composition may be, is called *average profit.* That price of a commodity which is equal to its cost price plus its share of the yearly average profit of the capital employed (not merely that consumed) in its production (regard being had to the quickness or slowness of turnover) is its *price of production* (III, 136).*

Identity Of Marxian Definition Of Price Of Production With Definitions Of Smith And Ricardo

This is in fact identical with Adam Smith's natural price, with Ricardo's price of production, and with the *prix nécessaire* of the physiocrats (III, 178). And the actual exchange relation of the separate commodities is *no longer determined by their values but by their prices of production;* or as Marx likes to put it "the values change into prices of production" (III, 176). Value and price of production are only exceptionally and accidentally coincident, namely, in those commodities which are produced by the aid of a capital, the organic composition of which chances to coincide exactly with the *average* composition of the whole social capital. In all other cases value and price of production necessarily and in principle part company.

> [According to Marx we call] capitals which contain a greater percentage of constant, and therefore a smaller percentage of variable capital than the social average capital, capitals of *higher* composition; and contrariwise those capitals in which the constant capital fills a relatively smaller, and the variable a relatively larger, space than in the social average capital are called capitals of *lower* composition.

So in all those commodities which have been created by the aid of capital of "higher" composition than the average composition the price of production will be *above* their value, and in the opposite case it will be *under* their value.

*Warning to readers by present publisher: the exact meaning of this term must be thoroughly understood and kept in mind, in all that follows, because the term is used repeatedly. For the most extensive definition, see page 247.

Or, commodities of the first kind will be necessarily and regularly sold *over* their value and commodities of the second kind *under* their value (III, 142ff. and often elsewhere).

Relation Of Individual Capitalists To Total Surplus Value

The relation of the individual capitalists to the total surplus value created and appropriated in the whole society is finally illustrated in the following manner:

> Although the capitalists of the different spheres of production in selling their commodities get back the value of the capital used up in the production of these commodities, they do not thereby recover the *surplus value,* and therefore profit, created in *their own particular spheres,* by the production of these commodities, but only so much surplus value, and therefore profit as falls by an equal division to every aliquot part of the whole capital, from the total surplus value or total profit which the entire capital of society has created in a given time, in all the spheres of production taken together. Every 100 of invested capital, whatever its composition, secures in every year, or other period of time, the profit which, for this period of time, falls due to a 100 as a given part of the total capital. So far as profit is concerned, the different capitalists are in the position of simple members of a joint stock company, in which the profits are divided into equal shares on every 100, and therefore for the different capitalists vary only according to the amount of capital invested by each in the common undertaking, according to the relative extent of his participation in the common business, according to the number of his shares (III, 136ff.).

Total profit and total surplus value are identical amounts (III, 151, 152). And the average profit is nothing else "than the total amount of surplus value divided among the amounts of capital in every sphere of production in proportion to their quantities" (III, 153).

An important consequence arising from this is that the profit which the individual capitalist draws is clearly shown not only to arise from the work performed by himself (III, 149), but often to proceed for the most part, and sometimes entirely (for example, in the case of mercantile capital), from laborers with whom the capitalist concerned has no connection whatever. Marx, in conclusion, puts and answers one more question, which he regards as the specially difficult question, namely, in what manner "does this adjustment of profits to a common rate of profit take place, since it is evidently a result and not a starting-point"?

Marx's Argument That In A Capitalist Society "Values" Are Changed Into "Prices Of Production"

He first of all puts forward the view that in a condition of society in which the capitalist system is not yet dominant, and in which, therefore the laborers themselves are in possession of the necessary means of production, commodities are actually exchanged according to their real value, and the rates of profit could *not* therefore be equalized. But as the laborers could always obtain and keep for themselves an equal surplus value for an equal working time, that is, an equal value over and above their necessary wants —the actually existing difference in the profit rate would be "a matter of indifference, just as today it is a matter of indifference to the hired laborer by what rate of profit the amount of surplus value squeezed out of him is represented" (III, 155). Now as such conditions of life in which the means of production belong to the worker are historically the earlier and are found in the old as well as in the modern world, with peasant proprietors, for instance, and artisans, Marx thinks he is entitled to assert that it is "quite in accordance with facts to regard the values of commodities as, not only theoretically but also historically, prior to the prices of production" (III, 156).

In societies organized on the capitalist system, however, this changing of values into prices of production and the equalization of the rates of profit which follows, certainly do take place. There are some long preliminary discussions, in which Marx treats of the formation of market value and market price with special reference to the production of separate parts of commodities produced for sale under conditions of varying advantage. And then he expresses himself as follows very clearly and concisely on the motive forces of this process of equalization and on its mode of action:

> If commodities are . . . sold according to their values . . . very different rates of profit are obtained. . . . Capital withdraws itself, however, from a sphere with a low rate of profit, and throws itself into another which yields a higher profit. By this continual interchange, or, in a word, by its apportionment between the different spheres, as the rate of profit sinks here and rises there, such a relation of supply to demand is created as to make the average profit in the different spheres of production the same, and thus values are changed into prices of production (III, 175-6).[7]

[7] W. Sombart in the classical, clear, and comprehensive account of the concluding volume of the Marxian system which he lately

CHAPTER III

The Question Of The Contradiction

Marx In His Third Volume Contradicts His Proposition In His First Volume

Many years ago, long before the above-mentioned prize essays on the compatibility of an equal average rate of profit with the Marxian law of value had appeared, the present writer had expressed his opinion on this subject in the following words:

> There are two possible alternatives. The first alternative is that a permanent system of exchange is really established whereby goods are exchanged at values which are in proportion to the labor that the respective goods represent, and whereby, furthermore, the magnitude of the surplus proceeds to be derived from production is really determined by the quantity of labor expended. If that alternative obtains, then any equalization of the ratio of surplus proceeds to capital is an impossibility. The second alternative is that such an equalization does take place. If that alternative obtains, then products cannot possibly continue to be exchanged at values which are in proportion to the labor they represent . . . [8]

From the Marxian camp the actual incompatibility of these two propositions was first acknowledged a few years ago by Conrad Schmidt.[9] Now we have the authoritative confirmation of the master himself. He has stated concisely and precisely that an equal rate of profit is only pos-

gave in the *Archiv für Soziale Gesetzgebung* (Vol. VII, part 4, pp. 555ff.), also regards the passages quoted in the text as those which contain the strict answer to the problem given (*Ibid.*, p. 564). We shall by and by have to deal more at large with this important and ingenious, but critically, I think, unsatisfactory essay.

[8] *History and Critique of Interest Theories* (Volume I of CAPITAL AND INTEREST), p. 277.

[9] See his work, *Die Durchshnittsprofitrate auf Grundlage des Marxschen Wertgesetzes*, Stuttgart, 1889, especially section 13; and my review of this work in the *Tübinger Zeitschrift fur die gesamte Staatswissenschaft*, 1890, pp. 590ff.

sible when the conditions of sale are such that some commodities are sold above their value, and others under their
value, and thus are not exchanged in proportion to the labor embodied in them. And neither has he left us in doubt
as to which of the two irreconcilable propositions conforms
in his opinion to the actual facts. He teaches, with a clearness and directness which merit our gratitude, that it is
the equalization of the gains of capital. And he even goes
so far as to say, with the same directness and clearness,
that the several commodities do not actually exchange with
each other in proportion to the labor they contain, but that
they exchange in that varying proportion to the labor, which
is rendered necessary by the equalization of the gains of
capital.

In what relation does this doctrine of the third volume stand to the celebrated law of value of the first volume?
Does it contain the solution of the seeming contradiction
looked for with so much anxiety? Does it prove "how not
only without contradicting the law of value, but even by
virtue of it, an equal average rate of profit can and must
be created"? Does it not rather contain the exact opposite
of such a proof, namely, the statement of an actual irreconcilable contradiction, and does it not prove that the equal
average rate of profit can only manifest itself if, and because, the alleged law of value does not hold good?

I do not think that anyone who examines the matter
impartially and soberly can remain long in doubt. In the
first volume it was maintained, with the greatest emphasis,
that all value is based on labor and labor alone, and that
values of commodities were in proportion to the working
time necessary for their production. These propositions
were deduced and distilled directly and exclusively from
the exchange relations of commodities in which they were
"immanent." We were directed "to start from the exchange
value, and exchange relation of commodities, in order to
come upon the track of the value concealed in them" (I, 23).
The value was declared to be "the common factor which
appears in the exchange relation of commodities" (I, 13).
We were told, in the form and with the emphasis of a
stringent syllogistic conclusion, allowing of no exception,
that to set down two commodities as equivalents in exchange
implied that "a common factor *of the same magnitude*"
existed in both, to which each of the two "*must* be reducible" (I, 11). Apart, therefore, from temporary and occasional variations which "appear to be a breach of the
law of the exchange of commodities" (I, 142), commodities which embody the same amount of labor *must* on prin-

ciple, in the long run, exchange for each other. And now in the third volume we are told briefly and drily that what, according to the teaching of the first volume *must* be, is not and never can be; that individual commodities do and must exchange with each other in a proportion different from that of the labor incorporated in them, and this not accidentally and temporarily, but of necessity and permanently.

Others Agree On The Illogic And Inconsistency Of The Marxian System

I cannot help myself; I see here no explanation and reconciliation of a contradiction, but the bare contradiction itself. Marx's third volume contradicts the first. The theory of the average rate of profit and of the prices of production cannot be reconciled with his theory of value. This is the impression which must, I believe, be received by every logical thinker. And it seems to have been very generally accepted. Loria, in his lively and picturesque style, states that he feels himself forced to the "harsh but just judgment" that Marx "instead of a solution has presented a mystification." He sees in the publication of the third volume "the Russian campaign" of the Marxian system, its "complete theoretic bankruptcy," a "scientific suicide," the "most explicit surrender of his own teaching" (*l'abdicazione più esplicita alla dottrina stessa*), and the "full and complete adherence to the most orthodox doctrine of the hated economists." [10]

And even a man who is so close to the Marxian system as Werner Sombart, says that a "general headshaking" best represents the probable effect produced on most readers by the third volume.

> Most of them [he says], will not be inclined to regard 'the solution' of 'the puzzle of the average rate of profit ' as a 'solution'; they will think that the knot has been cut, and by no means untied. For, when suddenly out of the depths emerges a 'quite ordinary' theory of cost of production, it means that the celebrated doctrine of value has come to grief. For, if I have in the end to explain the profits by the cost of production, wherefore the whole cumbrous apparatus of the theories of value and surplus value? [11]

[10] "L'opera postuma di Carlo Marx," *Nuova Antologia*, February 1, 1895, pp. 20, 22, 23.

[11] "Zur Kritik des ökonomischen Systems von Karl Marx," in the *Archiv für sociale Gesetzgebung*, Vol. VII, part 4, pp. 571ff.

Sombart certainly reserves to himself another judgment. He attempts to save the theory in a way of his own, in which, however, so much of it is thrown overboard that it seems to me very doubtful if his efforts have earned the gratitude of any person concerned in the matter. I shall by and by more closely examine this at all events interesting and instructive attempt. But, before the posthumous apologist, we must give the master himself the careful and attentive hearing which so important a subject deserves.

Marx's Inconsequent Observations And Explanations

Marx himself must, of course, have foreseen that his solution would incur the reproach of being no solution at all, but a surrender of his law of value. To this prevision is evidently due an anticipatory self-defense which, if not in form yet in point of fact, is found in the Marxian system; for Marx does not omit to interpolate in numerous places the express declaration that, in spite of exchange relations being directly governed by prices of production, which differ from the values, all is nevertheless moving within the lines of the law of value and this law, "in the last resort" at least, governs prices. He tries to make this view plausible by several inconsequent observations and explanations. On this subject he does not use his customary method of a formal close line of reasoning, but gives only a series of running, incidental remarks which contain different arguments, or turns of expression which may be interpreted as such. In this case it is impossible to judge on which of these arguments Marx himself intended to place the greatest weight, or what was his conception of the reciprocal relations of these dissimilar arguments. However that may be, we must, in justice to the master as well as to our own critical problem, give each of these arguments the closest attention and impartial consideration.

Marx's Four Arguments

The running remarks appear to me to contain the following four arguments in favor of a partly or wholly permanent validity of the law of value.

First argument: Even if the *separate* commodities are being sold either above or below their values, these reciprocal fluctuations cancel each other, and in the community itself—taking into account all the branches of production—the *total of the prices of production* of the commodities produced still remains *equal to the sum of their values* (III, 138).

Second argument: The law of value governs the *movement of prices*, since the diminution or increase of the requisite working time makes the prices of production rise or fall (III, 158; similarly III, 156).

Third argument: The law of value, Marx affirms, governs with undiminished authority the exchange of commodities in *certain "primary" stages*, in which the change of values into prices of production has not yet been accomplished.

Fourth argument: In a complicated economic system the law of value regulates the prices of production at least *indirectly and in the last resort*, since the total value of the commodities, determined by the law of value, determines the total surplus value. The latter, however, regulates the amount of the average profit, and therefore the general rate of profit (III, 159).

Let us test these arguments, each one on its own merits.

First Argument

It is admitted by Marx that separate commodities exchange with each other either over or under their value according as the share of constant capital employed in their production is above or below the average. Stress is, however, laid on the fact that these individual deviations which take place in opposite directions compensate or cancel each other, so that the sum total of all prices paid corresponds exactly with the sum of all values.

> In the same proportion in which one part of the commodities is sold above its value another part will be sold under its value (III, 135). The aggregate price of the commodities I to V [in the table given by Marx as an example] would therefore be equal to their aggregate values, and would therefore be, in fact, a money expression of the aggregate amount of labor, both past and recent, contained in the commodities I to V. And in this way in the community itself—when we regard the total of all the branches of production—the sum of the prices of production of the commodities manufactured is equal to the sum of their values (III, 138).

From this, finally, the argument is more or less clearly deduced that at any rate for the sum of all commodities, or for the community as a whole, the law of value maintains its validity.

Meanwhile it resolves itself into this—that by as much as there is too much surplus value in one commodity there is too little in another, and therefore the *deviations from value* which lurk in the prices of production *reciprocally cancel each other.* In capitalistic production as a whole *'the general law maintains itself as the governing tendency,'* only in a very complex and approximate manner, as the constantly changing average of perpetual fluctuations (III, 140).

This argument is not new in Marxian literature. In similar circumstances it was maintained, a few years ago, by Konrad Schmidt, with great emphasis, and perhaps with even greater clearness of principle than now by Marx himself. In his attempt to solve the riddle of the average rate of profit Schmidt also, while he employed a different line of argument from Marx, arrived at the conclusion that separate commodities *cannot* exchange with each other in proportion to the labor attaching to them. He too was obliged to ask the question whether, in face of this fact, the validity of Marx's law of value could any longer be maintained, and he supported his affirmative opinion on the very argument that has just been given. [12]

Rebuttal Of Marx's First Argument

I hold the argument to be absolutely untenable. I maintained this at the time against Konrad Schmidt, and I have no occasion today in relation to Marx himself to make any alteration in the reasoning on which I founded my opinion then. I may content myself now with simply repeating it word for word. In opposing Konrad Schmidt, I asked how much or how little of the celebrated law of value remained after so much had practically been given up, and then continued:

> That not much remains will be best shown by the efforts which the author makes to prove that, in spite of everything, the law of value maintains its validity. After he has admitted that the actual prices of commodities differ from their values, he remarks that this divergence only relates to those prices obtained by *separate commodities,* and that it disappears as soon as one considers the *sum* of all separate commodities, the yearly national product, and that the total price which is paid for the whole national product taken together does certainly coincide entirely with the amount of value actually embodied in it (p. 51). I do not know

[12] See text and footnote, p. 226, especially section 13.

whether I shall be able to show sufficiently the bearings of this statement, but I shall at least attempt to indicate them.

What then, we ask, is the chief object of the 'law of value'? It is nothing else than the elucidation of the exchange relations of commodities as they actually appear to us. We wish to know, for instance, why a coat should be worth as much in exchange as twenty yards of linen, and ten pounds of tea as much as half a ton of iron, etc. It is plain that Marx himself so conceives the explanatory object of the law of value. There can clearly only be a question of an exchange *relation* between different separate commodities *among each other*. As soon, however, as one looks at all commodities *as a whole* and sums up the prices, one must studiously and of necessity avoid looking at the relations existing inside of this whole. The internal relative differences of price do compensate each other in the sum total. For instance, what the tea is worth more than the iron, the iron is worth less than the tea and vice versa. In any case, when we ask for information regarding the exchange of commodities in political economy it is no answer to our question to be told, 'the total price which they bring when taken altogether,' any more than if, on asking by how many fewer minutes the winner in a prize race had covered the course than his competitor, we were to be told that all the competitors together had taken twenty-five minutes and thirteen seconds.

The state of the case is this: To the question of the problem of value the followers of Marx reply first with their law of value, that is, that commodities exchange in proportion to the working time incorporated in them. Then they—covertly or openly—revoke this answer in its relation to the domain of the exchange of separate commodities, the one domain in which the problem has any meaning, and maintain it in full force only for the whole aggregate national product, for a domain therefore in which the problem, being without object, could not have been put at all. As an answer to the strict question of the problem of value the law of value is avowedly contradicted by the facts, and in the only application in which it is not contradicted by them it is no longer an answer to the question which demanded a solution, but could at best only be an answer to some other question.

It is, however, not even an answer to another question; it is no answer at all; it is simple tautology. For, as every economist knows, commodities do eventually exchange with commodities—when one penetrates the disguises due to the use of money. Every commodity which comes into exchange is at one and the same time a commodity and the price of what is given in exchange for it. The aggregate of commodities therefore is identical with the aggregate of the prices paid for them; or, the price of the whole national product is nothing else than the national product itself. Under these circumstances, therefore, it is quite true that the total price paid for the entire national product coincides exactly with the total amount of value or labor incorporated in it. But this tautological declaration denotes no increase of true knowledge, neither does it serve as a special test of the correctness of the alleged law that commodities exchange in proportion to the labor embodied in them. For in this manner one might as well, or rather as unjustly, verify any other law one pleased —the law, for instance, that commodities exchange according to the measure of their specific gravity. For if certainly as a 'separate ware' one pound of gold does not exchange with one pound of iron, but with 40,000 pounds of iron; still, the *total price* for one pound of gold and 40,000 pounds of iron *taken together* is nothing more and nothing less than 40,000 pounds of iron and one pound of gold. The total weight, therefore, in the total price— 40,001 pounds—corresponds exactly to the like total weight of 40,001 pounds incorporated in the whole of the commodities. Is weight consequently the true standard by which the exchange relation of commodities is determined?

How Marx Confused The Issue Even Worse Than Schmidt

I have nothing to omit and nothing to add to this judgment in applying it now to Marx himself, except perhaps that in advancing the argument which has just been under criticism Marx is guilty of an additional error, which cannot be charged against Schmidt. For, in the passage just quoted from page 140 of the third volume, Marx seeks, by a general dictum concerning the way in which the law of value operates, to gain approval for the idea that a certain real authority may still be ascribed to it, even if it does not rule in separate cases. After saying that the "deviations" from value, which are found in the prices of production, cancel each other, he adds the remark that "in capitalistic production as a whole the general law maintains itself as the governing tendency, for the most part only in a very complex and approximate manner as the constantly changing *average of perpetual fluctuations*."

Here Marx confounds two very different things: an *average of fluctuations*, and an *average between permanently and fundamentally unequal quantities*. He is so far quite right, that many a general law holds good solely because an average resulting from constant fluctuations coincides with the rule declared by the law. Every economist knows such laws. Take, for example, the law that prices equal costs of production—that apart from special reasons for inequality there is a tendency for wages in different branches of industry, and for profits of capital in different branches of production, to come to a level, and every economist is inclined to acknowledge these laws as "laws," although perhaps there may be no absolutely exact agreement with them in any single case; and therefore even the power to refer to a mode of action operating on the whole, and on the average, has a strongly captivating influence.

But the case in favor of which Marx uses this captivating reference is of quite a different kind. In the case of prices of production which deviate from the "values," it is not a question of fluctuations, but of necessary and permanent divergences.

Two commodities, A and B, which contain the same amount of labor, but have been produced by capitals of different organic composition, do not fluctuate round the same average point, say, for example, the average of fifty shillings; but each of them assumes permanently a different level of price: for instance, the commodity A, in the production of which little constant capital, demanding but little interest, has been employed, the price level of forty shillings; and the commodity B, which has much constant capital to pay interest on, the price level of sixty shillings, allowance being made for fluctuation round each of these deviating levels. If we had only to deal with fluctuations round one and the same level, so that the commodity A might stand at one moment at forty-eight shillings and the commodity B at fifty-two shillings, and at another moment the case were reversed, and the commodity A stood at fifty-two shillings and the commodity B only reached forty-eight, then we might indeed say that in the average the price of both of these commodities was the same, and in such a state of things, if it were seen to obtain universally, one might find, in spite of the fluctuations, a verification of the "law" that commodities embodying the same amount of labor exchange on an equal footing.

When, however, of two commodities in which the same amount of labor is incorporated, one permanently and regularly maintains a price of forty shillings and the other as permanently and regularly the price of sixty shillings, a mathematician may indeed strike an average of fifty shillings between the two; but such an average has an entirely different meaning, or, to be more accurate, has no meaning at all with regard to our law. A mathematical average may always be struck between the most unequal quantities, and when it has once been struck the deviations from it on either side always "mutually cancel each other" according to their amount; by the same amount exactly by which the one exceeds the average the other must of necessity fall short. But it is evident that necessary and permanent differences of prices in commodities of the same cost in labor, but of unequal composition as regards capital, cannot by such playing with "average" and "deviations that cancel each other" be turned into a confirmation of the alleged law of value instead of a refutation. We might just as well try in this way to prove the proposition that animals of all kinds, elephants and May flies included, have the same length of life; for while it is true that elephants live on an average one hundred years and May flies only a single day, yet between these two quantities we can strike an average of fifty years. By as much time as the elephants live longer than the flies, the flies live shorter than the elephants. The deviations from this average "mutually cancel each other," and consequently on the whole and on the average the law that all kinds of animals have the same length of life is established!

Let us proceed.

Second Argument

In various parts of the third volume Marx claims for the law of value that it "governs the movement of prices," and he considers that this is proved by the fact that where the working time necessary for the production of the commodities decreases, there also prices fall; and that where it increases prices also rise, other circumstances remaining equal. [13]

Rebuttal Of Marx's Second Argument

This conclusion also rests on an error of logic so obvious that one wonders Marx did not perceive it himself. That in the case of "other circumstances remaining equal"

[13] Vol. III, 156; and quite similarly in the passage already quoted, III, 158.

prices rise and fall according to the amount of labor expended proves clearly neither more nor less than that labor is one factor in determining prices. It proves, therefore, a fact upon which all the world is agreed, an opinion not peculiar to Marx, but one acknowledged and taught by the classical and "vulgar economists." But by his law of value Marx had asserted much more. He had asserted that, barring occasional and momentary fluctuations of demand and supply, the labor expended was the sole factor which governed the exchange relations of commodities. Evidently it could only be maintained that *this* law governs the movement of prices if a permanent alteration in prices could not be produced or promoted by any other cause than the alteration in the amount of working time. This, however, Marx does not and cannot maintain; for it is among the results of his own teaching that an alteration in prices must occur when, for instance, the expenditure of labor remains the same, but when, owing to such circumstances as the shortening of the processes of production, the organic composition of the capital is changed. By the side of this proposition of Marx we might with equal justification place the other proposition, that prices rise or fall when, other conditions remaining equal, the length of time during which the capital is invested increases or decreases. If it is impossible to prove by the latter proposition that the length of time during which the capital is invested is the sole factor that governs exchange relations, it is equally impossible to regard the fact that alterations in the amounts of the labor expended affect the movements of prices as a confirmation of the alleged law that labor alone governs the exchange relations.

Third Argument

This argument has not been developed with precision and clearness by Marx, but the substance of it has been woven into those processes of reasoning, the object of which was the elucidation of the "truly difficult question," "how the adjustment of the profits to the general rate of profit takes place" (III, 153ff.).

The kernel of the argument is most easily extracted in the following way: Marx affirms, and must affirm, that "the rates of profits are originally very different" (III, 136), and that their adjustment to a general rate of profits is primarily "a result, and cannot be a starting point" (III, 153). This thesis further contains the claim that there exist certain "primitive" conditions in which the change of values into production prices, which leads to the adjustment of the rates of profit, has not yet taken place, and which therefore are still under the complete and literal dominion of the law of value. A certain area is consequently claimed for this law in which its authority is perfectly absolute.

Let us inquire more closely what this area is, and see what arguments Marx adduces to prove that the exchange relations in it are actually determined by the labor incorporated in the commodities.

According to Marx the adjustment of the rate of profit is dependent on two assumptions: firstly, on a capitalistic system of production being in operation (III, 154); and secondly, on the levelling influence of *competition* being in effect (III, 136, 151, 159, 175, 176). We must, therefore, logically look for the "primitive conditions" under which the pure regime of the law of value prevails, where one or other of these assumed conditions does not exist (or, of course, where both are absent).

Marx's Argument That Prices Are Determined By Their Values In Pre-Capitalist Production

On the first of these cases Marx has himself spoken very fully. By a very detailed account of the processes which obtain in a condition of society where capitalistic production does not yet prevail, but "where the means of production belong to the worker," he shows the prices of commodities in this stage to be exclusively determined by their values. In order to enable the reader to judge impartially how far this account is really convincing, I must give the full text of it:

> The salient point will be best shown in the following way: Suppose the workers themselves to possess each his own means of production, and to exchange their commodities with each other. These commodities would not then be the product of capital. The value of the tools and raw material employed in the different branches of labor would be different according to the special nature of the work; and also, apart from inequality of value in the means of production employed, different amounts of these means would be required for given amounts of labor, according as one commodity could be finished in an hour and another only in a day, etc.

> Let us suppose, further, that these laborers work the same time, on an average, allowing for the adjustments which result from differences of intensity, etc., in work. Of any two workers, then, both

would, firstly, in the commodities which represent
the product of their day's labor, have replaced
their outlays, that is, the cost prices of the consumed means of production. These would differ according to the technical nature of their branches
of industry. Secondly, both would have created the
same amount of new value, that is, the value of the
day's labor added to the means of production. This
would contain their wages plus the surplus value,
the surplus work above their necessary wants, of
which the result, however, would belong to themselves. *If we express ourselves in capitalistic
terms, both receive the same wages plus the same
profit*, but also the value, represented, for instance,
by the product of a working day of ten hours. But
in the first place the values of their commodities
would be different. In commodity I, for example,
there would be a larger share of value for the expended means of production than in commodity II.
The rates of profit also would be very different for
I and II, if we here consider as rates of profit the
proportion of the surplus value to the total value
of the employed means of production. The means
of subsistence which I and II consume daily during the process of production, and which represent the wages of labor, form here that part of the
advanced means of production which we usually
call variable capital. But the *surplus value would
be, for the same working time*, the same for I and
II; or, to go more closely into the matter, as I and
II, each, receive the value of the product of one
day's work, they receive, after deducting the value of the advanced 'constant' elements, equal
values, one part of which may be looked upon as
compensation for the means of subsistence consumed during the production, and the other as
surplus value—value over and above this. If I has
had more outlay it is made up to him by the greater value of his commodity, which replaces this
'constant' part, and he has consequently a larger
part of the total value to exchange back into the
material elements of this constant part; while if
II obtains less he has, on the other hand, the less
to exchange back. *Differences in rates of profit
would therefore, under this assumption, be a matter of indifference*, just as it is today a matter of
indifference to the wage earner by what rate of
profit the amount of surplus value derived from
him is represented, and just as in international
commerce the difference in the rates of profit in
the different nations is a matter of indifference for
the exchange of their commodities (III, 154ff.).

And now Marx passes at once from the hypothetical style of "supposition" with its subjunctive moods to a series of quite positive conclusions.

The exchange of commodities at their values, or approximately at their values, demands, *therefore,* a much lower stage of development than the exchange into prices of production, [and] it is, therefore, altogether in keeping with fact to regard the values as not only theoretically but *historically* prior to the prices of production. It holds good for circumstances where the means of production belong to the worker, and these circumstances are found *in the old and in the modern world,* in the cases of peasants who own land and work it themselves, and in the case of artisans (III, 155, 156).

Rebuttal Of Marx's Third Argument

What are we to think of this reasoning? I beg the reader above everything to notice carefully that the hypothetical part describes very consistently how exchange would present itself in those primitive conditions of society *if* everything took place according to the Marxian law of value; but that this description contains no shadow of proof, or even of an attempt at proof, that under the given assumptions things must so take place. Marx relates, "supposes," asserts, but he gives no word of proof. He consequently makes a bold, not to say naïve jump, when he proclaims as an ascertained result (as though he had successfully worked out a line of argument) that it is, *therefore,* quite consistent with facts to regard values, historically also, as prior to prices of production. As a matter of fact it is beyond question that Marx has not proved by his "supposition" the historical existence of such a condition. He has only hypothetically deduced it from his theory; and as to the credibility of that hypothesis we must, of course, be free to form our own judgment.

As a fact, whether we regard it from within or from without, the gravest doubts arise as to its credibility. It is inherently improbable, and so far as there can be a question here of proof by experience, even experience is against it.

Marx's Third Argument Involves An Assumption Altogether Improbable

It is inherently altogether improbable. For it requires that it should be a matter of complete indifference to the producers at what time they receive the reward of their activity, and that is economically and psychologically impossible. Let us make this clear to ourselves by considering

Marx's own example point by point. Marx compares two
workers—A and B. Laborer A represents a branch of production which requires technically a relatively large and
valuable means of production resulting from previous labor,
raw material, tools, and auxiliary material. Let us suppose,
in order to illustrate the example by figures, that the production of the previous material required five year's labor,
while the working of it up into finished products was effected in a sixth year. Let us further suppose—what is certainly not contrary to the spirit of the Marxian hypothesis,
which is meant to describe very primitive conditions—that
laborer A carries on both works, that he both creates the
previous material and also works it up into finished products. In these circumstances he will obviously recompense
himself for the previous labor of the first years out of the
sale of the finished products, which cannot take place till
the end of the sixth year. Or, in other words, he will have
to wait five years for the return on the first year's work.
For the return on the second year he will have to wait four
years; for the third year, three years, and so on. Or, taking the average of the six years' work, he will have to wait
nearly three years after the work has been accomplished
for the return on his labor. The second worker, on the other
hand, who represents a branch of production which needs
a relatively small means of production resulting from previous labor will perhaps turn out the completed product,
taking it through all its stages, in the course of a month,
and will therefore receive his compensation from the yield
of his product almost immediately after the accomplishment
of his work.

Now Marx's hypothesis assumes that the prices of the
commodities I and II are determined exactly in proportion
to the amounts of labor expended in their production, so
that the product of six years' work in commodity I only
brings as much as the total product of six years' work in
commodity II. And further, it follows from this that the laborer in commodity I should be satisfied to receive for every
year's work, with an average of three years' *delay* of payment, the *same* return that the laborer in commodity II
receives *without any delay;* that therefore delay in the receipt of payment is a circumstance which has no part to
play in the Marxian hypothesis, and more especially has
no influence on competition, on the crowding or understock-
ing of the trade in the different branches of production,
having regard to the longer or shorter periods of waiting
to which they are subjected.

I leave the reader to judge whether this is probable.

In other respects Marx acknowledges that the special accompanying circumstances peculiar to the work of a particular branch of production, the special intensity, strain, or unpleasantness of a work, force a compensation for themselves in the rise of wages through the action of competition. Should not a year's postponement of the remuneration of labor be a circumstance demanding compensation? And further, granting that all producers *would* as soon wait three years for the reward of their labor, as not at all, *could* they really all wait? Marx certainly assumes that "the laborers should possess their respective means of production"; but he does not and cannot venture to assume that each laborer possesses the amount of means of production which are necessary to carry on that branch of industry which for technical reasons requires the command of the greatest quantity of means of production. The different branches of production are therefore certainly not equally accessible to all producers. Those branches of production which demand the least advance of means of production are the most generally accessible, and the branches which demand larger capital are possible only for an increasingly smaller minority. Has this nothing to do with the circumstance that, in the latter branches, a certain restriction in supply takes place, which eventually forces the price of their products above the proportionate level of those branches in the carrying on of which the burdensome accompaniment of waiting does not enter and which are therefore accessible to a much wider circle of competitors?

Inadequacy Of Marx's Attempt To Bolster His Third Argument

Marx himself seems to have been aware that his case contains a certain improbability. He notes first of all, as I have done, though in another form, that the fixing of prices solely in proportion to the amount of labor in the commodities leads in another direction to a disproportion. He asserts this in the form (which is also correct) that the "surplus value" which laborers in both branches of production obtain over and above their necessary maintenance, calculated on the means of production advanced, shows *unequal rates of profit*. The question naturally obtrudes itself: Why should not this inequality be made to disappear by competition just as in "capitalistic" society? Marx feels the necessity of giving an answer to this, and here only does something of the nature of an attempt to give proofs instead of mere assertions come in. Now what is his answer?

The essential point (he says) is that both laborers should receive the same surplus value for the same working time; or, to be more exact, that for the *same working time* "they should receive the *same values* after deducting the value of the advanced constant element," and on this assumption the difference in the rates of profit would be a "matter of indifference, just as it is a matter of indifference to the wage earner by what rate of profit the quantity of surplus value squeezed out of him is represented."

Is this a happy simile? If I do not get a thing, then it may certainly be a matter of indifference to me whether that thing, which I do not get, estimated on the capital of another person, represents a higher or lower percentage. But when I get a thing as a settled right, as the worker (on the noncapitalistic hypothesis) is supposed to get the surplus value as profit, then it certainly is not a matter of indifference to me by what scale that profit is to be measured or distributed. It may, perhaps, be an open question whether this profit should be measured and distributed according to the expenditure of labor or to the amount of the advanced means of production, but the question itself can certainly not be a merely indifferent matter to the persons interested in it. And, when, therefore, the somewhat improbable fact is affirmed that unequal rates of profit can exist permanently side by side without being equalized by competition, the reason for this certainly cannot be found in the assumption that the height of the rate of profit is a matter of no importance whatever to the persons interested in it.

But are the laborers on the Marxian hypothesis treated alike even as laborers? They obtain for the same working time the same value and surplus value as wages, but they get it at different times. One obtains it immediately after the completion of the work; the other may have to wait years for the remuneration of his labor. Is this really equal treatment? Or does not the condition under which the remuneration is obtained constitute an inequality which cannot be a matter of indifference to the laborers, but which, on the contrary, as experience truly shows, they feel very keenly? To what worker today would it be a matter of indifference whether he received his weekly wages on Saturday evening, or a year, or three years hence? And such marked inequalities would not be smoothed away by competition. That is an improbability for the explanation of which Marx still remains in our debt.

Marx's Third Argument Also Contrary To The Facts Of Experience

His hypothesis, however, is not only inherently improbable, but it is also contrary to all the facts of experience. It is true that as regards the assumed case, in its full typical purity, we have, after all, no direct experience; for a condition of things in which paid labor is absent and every producer is the independent possessor of his own means of production can now no longer anywhere be seen in its full purity. Still, however, conditions and relationships are found in the "modern world," which correspond at least approximately to those assumed in the Marxian hypothesis. They are found, as Marx himself especially indicates (III, 156), in the case of the peasant proprietor, who himself cultivates his own land, and in the case of the artisan. According to the Marxian hypothesis, it ought to be a matter of observation that the incomes of these persons do not in the least depend on the amounts of capital they employed in production. They should each receive the same amount of wages and surplus value, whether the capital representing their means of production was 10 shillings or 10,000 shillings. I think, however, that my readers will all allow that though indeed in the cases just mentioned there is no such exact bookkeeping as to make it possible to determine proportions with mathematical exactitude, yet the prevailing impression does not confirm Marx's hypothesis, but tends on the contrary, to the view that in general and as a whole an ampler income is yielded by those branches of industry in which work is carried on with a considerable capital, than by those which have at their disposal only the hands of the producers.

Additional Evidence Against Marx's Third Argument

And finally this result of the appeal to fact, which is unfavorable to the Marxian hypothesis, receives not a little indirect confirmation from the fact that in the second case which he instances (a case much easier to test), in which, according to the Marxian theory, the law of value ought to be seen to be completely dominant, no trace of the process alleged by Marx is to be found.

Marx tells us, as we know, that even in a fully developed economy the equalization of the originally different rates of profit can be brought about only through the action of competition.

> If the commodities are sold according to their values [he writes in the most explicit of the passages concerning this matter],[14] very different rates of profit, as has been explained, occur in the different spheres of production, according to the different

[14] Vol. III, 175ff. Compare also the shorter statements, III, 136, 151, 159, and frequently.

organic compositions of the amounts of capital invested in them. But capital withdraws itself from
a sphere having a lower rate of profit, and throws
itself into another which yields a higher profit. By
this constant shifting from one sphere to another
—in short, by its distribution among the different
spheres according as the rate of profit rises in one
and sinks in another—it brings about such a proportion between supply and demand that the average profit in the different spheres of production
becomes the same.

We should therefore logically expect, wherever this
competition of capital was absent, or was at any rate not
yet in full activity, that the original mode of forming prices
and profits affirmed by Marx would be met with in its full,
or nearly its full, purity. In other words, there must be
traces of the actual fact that *before* the equalization of the
rates of profit the branches of production with the relatively
greater amounts of constant capital have won and do win
the smallest rates of profit, while those branches with the
smaller amounts of constant capital win the largest rates
of profit. As a matter of fact, however, there are no traces
of this to be found anywhere, either in the historical past
or in the present. This has been recently so convincingly
demonstrated by a learned professor who is in other respects extremely favorable to Marx, that I cannot do better
than simply quote the words of Werner Sombart:

Development never has and never does take place
in the way alleged. If it did, it would certainly be
seen in operation in the case of at least every new
branch of business. If this idea were true, in considering historically the advance of capitalism, one
would have to think of it as first occupying those
spheres in which human labor preponderated and
where, therefore, the composition of capital was
under the average (little constant and much variable), and then as passing slowly into other
spheres, according to the degree in which prices
had fallen in those first spheres in consequence of
overproduction. In a sphere having a preponderance of [material] means of production over human
labor, capitalism would naturally in the beginning have realized so small a profit, being limited
to the surplus value created by the individual, that
it would have had no inducement to enter into that
sphere. But capitalistic production at the beginning of its historical development occurs even to
some extent in branches of production of the latter kind, mining, etc. Capital would have had no

reason to go out of the sphere of circulation in which it was prospering, into the sphere of production, without a prospect of a 'customary profit' which, be it observed, existed in commercial profit previous to any capitalistic production. But we can also show the error of the assumption from the other side. If extremely high profits were obtained in the beginning of capitalistic production, in the spheres having a preponderance of human labor, it would imply that all at once capital had made use of the class of producers concerned (who had up to that time been independent), as wage earners, that is, at half the amount of gain they had hitherto procured, and had put the difference in the prices of the commodities, corresponding directly to the values, in its own pocket; and further it supposes, what is an altogether visionary idea, that capitalistic production began with rootless individuals in branches of production, some of which were quite new creations, and therefore was able to fix prices according to its own standard.

But if the assumption of an empirical connection between rates of profit and rates of surplus value is false historically, that is, false as regards the beginning of capitalism, it is even more so as regards conditions in which the capitalistic system of production is fully developed. Whether the composition of a capital by means of which a trade is carried on today is ever so high or ever so low, the prices of its products and the calculation (and realization) of the profits are based solely on the outlay of capital.

If in all times, earlier as well as later, capitals did, as a matter of fact, pass continually from one sphere of production to another, the principal cause of this would certainly lie in the inequality of profits. But this inequality most surely proceeds not from the organic composition of the capital, but from some cause connected with competition. Those branches of production which today flourish more than any others are just those with capitals of very high composition, such as mining, chemical factories, breweries, steam mills, etc. Are these the spheres from which capital has withdrawn and migrated until production has been proportionately limited and prices have risen? [15]

[15] "Zur Kritik des ökonomischen Systems von Karl Marx," *Archiv für sociale Gesetzgebung*, Vol. VII, pp. 584-586. I am bound, however, to make it clear that in the passage quoted Sombart in-

These statements will provide matter for many inferences against the Marxian theory. For the present I draw only one which bears immediately on the argument, which is the subject of our inquiry: the law of value, which, it is conceded, must give up its alleged control over prices of production in an economy where competition is in full force, has never exercised and could never exercise a real sway even in primitive conditions.

We have now seen, wrecked in succession, three contentions which affirmed the existence of certain reserved areas under the immediate control of the law of value. The application of the law of value to the sum total of all commodities and prices of commodities instead of to their several exchange relations (first argument) has been proved to be pure nonsense. The movement of prices (second argument) does not really obey the alleged law of value; and just as little does it exercise a real influence in "primitive conditions" (third argument). There is only one possibility left. Does the law of value, which has no real immediate power anywhere, have perhaps an indirect control, a sort of suzerainty? Marx does not omit to assert this also. It is the subject of the fourth argument, to which we now proceed.

Fourth Argument

This argument has been often hinted at by Marx, but so far as I can see he has explained it with any approach to fulness in one place only. The essence of it is this—that the "prices of production," which govern the actual formation of prices, are for their part in their turn under the influence of the law of value, which therefore, through the prices of production, governs the actual exchange relations. The values are "behind the prices of production and determine them in the last resort" (III, 188). The prices of production are, as Marx often expresses it, only "changed values" or "changed forms of value" (III, 142, 147, 152 and often). The nature and degree of the influence which the law of value exercises on the prices of production are more clearly explained, however, in a passage on pages 158 and 159.

tended to combat Marx, only on the assumption that Marx's doctrines did actually have the meaning attributed to them in the text. He himself ascribes to them, in his "attempt at rescue," already referred to by me, another, and, as I think, a somewhat exotic meaning, which I shall discuss in detail later on.

The average rate of profit which determines the price of production must, however, always be approximately equal to the amount of *surplus value* which falls to a given capital as an aliquot part of the total social capital. . . Now, as the total value of the commodities governs the total surplus value, and this again determines the amount of the average profit and consequently the general rate of profit—as a general law or a law governing fluctuation—the *law of value regulates the prices of production.*

Let us examine this line of argument point by point.

Marx says at the outset that the average rate of profit determines the prices of production. In Marx's sense this is correct but not complete. Let us make the connection quite clear.

The price of production of a commodity is first of all composed of the "cost price" to the employer of the means of production and of the average profit on the capital employed. The cost price of the means of production consists again of two component parts: the outlay of variable capital, that is, the money immediately paid in wages, and the outlay for consumed or used up constant capital—raw material, machines, and such-like. As Marx rightly explains, on pages 138ff., 144, and 186, in a society in which the values have already been changed into prices of production, the purchase or cost price of these means of production does not correspond with their value but with the total amount which has been expended by the producers of these means of production in wages and material appliances, plus the average profit on this expenditure. If we continue this analysis we come at last—as does Adam Smith in his *natural price,* with which, indeed, Marx expressly identifies his price of production (III, 178)—to resolve the price of production into two components or determinants: (1) the sum total of the wages paid during the different stages of production, which taken altogether represent the actual cost price of the commodities;[16] and (2) the sum total of the *profits* on all these wage outlays calculated *pro rata temporis,* and according to the average rate of profit.

Undoubtedly, therefore, *one* determinant of the price

[16] "The cost price of a commodity refers only to the amount of *paid* labor contained in it" (Marx, Vol. III, 144).

of production of a commodity is the average profit incidental to its production. In regard to the other determinant, the total of wages paid, Marx speaks no further in
this passage. In another place, however, to which we have
alluded, he says in a very general way that "the values
stand behind the prices of production," and "that the law
of value determines these latter in the last resort." In order to avoid a hiatus, therefore, we must subject this second factor also to our scrutiny and judge accordingly
whether it can rightly be said to be determined by the law
of value, and, if so, in what degree.

The Bearing Of Rate Of Wages On Marx's Fourth Argument

It is evident that the total expenditure in wages is
a product of the quantity of labor employed multiplied by
the average rate of the wages. Now as, according to the
[Marxian] law of value, the exchange relations must be
determined solely by the quantity of labor employed, and
Marx repeatedly and most emphatically denies that the rate
of wages has any influence on the value of the commodities,[17] it is also evident that, of the two components of the
factor, expenditure in wages, only the amount of labor employed is in harmony with the law of value, while in the
case of the second component, rate of wages, a determinant
alien to the law of value enters among the determinants of
the prices of production.

The nature and degree of the operation of this determinant may be illustrated, in order to avoid all misunderstanding, by one other example.

Let us take three commodities—A, B, and C—which, to
begin with, have the same price of production of 100 shillings, but which are of different types of composition as
regards the elements of their cost. Let us further suppose
that the wages for a day amount at first to five shillings,
and the rate of surplus value, or the degree of exploitation,
to 100%, so that from the total value of the commodities of
300 shillings, 150 falls to wages and another 150 to surplus
value; and that the total capital (invested in different proportions in the three commodities) amounts to 1,500 shillings. The average rate of profit would therefore be 10%.

The following table illustrates this assumption:

---

[17] For instance, Vol. III, 187, where Marx affirms "that in no
circumstances can the rise or fall of wages ever affect the value
of the commodities."

Commodity	Expended Time	Wages	Capital employed	Average profit accruing	Production price
A	10	50s.	500s.	50s.	100s.
B	6	30s.	700s.	70s.	100s.
C	14	70s.	300s.	30s.	100s.
Total	30	150s.	1,500s.	150s.	300s.

Now let us assume a rise in the wages from five to six shillings. According to Marx this can only take place at the expense of the surplus value, other conditions remaining the same.[18] Therefore of the total product of 300 shillings, which remains unaltered, there will fall (owing to a diminution in the degree of exploitation) 180 to wages and only 120 to surplus value, and consequently the average rate of profit on the capital employed falls to 8%. The following table shows the changes which take place, in consequence, in the compositions of the elements of capital and in the prices of production:

Commodity	Expended Time	Wages	Capital employed	Average profit accruing	Production price
A	10	60s.	500s.	40s.	100s.
B	6	36s.	700s.	56s.	92s.
C	14	84s.	300s.	24s.	108s.
Total	30	180s.	1,500s.	120s.	300s.

It appears from this that a rise in wages, when the amount of labor remains the same, brings with it a material alteration in the originally equal prices of production and relations of exchange. The alteration can partly, but obviously not altogether be traced to the contemporaneous necessary change produced in the average rate of profit by the alteration in the wages. I say "obviously not altogether," because the price of production of commodity C, for example, has really *risen* in spite of the fall in the amount of profit contained in it, therefore this change of price cannot be brought about by the change of profit *only*. I raise this really obvious point merely in order to show that in the rate of wages we have, indisputably, a price determinant which does not exhaust its force in its influence on the rate of profit, but also exerts a special and direct influence; and that therefore we have reason to submit this particular price determinant—which is passed over by Marx in the passage cited above—to a separate consideration. The summary of the results of this consideration I reserve for a

18 Compare Vol. III, p. 179 ff.

later stage, and in the meantime we will examine step by step Marx's assertion concerning the way in which the second determinant of the price of production, the average profit, is regulated by the law of value.

Analysis Of How Average Profit Enters The Marxian Argument

The connection is anything but a direct one. It is effected by the following links in his reasoning, some of which are indicated only elliptically by Marx, but which undoubtedly enter into his argument: The *law of value* determines the *aggregate value* of the whole of the commodities produced in the society;[19] the *aggregate value* of the commodities determines the *aggregate surplus value* contained in them; the latter distributed over the total social capital determines the *average rate of profit*: this rate applied to the capital employed in the production of a single commodity gives the *concrete average profit,* which finally enters as an element into the price of production of the commodity in question. In this way the first link in this sequence, the *law of value,* regulates the last link, the *price of production.*

Now for our running commentary on this series of arguments.

1. We are struck by the fact which must be kept in mind, that Marx after all does not affirm that there is a connection between the average profit entering into the price of production of the commodities and the values incorporated in single commodities by reason of the law of value. On the contrary, he says emphatically in numerous places that the amount of surplus value which enters into the price of production of a commodity is independent of and indeed fundamentally different from "the surplus value actually created in the sphere in which the separate commodity is produced" (III, 146; similarly III, 144, and often). He therefore does not after all connect the influence ascribed to the law of value with the characteristic function of the law of value, in virtue of which this law determines the exchange relations of the *separate commodities,* but only with another assumed function (concerning the highly questionable nature of which we have already passed an opinion), viz., the determination of the aggregate value *of all commodities taken together.* In this application, as we have convinced ourselves, the law of value has no meaning whatever. If the idea and the law of value are to be brought to bear—and Marx certainly means that they should—on

---

[19] This link is not expressly inserted by Marx in the passage quoted. Its insertion is nevertheless self-evident.

the exchange relations of goods,[20] then there is no sense in applying the idea and law to an aggregate which as such cannot be subject to those relations. As no exchange of this aggregate takes place, there is naturally neither a measure nor a determinant for its exchange, and therefore it cannot give material for a "law of value." If, however, the law of value has no real influence at all on a chimerical "aggregate value of all commodities taken together," there can be no further application of its influence to other relations, and the whole logical series which Marx endeavored to work out with such seeming cogency hangs therefore in the air.

2. But let us turn away altogether from this first fundamental defect, and let us independently of it test the strength of the other arguments in the series. Let us assume, therefore, that the aggregate value of the commodities is a real quantity, and actually determined by the law of value. The second argument affirms that this aggregate value of commodities determines the aggregate surplus value. Is this true?

The surplus value, unquestionably, represents no fixed or unalterable quota of the total national product, but is the difference between the "aggregate value" of the national product and the amount of the wages paid to the workers. That aggregate value, therefore, does not in any case rule the amount of the total surplus value by itself alone. It can at the most supply only *one* determinant of its amount, by the side of which stands a second, alien determinant, the rate of wages. But, it may be asked, does not this also, perhaps, obey the Marxian law of value?

In the first volume Marx had still unconditionally affirmed this.

The value of labor [he writes on page 155], is determined, like that of every other commodity, by the working time necessary to the production, and therefore also reproduction, of this specific article. [And on the next page he proceeds to define this proposition more fully:] For his maintenance the living individual needs a certain amount of means of subsistence. The working time necessary to the production of the labor power resolves itself, therefore, into the working time necessary to the production of these means of subsistence, or the value of the labor power is the value of the means

20. As I have already mentioned, p. 231ff., I shall take special notice later of the different view of W. Sombart; see p. 288ff.

of subsistence necessary to the maintenance of its possessor.

In the third volume Marx, however, is forced considerably to modify this statement. Thus, on page 186 of that volume, he rightly draws attention to the fact that it is possible that the necessary means of subsistence of the laborer also can be sold at prices of production which deviate from that of the necessary working time. In such a case, Marx says, the variable part of the capital (that is, the wages paid) may also deviate from its value. In other words, the wages (apart from purely temporary oscillations) may permanently deviate from the rate which should correspond to the quantity of work incorporated in the necessary means of subsistence, or to the strict requirements of the law of value. Therefore at least *one* determinant alien to the law of value is already a factor in determining the total surplus value.

3. The factor, aggregate surplus value, thus determined, "regulates," according to Marx, the average rate of profit, but obviously only in so far as the aggregate surplus value furnishes *one* determinant, while another—the amount of capital existing in a given society—acts as a second determinant, entirely independent of the first and of the law of value. If, as in the foregoing table, the total surplus value is 150 shillings, the surplus value being 100%, then, if and because the total capital expended in all its branches of production amounts to 1,500 shillings, the rate of profit amounts to 10%. If the total surplus value remained exactly the same, but the total capital participating in it amounted to 3,000 shillings, the rate of profit would obviously amount only to 5%; and it would be fully 20% if the total capital amounted only to 750 shillings. It is obvious, therefore, that again a determinant enters into the chain of influence which is entirely alien to the law of value.

4. We must, therefore, further conclude that the average rate of profit regulates the amount of the concrete average profit which accrues from the production of a special commodity. But this, again, is only true with the same restrictions as in the former arguments of the series. That is to say, the total amount of the average profit which accrues from the production of a separate commodity is the product of two factors: the quantity of invested capital multiplied by the average rate of profit. The quantity of the capital to be invested in the different stages is again determined by two factors, namely, by the quantity of the work to be remunerated (a factor which is of course not out of

harmony with Marx's law of value), and also by the rate of wages to be paid; and with this latter factor, as we have just convinced ourselves, a factor alien to the law of value comes into play. [See pages 248-250, and elsewhere.]

5. In the next argument of the series we go back again to the beginning: the average profit (defined in the fourth argument) must regulate the price of production of the commodity. This is true with the correction that the average profit is only *one* factor determining prices side by side with the expended wages in which, as we have repeatedly stated, there is an element, which is foreign to Marx's law of value, and which cooperates in determining prices.

Let us sum up. What is the proposition which Marx undertook to prove? It ran thus: "The law of value regulates the prices of production," or as otherwise stated, "The values determine in the last resort the prices of production," or if we formulate the meaning which Marx himself attached to value and law of value in the first volume the statement is: Prices of production are governed "in the last resort" by the principle that the quantity of labor is the only condition which determines the exchange relations of commodities.

And what do we find on examining the separate links of the argument? We find that the price of production is, first of all, made up of two components. One, the expended wages, is the product of two factors, of which the first—the quantity of work—is in harmony with the substance of the Marxian "value," and the other—the rate of wages—is not. Marx himself could only affirm of the second component—the total amount of accruing average profit—that it was connected with the law of value by means of a violent perversion of this law, alleging its operation in a domain in which no exchange relations exist at all. But apart from this, the factor "aggregate value of commodities" which Marx wishes to deduce from the law of value must, in any case, cooperate in determining the next link, the aggregate surplus value, along with a factor, "rate of wages," which is no longer homogeneous with the law of value. The "aggregate surplus value" would have to cooperate with a completely foreign element, the mass of social capital, in determining the average rate of profit; and, finally, the latter would have to cooperate with a partially foreign element, expended wages, in determining the accruing total profit.

The factor "aggregate value of all commodities," booked with doubtful correctness to the credit of the Marxian law of value, consequently cooperates after a triple homœopathic dilution of its influence (and naturally, therefore, with a share of influence diminished in proportion to this dilution) in determining the average profit, and also the prices of production. The following would, therefore, be a sober statement of the facts of the case. The quantity of labor which, according to the Marxian law of value, must entirely and exclusively govern the exchange relations of commodities proves itself as a matter of fact to be only *one* determinant of the prices of production side by side with other determinants. It has a strong, a tolerably direct influence on the one component of prices of production which consists of expended wages; a much more remote, weak, and, for the most part,[21] even questionable influence upon the second component, the average profit.

Now, I ask, do we find in this condition of things a confirmation or a contradiction of the claim that, in the last resort, the law of value determines the prices of production? I do not think that there can be a moment's doubt as to the answer. The law of value maintains that quantity of labor alone determines the exchange relations; facts show that it is *not* only the quantity of labor, or the factors in harmony with it, which determine the exchange relations. These two propositions bear the same relation to each other as Yes to No—as affirmation to contradiction. Whoever accepts the second proposition — and Marx's theory of the prices of production involves this acceptance — contradicts *de facto* the first. And if Marx really could have thought that he did not contradict himself and his first proposition, he allowed himself to be deluded by some strange mistake. He could not have seen that it is very different for one factor involved in a law to have some sort and degree of influence and for the law itself to be in full force.

The most trivial example will perhaps serve best in so obvious a matter. Suppose a discussion on the effect of cannon balls on ironclad vessels, and someone says that the degree of destructive power in the balls is due solely to the amount of powder with which the cannon is charged. When this statement is questioned and tested by actual experience it is seen that the effect of the shot is due not only to the amount of gunpowder in the charge, but also to the

---

[21] In so far, namely, as it is supposed to be brought about by the factor "aggregate value," which, in my opinion, has nothing to do with the embodied amount of labor. As, however, the factor "expended wages" (in determining which the amount of work to be remunerated certainly cooperates as an element) also appears in the following links, the amount of work always finds a place among the indirect determinants of average profit.

strength of the powder; and, further, to the construction, length, etc., of the barrel of the gun, the form and hardness of the balls, the distance of the object, and last, but not least, to the thickness and firmness of the plates on the vessel.

And now after all this has been conceded, could it still be said that nevertheless the first statement was true, because it had been proved that the alleged factor, the amount of gunpowder, does exert an important influence on the discharge, and that this was proved by the fact that, other circumstances being equal, the effect of the shot would be greater or less in proportion to the amount of gunpowder used in the charge?

This is what Marx does. He declares most emphatically that nothing can be at the root of exchange relations but quantity of labor alone; he argues strenuously with the economists who acknowledge other determinants of value and price besides the quantity of labor—the influence of which on the exchange value of goods freely reproduced no one denies. From the exclusive position of quantity of labor as the sole determinant of exchange relations he deduces in two volumes the most weighty and practical conclusions — his theory of surplus value and his denunciation of the capitalistic organization of society — in order, in the third volume, to develop a theory of prices of production which substantially recognizes the influence of other determinants as well. But instead of thoroughly analyzing these other determinants, he always lays his finger triumphantly on the points where his idol, quantity of labor, either actually, or in his opinion, exerts an influence: on such points as the change in prices when the amount of labor changes, the influence of "aggregate value" on average rate of profit, etc. He is silent about the coordinate influence of foreign determinants as well as about the influence of the amount of social capital on the rate of profit, and about the alteration of prices through a change in the organic composition of the capital, or in the rate of wages. Passages in which he recognizes these influences are not wanting in his book. The influence of the rate of wages on prices is, for instance, aptly treated on page 179ff., then on page 186; the influence of the amount of social capital on the height of the average rate of profit on pages 145, 184, 191ff., 197ff., 203, and often; the influence of the organic composition of capital on the prices of production on pages 142ff. It is characteristic that in the passages devoted to the justification of his law of value Marx passes silently over these other influences, and only mentions in a one-sided way the part played by quantity of labor, in order to deduce from the first and undisputed premise, that quantity of labor cooperates at many points to determine the prices of production, the utterly unjustifiable conclusion that, in the "last resort," the law of value, which proclaims the sole dominion of labor, determines the prices of production. This is to evade the admission of the contradiction; it is not to escape from the contradiction itself.

CHAPTER IV

The Error In The Marxian System — Its Origin And Ramifications

The evidence that an author has contradicted himself may be a necessary stage, but it cannot be the ultimate aim of a fruitful and well-directed criticism. To be aware that there is a defect in a system, which may possibly be accidental only and peculiar to the author, requires a comparatively low degree of critical intelligence. A firmly rooted system can only be effectually overthrown by discovering with absolute precision the point at which the error made its way into the system and the manner in which it spread and branched itself out. As opponents we ought to study the beginning, the development, and the final issue of the error which culminates in self-contradiction as thoroughly, I might almost say as sympathetically, as we would study the connection of a system with which we were in agreement.

Owing to many peculiar circumstances the question of self-contradiction has, in the case of Marx, gained a more than ordinary importance, and consequently I have devoted a considerable space to it. But in dealing with a thinker so important and influential as Marx it is incumbent upon us to apply ourselves to the second and, in this case I think, the actually more fruitful and instructive part of the criticism.

Section I

IN WHAT WAY DID MARX DEVELOP THE PROPOSITION THAT ALL VALUE DEPENDS ON INCORPORATED QUANTITIES OF LABOR?

We will begin with a question which will carry us straight to the main point: In what way did Marx arrive at the fundamental proposition of his teaching—the proposition that all value depends solely upon incorporated quantities of labor?

That this proposition is not a self-evident axiom, needing no proof, is beyond doubt. Value and effort, as I have stated at length in another place, are not ideas so intimately connected that one is forced immediately to adopt the view that effort is the basis of value.

That I have slaved to acquire a thing is *one* fact; that the thing is worth slaving for is a second and different fact. And that both facts do not always go hand in hand is far too well corroborated by experience to admit of any possible doubt. Every one of the countless unsuccessful efforts which are wasted every day on valueless results bears witness to this, quite regardless of whether the cause be technical ineptitude, misguided speculation, or merely bad luck. No less convincing is each of the many instances in which slight effort is rewarded with high value.[22]

When therefore it is affirmed that a necessary and natural correspondence between value and effort exists in any quarter, it behooves us to give ourselves and our readers some grounds in support of such a statement.

Marx's Argument Is Unnatural And Unsuited

Now Marx himself advances proofs of it in his system; but I think I shall be able to convince my readers that from the outset his line of argument is unnatural and not suited to the character of the problem; and further that the evidence which Marx advances in his system is clearly not the same as that by means of which he himself arrives at his convictions, but was thought out subsequently as an artificial support for an opinion which was previously derived from other sources; and finally—and this is the most decisive point—that the reasoning is full of the most obvious faults of logic and method which deprive it of all cogency.

Let us examine this more closely.

The fundamental proposition which Marx puts before his readers is that the exchange value of commodities—for his analysis is directed only to this, not to value in use— finds its origin and its measure in the quantity of labor incorporated in the commodities.

Marx Disingenuously Neglects Empirical Proof

Now it is certain that the exchange values, that is to say the prices of the commodities as well as the quantities

[22] *History and Critique of Interest Theories* (Volume I of CA-PITAL AND INTEREST), p. 288.

of labor which are necessary for their reproduction, are
real, external quantities, which on the whole it is quite possible to determine empirically. Obviously, therefore, Marx
ought to have turned to experience for the proof of a proposition the correctness or incorrectness of which must be
manifested in the facts of experience; or in other words,
he should have given a purely empirical proof in support
of a proposition adapted to a purely empirical proof. This,
however, Marx does not do. And one cannot even say that
he heedlessly passes by this possible and certainly proper
source of knowledge and conviction. The reasoning of the
third volume proves that he was quite aware of the nature
of the empirical facts, and that they were opposed to his
proposition. He knew that the prices of commodities were
not in proportion to the amount of incorporated labor, but
to the total costs of production, which comprise other elements besides. He did not therefore accidentally overlook
this the most natural proof of his proposition, but turned
away from it with the full consciousness that upon this
road no issue favorable to his theory could be obtained.

Marx Also Neglects
Psychological Analysis

But there is yet another and perfectly natural way of
testing and proving such propositions, namely, the psychological. We can by a combination of induction and deduction, much used in our science, investigate the motives
which direct people in carrying on the business of exchange
and in determining exchange prices on the one hand, and
on the other hand which guide them in their cooperation
in production; and from the nature of these motives a typical mode of action may be inferred through which among
other things, it is conceivable that a connection should result between the regularly demanded and accepted prices
and the quantity of work necessary for the production of
the commodities. This method has often been followed with
the best results in exactly similar questions—for instance,
the usual justification of the law of supply and demand and
of the law of costs of production, and the explanation of
ground rents, rests upon it. And Marx himself, in a general
way at least, has often made use of it; but just in dealing
with his fundamental proposition he avoids it. Although,
obviously, the affirmed external connection between exchange relations and quantities of work could only be fully
understood by the discovery of the psychological links which
connect the two, he forgoes all explanation of these internal
connections. He even once says, incidentally, that "the

deeper analysis" of the two social forces, "demand and sup-ply"—which would have led to this internal connection—"is not apposite here" (III, 169), where the "here" refers only to a digression on the influence of supply and demand on the formation of prices. In reality, however, nowhere in the whole Marxian system is a really "deep" and thorough analysis attempted; and most of all is the absence of this analysis noticeable where he is preparing the ground for his most important leading idea.

But here again we notice something strange. Marx does not, as might have been expected, pass over this sec-ond possible and natural method of investigation with an easy carelessness. He studiously avoids it, and with a full consciousness of what the results of following it would be, and that they would not be favorable to his thesis. In the third volume, for instance, he actually brings forward, un-der their roughly collective name of "competition," those motives operative in production and exchange, the "deeper analysis" of which he forgoes here and elsewhere, and dem-onstrates that these motives do not in reality lead to an adjustment of the prices to the quantities of labor incor-porated in the commodities, but that, on the contrary, they force them away from this level to a level which implies at least one other coordinating factor. Indeed it is compe-tition which, according to Marx, leads to the formation of the celebrated average rate of profit and to the "transfer" of pure labor values into prices of production, which differ from them and contain a portion of average profit.*

Marx's Erroneous Dialectical Deduction Based On Aristotle

Now Marx, instead of proving his thesis from experi-ence or from the motivations of the actors—that is, empir-ically or psychologically—prefers another, and for such a subject somewhat singular line of evidence—the method of a purely logical proof, a dialectic deduction from the very nature of exchange.

Marx had found in old Aristotle the idea that "exchange cannot exist without equality, and equality cannot exist without commensurability" (I, 35). Starting with this idea he expands it. He conceives the exchange of two commodi-ties under the form of an equation, and from this infers that "a common factor of the same amount" must exist in the things exchanged and thereby equated, and then proceeds to search for this common factor to which the two equated things must as exchange values be "reducible" (I, II).

* Present publisher's note: see Chapter II, p. 219ff.

Equality In Exchange Is An Idea Plainly Wrong

I should like to remark, in passing, that the first assumption, according to which an "equality" must be manifested in the exchange of two things, appears to me to be very old-fashioned, which would not, however, matter much were it not also very unrealistic. In plain English, it seems to me to be a wrong idea. Where equality and exact equilibrium obtain no change is likely to occur to disturb the balance. When, therefore, in the case of exchange the matter terminates with a change of ownership of the commodities, it points rather to the existence of some inequality or preponderance which produces the alteration. When composite bodies are brought into close contact with each other new chemical combinations are produced by some of the constituent elements of one body uniting with those of another body, not because they possess an exactly equal degree of chemical affinity, but because they have a stronger affinity with each other than with the other elements of the bodies to which they originally belonged. So here. And as a matter of fact modern political economists agree that the old scholastico-theological theory of "equivalence" in the commodities to be exchanged is untenable. I will not, however, dwell any longer on this point, but will proceed to the critical investigation of the logical and systematic processes of distillation by means of which Marx obtains the sought-for "common factor" in labor.

It is these processes which appear to me to constitute, as I have before said, the most vulnerable point in the Marxian theory. They exhibit as many cardinal errors as there are points in the arguments—of which there are not a few —and they bear evident traces of having been a subtle and artificial afterthought contrived to make a preconceived opinion seem the natural outcome of a prolonged investigation.

The Bias In Marx's Attempted Negative Proof

Marx searches for the "common factor" which is the characteristic of exchange value in the following way: He passes in review the various properties possessed by the objects made equal in exchange, and according to the method of exclusion separates all those which cannot stand the test, until at last only one property remains, that of being the product of labor. This, therefore, must be the sought-for common property.

This line of procedure is somewhat singular, but not in itself objectionable. It strikes one as strange that instead of submitting the supposed characteristic property to a positive test—as would have been done if either of the other methods studiously avoided by Marx had been employed—Marx tries to convince us that he has found the sought-for property, by a purely negative proof, namely, by showing that it is not any of the other properties. This method can always lead to the desired end if attention and thoroughness are used—that is to say, if extreme care is taken that everything that ought to be included is actually passed through the logical sieve and that no mistake has been made in leaving anything out.

But how does Marx proceed?

From the beginning he only puts into the sieve those exchangeable things which contain the property which he desires finally to sift out as "the common factor," and he leaves all the others outside. He acts as one who urgently desiring to bring a white ball out of an urn takes care to secure this result by putting in white balls only. That is to say he limits from the outset the field of his search for the substance of the exchange value to "commodities," and in doing so he forms a conception with a meaning narrower than the conception of "goods" (though he does not clearly define it), and limits it to products of labor as against gifts of nature. Now it stands to reason that if exchange really means an equalization, which assumes the existence of a "common factor of the same amount," this common factor must be sought and found in every species of goods which is brought into exchange, not only in products of labor but also in gifts of nature, such as the soil, wood in trees, water power, coal beds, stone quarries, petroleum reserves, mineral waters, gold mines, etc.[23] To exclude the exchangeable goods which are not products of labor in the search for the common factor which lies at the root of exchange value is, under the circumstances, a great error of method. It is just as though a natural philosopher, desiring to discover a property common to all bodies—weight, for instance —were to sift the properties of a single group of bodies— transparent bodies, for instance—and after passing in review all the properties common to transparent bodies were to declare that transparency must be the cause of weight, for the sole reason that he could demonstrate that it could not be caused by any of the other properties.

[23] Karl Knies makes the following pertinent objection against Marx: "There is no reason apparent in Marx's statement why the equation, eight bushels of wheat = a cwts. of virgin-forest wood = b acres of virgin soil = c acres of natural pasture-land, should not be as good as the equation, eight bushels of wheat = a cwts. of cultivated-forest wood" (*Das Geld*, 1st edition, p. 121; 2nd edition, p. 157).

Marx Excludes Gifts Of Nature

The exclusion of the gifts of nature (which would never have entered the head of Aristotle, the father of the idea of equality in exchange) is the less to be justified because many natural gifts, such as the soil, are among the most important objects of property and commerce, and also because it is impossible to affirm that in nature's gifts exchange values are always established arbitrarily and by accident. On the one hand, there are such things as accidental prices among products of labor; and on the other hand the prices in the case of nature's gifts are frequently shown to be distinctly related to antecedent conditions or controlling motives. For instance, that the sale price of land is a multiple of its rent calculated on an interest usual in the country of sale is as well known a fact as that the wood in a tree, or the coal in a pit, brings a higher or lower price according to differences of quality or of distance from market, and not by mere accident.

Marx's Definition Of Commodities
Is Narrower Than Exchangeable Goods

Marx also takes care to avoid mentioning or explaining the fact that he excludes from his investigation a part of exchangeable goods. In this case, as in many others, he manages to glide with dialectic skill over the difficult points of his argument. He omits to call his readers' attention to the fact that his idea of "commodities" is narrower than that of exchangeable goods as a whole. He very cleverly prepares us for the acceptance of the subsequent limitation of the investigation to commodities by placing at the beginning of his book the apparently harmless general phrase that "the wealth of the society in which a capitalistic system of production is dominant appears as an immense *collection of commodities.*" This proposition is quite wrong if we take the term "commodity" to mean products of labor, which is the sense Marx subsequently gives to it. For the gifts of nature, inclusive of the *soil*, constitute a by no means insignificant, but on the contrary a very important element of national wealth. The ingenuous reader easily overlooks this inaccuracy, however, for of course he does not know that later Marx will give a much more restricted meaning to the term "commodity."

Nor is this made clear in what immediately follows. On the contrary, in the first paragraphs of the first chapter we read, in turn, of a "thing," a "value in use," a "good," and a "commodity," without any clear distinction being made between the last and the three former. " The usefulness of a *thing*," it says on page 10, makes it a *value in use*": "the commodity . . . is a *value in use* or *good*." On page 11 we read, "Exchange value appears . . . as the quantitative proportion . . . in which *values in use* of one kind exchange with *values in use* of another kind." And here let it be noticed that it is just the *value in use* = *good* which is still directly indicated as the main factor of the exchange phenomenon. And with the phrase "Let us look into the matter more closely," which surely cannot be meant to prepare us for a leap into another and a narrower field of research, Marx continues, "a single *commodity*, eight bushels of wheat, for instance, exchanges in the most varying proportions with other *articles*." And "Let us further take two *commodities*," etc. In the same paragraph the term "things" occurs again, and indeed with the application which is most important for the problem, namely, "that a common factor of equal amount exists in two different *things*" (which are made equal to each other in exchange).

On the next page (p. 12), however, Marx directs his search for the "common factor" only to the "exchange value of *commodities*," without hinting, even in the faintest whisper, that he has thereby limited the field of research to a part only of the things possessing exchange value.[24] And immediately, on the next page (p. 13), the limitation is again abandoned and the results just obtained in the narrower area are applied to the wider sphere of values in use, or goods. "A *value in use*, or a *good*, has therefore only a value because abstract human labor is stored up or materialized in it."

If Marx had not confined his research, at the decisive point, to products of labor, but had sought for the common factor in the exchangeable gifts of nature as well, it would have become obvious that labor cannot be the common factor. If he had carried out this limitation quite clearly and openly, this gross fallacy of method would inevitably have struck both himself and his readers; and they would have been forced to laugh at the naïve juggle by means of which the property of being a product of labor has been successfully distilled out as the common property of a group from which all exchangeable things which naturally belong to it, and which are not the products of labor, have been first of all eliminated. The trick could only have been performed, as Marx performed it, by gliding unnoticed over the knotty point with a light and quick dialectic. But while I express

---

[24] In a quotation from Barbon, in this same paragraph, the difference between commodities and things is again effaced: "One sort of *wares* are as good as another, if the value be equal. There is no difference or distinction in *things* of equal value."

my sincere admiration of the skill with which Marx managed to present so faulty a mode of procedure in so specious a form, I can of course only maintain that the proceeding itself is altogether erroneous.

But we will proceed. By means of the artifice just described Marx has merely succeeded in convincing us that labor can in fact enter into the competition. And it was only by the artificial narrowing of the sphere that it could even have become *one* "common" property of this narrow sphere. But by its side other properties could claim to be as common. How now is the exclusion of these other competitors effected? It is effected by two arguments, each of a few words only, but which contain one of the most serious of logical fallacies.

How Marx Confused A Factor Generally With Phases Of A Factor

In the first of these Marx excludes all "geometrical, physical, chemical, or other natural properties of the commodities," for "their physical properties only come into consideration in so far as they make the commodities useful —make them values in use, therefore. *On the other hand, the exchange relation of commodities evidently involves our disregarding their values in use*"; because "*within this relation* (the exchange relation) *one value in use is worth exactly as much as every other, provided only it is present in proper proportions*" (I, 12).

In making clear what this argument involves may I be permitted to quote from my *History and Critique of Interest Theories* (Volume I of CAPITAL AND INTEREST), page 295:

> What would Marx have said to the following argument? In an opera company there are three excellent singers, a tenor, a bass, and a baritone, who receive a salary of $20,000 a year each. The question is 'What is the element possessed in common which causes them all to be paid the same salary?' My answer is, that in the matter of salaries one good voice is worth as much as any other, a good tenor voice is worth the same as a good bass voice or a good baritone, provided only it is available in the proper proportion. Consequently there is 'aprently' an elimination, in the matter of salary, of the factor of good voice, and consequently the good voice cannot be the common cause of the high salaries.
> It is obvious that this line of reasoning is fallacious. It is equally obvious that the Marxian logical sequence, of which it is an exact copy, is no whit more correct. Both contain the same error.

They confuse elimination *of a factor generally,* with elimination *of the special phases* the factor exhibits in special instances. The factor which can be disregarded in our problem is the special phase in which the factor 'good voice' manifests itself. It may be immaterial whether we are paying for a tenor, a bass, or a baritone. But rest assured it is not so as to 'any good voice.' In the same way, consideration of the exchange relation of commodities may disregard the special phase in which their use value manifests itself, for instance whether the commodity serves to provide food or clothing or shelter, but it certainly may not disregard the use value itself. The utter impropriety of summarily dismissing use value from consideration could have been deduced by Marx from the very fact that there can be no exchange value where there is no use value. Indeed, that is a fact which Marx himself is repeatedly compelled to admit.[25]

Marx's False Conclusion That Labor Is The Only Common Factor In Commodities

The second step in the argument is still worse: "If the use value of commodities be disregarded"—these are Marx's words—"there remains in them *only one other property, that of being products of labor.*" Is it so? I ask today as I asked twelve years ago: Is there only one other property? Is not the property of being scarce in proportion to demand also common to all exchangeable goods? Or that they are the subjects of demand and supply? Or that they are appropriated? Or that they are natural products? For that they are products of nature, just as they are products

---

[25] For example, p. 15, at end: "Lastly, nothing can be a value without also being an object of use. If it is useless, the labor contained in it is also useless; it does not count as labour (*sic!*), and therefore creates no value." Knies has already drawn attention to the logical fallacy animadverted upon in the text. (See *Das Geld,* Berlin, 1873, pp. 123ff.; 2nd edition, pp. 160ff.) Adler (*Grundlagen der Karl Marxschen Kritik,* Tübingen, 1887, pp. 211ff.) has strangely misunderstood my argument when he contends against me that good voices are not commodities in the Marxian sense. It did not concern me at all whether "good voices" could be classed as economic goods under the Marxian law of value or not. It only concerned me to present an argument of a logical syllogism which showed the same fallacy as that of Marx. I might for this purpose just as well have chosen an example which was in no way related to the domain of economics. I might, for example, just as well have shown that according to Marx's logic the common factor of *variously colored* bodies might consist in heaven knows what, but not in the blending of various colors. For any *one* combination of colors—for example, white, blue, yellow, black, violet—is as regards variety worth just as much as any other combination, say green, red, orange, sky-blue, etc., if only it is present "in proper proportion"; we therefore apparently abstract from the color and combination of colors!

of labor, no one asserts more plainly than Marx himself, when he declares in one place that "commodities are combinations of two elements, natural material and labor." Or is not the property that they cause expense to their producers—a property to which Marx draws attention in the third volume—common to exchangeable goods?

Why then, I ask again today, may not the principle of value reside in any of these common properties as well as in the property of being products of labor? For in support of this latter proposition Marx has not adduced a shred of positive evidence. His sole argument is the negative one, that the value in use, from which we have happily abstracted, is not the principle of exchange value. But does not this negative argument apply equally to all the other common properties overlooked by Marx? And this is not all. On page 12, in which Marx has abstracted from the influence of the value in use on exchange value by arguing that any one value in use is worth as much as any other if only it is present in proper proportion, he writes as follows about products of labor:

> But even as the product of labor they have already changed in our hand. For if we abstract from a commodity its value in use, we at the same time take from it the material constituents and forms which give it a value in use. It is no longer a table, or a house, or yarn, or any other useful thing. All its physical qualities have disappeared. *Nor is it any longer the product of the labor of the carpenter, or the mason, or the spinner, or of any other particular productive industry.* With the useful character of the labor products there disappears the useful character of the labor embodied in them, and there vanish also the different concrete forms of those labors. *They are no longer distinguished from each other, but are all reduced to identical human labor—abstract human labor.*

Is it possible to state more clearly or more emphatically that for an exchange relation not only any one value in use, but also any one kind of labor or product of labor is worth exactly as much as any other, if only it is present in proper proportion? Or, in other words, that exactly the same evidence on which Marx formulated his verdict of exclusion against the value in use holds good with regard to labor. Labor and value in use have a qualitative side and a quantitative side. As the value in use is different qualitatively as table, house, or yarn, so is labor as carpentry, masonry, or spinning. And just as one can compare different kinds of labor according to their quantity, so one can compare values in use of different kinds according to the amount of the value in use. It is quite impossible to understand why the very same evidence should result in the one competitor being excluded and in the other getting the crown and the prize. If Marx had chanced to reverse the order of the examination, the same reasoning which led to the exclusion of the value in use would have excluded labor; and then the reasoning which resulted in the crowning of labor might have led him to declare the value in use to be the only property left, and therefore to be the sought-for common property, and value to be "the cellular tissue of value in use." I think it can be maintained seriously, not in jest, that, if the subjects of the two paragraphs on page 12 were transposed (in the first of which the influence of value in use is thought away, and in the second labor is shown to be the sought-for common factor), the seeming justness of the reasoning would not be affected; then labor and *products of labor* could be substituted everywhere for *value in use* in the otherwise unaltered structure of the first paragraph, and then in the structure of the second paragraph *value in use* could be substituted throughout for *labor*.

The Source Of Marx's Error — Doctrines
Borrowed From Smith And Ricardo, Which Were Wrong

Of such a nature are the reasoning and the method employed by Marx in introducing into his system his fundamental proposition that labor is the sole basis of value. In my opinion it is quite impossible that this dialectical hocus-pocus constituted the ground and source of Marx's own convictions. It would have been impossible for a thinker such as he was (and I look upon him as an intellectual force of the very highest order), to have followed such tortuous and unnatural methods had he been engaged, with a free and open mind, in really investigating the actual connections of things, and in forming his own conclusions with regard to them; it would have been impossible for him to fall successively by mere accident into all the errors of thought and method which I have described, and to arrive at the conclusion that labor is the sole source of value as the natural outgrowth, not the desired and predetermined result, of such a mode of inquiry.

I think the case was really different. That Marx was truly and honestly convinced of the truth of his thesis I do not doubt. But the grounds of his conviction are not those which he gives in his system. They were in reality opinions rather than thought-out conclusions. Above all they were opinions derived from authority. Smith and Ricardo, the great authorities, as was then at least believed, had taught the same doctrine. They had not *proved* it any more than Marx. They had only postulated it from certain general and confused impressions. But they explicitly contradicted it when they examined things more closely and in quarters where a closer examination could not be avoided. Smith, in the same way as Marx in his third volume, taught that in a developed economic system values and prices gravitate towards a level of costs which besides labor comprises an average profit of capital. And Ricardo, too, in the celebrated fourth section of the chapter "On Value," clearly and definitely stated that by the side of labor, mediate or immediate, the amount of capital invested and the duration of the investment exercise a determining influence on the value of the goods. In order to maintain without obvious contradiction their cherished philosophical principle that labor is the "true" source of value, they were obliged to beat a retreat to mythical times and places in which capitalists and landed proprietors did not exist. There they could maintain it without contradiction, for there was nothing to restrain them. Experience, which does not support the theory, was not there to refute them. Nor were they restrained by a scientific, psychological analysis, for like Marx they avoided such an analysis. They did not seek to prove but they postulated, as a "natural" state, an idyllic state of things where labor and value were one.[26]

While Smith And Ricardo Were Confused, Marx Blundered Egregiously

It was to tendencies and views of this kind, which had acquired from Smith and Ricardo a great but not undisputed authority, that Marx became heir, and as an ardent socialist he willingly believed in them. It is not surprising that he did not take a more skeptical attitude, with regard to a view which was so well adapted to support his economic theory of the world, than did Ricardo, to whom it must have gone sorely against the grain. It is not surprising, too, that he did not allow those views of the classical writers which were against him to excite any critical doubts in his own mind on the doctrine that value is wholly labor, but considered that they were only attempts on their part to escape in an indirect way from the unpleasant conse-

[26] The position which is taken by Smith and Ricardo towards the doctrine that value is wholly labor I have discussed exhaustively in *History and Critique of Interest Theories*, (Volume I of CAPITAL AND INTEREST) p. 287ff. and have there also shown especially that no trace of a proof of this thesis is to be found in the so-called classical writers. Compare also Knies, *Der Kredit*, 2nd section, pp. 60ff.

quences of an inconvenient truth. In short, it is not surprising that the same material on which the classical writers had grounded their half-confused, half-contradictory, and wholly unproved opinions should have served Marx as foundation for the same assumption, believed in unconditionally and with earnest conviction. For himself he needed no further evidence. Only for his system he needed a formal proof.

It is clear that he could not rely simply on the classical writers for this, as they had not proved anything; and we also know that he could not appeal to experience, or attempt an economico-psychological proof, for these methods would have straightway led him to a conclusion exactly opposite to the one he wished to establish. So he turned to dialectical speculation, which was, moreover, in keeping with the bent of his mind. And here it was a case of the end justifying the means. He knew the result that he wished to obtain, and must obtain, and so he twisted and manipulated the malleable ideas and logical premises with admirable skill and subtlety until they actually yielded the desired result in a seemingly respectable syllogistic form. Perhaps he was so blinded by his convictions that he was not aware of the monstrosities of logic and method which had necessarily crept in, or perhaps he was aware of them and thought himself justified in making use of them simply as formal supports, to give a suitable systematic dress to a truth which, according to his deepest convictions, was already substantially proved. Of that I cannot judge, neither is it now possible for any one else to do so. What I will say, however, is that no one, with so powerful a mind as Marx, has ever exhibited a logic so continuously and so palpably wrong as he exhibits in the systematic proof of his fundamental doctrine.

Section II

MARX'S METHODOLOGY WHICH CONCEALS HIS FALLACIES

Marx's Problem Of Reconciling His Theories With The Facts

This wrong thesis he now weaves into his system with admirable tactical skill. Of this we have a brilliant example in the next step he takes. Although he has carefully steered clear of the testimony of experience and has evolved his doctrine entirely "out of the depths of his mind," yet the wish to apply the test of experience cannot be altogether suppressed. If Marx himself would not do it, his readers would certainly do it on their own account. What does he do? He divides and distinguishes. At one point the disagreement between his doctrine and experience is flagrant. Taking the bull by the horns he himself seizes upon this point. He had stated as a consequence of his fundamental principle that the value of different commodities is in proportion to the working time necessary to their production (I, 14). Now it is obvious even to the casual observer that this proposition cannot maintain itself in the face of certain facts. The day's product of a sculptor, of a cabinet-maker, of a violin-maker, of an engineer, etc., certainly does not contain an equal value, but a much higher value than the day's product of a common workman or factory hand, although in both the same amount of working time is "embodied." Marx himself, with a masterly dialectic, now brings these facts up for discussion. In considering them he seeks to suggest that they do not contain a contradiction of his fundamental principle, but are only a slightly different reading of it which still comes within the limits of the rule, and that all that is needed is some explanation or more exact definition of the latter. That is to say he declares that labor in the sense of his proposition means the "expenditure of simple [unskilled] labor power, an average of which is possessed in his physical organism by every ordinary man, without special cultivation"; or in other words *simple average labor*" (I, 19, and also previously in I, 13).

> Skilled labor [he continues] *counts only as concentrated or rather multiplied unskilled labor,* so that a small quantity of skilled labor is equal to a larger quantity of unskilled labor. *That this reduction is constantly made experience shows.* A commodity may be the product of the most highly skilled labor, but *its value makes it equal to the product of unskilled labor, and represents therefore only a definite quantity of unskilled labor.* The different proportions in which different kinds of labor are reduced to unskilled labor as their unit of measure are fixed by a social process beyond the control of the producers, and therefore seem given to them by tradition.

This explanation may really sound quite plausible to the hasty reader, but if we look at it coolly and soberly we get quite a different impression.

Marx's Substitution Of "To Count" For "To Be"

The fact with which we have to deal is that the product of a day's or an hour's skilled labor is more valuable than the product of a day's or an hour's unskilled labor;

that, for instance, the day's product of a sculptor is equal to the five days' product of a stone-breaker. Now Marx tells us that things made equal to each other in exchange must contain "a common factor of the same amount," and this common factor must be labor and working time. Does he mean labor in general? Marx's first statements up to page 13 would lead us to suppose so; but it is evident that something is wrong, for the labor of five days is obviously not "the same amount" as the labor of one day. Therefore Marx, in the case before us, is no longer speaking of labor as such but of unskilled labor. The common factor must therefore be the possession of an equal amount of labor of a particular kind, namely, unskilled labor.

If we look at this dispassionately, however, it fits still worse, for in sculpture there is no "unskilled labor" at all embodied, much less therefore unskilled labor equal to the amount in the five days' labor of the stone-breaker. The plain truth is that the two products embody *different kinds* of labor in *different amounts,* and every unprejudiced person will admit that this means a state of things exactly contrary to the conditions which Marx demands and must affirm, namely, that they embody labor of the *same kind* and of the *same amount!*

Marx certainly says that skilled labor "counts" as multiplied unskilled labor, but to "count as" is not "to be," and the theory deals with the being of things. Men may naturally consider one day of a sculptor's work as equal in some respects to five days of a stone-breaker's work, just as they may also consider a deer as equal to five hares. But a statistician might with equal justification maintain, with scientific conviction, that there were one thousand hares in a cover which contained one hundred deer and five hundred hares, as a statistician of prices or a theorist about value might seriously maintain that in the day's product of a sculptor five days of unskilled labor are embodied, and that this is the true reason why it is considered in exchange to be equal to five day's labor of a stone-breaker. I will presently attempt to illustrate, by an example bearing directly on the problem of value, the multitude of things we might prove if we resorted to the verb "to count" whenever the verb "to be," etc., landed us in difficulties. But I must first add one other criticism.

How Marx Reasons In A "Vicious Circle"

Marx makes an attempt in the passages quoted to justify his maneuver of reducing skilled labor to common labor, and to justify it by experience.

That this reduction is constantly made experience shows. A commodity may be the product of the most highly skilled labor, but its value makes it equal to the product of unskilled labor, and represents therefore only a definite quantity of unskilled labor.

Good! We will let that pass for the moment and will only inquire a little more closely in what manner and by what means we are to determine the standard of this reduction, which, according to Marx, experience shows is constantly made. Here we stumble against the very natural, but for the Marxian theory the very compromising circumstance that the standard of reduction is determined solely *by the actual exchange relations themselves.* But in what proportions skilled is to be translated into terms of simple labor in the valuation of their products is not determined, nor can it be determined *à priori* by any property inherent in the skilled labor itself, but it is the actual result alone which decides the actual exchange relations. Marx himself says "their value makes them equal to the product of unskilled labor," and he refers to a "social process beyond the control of the producers which fixes the proportions in which different kinds of labor are reduced to unskilled labor as their unit of measure," and says that these proportions therefore *"seem to be given by tradition."*

Under these circumstances what is the meaning of the appeal to "value" and "the social process" as the determining factors of the standard of reduction? Apart from everything else it simply means that Marx is arguing in a complete circle. The real subject of inquiry is the exchange relations of commodities: why, for instance, a statuette which has cost a sculptor one day's labor should exchange for a cart of stones which has cost a stone-breaker five days' labor, and not for a larger or smaller quantity of stones, in the breaking of which ten or three days' labor have been expended. How does Marx explain this? He says the exchange relation is this, and no other—because one day of sculptor's work is reducible exactly to five days of unskilled work. And why is it reducible to exactly five days? Because experience shows that it is so reduced by a social process. And what is this social process? The same process that has to be explained, that very process by means of which the product of one day of sculptor's labor has been made equal to the value of the product of five days of common labor. But if as a matter of fact it were exchanged regularly against the product of only three days of simple labor, Marx would equally bid us accept the rate of reduction of 1:3 as the one derived from experience, and would found upon it and explain by it the assertion that a statuette must be equal in exchange to the product of exactly three days of a stone-breaker's work—not more and not less. In short, it is clear that we shall never learn in this way the actual reasons why products of different kinds of work should be exchanged in this or that proportion. They exchange in this way, Marx tells us, though in slightly different words, because, according to experience, they do exchange in this way!

Efforts Of Others To Salvage Marx's Reasoning Are Unsuccessful

I remark further in passing that the followers (*epigoni*) after Marx, having perhaps recognized the circle I have just described, have made the attempt to place the reduction of complicated to simple work on another, a real, basis.

"It is no fiction but a fact," says Grabski,[27] "that an hour of skilled labor contains several hours of unskilled labor." For "in order to be consistent, we must also take into account the labor which was used in acquiring the skill." I do not think it will need many words to show clearly the complete inadequacy also of this explanation. I have nothing to say against the view that to labor in actual operation should be added the quota due to the acquirement of the power to labor. But it is clear that the difference in value of skilled labor as opposed to unskilled labor could only then be explained by reference to this additional quota if the amount of the latter corresponded to the amount of that difference. For instance, in the case we have given, there could only be actually five hours of unskilled labor in one hour of skilled labor, if four hours of preparatory labor went to every hour of skilled labor; or, reckoned in greater units, if out of fifty years of life which a sculptor devotes to the learning and practicing of his profession, he spends forty years in educational work in order to do skilled work for ten years. But no one will maintain that such a proportion or anything approaching to it is actually found to exist. I turn therefore again from the obviously inadequate hypothesis of a follower to the teaching of the master himself in order to illustrate the nature and range of its errors by one other example, which I think will bring out most clearly the fault in Marx's mode of reasoning.

Marx's Argument Extended To Materials In Order To Demonstrate Its Absurdity

With the very same reasoning one could affirm and argue the proposition that the quantity of material contained in commodities constitutes the principle and meas-

27 *Deutsche Worte*, Vol. XV, part 3, March, 1895, p. 155.

ure of exchange value—that commodities exchange in proportion to the *quantity of material incorporated in them*. Ten pounds of material in one kind of commodity exchange against 10 pounds of material in another kind of commodity. If the natural objection were raised that this statement was obviously false because 10 pounds of gold do not exchange against 10 pounds of iron but against 40,000 pounds, or against a still greater number of pounds of coal, we may reply after the manner of Marx, that it is the amount of *common average material* that affects the formation of value, that acts as unit of measurement. Skilfully wrought costly material of special quality *counts* only as compound or rather multiplied common material, so that a small quantity of material fashioned with skill is equal to a larger quantity of common material. *That this reduction is constantly made experience shows.* A commodity may be of the most exquisite material; its *value* can be equated to commodities formed of common material, and *therefore represents only a particular quantity of common material*. A "social process," the existence of which cannot be doubted, is persistently reducing the pound of raw gold to 40,000 pounds of raw iron, and the pound of raw silver to 1,500 pounds of raw iron. The working up of the gold by an ordinary goldsmith or by the hand of a great artist gives rise to further variations in the character of the material to which use, in conformity with experience, does justice by means of special standards of reduction. If 1 pound of bar gold, therefore, exchanges against 40,000 pounds of bar iron, or if a gold cup of the same weight, wrought by Benvenuto Cellini, exchanges against 4,000,000 pounds of iron, it is not a violation but a confirmation of the proposition that commodities exchange in proportion to the "average" material they contain!

I think the impartial reader will easily recognize once more in these two arguments the two ingredients of the Marxian recipe—the substitution of "to count" for "to be," and the explanation in a circle which consists in obtaining the standard of reduction from the actually existing social exchange relations which themselves need explanation. In this way Marx has settled his account with the facts that most glaringly contradict his theory with great dialectical skill, certainly, but, as far as the matter itself is concerned, naturally and inevitably in a quite inadequate manner.

Ricardo Acknowledged Exceptions To His (Erroneous) Law Of Value, But Marx First Ignores And Then Condemns Them

But there are, besides, contradictions with actual experience rather less striking than the foregoing; those, namely, which spring from the part that the *investment of capital* has in determining the actual prices of commodities, the same which Ricardo—as we have already noticed—treats of in Section IV of the chapter "On Value." Towards them Marx adopts a change of tactics. For a time he completely shuts his eyes to them. He ignores them, by a process of abstraction, through the first and second volumes, and pretends that they do not exist; that is to say, he proceeds throughout the whole detailed exposition of his doctrine of value, and likewise throughout the development of his theory of surplus value, on the "assumption"—in part tacitly maintained, in part clearly asserted—that commodities really exchange according to their values, which means exactly in proportion to the labor embodied in them.[28]

This hypothetical abstraction he combines with an uncommonly clever dialectical move. He gives certain actual deviations from the law, from which a theorist may really venture to abstract, namely, the accidental and temporary fluctuations of the market prices round their normal fixed level. And on the occasions when Marx explains his intention to disregard the deviations of the prices from the values he does not fail to direct the reader's attention to those "accidental circumstances" which have to be ignored as "the constant oscillations of the market prices," whose "rise and fall compensate each other," and which "reduce themselves to an average price as their inner law."[29] By this reference he gains the reader's approval of his abstraction, but the fact that he does not abstract merely from accidental fluctuations but also from regular, permanent, typical "deviations," whose existence constitutes an integral part of the rule to be elucidated, is not made manifest to the reader who is not closely observant, and he glides unsuspectingly over the author's fatal error of method.

For it is a fatal error of method to ignore in scientific investigation the very point that demands explanation. Now Marx's theory of surplus value aims at nothing else than the explanation, as he conceives it, of the profits of capital. But the profits of capital lie exactly in those regular deviations of the prices of commodities from the amount of their mere costs in labor. If, therefore, we ignore those deviations, we ignore just the principal part of what has to be explained. Rodbertus[30] was guilty of the same error

[28] For example, 141ff., 150, 151, 158, and often; also in the beginning of the third volume, III, 25, 128, 132.

[29] For example, volume I, 150, note 37.

[30] As to Rodbertus, see the exhaustive account in my *History and Critique of Interest Theories* (Volume I of Capital and Interest) pp. 272ff., and more especially Note 62 on p. 469f.

of method, and twelve years ago I taxed him, as well as Marx, with it; and I venture now to repeat the concluding words of the criticism I then made:

> And the socialist adherents of the exploitation theory seek to maintain such a proposition, built on sand as it is! Nor do they employ it just incidentally, and to shore up some inconsequential angle of the structure of their theory. Indeed, they make of it a keystone to support the very facade of their most vital and practical claims. They uphold the law that the value of all goods consists in the labor time they represent. Then the next moment they attack any creation of wealth that is in conflict with this "law," such as the differences in exchange value which accrue to the capitalist as a surplus value. They call it "contrary to the law," "unnatural," "unjust," and recommend that it be abolished. That is to say, first they ignore the exception, in order to be able to proclaim their law of value as having universal validity. And after their furtive theft of that quality of universal validity, they revive their memories of the exceptions, to brand them as violations of the law. This method of argumentation is truly just as bad as that which would be followed by one who, observing that they are many foolish men, ignores the fact that there are also some wise men, in order to derive the "universally valid law," that "all men are foolish," and then demands the extirpation of the "unlawfully" existent wise men.[31]

When Marx's Theories And The Facts Are In Harmony He Reasons Well, But Otherwise Disingenuously

By his maneuver of abstraction Marx certainly gained a great tactical advantage for his own version of the case. He, "by hypothesis," shut out from his system the disturbing real world, and did not therefore, so long as he could maintain this exclusion, come into conflict with it; and he does maintain it through the greater part of the first volume, through the whole of the second volume, and through the first quarter of the third volume. In this middle part of the Marxian system the logical development and connection present a really imposing closeness and intrinsic consistency. Marx is free to use good logic here because, by means of hypothesis, he has in advance made the facts to square with his ideas, and can therefore be true

[31] *Ibid.*, p. 302.

to the latter without knocking up against the former. And when Marx is free to use sound logic he does so in a truly masterly way. However wrong the starting point may be, these middle parts of the system, by their extraordinary logical consistency, permanently establish the reputation of the author as an intellectual force of the first rank. And it is a circumstance that has served not a little to increase the practical influence of the Marxian system that during this long middle part of his work, which, as far as intrinsic consistency is concerned, is really essentially faultless, the readers who have got happily over the difficulties at the beginning get time to accustom themselves to the Marxian world of thought and to gain confidence in his connection of ideas, which here flow so smoothly one out of the other, and form themselves into such a well-arranged whole. It is on these readers, whose confidence has been thus won, that he makes those hard demands which he is at last obliged to bring forward in his third volume. For, long though Marx delayed to open his eyes to the facts of real life, he had to do it some time or other. He had at last to confess to his readers that in actual life commodities do not exchange, regularly and of necessity, in proportion to the labor time incorporated in them, but in part exchange above and in part below this proportion, according as the capital invested demands a smaller or a larger amount of the average profit; in short that, besides labor time, investment of capital forms a coordinate determinant of the exchange relation of commodities. From this point he was confronted with two difficult tasks. In the first place he had to justify himself to his readers for having in the earlier parts of his work and for so long taught that labor was the sole determinant of exchange relations; and secondly—what was perhaps the more difficult task—he had also to give his readers a theoretical explanation of the facts which were hostile to his theory, an explanation which certainly could not fit into his labor theory of value without leaving a residuum, but which must not, on the other hand, contradict it.

One can understand that good straightforward logic could no longer be used in these demonstrations. We now witness the counterpart to the confused beginning of the system. There Marx had to do violence to facts in order to deduce a theorem which could not be straightforwardly deduced from them, and he had to do still greater violence to logic and commit the most incredible fallacies into the bargain. Now the situation repeats itself. Now again the propositions which through two volumes have been in undisturbed possession of the field come into collision with the facts with which they are naturally as little in agreement as they were before. Nevertheless the harmony of the system has to be maintained, and it can only be maintained at the cost of the logic. The Marxian system, therefore, presents us now with a spectacle at first sight strange, but, under the circumstances described, quite natural, namely, that by far the greater part of the system is a masterpiece of close and forcible logic worthy of the intellect of its author, but that in two places—and those, alas! just the most decisive places—incredibly weak and careless reasoning is inserted. The first place is just at the beginning when the theory first separates itself from the facts, and the second is after the first quarter of the third volume when facts are again brought within the horizon of the reader. I here refer more especially to the tenth chapter of the third volume (pp. 151-79).

*   *   *

We have already become acquainted with one part of its contents, and we have subjected it to our criticism, the part, namely, where Marx defends himself against the accusation that there is a contradiction between the law of the price of production and the "law of value."[32] It still remains, however, to glance at the second object with which the chapter is concerned, the explanation with which Marx introduces into his system that theory of the price of production which takes account of actual conditions.[33] This consideration leads us also to one of the most instructive and most characteristic points of the Marxian system—the position of *"competition"* in the system.

Section III

MARX'S MINIMIZATION OF COMPETITION; HIS FALLACIES CONCERNING IT

**How Psychological Motivation Is
The Prime Factor In Competition**

"Competition," as I have already hinted, is a sort of collective name for all the psychical motives and impulses which determine the action of the dealers in the market, and which thus influence the fixing of prices. The buyer

[32] See foregoing p. 229ff.

[33] Of course I here quite disregard comparatively small differences of opinion. I have especially refrained in the whole of this essay from emphasizing or even mentioning the finer shades of difference which obtain in relation to the conception of the "law of costs."

has his motives which actuate him in buying, and which
provide him with a certain guide as to the prices which
he is prepared to offer either at once or in the last resort.
And the seller and the producer are also actuated by certain motives—motives which determine the seller to part
with his commodities at a certain price and not at another
price, and the producer to continue and even to extend his
production when prices reach a certain level, or to suspend
it when they are at a different level. In the competition
between buyer and seller all these motives and determinants
encounter each other, and whoever refers to competition
to explain the formation of prices appeals in effect to
what under a collective name is the active play of all the
psychical impulses and motives which had directed both
sides of the market.

Marx's Minimization Of Competition

Marx is now, for the most part, engaged in the endeavor to give to competition and the forces operating in it
the lowest possible place in his system. He either ignores
it, or, if he does not do this, he tries to belittle the manner
and degree of its influence where and whenever he can. This
is shown in a striking way on several occasions.

First of all he does this when he deduces his law that
value is wholly labor. Every impartial person knows and
sees that that influence which the quantity of labor employed exerts on the permanent level of prices of goods
(an influence not really so special and peculiar as the
Marxian law of value makes it appear) acts only through
the play of supply and demand, that is to say, through competition. In the case of exceptional exchanges, or in the
case of monopoly, prices may come into existence which
(even apart from the claim of the capital invested) are out
of all proportion to the working time incorporated. Marx
naturally knows this too, but he makes no reference to it
in his deduction of the law of value. If he had referred
to it, then he would have been unable to put aside the question in what way and by what middle steps labor time
should come to be the sole influence determining price
among all the motives and factors which play their part
under the flag of competition. The complete analysis of
those motives, which then could not have been avoided,
would inevitably have placed the value in use much more
in the foreground than would have suited Marx, and would
have cast a different light on many things, and finally would
have revealed much to which Marx did not wish to allow
any weight in his system.

And so on the very occasion when, in order to give

a complete and systematic explanation of his law of value, it would have been his duty to have shown the part which competition plays as intermediary, he passes away from the point without a word. Later on he does notice it, but, to judge from the place and the manner, not as if it were an important point in the theoretical system; in some casual and cursory remarks he alludes to it in a few words as something that more or less explains itself, and he does not trouble himself to go further into it.

But Marx Contrarily Assumes Active Competition

I think that the said facts about competition are most clearly and concisely set forth by Marx on page 156 of the third volume, where the exchange of commodities at prices which approximate to their "values" and correspond therefore to the working time incorporated in them is said to be subject to the three following conditions: (1) That the exchange of commodities be not merely an *"accidental or occasional one."* (2) That commodities "on both sides should be produced in quantities nearly proportionate to the reciprocal demand, *which itself results from the experience of both sides of the market, and which therefore grows as a result out of a sustained exchange itself";* and (3) *"That no natural or artificial monopoly* should give to either of the contracting parties the power to sell above the value, or should force either of them to sell below the value." And so what Marx demands as a condition of his law of value coming into operation is a brisk competition on both sides which should have lasted long enough to adjust production relatively to the needs of the buyer according to the experience of the market. We must bear this passage well in mind.

No more detailed proof is added. On the contrary, a little later—indeed, just in the middle of those arguments in which, relatively speaking, he treats most exhaustively of competition, its two sides of demand and supply, and its relation to the fixing of prices—Marx expressly declines a "deeper analysis of these two social impelling forces" as "not apposite here."[34]

Marx's Method Of Negating The Influence Of Competition On Prices, By His Peculiar Dialectics

But this is not all. In order to belittle the importance of supply and demand for theory, and perhaps also to justify his neglect of these factors, Marx thought out a peculiar and remarkable theory which he developes on pages 169-70 of the third volume, after some previous slight allusions to it. He starts by saying that when one of the two

[34] Vol. III, 169. See also foregoing, p. 259.

factors preponderates over the other, demand over supply, for instance, or vice versa, irregular market prices are formed which deviate from the "market value," which constitutes the "point of equilibrium" for these market prices; that on the other hand, if commodities should sell at this their normal market value, demand and supply must exactly balance each other. And to that he adds the following remarkable argument: "If demand and supply balance each other *they cease to act*. If two forces act equally in opposite directions they cancel each other—they produce no result, and phenomena occurring under these conditions *must be explained by some other agency than either of these forces*. If supply and demand cancel each other *they cease to explain anything, they do not affect the market value*, and they leave us altogether in the dark as to the reasons why the market value should express itself in just this and no other sum of money." The relation of demand to supply can be rightly used to explain the "deviations from the market value" which are due to the preponderance of one force over the other, but not the level of the market value itself.

That this curious theory squared with the Marxian system is obvious. If the relation of supply to demand had absolutely no bearing on the level of permanent prices, then Marx was quite right, in laying down his principles, not to trouble himself further with this unimportant factor, and straightway to introduce into his system the factor which, in his opinion, exercised a real influence on the degree of value, that is, labor.

Marx's Misunderstanding Regarding In What Part Of The Market Supply And Demand Balance

It is, however, not less obvious, I think, that this curious theory is absolutely false. Its reasoning rests, as is so often the case with Marx, on a play upon words.

It is quite true that when a commodity sells at its normal market value, supply and demand must in a certain sense balance each other: that is to say, at this price, just the same quantity of the commodity is effectively demanded as is offered. But this is not only the case when commodities are sold at a normal market value, but at whatever market value they are sold, even when it is a varying, irregular one. Moreover, every one knows quite well, as does Marx himself, that supply and demand are elastic quantities. In addition to the supply and demand which enters into exchange, there is always an "excluded" demand or supply, that is, a number of people who equally desire the commodities for their needs, but who will not or cannot offer the

prices offered by their stronger competitors; and a number of people who are also prepared to offer the desired
commodities, only at higher prices than can be obtained
in the then state of the market. But the saying that demand and supply "balance each other" does not apply absolutely to the *total* demand and supply, but only to the
successful part of it. It is well known, however, that the
business of the market consists just in selecting the successful part out of the total demand and the total supply, and
that the most important means to this selection is the fixing of price. More commodities cannot be bought than are
sold. Hence, on the two sides, only a certain fixed number
of reflectors (that is, reflectors for only a certain fixed number of commodities) can arrive at a focus. The selection
of this number is accomplished by the automatic advance
of prices to a point which excludes the excess in number
on both sides; so that the price is at the same time too
high for the excess of the would-be buyers and too low
for the excess of the would-be sellers. It is not, therefore,
the successful competitors only who take part in determining the level of prices, but the respective circumstances of
those who are excluded have a share in it as well;[35] and
on that account, if on no other, it is wrong to argue the
complete suspension of the action of supply and demand
from the equilibrium of the part which comes effectively
into the market.

The Balancing Of Supply And Demand Does Not Mean The Elimination Of Those Forces

But it is wrong also for another reason. Assuming
that it is only the successful part of supply and demand,
being in quantitative equilibrium, that affects the fixing
of price, it is quite erroneous and unscientific to assume
that forces which hold each other in equilibrium therefore
"cease to act." On the contrary, the state of equilibrium is
just the result of their action, and when an explanation has
to be given of this state of equilibrium with all its details
— one of the most prominent of which is the height of
the level in which the equilibrium was found—it certainly
cannot be given "in some other way than by the agency
of the two forces." On the contrary, it is only by the

---

[35] A closer analysis shows that the price must fall between
the money estimates of the so-called marginal pairs, that is, between
the amounts which the last actual buyer and the first would-be buyer
who is excluded from the market are prepared to offer, and the
amounts which the last actual seller and the first would-be seller
who is excluded are prepared to take in the last resort for the commodities. For further details see my *Positive Theory of Capital*
(Volume II of CAPITAL AND INTEREST) p. 220ff.; especially, p. 224.

agency of the forces which maintain the equilibrium that it can be explained. But such abstract propositions can best be illustrated by a practical example.

Suppose we send up an air balloon. Everybody knows that a balloon rises if and because it is filled with a gas which is lighter than air. It does not rise indefinitely, however, but only to a certain height, where it remains floating so long as nothing occurs, such as an escape of gas, to alter the conditions. Now how is the degree of altitude regulated, and by what factor is it determined? This is transparently evident. The density of air diminishes as we rise. The balloon rises only so long as the density of the surrounding stratum of atmosphere is greater than its own density, and it ceases to rise when its own density and the density of the atmosphere hold each other in equipoise. The less dense the gas, therefore, the higher the balloon will rise, and the higher the stratum of air in which it finds the same degree of atmospheric density. It is obvious, under these circumstances, therefore, that the height to which the balloon rises cannot be explained in any other way than by considering the relative density of the balloon on one side and of the air on the other.

How does the matter appear, however, from the Marxian point of view? At a certain height both forces, density of the balloon and density of the surrounding air, are in equipoise. They, therefore, "cease to act," they "cease to explain anything," they do not affect the degree of ascent, and if we wish to explain this we must do it by "something else than the agency of these two forces." "Indeed," we say, "By what then?" Or again, when the index of a weighing machine points to 100 pounds when a body is being weighed, how are we to account for this position of the index of the weighing machine? We are *not* to account for it by the relation of the weight of the body to be weighed on the one side and the weights which serve in the weighing machine on the other, for these two forces, when the index of the weighing machine is in the position referred to, hold each other in equipoise; they therefore cease to act, and nothing can be explained from their relationship, not even the position of the index of the weighing machine.

I think the fallacy here is obvious, and that it is not less obvious that the same kind of fallacy lies at the root of the arguments by which Marx reasons away the influence of supply and demand on the level of permanent prices. Let there be no misunderstanding, however. It is by no means my opinion that a really complete and satisfying explanation of the fixing of permanent prices is contained in a reference to the formula of supply and demand. On the contrary, the opinion, which I have elsewhere often expressed at length,[36] is that the elements which can only be roughly comprehended under the term "supply and demand" ought to be closely analyzed, and the manner and measure of their reciprocal influence exactly defined; and that in this way we should proceed to the attainment of the knowledge of those elements which exert a special influence on the state of prices. But the influence of the relation of supply and demand which Marx reasons away is an indispensable link in this further and more profound explanation; it is not a side issue, but one that goes to the heart of the subject.

Marx's Employment Of The Idea Of Competition For Arguing Toward Opposite, Conflicting Ends

Let us take up again the threads of our argument. Various things have shown us how hard Marx tries to make the influence of supply and demand retire into the background of his system, and now at the remarkable turn which his system takes after the first quarter of the third volume he is confronted by the task of explaining why the permanent prices of commodities do not gravitate towards the incorporated quantity of labor but towards the "prices of production" which deviate from it.

He declares competition to be the force which causes this. Competition reduces the original rates of profit, which were different for the different branches of production according to the different organic compositions of the capitals, to a common average rate of profit,[37] and consequently the prices must in the long run gravitate towards the prices of production yielding the one equal average profit.

Let us hasten to settle some points which are important to the understanding of this explanation.

Firstly, it is certain that a reference to competition is in effect nothing else than a reference to the action of supply and demand. In the passage already mentioned, in which Marx describes most concisely the process of the equalization of the rates of profit by the competition of capitals (III, 175), he expressly says that this process is brought about by "such a relation of supply to demand, that the average profit is made equal in the different spheres of production, and that therefore values change into prices of production."

[36] *Positive Theory of Capital* (Volume II of CAPITAL AND INTEREST), Book III, pp. 207-256.

[37] See foregoing pp. 223ff.

Secondly, it is certain that, as regards this process, it is not a question of mere *fluctuations* round the center of gravitation contemplated in the theory of the first two volumes, that is, round the incorporated working time, but a question of a *definitive forcing* of prices to another permanent center of gravitation, namely, the price of production.

And now question follows on question.

The High Point Of Inconsistency In Marx's Argument

If, according to Marx, the relation of supply and demand exerts no influence at all on the level of permanent prices, how can competition, which is identical with this relation, be the power which shifts the level of the permanent prices from the level of "value" to a level so different as that of the price of production?

Do we not rather see, in this forced and inconsistent appeal to competition as the *deus ex machina* which drives the permanent prices from that center of gravitation which is in keeping with the theory of embodied labor to another center, an involuntary confession that the social forces which govern actual life contain in themselves, and bring into action, some elementary determinants of exchange relations which *cannot* be reduced to working time, and that consequently the analysis of the original theory which yielded working time alone as the basis of exchange relations was an incomplete one which did not correspond with the facts?

And further: Marx has told us himself, and we have carefully noted the passage,[38] that commodities exchange approximately to their values only when a brisk competition exists. Thus he, at that time, appealed to competition as a factor which tends to push the prices of commodities towards their "values." And now we learn, on the contrary, that competition is a force which pushes the prices of commodities away from their values and on to their prices of production. These statements, moreover, are found in one and the same chapter—the tenth chapter, destined, it would seem, to an unhappy notoriety. Can they be reconciled? And, if Marx perhaps thought that he could find a reconciliation in the view that one proposition applied to primitive conditions and the other to developed modern society, must we not point out to him that in the first chapter of his work he did not deduce his theory that value was wholly labor from a Robinson Crusoe situation, but

[38] See foregoing pp. 280f.

from the conditions of a society in which a "capitalistic mode of production prevails" and the "wealth" of which "appears as an immense collection of commodities?" And does he not demand of us throughout his whole work that we should view the conditions of our modern society in the light of his theory of labor, and judge them by it? But when we ask where, according to his own statements, we are to seek in modern society for the region in which his law of value is in force, we ask in vain. For either there is no competition, in which case commodities do not at all exchange according to their values, says Marx (III, 156); or competition exists, and precisely then, he states, they exchange still less according to their values, but according to their prices of production (III, 176).

Marx's Deplorable Tenth Chapter

And so in the unfortunate tenth chapter contradiction is heaped upon contradiction. I will not prolong the already lengthy inquiry by counting up all the lesser contradictions and inaccuracies with which this chapter abounds. I think every one who reads the chapter with an impartial mind will get the impression that the writing is, so to say, demoralized. Instead of the severe, pregnant, careful style, instead of the iron logic to which we are accustomed in the most brilliant parts of Marx's works, we have here an uncertain and desultory manner not only in the reasoning but even in the use of technical terms. How striking, for instance, is the constantly changing conception of the terms "supply" and "demand," which at one time are presented to us, quite rightly, as elastic quantities, with differences of intensity, but at another are regarded, after the worst manner of a long-exploded "vulgar economy," as simple quantities. Or how unsatisfying and inconsistent is the description of the factors which govern the market value, if the different portions of the mass of commodities which come into the market are created under unequal conditions of production, etc.

The explanation of this feature of the chapter cannot be found simply in the fact that it was written by Marx when he was growing old; for even in later parts there are many splendidly written arguments; and even this unfortunate chapter, of which obscure hints were already scattered here and there in the first volume,[39] must have been *thought out* in early times. Marx's writing is confused and vacillating here because he could not venture to write clearly and definitely without open contradiction and retraction. If at the time when he was dealing with actual

[39] For example, Vol. I, p. 151, note 37 at foot; p. 210, note 31.

exchange relations—those manifested in real life—he had pursued the subject with the same luminous penetration and thoroughness with which he followed, through two volumes, to its utmost logical conclusion, the hypothesis that value is labor; if at this juncture he had given to the important term "competition" a scientific import, by a careful economico-psychological analysis of the social motive forces which come into action under that comprehensive name; if he had not halted or rested, so long as a link in the argument remained unexplained, or a consequence not carried to its logical conclusion; or so long as one relation appeared dark and contradictory—and almost every word of this tenth chapter challenges a deeper inquiry or explanation such as this—he would have been driven step by step to the exposition of a system altogether different in purport from that of his original system, nor would he have been able to avoid the open contradiction and retraction of the main proposition of the original system. This could only be avoided by confusion and mystification. Marx must often instinctively have felt this, even if he did not know it, when he expressly declined the deeper analysis of the social motive forces.

Herein lies, I believe, the Alpha and Omega of all that is fallacious, contradictory, and vague in the treatment of his subject by Marx. His system is not in close touch with facts. Marx has not deduced from facts the fundamental principles of his system, either by means of a sound empiricism or a solid economico-psychological analysis; but, he founds it on no firmer ground than a formal dialectic. This is the great radical fault of the Marxian system at its birth; from it all the rest necessarily springs. The system runs in one direction, facts go in another; and they cross the course of the system sometimes here, sometimes there, and on each occasion the original fault begets a new fault. The conflict of system and facts must be kept from view, so that the matter is shrouded either in darkness or vagueness, or it is turned and twisted with the same tricks of dialectic as at the outset; or where none of this avails we have a contradiction. Such is the character of the tenth chapter of Marx's third volume. It brought the long-deferred bad harvest, which had to grow inevitably out of the bad seed.

CHAPTER V

Werner Sombart's Apology

Sombart's View: Marx's Value As Nothing More Than A "Fact Of Thought" And Not Of "Experience"

An apologist of Marx, as intelligent as he is ardent, has lately appeared in the person of Werner Sombart.[40] His apology, however, shows one peculiar feature. In order to be able to defend Marx's doctrines he has first to put a new interpretation upon them.

Let us go at once to the main point. Sombart admits (and even adds some very subtle arguments to the proof)[41] that the Marxian law of value is false if it claims to be in harmony with actual experience. He says (p. 573) of the Marxian law of value that it "is *not* exhibited in the exchange relation of capitalistically produced commodities," that it "does *not* by any means indicate the point towards which market prices gravitate," that "*just as little* does it act as a factor of distribution in the division of the yearly social product," and that "it *never comes into evidence anywhere*" (p. 577). The "outlawed value" has only "one place of refuge left—*the thought of the theoretical economist. . . .* If we want to sum up the characteristics of Marx's value, we would say, *his value is a fact not of experience but of thought*" (p. 574).

What Sombart means by this "existence in thought" we shall see directly; but first we must stop for a moment to consider the admission that the Marxian value has no existence in the world of real phenomena. I am somewhat curious to know whether the Marxists will ratify this admission. It may well be doubted, as Sombart himself had to quote a protest from the Marxian camp, occasioned by an utterance of K. Schmidt and raised in advance against such a view. "The law of value is not a law of our thought merely; . . . the law of value is a law of a very real nature: it is a natural law of human action."[42] I think it also very questionable whether Marx himself would have ratified the admission. It is Sombart himself who again, with note-

---

[40] See the already repeatedly mentioned article "Zur Kritik des Ökonomischen Systems von Karl Marx" in the *Archiv für Sociale Gesetzgebung und Statistik*, Vol. VII, part 4, pp. 555ff. See also Publisher's Note on p. 301f.

[41] See foregoing, pp. 244f.

[42] Hugo Landé, *Die Neue Zeit*, Vol. XI.

worthy frankness, gives the reader a whole list of passages from Marx which make this interpretation difficult.[43] For my own part I hold it to be wholly irreconcilable with the letter and spirit of the Marxian teaching.

Sombart's Views Are Not Reconcilable With Marx's

Let anyone read without bias the arguments with which Marx develops his theory of value. He begins his inquiry, as he himself says, in the domain of "capitalistically organized society, whose wealth is an immense collection of commodities," and with the analysis of a commodity (I, 9). In order to "get on the track" of value he starts from the exchange relation of the commodity (I, 23). Does he start from an actual exchange relation, I ask, or from an imaginary one? If he had said or meant the latter, no reader would have thought it worth while to pursue so idle a speculation. He does indeed make very decided reference—as was inevitable—to the phenomena of the actual economic world. The exchange relation of two commodities, he says, can always be represented by an equation: thus 8 bushels wheat= 1 cwt. iron. "What does this equation prove? *That a common factor of the same magnitude exists* in both things, and each of the two, *in so far as it is an exchange value, must be* reducible to this third," which third, as we learn on the next page, is labor of the same quantity.

If you maintain that the same quantity of labor *exists* in things made equal in exchange, and that these things *must* be reducible to equal amounts of labor, you are claiming for these conditions an existence in the real world and not merely in thought. Marx's former line of argument, we must bear in mind, would have been quite impossible if beside it he had wished to propound, for actual exchange relations, the dogma that products of *unequal* amounts of labor exchange, on principle, with each other. If he had admitted this notion (and the conflict with facts with which I reproach him lies in his not admitting it), he would certainly have to come to quite different conclusions. Either he would have been obliged to declare that the so-called equalization in exchange is no true equation, and does not admit of the conclusion that "a common factor *of equal magnitude*" is present in the exchanged things, or he would have been obliged to come to the conclusion that the sought-for common factor of equal magnitude is *not*, and could not be, labor. In any case it would have been impossible for him to have continued to reason as he did.

And Marx goes on to say very decidedly on numerous

[43] *Loc. cit.*, p. 575, then pp. 584ff.

occasions that his "value" lies at the root of exchange relations, so that indeed products of equal amounts of labor are "equivalents," and as such exchange for each other.[44] In many places, some of which are quoted by Sombart himself,[45] he claims that his law of value possesses the character and the potency of a *law of nature*, "it forces its way as the law of gravity does when the house comes down over one's head."[46] Even in the third volume he distinctly sets forth the actual conditions (they amount to a brisk competition on both sides) which must obtain "in order that the prices at which commodities exchange with each other should correspond approximately to their value," and explains further that this "naturally only signifies that their value is the center of gravitation round which their prices move" (III, 156).

We may mention in this connection that Marx also often quotes with approval older writers who maintained the proposition that the exchange value of goods was determined by the labor embodied in them, and maintained it undoubtedly as a proposition which was in harmony with actual exchange relations. [47]

Sombart himself, moreover, notes an argument of Marx in which he quite distinctly claims for his law of value an "empirical" and "historical" truth (III, 155 in connection with III, 175ff.).

And finally, if Marx claimed only a validity in thought and not in things for his law of value, what meaning would there have been in the painful efforts we have described, with which he sought to prove that, in spite of the theory

[44] For example, Vol. I, 25; Equivalent = *Exchangeable*. "It is only as a value that it (linen) can be brought into relation with the coat as possessing an *equal value* or *exchangeability with it*." . . . "When the coat as a thing of value is placed on an equality with the linen, the work existing in the former is made equal to the work existing in the latter." See besides pp. 27, 31 (the proportion in which coats and linen are exchangeable depends on the degree of value of the coats), p. 35 (where Marx declares human work to be the "real element of equality" in the house and the beds which exchange with each other), pp. 39, 40, 41, 42, 43, 50, 51, 52, 53 (Analysis of the price of commodities [but of actual prices only!—B-B] leads to the determining of the amount of value), p. 60 (exchange value is the social contrivance for *expressing the labor* expended on a thing), p. 80 ("the price is the money name for the work realized in a commodity"), p. 141 ("the same exchange value, that is, the same quantum of realized social work"), p. 174 ("According to the universal law of value, for example, 10 lbs. of yarn are an equivalent for 10 lbs. of cotton and a quarter of a spindle . . . if the same working time is needed to produce both sides of this equation"), and repeatedly in the same sense.

[45] *Ibid.*, p. 575.   [46] Vol. I, 52.

[47] For example, Vol. I, 14, note 9.

of the price of production, his law of value governed actual exchange relations, because it regulated the movement of prices on the one side, and on the other the prices of production themselves?

In short, if there is any rational meaning in the tissue of logical arguments on which Marx founds his theory of labor value I do not believe he taught or could have taught it in the less pretentious sense which Sombart now endeavors to attribute to it. For the rest, it is a matter which Sombart may himself settle with the followers of Marx. For those who, like myself, consider the Marxian theory of value a failure, it is of no importance whatever. For either Marx has maintained his law of value in the more pretentious sense that it corresponds with reality, and if so we agree with Sombart's view that, maintained in this sense, it is false; or he did not ascribe any real authority to it, and then, in my opinion, it cannot be construed in any sense whatever which would give it the smallest scientific importance. It is practically and theoretically a nullity.

Critique Of Sombart's Theory Of Value

It is true that about this Sombart is of a very different opinion. I willingly accept an express invitation from this able and learned man (who expects much for the progress of science from a keen and kindly encounter of opinions) to reconsider the "criticism of Marx" on the ground of his new interpretation. I am also quite pleased to settle this particular point with him. I do so with the full consciousness that I am no longer dealing with a "criticism of Marx," such as Sombart invited me to revise on the strength of his new interpretation, but am presenting purely a "criticism of Sombart."

What, then, according to Sombart, does the existence of value as a "fact of thought" mean? It means that the "idea of value is an aid to our thought which we employ in order to make the phenomena of economic life comprehensible." More exactly, the function of the idea of value is

> to cause to pass before us, defined by quantity, the commodities which, as goods for use, are different in quality. It is clear that I fulfill this postulate if I imagine cheese, silk, and blacking as nothing but products of human labor in the abstract, and only relate them to each other quantitatively as quantities of labor, the amount of the quantity being determined by a third factor, common to all and measured by units of time.[48]

[48] "Zur Kritik des Ökonomischen Systems von Karl Marx," p. 574.

So far all goes well, till we come to a certain little hitch. For certainly it is admissible in itself for some scientific purposes, to abstract from all sorts of differences, which things may exhibit in one way or another, and to consider in them only one property, which is common to them all, and which, as a common property, furnishes the ground for comparison, commensurability, etc. In this very way mechanical dynamics, for instance, for the purpose of many of its problems rightly abstracts altogether from the form, color, density, and structure of bodies in motion, and regards them only as masses; propelled billiard-balls, flying cannon-balls, running children, trains in motion, falling stones, and moving planets, are looked upon simply as moving bodies. It is not less admissible or less to the purpose to conceive cheese, silk, blacking, as "nothing but products of human labor in the abstract."

Abstracting A Characteristic Of A Commodity Is Not The Same As Explaining Its Value

The hitch begins when Sombart, like Marx, claims for *this* idea the name of the idea of *value*. This step of his —to go closely into the matter—admits conceivably of two constructions. The word "value," as we know it, in its double application to value in use and value in exchange, is already used in scientific as well as in ordinary language to denote definite phenomena. Sombart's nomenclature, therefore, involves the claim either that that property of things, namely, the being a product of labor, which is alone taken into consideration, is the deciding factor for all cases of value in the ordinary scientific sense, and thus represents, for example, the phenomena of exchange value; or, without any *arrière pensée* of this kind, his nomenclature may be a purely arbitrary one; and, unfortunately for nomenclatures of that kind, there is as guide no fixed compulsory law, but only good judgment and a sense of fitness.

If we take the second of the two constructions, if the application of the term "value" to "embodied labor" does not carry with it the claim that embodied labor is the substance of exchange value, then the matter would be very harmless. It would be only a perfectly admissible abstraction, connected, it is true, with a most unpractical, inappropriate, and misleading nomenclature. It would be as if it suddenly occurred to a natural philosopher to give to the different bodies which, by abstraction of form, color, structure, etc., he had conceived of solely as masses, the name of "active forces," a term which we know has already established rights, denoting a function of mass and velocity, that is to say, something very different from mere mass.

There would be no scientific error in this, however, only a (practically very dangerous) gross inappropriateness of nomenclature.

But our case is obviously different. It is different with Marx and different with Sombart. And here, therefore, the hitch assumes larger proportions.

Arbitrary Abstractions Are Not Permissible

My esteemed opponent will certainly admit that we cannot make any abstraction we like to suit any scientific purpose we like. For instance, to start by conceiving the different bodies as "nothing but masses," which is legitimate in certain dynamic problems, would be plainly inadmissible in regard to acoustic or optical problems. Even within dynamics it is certainly inadmissible to abstract from shape and consistency, when setting forth, for instance, the law of wedges. These examples prove that even in science "thoughts" and "logic" cannot proceed independent of facts. For science, too, the saying holds good, *Est modus in rebus, sunt certi denique fines* [There is a limit in things; there are certain and definite limits; that is, facts are not to be ignored]. And I think that I may show, without danger of a contradiction from my esteemed opponent, that those "definite limits" consist in this, that in all cases only those peculiarities may be disregarded which are irrelevant to the phenomenon under investigation: that is, *really, actually* irrelevant. On the other hand, one must leave to the remainder — to the skeleton, as it were — of the conception which is to be subjected to further study everything that is actually relevant on the concrete side. Let us apply this to our own case.

The Marxian teaching in a very emphatic way bases the scientific investigation and criticism of the *exchange relations of commodities* on the conception of commodities as "nothing but products." Sombart endorses this, and in certain rather indefinite statements—which, on account of their indefiniteness, I do not discuss with him—he even goes so far as to view the foundations of the whole *economic existence* of man in the light of that abstraction.[49]

Other Abstractions Besides Labor
Are Relevant And Important

That embodied labor alone is of importance in the first (exchange), or even in the second case (economic existence), Sombart himself does not venture to affirm. He contents himself by asserting that with that connection the "fact *most important* economically and objectively" is

[49] For example, pp. 576, 577.

brought into prominence.[50] I will not dispute this statement, only it must certainly not be taken to mean that all the other important facts besides labor are so completely subordinate that they might be almost, if not altogether disregarded, from their insignificance. Nothing could be less true. It is in the highest degree important for the economic existence of human beings whether, for instance, the land which they inhabit is like the valley of the Rhone, or the desert of Sahara, or Greenland; and it is also a matter of great importance whether human labor is aided by a previously accumulated stock of goods—a factor which also cannot be referred exclusively to labor. Labor is certainly *not* objectively the most important circumstance for many goods, especially as regards exchange relations. We may mention, as instances, trunks of old oaktrees, beds of coal, and plots of land; and even if it be admitted that labor is most important for the greater part of commodities, still the fact must be emphasized that the influence of the other factors, which are determinative together with labor, is so important that actual exchange relations diverge considerably from the line which would correspond with the embodied labor by itself.

But if work is not the sole important factor in exchange relations and exchange value, but only *one*, even though the most powerful, important factor among others—a *primus inter pares* ["first among equals"], as it were—then, according to what has been already said, it is simply incorrect and inadmissible to base upon labor alone a conception of value which is synonymous with exchange value; it is just as wrong and inadmissible as if a natural philosopher were to base the "active force" on the mass of the bodies alone, and were by abstraction to eliminate velocity from his calculation.

Sombart's Propositions Are Inconsistent With Each Other

I am truly astonished that Sombart did not see or feel this, and all the more so because in formulating his opinions he incidentally made use of expressions the incongruity of which, with his own premises, is so striking that one would have thought he could not fail to be struck by it. His starting point is that the character of commodities, as products of social labor, represents the economically and objectively most important feature in them, and he proves it by saying that the supply to mankind of economic goods, *"natural conditions being equal,"* is *in the main* dependent on the development of the social productive power of labor, and

[50] P. 576.

thence he draws the conclusion that this feature finds its adequate economic expression in the conception of value which rests upon labor alone. This thought he twice repeats on pages 576 and 577 in somewhat different terms, but the expression "adequate" recurs each time unchanged.

Now, I ask, is it not on the contrary evident that the conception of value as grounded upon labor alone is *not* proper on the premise that labor is merely the most important among several important facts, but goes far beyond it? It would have been adequate only if the premise had affirmed that labor is the only important fact. But this Sombart by no means asserted. He maintains that the significance of labor is very great in regard to exchange relations and for human life generally, greater than the significance of any other factor; and for such a condition of things the Marxian formula of value, according to which labor alone is all-important, is an expression as little adequate as it would be to put down $1+\frac{1}{2}+\frac{1}{4}$ as equal to 1 only.

Not only is the assertion of the "adequate" conception of value not apposite, but it seems to me that there lurks behind it a little touch of wiliness — quite unintended by Sombart. While expressly admitting that the Marxian value does *not* stand the test of facts, Sombart demanded an asylum for the "outlawed" value in the *thought* of the economic theorist. From this asylum, however, he unexpectedly makes a clever sally into the concrete world when he again maintains that his conception of value is adequate to the objectively most relevant fact, or in more pretentious words —that "a *technical fact which objectively governs* the economic existence of human society has found in it its adequate economic expression" (p. 577).

I think one may justly protest against such a proceeding. It is a case of one thing or the other. Either the Marxian value claims to be in harmony with actual facts, in which case it should come out boldly with this assertion and not seek to escape the thorough test of facts by entrenching itself behind the position that it had not meant to affirm any actual fact but only to construct "an aid for our thought"; or else it does seek to protect itself behind this rampart, it does avoid the thorough test of fact, and in that case it ought not to claim by the indirect means of vague assertions a kind of concrete significance which could justly belong to it only if it had stood that testing by facts which it had distinctly avoided. The phrase "the adequate expression of the *ruling fact*" signifies nothing less than that Marx is *in the main* even *empirically right*. Well and good. If Sombart or any one else wishes to affirm that, let him do so openly. Let him leave off playing with the mere "fact of thought" and put the matter plainly to the test of actual fact. This test would show what the difference is between the complete facts and the "adequate expression of the ruling fact." Until then, however, I may content myself with asserting that in regard to Sombart's views we have to deal not with a harmless variation of a permissible but merely inappropriately named abstraction, but with a pretentious incursion into the domain of the actual, for which all justification by evidence is omitted and even evaded.

The Labor Ingredient In The Value Of Commodities Is Not What Makes Their Values Commensurable

There is another inadmissibly pretentious assertion of Marx's which I think Sombart has accepted without sufficient criticism; the statement, namely, that it is only by conceiving commodities as "nothing but products" of social labor that it becomes possible to our thought to bring them into quantitative relation with each other—to make them "commensurable," and, therefore, "to render" the phenomena of the economic world "accessible" to our thought.[51] Would Sombart have found it possible to accept this assertion if he had subjected it to criticism? Could he really have thought that it is only by means of the Marxian idea of value that exchange relations are made accessible to scientific thought, or not at all? I cannot believe it. Marx's well-known dialectical argument on page 12 of the first volume can have had no convincing power for a Sombart. Sombart sees and knows as well as I do that not only products of labor, but pure products of nature too, are put into quantitative relation in exchange, and are therefore practically conmensurable with each other as well as with the products of labor. And yet, according to him, we cannot conceive of them as commensurable except by reference to an attribute which they do not possess, and which, though it can be ascribed to products of labor as far as character is concerned, cannot be imputed to them in regard to quantity since, as has been admitted, products of labor too do *not* exchange in proportion to the labor embodied in them. Should not that rather be a sign to the unbiassed theorist that, in spite of Marx, the true common demoninator—the

[51] *Ibid.*, pp. 574, 582. Sombart has not asserted this in so many words in his own name, but he approves a statement of K. Schmidt to this effect, and of which he only corrects an unimportant detail (p. 574). He says, moreover, that Marx's doctrine of value "performs" just this "service" (p. 582), and at all events he refrains entirely from denying it.

true common factor in exchange—has still to be sought for, and sought for in another direction than that taken by Marx?

The Conflict Of The Socialists And The Austrians Is Not Merely One Of Objectivity Versus Subjectivity

This leads me to a last point on which I must touch in regard to Sombart. Sombart wishes to trace back the opposition which exists between the Marxian system on the one side, and the adverse theoretical systems—especially of the so-called Austrian economists—on the other, to a dispute about method. Marx, he says, represents an extreme objectivity. We others represent a subjectivity which runs into psychology. Marx does not trace out the motives which determine individual subjects as economic agents in their mode of action, but he seeks the objective factors, the "economic conditions," which are *independent* of the will, and, I may add,. often also of the knowledge, of the individual. He seeks to discover "what goes on beyond the control of the individual by the power of relations which are *independent* of him." We, on the contrary, "try to explain the processes of economic life in the last resort by a reference to the mind of the economic subject," and "plant the laws of economic life on a psychological basis."[52]

That is certainly one of the many subtle and ingenious observations which are to be found in Sombart's writings; but in spite of its essential soundness it does not seem to me to meet the main point. It does not meet it in regard to the past by explaining the position taken up hitherto by the critics towards Marx, and therefore it does not meet it as regards the future, demanding, as it does, an entirely new era of Marxian criticism, which has still to begin, for which there is "as good as no preparatory work done,"[53] and in regard to which it would be necessary to decide first of all what is to be its method.[54]

The state of things appears to me to be rather this: The difference pointed out by Sombart in the method of investigation certainly exists. But the "old" criticism of Marx did not, so far as I personally can judge, attack his choice of method, but his mistakes in the application of his chosen method. As I have no right to speak of other critics of Marx I must speak of myself. Personally, as regards the question of method, I am in the same position as that of the literary man in the story in regard to literature: he allowed every kind of literature with the exception of

[52] *Ibid.*, pp. 591ff.   [53] *Ibid.*, p. 556.

[54] Pp. 593ff.

the *genre ennuyeux* ["vexing type"]. I allow every kind of method so long as it is practiced in such a way as to produce some good results. I have nothing whatever to say against the objective method. I believe that in the region of those phenomena which are concerned with human action it can be an aid to the attainment of real knowledge. That certain objective factors can enter into systematic connection with typical human actions, while those who are acting under the influence of the connection are not clearly conscious of it, I willingly admit, and I have myself drawn attention to such phenomena. For instance, when statistics prove that suicides are specially numerous in certain months, say July and November, or that the number of marriages rises and falls according as harvests are plentiful or the reverse, I am convinced that most of those who swell the contingent of suicides that occur in the months of July and November never realize that it is July and November; and also that the decision of those who are anxious to marry is not directly affected by the consideration that the means of subsistence are temporarily cheaper.[55] At the same time the discovery of such an objective connection is undoubtedly of scientific value.

At this juncture, however, I must make several reservations—self-evident reservations, I think.

1. First, it seems clear to me that the knowledge of such an objective connection, without the knowledge of the subjective links which help to form the chain of causation, is by no means the highest degree of knowledge, but that a full comprehension will only be attained by a knowledge of both the internal and external links of the chain. And so it seems to me that the obvious answer to Sombart's question ("whether the objective movement in the science of political economy is justified as exclusive, or as simply

[55] Somehow or other indeed an influence proceeding from the objective factor, and having a symptomatic connection with it, must produce effects on the actors; for instance, in the examples given in the text, the effect on the nerves of the heat of July, or the depressing melancholy autumn weather, may increase the tendency to suicide. Then the influence coming from the "objective factor," issues, as it were, in a more general typical stimulus, such as derangement of the nerves or melancholy, and in this way affects action. I maintain firmly (in opposition to Sombart's observation, p. 593), that conformity to law in outward action is not to be expected without conformity to law in inward stimulus; but at the same time (and this will perhaps satisfy Sombart from the standpoint of his own method) I hold it to be quite possible that we can observe objective conformities to law in human action, and fix them inductively without knowing and understanding their origin in inward stimulus. Therefore there is no law-determined action without law-determined stimulus, but yet there is law-determined action without knowledge of the stimulus of it.

complementary?"[56]) is, that the objective movement can be justified only as complementary.

2. Second, I think, but as it is a matter of opinion, I do not wish to press the point with opponents, that it is just in the region of economics, where we have to deal so largely with conscious and calculated human action, that the first of the two sources of knowledge, the objective source, can at the best contribute a very poor and, especially when standing alone, an altogether inadequate part of the total of attainable knowledge.

3. Third—and this concerns the criticism of Marx in particular—I must ask with all plainness that if any use is made of the objective method it should be the right use. If external objective connections are shown to exist, which, like fate, control action with or without the knowledge, with or without the will of the doer, let them be shown to exist in genuine reality. And Marx has not done this. He has not proved his fundamental proposition that labor alone governs exchange relations either objectively, from the external, tangible, objective world of facts, with which on the contrary it is in opposition, or subjectively, from the motives of the exchanging parties; but he gives it to the world in the form of an abortive dialectic, more arbitrary and untrue to facts than has probably ever before been known in the history of our science.

4. And one thing more. Marx did not hold fast to the "objective" pale. He could not help referring to the motives of the operators as to an active force in his system. He does this pre-eminently by his appeal to "competition." Is it too much to demand that if he introduces subjective interpolations into his system they should be correct, well founded, and noncontradictory? And this reasonable demand Marx has continually contravened. It is because of these offenses with which, I say again, the choice of method has nothing to do, but which are forbidden by the laws of every method, that I have opposed and do oppose the Marxian theory as a wrong theory. It represents, in my opinion, the one forbidden *genre*—the genre, *wrong* theories.

I am, and have long been, at the standpoint towards which Sombart seeks to direct the future criticism of Marx, which he thinks has still to be originated. He thinks

> that a sympathetic study and criticism of the Marxian system ought to be attempted in the following way: Is the objective movement in the science of political economy justified as exclusive or as complementary? If an affirmative answer be given,

[56] *Ibid.*, p. 593.

then it may further be asked: Is the Marxian method of a quantitative measurement of the economic facts by means of the idea of value as an aid to thought demanded? If so, is labor properly chosen as the substance of the idea of value? . . . If it is, can the Marxian reasoning, the edifice of system erected on it, its conclusions, etc., be disputed?

In my own mind I long ago answered the first question of method in favor of a justification of the objective method as "complementary." I was, and am, also equally certain that, to keep to Sombart's words, "a quantitative measurement of economic facts" does require "*an* idea of value as an aid to thought." To the third question, however, the question whether it is right to select labor as the substance of this idea of value, I have long given a decidedly negative answer; and the further question, the question whether the Marxian reasoning, conclusions, etc., can be disputed, I answer as decidedly in the affirmative.

Eventually The Fallacies In The Marxian System Will Discredit It

What will be the final judgment of the world? Of that I have no manner of doubt. The Marxian system has a past and a present, but no abiding future. Of all sorts of scientific systems those which, like the Marxian system, are based on a hollow dialectic, are most surely doomed. A clever dialectic may make a temporary impression on the human mind, but cannot make a lasting one. In the long run facts and the secure linking of causes and effects win the day. In the domain of natural science such a work as Marx's would even now be impossible. In the very young social sciences it was able to attain influence, great influence, and it will probably only lose it very slowly, and that because it has its most powerful support not in the convinced intellect of its disciples, but in their hearts, their wishes, and their desires. It can also subsist for a long time on the large capital of authority which it has gained over many people. In the prefatory remarks to this article I said that Marx had been very fortunate as an author, and it appears to me that a circumstance which has contributed not a little to this good fortune is the fact that the conclusion of his system has appeared ten years after his death, and almost thirty years after the appearance of his first volume. If the teaching and the definitions of the third volume had been presented to the world simultaneously with the first volume, there would have been few unbiassed readers, I think, who would not have felt the logic of the first volume to be somewhat doubtful. Now a belief in an authority which has been rooted for thirty years forms a bulwark against the incursions of critical knowledge—a bulwark that will surely but slowly be broken down.

But even when this will have happened socialism will certainly not be overthrown with the Marxian system— neither practical nor theoretical socialism. As there was a socialism before Marx, so there will be one after him. That there is vital force in socialism is shown, in spite of all exaggerations, not only by the renewed vitality which economic theory has undeniably gained by the appearance of the theoretical socialists, but also by the celebrated "drop of social oil" with which the measures of practical statesmanship are nowadays everywhere lubricated, and in many cases not to their disadvantage. What there is, then, of vital force in socialism, I say, the wiser minds among its leaders will not fail in good time to try to connect with a scientific system more likely to live. They will try to replace the supports which have become rotten. What purification of fermenting ideas will result from this connection the future will show. We may hope perhaps that things will not always go round and round in the same circle, that some errors may be shaken off for ever, and that some knowledge will be added permanently to the store of positive attainment, no longer to be disputed even by party passion.

Marx's System, Like Hegel's, Is A House Of Cards

Marx, however, will maintain a permanent place in the history of the social sciences for the same reasons and with the same mixture of positive and negative merits as his prototype Hegel. Both of them were philosophical geniuses. Both of them, each in his own domain, had an enormous influence upon the thought and feeling of whole generations, one might almost say even upon the spirit of the age. The specific theoretical work of each was a most ingeniously conceived structure, built up by a legerdemain of combination, of numerous stories of thought, held together by a marvellous mental grasp, but—a house of cards.

Publisher's Note to Note 40 on page 288:

In general Böhm-Bawerk was a mild critic of ideas with which he disagreed, and he was gentle with Marx, Sombart and the others. In regard to Sombart, the fact adverted to in the following (from Mises's *Planning For Freedom*, Libertarian Press, 1952, p. 43) indicates to what extent Sombart could be influenced by the prevailing climate of thought:

"The theocratic doctrine is consistent in attributing to the head of the government superhuman powers. The French royalists contend that the solemn consecration at Rheims conveys to the King of France, annointed with the sacred oil which a dove from Heaven brought down for the consecration of Clovis, divine dispensation. The legitimate king cannot err and cannot do wrong, and his royal touch miraculously cures scrofula. No less consistent was the late German Professor Werner Sombart in declaring that *Führertum* is a permanent revelation and the the *Führer* gets his orders directly from God, the supreme *Führer* of the Universe.* Once you admit these premises, you can no longer raise any objections against planning and socialism. Why tolerate the incompetence of clumsy and ill-intentioned bunglers if you can be made happy and prosperous by the God-sent authority?"

*Cf W. Sombart, *Deutscher Sozialismus*, Charlottenburg 1934, p. 213. (American edition: *A New Social Philosophy*, translated by K. F. Geiser, Princeton 1937, p. 194.)

V

The Ultimate
Standard of Value

C. W. Macfarlane Translation

*The title of the German original is "Der letzte Massstab
der Güterwertes." This essay first appeared in *Zeitschrift
für Volkswirtschaft, Sozialpolitik und Verwaltung*, Vienna,
Austria, Volume III, 1894, pp. 185-230. A translation by
C. W. Macfarlane was printed in *The Annals* of the American Academy of Political and Social Science, Philadelphia,
Pennsylvania, September 1894, pp. 1-60. Reprinted here
by permission of *The Annals*.

Contents

Present Publisher's Preface To "The Ultimate Standard Of Value"

The old cliché answer to the question, what determines price, is *supply and demand*. Whether that is adequate depends on what is understood by the term.

Price reflects, in terms of money or some other commodity, the *value* of something. A high price is associated with high value; a low price, with low value. The question in regard to what determines price, can therefore be expressed in a different form by asking, what determines *value?*

When the question is asked, what determines value, or using Böhm-Bawerk's term, what is the "ultimate standard of value," several answers can be given: (1) demand, (2) supply; or (3) a combination of the two. Or the terminology can be changed to the terms: (1) *utility*, in place of demand; (2) *cost*, in place of supply; or (3) *utility and cost*, in place of demand and supply. Each of these three answers has its advocates.

(1) The oldest answer is the combination answer, *demand and supply*, or *utility and cost*. That was Adam Smith's answer; and David Ricardo's too (although Ricardo did not fail to note a group of exceptions). A leading modern economist who gave his dual answer was the late Alfred Marshall. He settled the question, in the minds of many, by his easily remembered metaphor, that demand and supply (or utility and cost) were like the two blades of a scissors. Metaphors, however, do not substantiate a proposition, and Marshall's answer, although expressed in a somewhat new form, is a confused and unsatisfactory answer. (Marshall was an eclectic; the solutions of eclectics are not genuinely satisfying.)

(2) Strangely, people, who are of radically different stamp among each other, are agreed on the answer that *cost* is the *ultimate* determinant of value and of price. A modern *manufacturer*, when pressed hard for his unequivocal answer regarding what determines value or price, will usually finally say, *cost*. *Socialist theorists* give the same answer; but they narrow the cost factor down to one type of cost only, namely, *labor* cost. Marx, as is elucidated in one of the other essays in this volume, *Unresolved Contradiction in the Marxian Economic System*, declared that labor (a cost factor) is the sole, ultimate source of all value.

(3) In contradiction to both of the foregoing explanations of value (and price,) Böhm-Bawerk (and also his colleagues in the Austrian School of economic thought) affirm that the ultimate determinant of value is *demand,* or to use the alternative term, *utility.* This answer of Böhm-Bawerk (and also the answer of Jevons, Menger, and others of the Neoclassicists) is a relatively new answer. Few really accept it. Others profess to accept it, but it is often a sterile intellectual acceptance, lacking genuine significance in their thinking.

Böhm-Bawerk's unequivocal answer is: value is *never* ultimately determined by cost; nor by a combination of cost and utility; instead it is always exclusively determined by utility.

The essence of Böhm-Bawerk's formulation of his explanation is expressed in the following, taken from this essay (page 361 f.):

> The figure of the two blades [but Böhm-Bawerk is merely using Alfred Marshall's metaphor, not his concepts] of a pair of shears still holds good. One of the two blades, whose coming together determines the height of the price of any species of product, is in truth the marginal utility of this particular product. The other, which we are wont to call "cost," is the marginal utility of the products of other communicating branches of production. Or according to Wieser, the marginal utility of "production-related goods" (*productionsverwandten Güter*).

> It is, therefore, utility and not disutility which, as well on the side of supply as of demand, determines the height of the price. This, too, even where the so-called law of cost plays its role in giving value to goods.

> Jevons, therefore, did not exaggerate the importance of the one side, but came very near the truth when he said "value depends entirely upon utility."

This is an idea radically different from what is usually understood and accepted. Value is, so Böhm-Bawerk declares, determined not by utility and cost, but by two utilities—one, the *utility of the product itself;* and the other, the utilities *of the alternative uses of the factors of production pertaining to that product.* The scissors indeed has two blades, but both are *demand* blades.

This new, and in a sense abstruse, idea is analyzed in characteristic Böhm-Bawerkian manner, systematically and meticulously. A careless reader will find the argument tedious; a disinterested reader will believe that some of the steps in the argument are unnecessary or irrelevant; a competent and careful reader will be well-rewarded.

After all, it is this idea that utility is the sole determinant of value, which is the "revolution" that occurred in economics with the advent of Neoclassicism, as expressed in the writings of Jevons, Menger, Böhm-Bawerk and others. A "revolution" in thought cannot be a trifle. And, therefore, an essay as this one is worth more than reading; it is worth study.

The original American title of this essay is "The Ultimate Standard of Value" and this dignified formulation is not worthy of change. In the original German, the key word is *Massstab,* which can be translated as "measuring stick." An alternate term for "Standard" is "Determinant." "Standard" has a static connotation; but "Determinant" sounds dynamic. The determination of prices is a very dynamic activity. The title could, therefore, well have read, "The Ultimate Determinant of Value." That ultimate determinant, according to Böhm-Bawerk, is *demand* in its varying manifestations.

THE ULTIMATE STANDARD

OF VALUE

The Old Unsettled Question — What Is The "Ultimate Standard Of Value"?

There are certain unsettled questions in economic theory that have been handed down as a sort of legacy from one generation to another. The discussion of these questions is revived twenty or it may be a hundred times in the course of a decade, and each time the disputants exhaust their intellectual resources in the endeavor to impress their views upon their contemporaries. Not unfrequently the discussion is carried far beyond the limits of weariness and satiety, so that it may well be regarded as an offence against good taste to again recur to so well-worn a theme. And yet these questions return again and again, like troubled spirits doomed restlessly to wander until the hour of their deliverance shall appear. It may be that since the last discussion of the question we have made some real or fancied discoveries in the science, and some may think that these throw new light upon the old question. Instantly the old strife breaks forth anew, with the same liveliness as if it possessed the charm of entire novelty, and so it continues year after year, and will continue, until the troubled spirit is at last set free.   In this class we find the question—What is the "ultimate standard of value," (*dem letzten Bestimmgrunde des Wertes der Güter*)? The contest over this question began as early as the days of Say and Ricardo.   More recently the German, Austrian, Danish and American, English and Italian Economists have taken it up, so that the contest has assumed an international character.

A Fatal Misunderstanding Has Kept That Question Moot

The present generation has indeed some justification for again renewing the discussion.   It cannot be denied that of late we have made some important additions to the sum of our knowledge in regard to the theory of value.   This at first resulted in an increase in the number of conflicting opinions, but if we are not greatly mistaken, the present phase of this difference in opinion is due to a positive misunderstanding, which stands as a rock of offence in the path of explanation.

I believe that this fatal misunderstanding may now be definitely and finally removed, by an investigation which need possess no other merits than those of care and exactness, and that this will result in permanently advancing the controversy by several paces.   In this belief I venture upon a step which otherwise it would be difficult to justify, and propose to add yet another victim to the hecatombs already offered upon the altar of economic theory, though, owing to the necessity of pedantic thoroughness in such an investigation, it is a sacrifice which may not commend itself to some of our readers.

I
Progress And Present Position Of Opinion

The Classical Theory's Solution — First, To Divide The Domain Of The Phenomena Of Value

Since the time when Economics first became a science, there have been two rivals for the honor of being considered the "ultimate standard of value," the utility that the goods afford, and the cost of their attainment. Any tyro who takes up this question of the " value of goods" will invariably start out with the idea that we value goods because, and in the measure that, they are useful to us. He will, therefore, incline to the opinion that the ultimate cause of the value of goods is to be found in their utility. But this naïve opinion is soon disturbed by a thousand practical experiences. It is not the most useful things, as air and water, but the most costly things that show the highest value. Again, in innumerable instances, it is undoubtedly true that value and price do accommodate themselves to cost of attainment, and so at the very outset the spirit of dissent was introduced into the theory of value, and has remained there until the present day. There was either this divergence of opinion, or a division of the field of value phenomena into two sections, that of utility and that of cost; or, finally, both domain and opinions were divided.

Secondly, How That Attempted Solution Led To Cost Being The Prevailing Ultimate Standard

The classical theory of value, as is well known, divided the domain of the phenomena of value. A distinction was drawn between " value in use " and " value in exchange." The " value in use " of goods was thought to rest entirely upon utility, but beyond this passing reference to the domain of utility the classical theory did not trouble itself about value in use. In " value in exchange," a distinction was made between monopoly or scarcity goods on the one hand, and freely reproducible goods on the other. The value of goods of the first class, e. g., wines of rare vintage, statues or pictures by leading artists, rare old coins, patented inventions, was thought to depend upon the demand for them, and this in turn depended upon their utility. The value of goods of the second class was thought to depend upon their cost of production, or, as it has been more accurately stated, since the time of Carey, upon their cost of reproduction. To this, as we know from experience, the value and price of all freely reproducible goods tends, in the long run, to conform.

Pro-Cost Arguments

As we have said, the classical theory does not enter into any discussion of "value in use." It also practically ignores the value of scarcity goods, holding, that instances of such value are few in number and of little importance. The stress was thus thrown upon the value of freely reproducible goods. In this way it came about that "cost" was held to be the "ultimate standard of value." This view did not escape frequent and serious, though for the most part, unsuccessful attacks. Say, MacLeod and many other celebrated or little known writers have, at one time or another, attacked this cost theory of value.

Pro-Utility Arguments

It was urged that things that are not useful do not have value, no matter how high their cost of production or of reproduction may be, and therefore that high cost can only result in high value, when associated with a correspondingly high utility. From this the further conclusion was eagerly drawn, that the correspondence between value and cost, which is not to be denied, does not result from value regulating itself according to cost, but rather from cost regulating itself according to value, since higher costs are only undergone when, from the outset, correspondingly higher values are anticipated.

The Salient Feature Of The Marginal Utility Concept

This line of argument, however, is itself open to serious and very manifest objections. It might be urged that just as there can be no value without utility, no matter how great the cost may be, so there can be no value without cost, no matter how great the utility may be. This is manifest in the familiar instances of air and water. The adherents of the cost theory had so much of direct experience in their favor, confirmed as this was by the undeniable interdependence of cost and value, that they for a long time had the advantage in this constantly recurring strife.

A remarkable shifting of the scene was brought about by the appearance of the theory of marginal utility. The main points in this theory I may safely assume to be well known. Its corner-stone is the distinction between usefulness in general, and that very definite and concrete utility, which, under given economic conditions, is dependent upon the control over the particular good whose value is to be determined. According to this theory, value arises as a rule—that there are exceptions is expressly emphasized—from the utility of goods, not however from some abstract and ever-varying usefulness which cannot be definitely measured, but from that use or useful employment (*Nutz Verwendung*), which in a definite concrete case is dependent upon the control over the particular good.

Since of all the possible useful employments to which the good may be put, it is not the most important, but the least important, that a rational being would dispense with first, the determining utility is the smallest or least important utility among all the useful employments to which a good may be put. This determines its value and is called the marginal utility.

This more exact form of the use theory of value meets in a clear and definite way the objection urged against the older " use " theory of value ; namely, that free goods, no matter how useful they may be, have no value.   The answer is, that since these free goods exist in superabundant quantities, there is for us no utility dependent upon a concrete quantity of the same, as a single glass of water or a single cubic metre of air.   Their marginal utility therefore is zero. Again, this theory of marginal utility gives us the basis for a new and vigorous attack upon the cost theory of value. Considered from one point of view, the cost that determines the value of any product represents nothing else than the value of the producers' goods.   If now, as we are compelled to do in a scientific investigation, we inquire how we are to determine the value of these producers' goods, we find that this, too, in the last resort is determined by marginal utility. The cost therefore exercises, as it were, only a vice-regency. It cannot be denied that under certain circumstances it governs the value of certain products, but it is itself, at least in most cases, governed by a still higher ruler, namely, "marginal utility." Cost, therefore, is for the most part merely a province in the general kingdom of utility, and it is to this last that we must concede the position of the universal "ultimate standard of value." This proposition was first placed in opposition to the prevailing classical theory, in a bold and uncompromising way, by Jevons. "Value depends entirely upon utility," this writer emphatically declares in the very beginning of his great work on "The Theory of Political Economy." This proposition has since found even clearer and more exact statement at the hands of the Austrian Economists, nor have we even yet entirely escaped from this newest phase of the old struggle between cost and utility as the ultimate determinants of value. The present contest is notable, not merely for the number and scientific rank of those who are parties to it, among whom may be found many of the ablest economists of all countries, but also because of the extraordinary variety of opinions advanced. Instead of two opposing conceptions, we find a whole series of separate and seemingly unrelated opinions, each of which is held with the greatest persistence.

The Gamut Of Opinions — From Jevons And The Austrians To Scharling And J. B. Clark

The most extreme opinion at one end of the series is that which finds statement in Jevons' proposition, that "value depends entirely upon utility." It must, however, be added that while Jevons occasionally gives statement to this proposition in the above sweeping and uncompromising terms, yet the doctrine as expounded by him contains elements which necessarily lead to a limitation of this proposition. The addition of these necessary, though not highly important limitations, gives us the doctrine as taught by the Austrian economists.* They, therefore, stand next to

---

*This name, given us by our opponents, includes a certain group of theoretic economists. Not all of those included are Austrians, nor does the group include all the Austrian economists. I would also take occasion to remark that when in the following I speak in the name of the Austrian economists, I do not wish that anyone else shall be held responsible for what I may say or for the manner of saying it. Conversely I do not wish to place myself in the position of being responsible for the statements of every member of that group. Again, while I

Jevons in the series of opinions. Their position is that cost does not officiate as the original and ultimate determinant of value, except in a comparatively limited number of unimportant cases.* The great majority of value phenomena are subject to the dominion of utility. This dominion is exercised in some cases directly, but in a still greater number of cases indirectly. When exercised indirectly the value is, of course, first determined by certain costs, but closer analysis shows that these costs are themselves determined by utility.

At the other extreme end of the series, we find the eminent Danish economist, Scharling, who would establish cost (under the title of "difficulties of attainment") as the sole ruler over the entire domain of value; over value in use, as well as over value in exchange; over the value of freely reproducible goods, as well as over the value of scarcity goods.†

Quite close to Scharling, who is a very pronounced opponent of the theory of marginal utility, we find the acute American thinker, J. B. Clark, who is a no less decided adherent of that theory. This illustrates how strangely confused the controversy has become. Clark also makes cost the general and ultimate "standard of value," though in a different sense from Scharling. According to Clark, the final and determining condition is the amount of personal fatigue, pain or disutility which is imposed upon the laborer by the last and most fatiguing increment of his day's work.‡

have given statement to certain general doctrines of the Austrian economists, yet I would expressly state that the kernel of the doctrine does not belong to me, but is, to a large degree, the outcome of the investigations of my able colleagues, especially Menger and Wieser.

* Wieser's "*Ursprung und Hauptgesetze des Wirtschaftlichen Wertes*," Wien, 1884, p. 104. Then my "*Grundzüge der Theorie des Wirthshaftlichen Güterwertes*," in Conrad's *Jahrbücher für Nat-Oek.* N. F. B. XIII, 1886, p. 42. Then my article, "*Wert*," in Conrad-Lexischen *Handwörterbuch der Staatswissenschaften.*

† Essay on the "*Werttheorien und Wertgesetze*," in Conrad's *Jahrbücher*, N. F. B. XVI.

‡ "Ultimate Standard of Value," *Yale Review*, November, 1892.

Writers Who Are Not Far From The Cost Explanation

Somewhat nearer the middle of our series, though still not far from the cost end, we find those writers who, with certain modifications, uphold the old classical theory. It is here that we find the learned and contentious Dietzel,* of Bonn, who so divides the field of value that the value of scarcity goods is determined by utility, while the value of freely reproducible goods is determined by the cost. His position differs from the classical theory, in that he divides the domain of value in use between utility and cost, in the same way that he divides the domain of value in exchange. The classical theory, on the other hand, puts the use value entirely under the dominion of utility. Quite close to Dietzel, we find the Italian economist, Achille Loria, and the able American defender of the classical school, Professor Macvane. The latter has recently attacked the position of the Austrian economists, in two polemical papers of great acuteness. His interpretation of the Austrian theory, however, is not always accurate, nor always free from polemic exaggeration. His chief objection is that their conception of cost as "a sum of producer's goods possessing value" is obsolete and untenable. He holds that the only genuine economic cost of production is labor and abstinence (more correctly, waiting), which, in the case of freely reproducible goods, are the final and entirely independent regulators of value.†

Economists, In The Middle Of The Road

Where opinions vary so widely from one another, some one is usually found who will take a middle course, hoping to find a solution for the problem in the golden mean. This mission of conciliation has been undertaken in this case by no less eminent economists than Professor Marshall, of

* Die Classiche Werttheorie und die Theorie vom Grenznutzin," Conrad's Jahrbücher. " Zur classichen Wert und Preistheorie," N. F., Vol. 20, in the same Jahrbücher, third edition, Bd. 1.

†" Böhm-Bawerk on Value and Wages," in the Quarterly Journal of Economics, October, 1890; also "Marginal Utility and Value," in the same journal, April, 1893. Near the completion of the present paper, a third paper by Professor Macvane came to hand, "The Austrian Theory of Value," ANNALS OF THE AMERICAN ACADEMY, November, 1893.

Cambridge,* and Professor Edgeworth, of Oxford.† Both of these writers incline toward the theory of marginal utility, but have perched themselves very nicely upon the middle round of the ladder, from which vantage-ground they send forth gentle blame and conciliating applause to both parties in the discussion. Jevons and the Austrian economists are censured for exaggerating the importance of marginal utility, while the adherents of the classical theory are taken to task for underrating its importance; the truth, they say, lies in the middle. Scarcity goods, without doubt, have their value determined entirely by utility. In the case of freely reproducible goods the demand is governed by utility, and the supply by cost; since the price is determined by the inter-action of these two factors, one cannot say either that utility alone or that cost alone determines value; but rather that utility and cost co-operate with each other in the determination of price, like, to use Professor Marshall's figure, the two blades of a pair of shears.‡

Cherchez la femme — In This Case, An Ambiguity In The Term, Cost

Criminal lawyers of long experience are wont to apply to obscure and complicated cases the motto: *Cherchez la femme!*

For my own part, when, in our science, I find many clear and able thinkers at odds about a given point, I usually ask myself, where is the ambiguous or elusive concept with which

---

*"Principles of Economics," London, 1890 (second edition, 1891), and "Elements of Economics of Industry," London, 1892, *passim*.

†A very able criticism of my "Positive Theory of Capital," in the *Economic Journal*, June, 1892, page 328. Also in the same number a criticism of Smart's "Introduction to the Theory of Value," by the same writer.

‡Among other noteworthy contributions to the discussion of this theme I would mention Patten's "Theory of Dynamic Economics," 1892; also a paper by the same writer in a recent number of the Annals of the American Academy on "Cost and Expense." Patten takes a position which in the main is not far from that of the Austrian economists. His point of view is, however, peculiar, in that he throws special emphasis upon the influence of consumption upon the value of goods. This is a special theme which lies outside of the province of this paper. It still remains to notice the work of Irving Fisher ("Mathematical Investigations in the Theory of Value and Prices"), Connecticut Academy, 1892; also a very able work of Benini ("*Il valore e la sua attribuzione ai beni strumentali*"), Bari, 1893. The views of the Austrian economists have found very able and, because of many original features very interesting statement, at the hands of W. Smart ("Introduction to the Theory of Value," London, 1891).

they are playing.   In this case we need not search far afield; it is the concept of "cost."

II
The Various Meanings Of The Word "Cost"

The term "cost," like many of the other terms employed in political economy, is used, both in scientific discussions and in practical life, in several different senses.   Even when in a general way we agree in saying that the "cost of production of a good is the sum of the sacrifices involved in the creation of the good, this, by no means, guarantees that we all have the same thing in mind.   In the estimation of these sacrifices, we may employ several different methods of measurement.   These give us results which, under certain circumstances, will differ not merely with reference to the terms employed, but also with reference to the phenomena indicated by these terms.

Cost In The "Synchronous" Sense — As Understood By The Businessman

First of all, we may distinguish between what might be called the "synchronous" and the "historical" methods of estimating sacrifices.   According to the former, we take a unit of the total sacrifices as the basis for our reckoning, a unit which contains an increment of all the forms of sacrifices, which, at any instant, must enter into the production of the commodity.   In the production of cloth, for instance, we consume at the same time, yarn, looms (wear and tear), the labor of weavers, coal, etc., besides a great many subordinate aids to production.   By this method we usually arrive at a very extensive list of production sacrifices.   In order to obtain a single expression for this aggregate, or for the height of the cost, we must bring these various elements in production under a common denominator.   This may be done by estimating them all according to their value or price. Hence, by this synchronous method of reckoning, the cost equals the aggregate of the means of production, that have been sacrificed in the creation of the commodities, estimated according to their value.

Cost In The "Historical" Sense — Labor, Abstinence, And Original Natural Power

This is undoubtedly the sense in which the term cost is understood in practical business life. It is in this way, that the manufacturer, the farmer and the merchant reckon their cost. This, too, is the sense in which Professor Marshall employs the term when he speaks of the "money cost of production,"* and in my own writings about value and capital, I usually employ the term cost in the same way. Usually but not always, because for certain purposes another mode of estimating sacrifices, becomes important and may not be neglected. This is the historical method. It is quite manifest that many of the concrete forms of goods, which we to-day are compelled to sacrifice to purposes of production, are themselves the product of past and more original sacrifices. For example, the wood and coal that we consume to-day in the production of cloth, and likewise the machine which we wear out, are themselves the product of previous sacrifices of labor. If we go behind these material commodities to the sacrifices which the human race has suffered in successive periods of time, in bringing them into existence, or if you like the sacrifices necessary to reproduce them, the list of the historical production sacrifices would be greatly simplified. It would include two, or at most three, elements. First of all comes *labor*, which without doubt is the most important of these elements. Then comes a second to which many economists have given the name, *abstinence*. Perhaps a third might be added, namely, *valuable original natural power;* though many might decline to regard this last as a sacrifice.

For our present purpose, the extension of the discussion to the last two elements, about which there may be some question, is not at all necessary. We may indeed leave them entirely out of the discussion, and take the most important of the above elements—labor—as the representative of the elementary production sacrifices. Of course we do not mean

* "Elements" vol. i, p. 214. Compare especially the enumeration of the elements of cost on p. 217.

that we would either deny or overlook the co-operation of the other elements; but, in the question which here interests us, these elements play a part in no way different from that played by labor, so that the result obtained for the latter may in a general way be regarded as true of the other elementary production sacrifices.   It is therefore hardly necessary to repeat the same argument for the other elements.

As I have already remarked, the historical mode of viewing cost is regarded by Professor Macvane as the only correct method;* whether or not he is right we have yet to inquire.   It is employed by Professor Marshall in the statement of his conception, of "the real cost of production."†   In numerous instances I also have had occasion to make use of it, as when I endeavor to show that capital does not possess original productive power.   Again, when in explaining the operation of the law of cost,‡ say in the iron industry, I declare in a brief way, that the necessary means of production are mines, direct, and indirect labor.§

Three Ways Of Measuring The Cost Of Labor

According to this historical method of reckoning cost, labor may be regarded as the chief representative of all production costs.   But the sacrifice arising from the expenditure of labor may itself be measured by different standards or scales.   We can measure it either according to the amount of the labor (i. e., the duration of the labor), according to the value of the labor, or, finally according to the amount of the pain or disutility, which is associated with the labor.

* In his paper, "Böhm-Bawerk on Value and Wages," pages 27 and 28, and more recently in his paper on "The Austrian Theory of Value," page 14.   In order to avoid any possible misunderstanding that might result from a difference in the use of the term "historical cost" by Professor Macvane ("Marginal Utility," page 262), I would expressly state, that I apply the term "historical" as antithetical to "synchronous."   I therefore include under this term not only that cost of production, which has actually been expended in the past, but also the cost of reproduction, in so far as this "historical" may be resolved into the single state of primary productive power, which must in successive periods of time be applied or expended.

† "Elements," page 214.   "The exertions of all the different kinds of labor that are directly or indirectly involved in making it, together with the abstinences or rather the waitings required for saving the capital used in making it: all these efforts and sacrifices together will be called its real cost of production."

‡ Positive Theory of Capital (Volume II of CAPITAL AND INTEREST), p. 97, English translation by Libertarian Press, South Holland, Illinois, U.S.A., 1959.

§ Ibid. p. 252.

Obviously, through the use of these different standards of measurements, one will arrive at very different formulas for expressing the amount of the costs.   If, for instance, one were asked: What is the cost of production of a certain piece of cloth? he would answer according to the first scale or standard, twenty days' labor; according to the second (if a day's labor cost say eighty cents), labor to the value of sixteen dollars, and according to the third, a certain sum of pain or disutility, which the laborer must endure.

But it is important that we should here see clearly, that this involves more than a mere difference in the terms employed.   For according as we employ one or the other of these scales or standards, our estimates of the actual amount of the cost of any commodity will vary.   They will not only be different, but may even positively contradict each other.   Suppose, for instance, that a certain commodity A requires for its production twenty days' labor, which is paid for at the rate of eighty cents per day; again let us assume that a certain other commodity, B, requires thirty days' labor, which is paid for at the rate of forty cents per day.   Now if we employed the first scale or standard, we would reach the conclusion that the cost of A was less than the cost of B, (twenty against thirty days' labor).   By the application of the second, we reach the directly opposite conclusion, that the cost of A is greater than the cost of B (labor to the value of sixteen dollars against labor to the value of twelve dollars).   It is also clear that even though we assume that the labor in these cases is equal, either in amount or in value, this does not necessitate the conclusion that the amounts of pain or disutility are equal.   The labor of a great artist, which perhaps is paid the highest of any form of labor, may not only not cause him any pain, but may even yield him, quite independent of all economical considerations, a large measure of pleasure.   It might therefore very readily happen that by the application of the third standard, the cost of a commodity would seem very small, while its cost, according to the other two standards, would seem very large, and conversely.

The Real Question Pertains To The "Deeper Meaning" Of The Law Of Cost

This short resumé of the uses that have been made of the term "cost of production" makes it clear, that if we would avoid idle disputation, all further discussion of this subject must be preceded by the consideration of a preliminary question. A question which, for the most part, has been neglected by those who have taken part in the general discussion. The whole controversy, in its final issue, turns upon the famous "law of cost," which holds that the value of the majority of goods, namely, those which may be regarded as freely reproducible, adjusts itself in the long run according to the cost of production. As to the actual manifestation of such a law, there can be no question. Its existence is empirically proven, and so far as the actual fact is concerned is unanimously acknowledged by all parties to the discussion. The real question is as to the deeper meaning, the final theoretical conclusions, which may be deduced from this empirically established law of cost. But before we can enter upon any inquiry in regard to this deeper meaning, we must first know in what sense the term "cost" is to be employed.

That it cannot at one and the same time, have all of the above enumerated meanings, the preceding examples make very manifest. If the cost of a commodity A, taken in one sense is higher, and taken in another sense is lower, than the cost of a commodity B, it is manifest that the price cannot, at one and the same time, be adjusted in both senses according to the cost. In that event the price of the commodity A would at one and the same time be higher and lower than the price of the commodity B. Our most pressing problem, therefore, is to find a solution for that preliminary question, to which we have referred, a question which finds statement in the title of the following chapter.

III

For Which Of The Different Meanings Of The Word "Cost" Is It Really True That, According To The Experience Of Industrial Life, Prices Adjust Themselves According To Cost

Prices Adjust Themselves To Synchronously Reckoned Costs

It is undoubtedly true for the value sum of the synchronously reckoned cost; or for what Professor Marshall calls the "money cost of production." This is the cost from which, in practical life, the "law of cost" receives its most direct and effective confirmation. The action of the merchant is determined by the amount which he must expend for all the necessaries of production. If the price of the ware is not sufficient to cover this outlay, he ceases to bring the ware to market; conversely, if the price yields a fair surplus over and above this outlay, the producers increase the supply until the price, in the above sense, is adjusted according to the cost. It is therefore, from the standpoint of the practical man's estimate of the money cost of production, that the "law of cost" is always demonstrated. Even such writers as Professor Marshall have recourse in the first instance, to this method of proof.*

Prices Adjust Themselves, In A Sense, To One Type Of Historically Reckoned Cost — To Wit, Abstracted Wages For Labor And Interest For Waiting

We do not mean to say that this "law of cost" is only true for the synchronous method of reckoning money cost. On the contrary, it is in a certain sense applicable also to the historically reckoned cost; and it is this extension of it which, since the time of Adam Smith, has excited the greatest interest among writers on the theory of value. The only question is, to which of the different conceptions that are included under the historical method of reckoning cost may this be applied.

There is no doubt that it is true—in that approximate way in which any "law of cost" can be true—of the primary

* For instance, "Elements," page 222, "the normal level about which the market price fluctuates will be this definite and fixed (money) cost of production." Compare also the explanation of "equilibrium," on page 219.

elements of cost, labor and abstinence, measured according to their value.   We might put this in a more concrete form as follows:

In those goods that generally obey the "law of cost," the price of the finished product tends to an approximate equality with the total sum, that must be expended in wages and interest during the whole course of its production.

This proposition, I believe, is common to all theories of value including the classical (see A. Smith and J. S. Mill), and really follows as a logical consequence from the older theories.   We have said that the price, say of cloth, tends to adjust itself to the money cost of producing cloth.   This consists in part of the wages and interest, which are paid directly in this industry (the wages of weavers); also, in part, of the money expended for the consumption and durable goods sacrificed in its production, for instance, the yarn consumed.   But here again, the money price of yarn, according to our proposition, would tend to adjust itself to the spinner's money cost.   This again consists, in part, of interest and wages of spinners, and in part, of the money expended upon consumption and durable goods, say the wool consumed.

It is manifest that the analysis may be continued in this way until finally the money cost of every single stage of production is resolved into interest and wages.   In so far as the prices of the finished product or of the intermediate products (cloth, yarn, wool, etc.), actually conform to their money cost of production, they cannot fail, in the end, to coincide with the total sum of the interest and wages expended in their production.   Or what is the same thing, they will agree with the total outlay of the original elements of production—labor and abstinence—rated according to their value or price.

The primary outlay in production, especially the labor, to whose consideration we will, for the sake of brevity, confine ourselves, can, as we know, be measured by other scales or standards.

For The Other Two Kinds Of Historical Costs, The Principle Comes To Grief

If we attempt to verify the law of cost, with reference to these other methods of measuring costs, we soon come to grief.

It is very clear, for example, that the "law of cost," in the sense that the price tends to conform to the quantity or duration of the labor expended, will not hold good. To prove this, we need only advert to the simple fact that the product of a day's labor of a machinist or cabinetmaker is much higher in value than the product of a day's labor of an ordinary ditch-digger. This holds good, not only for the difference between skilled and unskilled labor, but also for the less pronounced differences that exist between the various groups or grades of common labor. The well-known doctrine of the socialists, which bases all value upon the quantity of labor expended, must either do violence to the facts or be untrue to itself; and this entirely independent of the fact that it ignores the cost element—abstinence. When, for example, Marx concedes that skilled labor must be translated into terms of common average labor, and so, for the purposes of estimating cost, must be regarded as some multiple of this common average labor, he is only verbally faithful to the proposition that the duration of labor is the true measure of cost. As a matter of fact, he makes, the *value* of the labor expended the measure of the cost.

Our investigation becomes far more difficult when we come to consider the fourth of the above enumerated meanings of the word cost; this meaning understands by the word cost, the sum of the pains or disutilities which the laborer must endure in production. This brings us to the cardinal point of the whole question, a point, however, which requires the most careful investigation.

It is quite conceivable that the correspondence which we have already noted between the value of freely reproducible goods and their synchronously reckoned cost, and again between that value and the value of the labor expended, may extend to a third member. In this case the law of cost would be true in a threefold sense.   To establish this it would be only necessary to show, that the value of the labor corresponds with reasonable accuracy to the amount of pain that the laborer endures.

Attainment Of Coincidence Of The Value Of The Product Of Labor With The Disutility Of The Labor Expended

Such a correspondence actually occurs under a certain definite assumption.   This assumption depends upon the facts, first, that the pain of labor increases with its duration, and second, that the labor is continued until the pain of the last increment of labor (*Arbeitstheilchen*), say the last quarter of an hour, is in exact equilibrium with the marginal utility of the product of that final increment of labor.   In this event we have here a common rendezvous for our several items—the utility of the product, the pain endured by the laborer, the value of the labor, and finally the value of the product.

Let us illustrate this by an example.   We will take a man engaged in one of the ordinary trades, say a cabinetmaker or a locksmith.   A certain amount of money, say five cents, which he obtains for a quarter of an hour's labor, has for him a definite value.   This is determined by its marginal utility, or by the importance of the last need which he is in a position to satisfy through the outlay of five cents. Now, according to well-known principles, about which my English and American colleagues and myself are in entire agreement,* this marginal utility will be smaller, as the daily pay of the laborer increases.   It will, for instance, be smaller when the laborer receives two dollars and forty cents for twelve hours of work, than when he receives one dollar and

---

* The very nature of my problem specially compels me to seek some settlement or agreement with the representatives of English and American science.   Partly because their rival opinions touch most nearly the salient points of the controversy ; partly because they already, in consequence of the great weight of scientific authority which they have upon their side, and of the exceptionally able representatives which they have found, are in advance of all others.   Besides, I have elsewhere taken occasion to refer to some of the others whose opinions bear upon this point.   I referred to Scharling's theory in my " Theory of Capital," p. 160, English edition ; to Dietzel in two papers, "*Zwischenwort zur Werttheorie*," and "*Wert, Kosten und Grenznutzen*," in Conrad's *Jahrbücher*, N.F.,vol. xxi, and third edition, vol. iii.

sixty cents for eight hours of work. Again, according to equally well-known principles, about which there is a no less complete agreement among all parties to the controversy, the fatigue and strain of the laborer grows with the increase in the duration of labor. Other things being equal, the tenth hour of labor is unquestionably more fatiguing than the third or sixth, and a fourteenth or an eighteenth would certainly be still more fatiguing. Now, since the marginal utility of every five cents added to the pay of the laborer is less than the utility of the last preceding five cents, and since with each additional quarter of an hour of labor the pain increases, there must come a point where the two will meet or be in equilibrium with each other. It is also undoubtedly true that when the laborer is entirely free to determine the length of his labor day, he will continue his labor until this point of equilibrium is reached. He will work nine and one-half hours when and because to his mind five cents is just sufficient indemnification for the disutility of the thirty-eighth quarter-hour of labor, but not sufficient for the somewhat greater disutility of the thirty-ninth quarter hour.

This point of equilibrium will, of course, vary for different laborers. A laborer, for instance, who must provide for a large family, and to whom the addition of five cents means the satisfaction of a quite important want, will be inclined to work longer, as will also a strong, vigorous laborer, who feels less fatigue from this labor. On the other hand, the sickly or lazy laborer, or the one who has fewer, or less pressing wants, will stop at an earlier point. He will prefer a longer period of leisure to the increased amount of wages, which he would have obtained had he continued to work.

It is just as manifest that, other things being equal, the point of equilibrium will vary for one and the same laborer, according to the amount of the wage which he will receive for the additional quarter hour. A laborer who would work thirty-eight quarter hours, for five cents per quarter hour, would perhaps work forty-two quarter hours, if he could obtain seven and a half cents per quarter hour, while if he received only two and a half cents, he might only work thirty quarter hours.* Or the number of hours of labor and the degree of fatigue, which the laborer will endure, will vary with the rate of wages.

Under Simple Conditions Of Robinson Crusoe, Rate Of Wages And Value Of Product Will Coincide

Upon what then, under the above assumption, will the rate of wages (in other words the value of the labor) and the value of the created products depend? For the simple conditions of a Robinson Crusoe this question is already answered. The value of the goods produced, which for a Crusoe have no price, but merely a subjective value, will equal their marginal utilities to. him. Since the product constitutes his wages or the recompense for his labor, the rate of wages or the value of his labor is identical with the value of the product.

Finally, Crusoe, as a reasonable being, will continue his labor to that quarter of an hour, the disutility of which will be exactly counterbalanced by the utility of the goods produced in this quarter of an hour. All four of the items which we have been considering would then be equal. Value of product—value of labor—marginal utility—pain of labor. If it is asked: What, in this case, are the factors that determine the value of the product? We must reply that "utility" and "disutility" are here of equal importance. The utility of the goods produced and the pain of the labor undergone. This point of equilibrium by which the marginal utility, and therefore the value, is determined, is in reality the marginal point for both utility and disutility. We might therefore, in this case, say with Professor Marshall,

---

* I would not maintain that low wages must always result in a sinking of the point of equilibrium. It may very readily happen, that with very low wages the necessities of the laborer and so the marginal utility of the unit of money, which he receives, is so great that he is compelled, even to satisfy the most pressing wants, to endure long hours of labor. This occurs with us in the case of the miserably paid sewing women, who not unfrequently work from fourteen to fifteen hours a day. But, as a rule, and especially where the payment of wages is so arranged that the overtime is paid for as a separate item from the regular time, the advance in wages will result in an increase in the supply of labor. This is always under the assumption that the laborer is free to determine how long he will work.

that, in the determination of value, utility and disutility, or pleasure and pain, work together like the two blades of a pair of shears.

Complications Which Arise In Actual Economic World; A Specific Computation

Though essentially the same thing, the matter takes a somewhat more complicated form, when we turn to the consideration of a laborer in our actual economic world; still assuming of course that the laborer is free to continue, or to terminate his labor when he pleases. Here also, the value of the product will equal the value or wages of labor. This will be true, even though the laborer does not receive his reward directly in the form of the created product, but receives a certain money consideration, in lieu of his share of the product. When competition has done its work, and forced the value of the product down, until it equals its cost, then the wages which the entrepreneur has paid out either directly or indirectly, must equal the value of the product, (we here ignore all payments for abstinence). How high will the value of both product and labor go? We would again answer, to the point at which marginal utility and marginal disutility coincide. Here, however, a new element enters into the problem. We have to consider, not only the marginal utility which the wages have for the laborer, but also the marginal utility which the product of labor has for the general public or for the consumer.

Every consumer continues to buy so long as the marginal utility of the ware exceeds the price sacrifice. Since the marginal utility decreases as the supply increases, an increase in the amount produced cannot find a market except at a lower price. When, for instance, thirty million pieces of a product, each of which cost one-quarter hour's labor, will find purchasers at a price of seven and one-half cents; thirty-five million pieces will perhaps bring only six cents each; thirty-eight million only five cents; forty-two million only four cents, while fifty million might only find buyers at two or at one and one-half cents. On the other hand, the amount that will be produced will depend, *ceteris paribus*, upon

the length of the working day.   But this again, as we have
seen, depends in part upon the rate of wages, or upon the
amount which the laborer will receive for an additional quarter hour of work.   With a wage of two and one-half cents
per quarter hour, every worker, according to the figures of a
previous example, would be willing to work thirty quarter
hours per day: with a wage of five cents per quarter hour,
they would work thirty-eight quarter hours; with a wage of
seven and one-half cents per quarter hour, they would work
forty-two quarter hours.   If the number of workers be taken
as a million, then with a wage of two and one-half cents per
quarter hour, they will produce thirty million pieces; with a
wage of five cents, thirty-eight million, and with a wage of
seven and one-half cents, they will produce forty-two million
pieces of a product of which each piece costs one-quarter
hour of labor.   It is manifest that under these conditions
supply and demand will be in equilibrium when we have a
product of thirty-eight million pieces with a value of product, and a wage of labor equal to five cents.   This would
be the price of the commodity and the level of wages at
which demand and supply would come into equilibrium.
All those who desire to purchase at that price would be
satisfied, and, at the same time, the price would afford sufficient indemnification for the pain endured by just the right
number of workmen.   It must not, however, be forgotten
that in the fixing of this level the utility of the ware is just
as important a factor as the disutility of the labor, or that in
the determination of this level they work together like the
two blades of a pair of shears.

Where Bohm-Bawerk And English And American Contemporaries Part Company

Here, however, my English and American colleagues and
myself must part company.   They seem to regard this rule
as capable of quite general application.*   They even seem

---

* Professor J. B. Clark, in his paper on the "Ultimate Standard of Value," has
set forth with great clearness and elegance, nearly the same thought which I
have employed in the text.   He certainly draws from it a conclusion which I am
no more prepared to accept than his brilliant statement of a part of their premises.

disposed to hold that it is the great law itself. I hold, on the other hand, that this rule has no wider application than is justified by the assumption upon which it is based; namely, that the laborer is entirely free to determine how long he will continue his daily labor. When, however, we turn to the actual facts of our present industrial life, we find first that this assumption does not obtain, save as an exception, and that it does not correspond at all with the other assumptions upon which our empirical law of cost is based.

IV
The Relation Of The "Law Of Cost" To Disutility (Continued)

Assumption That Laborer Is Free To Determine Length Of Working Time Is Not Correct

To demonstrate the first of the two propositions with which I closed the preceding chapter, I need only advert to well-known facts. It is, for instance, a fact of common experience, that in most branches of production the laborer is not free to determine the length of his working day. The hours of labor are fixed more or less by custom or law. This is true in factory and workshop, as well as in agriculture. In some countries it is the eleven-hour day, in others the ten-hour day, that prevails. If the present labor agitation should be at all successful, we may see the eight-hour day quite generally adopted. In any event, the amount of the pain of labor is more or less fixed. When changes occur in the rate of wages or in the value of the product, the laborer is not free to make a corresponding change in the length of his working day, and thus restore the equilibrium between utility and disutility. If the ten-hour day prevails, we cannot say that with a wage of seven and one-half cents per quarter hour, a million laborers will work forty-two million quarter hours, and hence that forty-two million pieces of commodity will be produced, while with a wage of five cents, they will labor thirty-eight million quarter hours, and produce thirty-eight million pieces of commodity. But whether the wage was five or seven and one-half cents, they would, in all probability, work forty million quarter hours and produce forty million pieces of commodity. In this way the equilibrium, in the case of the individual laborer, between the wages and the disutility of labor is disturbed. With many the disutility of the last quarter hour of labor will be less than the utility of the wage received, while for others it will be in excess of the same, *i. e.*, the laborer in this last instance, will find that the disutility of the last quarter hour of labor (or it may well be of several of the last quarter hours) is greater than the utility of the wage that he receives for it, and this whether the rate of pay is five or seven and one-half cents per quarter hour. If he were free to determine the length of his working day, he would, of course, work that many quarter hours less. But, as a matter of fact, he is not free to do this. He must either work the regular ten hours or not work at all. He naturally chooses the former, because the total utility of his entire wage (which means for him protection from hunger, etc.), is undoubtedly greater than the total disutility of the entire ten hours of labor.

Value Of Product Will Vary With Wages Paid But Not With The Disutility Of Labor

In this way the disutility of the labor fails to operate as a correct measure, either for the amount of the labor supply or for the quantity of the product. It also fails in the same way as a correct measure for the height of wages and the value of the product. In so far as free competition may prevail in the determination of cost, the value of the product will vary with the wages paid, but it will not vary with the disutility of the labor. A careful examination of the actual facts of life will show that the influence of this disutility or pain of labor only appears in the following special cases :

(*a*) In the case of those goods that are produced outside of the time devoted to the regular occupation. An instance of this may be found in the making or repairing of tools during leisure time, these tools being intended, not for sale, but for home use. Their cost is the pain or disutility of the labor devoted to them, and they will be valued according to the amount of this disutility.

(*b*) This is also true in the case of some regular occupations, in which men produce on their own account as artists and authors.   It is also true in the case of industries carried on at home, where men are free to continue or to stop working as they may themselves determine.   That the degree of their fatigue will exert an influence upon this determination may be granted.

(*c*) This is likewise true in those industries in which men voluntarily work overtime and receive special payment for the same.   But such overtime is neither general nor fixed. It is a more or less temporary and exceptional arrangement, which only continues during the period of special pressure. Therefore the influence of this case upon the supply of labor and the value of the product is neither deep nor lasting.

(*d*) Differences in agreeableness or disagreeableness of the various occupations will (unless offset by other conditions) tend to give rise to differences in the rate of wages. Those which involve less than the average laboriousness or unpleasantness, or which have associated with them certain advantages or perquisites will yield a less than normal wage. Occupations of more than the average laboriousness or unpleasantness will, on the other hand, yield a more than normal wage.   I must, however, expressly declare, that in these cases the absolute amount of the pain of labor does not determine the absolute amount of the wages.   Differences in the disutility or pain of labor can only give rise to variations from a normal wage, and as we shall take occasion to show, this normal wage is determined by an entirely different set of conditions.

The influence of the laboriousness or disagreeableness of the labor is often greatly modified and in some instances is entirely offset by opposite tendencies.   In Professor Marshall's " evil paradox " * we have one of the earliest

* "Elements," page 275.

recognized facts of our economic experience. This is the fact that unpleasant occupations, unless they demand some rare quality, usually bring in a wage that is not only no higher, but is ofttimes lower, than that paid in more pleasant occupations.

(*e*) Under normal wage I include the wage in all those occupations that do not require any rare or exceptional qualities. This, of course, includes the great mass of all occupations. With this understood, it becomes clear that the disutility of labor has but an indirect, and in one sense crude influence upon the absolute height of the normal wage. It undoubtedly prevents the introduction of an eighteen-hour labor day or even of a fifteen-hour day, but it has not been able to prevent the introduction of a thirteen or fourteen-hour day, as is shown by the history of the condition of the laboring classes. No one would claim that the progress of humanity from a thirteen to an eight-hour labor day has corresponded step for step with a similar progressive movement in the subjective feelings of the laborer. Nor will any one claim that the laborer will find in his wages an exact equivalent or recompense for the pain or disutility of his labor when he works thirteen hours per day. Again, when he works twelve hours per day, and so on for eleven, ten, nine and finally for eight hours per day. It is no nice variation in the point of equilibrium between utility and disutility that determines the length of the working day. It is the changing of the relative strengths of the various social factors that plays the principal part in this determination. This, within certain limits, which we cannot here stop to discuss, it will probably continue to do in the future.

(*f*) Finally the absolute height of the wages of skilled labor is manifestly still more independent of the disutility or pain of such labor. I take it that no economist would urge that this is the element which finally determines the salary of the higher officials, great actors or singers, specially skilled workmen, managers of factories, lawyers, doctors, etc.

These various points taken together certainly justify the assertion made above, viz., that the actual conditions which make possible an equilibrium of wages and pain, or of value and pain (so far as the value of the product is dependent upon the height of the wages), do not obtain in our industrial life. On the contrary, these conditions are only found in a relatively limited number of unimportant and exceptional cases.

The Empirical Law Of Cost Of Necessity Excludes Assumption That There Is Correspondence Of Value Of Goods With Disutility Of Labor

This alone would be sufficient to show that in tracing the influence of disutility upon the value of goods, we have quite a different and indeed much narrower trail to follow, than that which leads to the great empirical law of cost. This may be shown in the clearest and most convincing way from several different standpoints, and with this we are brought to the second proposition advanced at the end of the preceding section. First, it may be shown that in many instances the correspondence of the value of goods with their cost, in the sense of the great empirical law of cost, not only does not imply that the value of the goods corresponds to the disutility or pain of labor, but actually excludes this assumption. Excludes it not merely by chance or temporarily, but of necessity and permanently.

In order to avoid needless repetition, we will take an example that is sufficiently comprehensive to include nearly all possible cases. In the production of nearly all wares there comes into play, besides the commoner sorts of labor, some better paid skilled labor. In the making of a common cloth coat, we will have the labor of some skilled cutter, or of a manager with a higher standard of life. Again, in the weaving of the cloth, we find the better paid labor of factory bookkeeper, manager, etc. If we go back to still earlier stages—the manufacture of the machines or looms, the mining or preparation of the steel, etc.—it is clear that the better paid labor of the engineer, foreman and manager will enter into the cost.

Let us now assume that the production of a cloth coat, including all stages, costs three days of common labor at eighty cents and one day of skilled labor at one dollar and sixty cents. Let us also assume, for the sake of the argument, that the wage of eighty cents is an exact equivalent or recompense for the pain of a day's labor. If the amount of this pain of labor is to figure as the regulator of price, then under the above assumptions, the price of the coat should not exceed three dollars and twenty cents, for the skilled labor of the engineer or bookkeeper is not more painful than that of the common miner or tailor. Hence, if we take the pain as the standard, we cannot reckon the former as greater than the latter. And yet we all know that under the above assumptions, a cloth coat could not, for any long time, be put upon the market for less than four dollars (not including interest). This is manifestly out of proportion with the disutility of the labor. And yet, according to the law of cost, the price of the coat in the long run, and under conditions of free competition, should tend or gravitate toward this disutility.*

A Laborer With Talents Enabling Monopolistic Control Can Strike Equilibrium Between Utility And Disutility

The lack of agreement of the cost, in the sense of the classical law of cost, with the disutility of labor, may be shown by approaching the question from an entirely different point of view. This brings us to an interesting counter test, which, if I am not greatly mistaken, has hitherto entirely escaped the attention of Economists.

We have occasionally remarked that the wages of skilled laborers, as a rule, are determined upon other grounds than the amount of pain which these persons endure. In particular

---

*We might compare the coat that cost three days of common labor at eighty cents and one day of skilled labor at one dollar and sixty cents with another coat that cost four days of common labor at eighty cents. If the law of cost is interpreted as meaning the sum of the pain or disutility endured, then these coats should have about the same value. It is manifest, however, that the fulfilling of the law of cost actually demands the opposite of this: that the coats should exchange in the ratio of ten to eight. The empirical law of cost is by no means the same thing as the regulation of price through the disutility of labor, and cannot be so. Or as Professor Green says in a paper on "Pain Cost and Opportunity Cost," "We shall certainly find that the rule of equal values for equal pains is not the law which actually determines exchange ratios."—*Quarterly Journal of Economics,* January, 1894.

cases, it is possible to find a justification for the casuistical assumption which regards utility and disutility as exercising an equal influence, both upon the remuneration of labor and the value of the goods produced. This is just as true as regards the ordinary carpenter or locksmith, as in the case of some famous artist, such as Titian or Van Dyck. In short, it is true of all men who, because of the scarcity of their talents, possess a sort of monopoly in the production of certain goods. How long they will work per day will depend, in part at least, upon the degree of fatigue that they must undergo. This, however, does not give us a fixed limit. How long a great artist will work depends, as in the case of the common laborer, upon several conditions. Among others upon the rate of pay that he can obtain for the product of his more prolonged effort. An artist may not be willing to work overtime to paint a picture, for which he will receive forty dollars. He might, however, not only willingly but gladly prolong his working day if he were offered four thousand dollars for the completed picture.

In short, there is nothing to prevent the producer of a monopoly good from so prolonging his day's labor, and thereby the daily supply of his monopoly ware,* until the marginal utility, of the money received for the last unit of labor time, is in exact equilibrium with the disutility of this last unit of labor time. It cannot be denied that under such circumstances the disutility exercises a determining or co-determining influence upon the amount of the supply, the height of the marginal utility, and the price of the product. This, too, is done in just the same way as in the illustration given in the last chapter, in which the ware was the product of common labor. At the same time, economists are agreed that such monopoly prices do not come under the classic law of cost. Here again, as I believe, we are brought to the conclusion, that the disutility which we are investigating is

---

* It would be easy to find many other and possibly better examples than that of the artist. In his case the artistic impulse is always strongly opposed to the action of the purely economic motives. Possibly the best example would be an inventor. He is in a position to produce a useful object, without any help from others, and is entirely free to determine the length of his working day.

something different from the cost which is operative in the empirical law of cost, and, therefore, that those economists are on the wrong path who think that the occasional agreement of value and disutility may be explained as a manifestation of the great empirical law of cost, and *vice versa*.

Adam Smith's Explanation Of Law Of Cost Was Confused And Erroneous

This erroneous confounding of two quite different phenomena has been, as it were, in the air of theoretic economics since the time of Adam Smith. The latter, according to the very apt and ingenious observation of Wieser,* really gives two parallel explanations of the phenomenon of value, viz.: a philosophical explanation, which is especially applicable to primitive conditions; and an empirical explanation, which is better suited to the more fully developed conditions of our present industrial life. Adam Smith also gives us two similarly related explanations of cost. According to the philosophical, he puts the personal pain associated with labor, "the toil and trouble," as the cost which really determines the price of the product. Later, in explaining his famous law of cost, which belongs to the empirical part of his theory of value, he holds that the "natural price" of the product gravitates toward the empirical cost. This, he declares to be wages of labor and interest.† To the mind of Adam Smith, of course, there was no opposition between these two explanations, and accordingly it was impossible to escape the conclusion, that, at least so far as labor is concerned, they really have to do with the same thing. By eliminating the modern economic conditions, as modified by exchange, we get the real kernel of the matter. And this kernel, according to the empirical law of cost, is nothing else than "the toil and trouble" of labor.

Ricardo Was Quite Wrong In His Explanation Of Price Formation; Gossen And Jevons Made Correction In Part; But Old Confusion Remained Even In Marshall's Works

The well-known controversy that long monopolized the attention of the classical economists, whether the price of

---

*" *Der Natürliche Wert*," Wien, 1889, Preface, p. iii. (Translation: *Natural Value*, p. xxvii f., Kelley & Millman, Inc., New York, 1956.)

†" Wealth of Nations," Bk. i., Ch. v. and vii.

goods depends upon the quantity of labor expended, as Ricardo taught, or upon the amount of wages, as Mill correctingly suggested, afforded ample opportunity to correct this error. They failed, however, to do so. The old Smithian "toil and trouble" remained in a sort of scientific haziness, until, through Gossen, and especially through Jevons, it was brought to full and clear recognition. Then, for the first time under the name of the "disutility of labor," it was raised to the rank of an elementary economic power, while its counterpart, the utility of the good, was set over against it. The old confusion, however, attached itself to the new names. If I am not greatly mistaken, not only the followers of the old classical school, but also many of the adherents of the newer theory, developed by Jevons, still stand under this ban.

In the case of Professor Macvane, the confusion is quite pronounced, as when he explains the cost of the classical law of cost as "pain of labor and fatigue of muscles."* Professor Edgeworth takes substantially the same position when he occasionally explains the "disutility" in terms of "cost and sacrifice."† Or when he sets first utility and cost,‡ and again, utility and disutility over against one another.§ Again, when he indulges in a polemic against the Austrian school of economists, and urges that they have neglected the great Ricardian law of cost and stripped it of its significance, and that they have not properly recognized the function of disutility in the determination of the economic equilibrium and the value of goods.|| Professor Marshall, as it seems to me, also becomes involved, to some degree, in this confusion. While Ricardo held that cost of production, and Jevons held that marginal utility was the determinant of value, Marshall holds that both enter

---

* "Marginal Utility and Value," pp. 262, 269.
† *Economic Journal*, June, 1892, p. 334.
‡ *Ibid.*, p. 335.
§ *Ibid.*, p. 337.
|| *Ibid.*, *passim*, especially p. 334.

into the determination of value, and that, like the two blades of a pair of shears, they are co-equal factors in this determination. Nor does he assume this position in any tentative way, but rather holds that he has found the solution for a problem long in dispute.*

Confounding Of "Pain Involved In Production" With The "Great Empirical Law Of Costs"

No matter who is responsible for this confounding of the cost of the empirical law of cost with the disutility of labor, the fact remains that the confusion does exist. In order to distinguish as sharply as possible between the two principles referred to, I may remark that there is a rule which may be called the law of disutility, according to which the value of all goods that come under its influence tend to be in equilibrium with the amount of the pain involved in their production. But this is far from being the same as the great empirical law of cost. It depends upon quite different assumptions, and upon the play of other and intermediate motives. Finally, it has a different and much smaller field of operation. On the one side, it includes but a small part of the territory covered by the empirical law of cost, and on the other, it includes a certain portion of territory which is not covered by the law of cost.

Summary Of All That Precedes

This somewhat minute and pedantic, though none the less necessary, examination of the famous law of cost leads us to the following conclusion. The law of cost, as applied to the actual facts of our economic life, is susceptible of verification, in the sense that the synchronously reckoned cost, or the sum of the values of goods expended in production, coincides with the price of the product. Again, under the assumption that this synchronously reckoned cost can all be resolved historically into labor, it is possible to verify the proposition that the price of the product is determined by the sum of the labor expended, measured in terms of the *value* of this labor. But the law of cost is certainly *not* true in the sense that the price of those goods which are within

---

*"Principles," note on Ricardo's Theory of Cost in Relation to Value, Bk. vi., Ch. vi.

the domain of the law of cost is determined by the amount of the pain involved in their production.

V
The Law Of Cost And The Value Of Labor

Two Unresolved Problems

I would now ask, and my colleagues of the Austrian school ask with me, what advance have we made toward a solution of our problem. Even though it be shown by means of the famous law of cost, that the value of freely reproducible goods may be resolved into the value of their means of production, or into the value of the most ultimate or elementary factor in production, *i. e.*, labor, we still must ask, what progress has been made in explaining the value of goods?

Manifestly this translation of the value of goods into the value of the means of production, does not give us the final solution for our problem, for we must still further inquire, how we are to determine the value of these means of production; or if we regard the means of production as resolvable historically into the labor previously expended, how are we to determine the value of this labor?

Let us proceed immediately to the consideration of the second half of our question. This will bring us at once to the root of the problem. For the sake of clearness I will accept as the basis of the argument the doctrines proposed by those who are in opposition to me in this matter.

Marshall, Representative Of One School Of Thought, Presents Two Conflicting Explanations Of The Ultimate Source Of Value. First Explanation

In Professor Marshall's most admirable book which may fairly be taken as representative of the present status of economic theory in England, may be found several answers to the question: What determines the value of labor? In one place, he teaches that "free° competition tends in the direction of making each man's wages equal to the *net product* of his own labor; by which is meant, the value of the produce which he takes part in producing, after deducting all the other expenses of producing it."* He also holds, that " the

* " Elements," Bk. vi., Ch. ii., § 2, and corresponding place in " Principles."

wages of every class of labor tend to be equal to the net produce due to the additional labor of the marginal laborer of that class. It may be remarked, that in obtaining the value of labor out of the value of the product of labor, one is in entire harmony with the conceptions of the Austrian school. What effect this has upon the law of cost will appear later on in the discussion.

Marshall's Second, And Ambiguous, Explanation

In another place* Professor Marshall gives us quite a different standard for determining the value of labor. He holds, that in the case of every agent of production: "there is a constant tendency toward a position of normal equilibrium, in which the supply of each of these agents shall stand in such a relation to the demand for its services, as to give to those who have provided the supply a sufficient reward for their efforts and sacrifices. If the economic condition of the country remain stationary sufficiently long this tendency would realize itself in such an adjustment of supply to demand, that both machines and human beings would earn generally an amount that corresponds fairly with their cost of production."

I am not quite sure how wide an application Professor Marshall would give to this statement. This much, however, is clear, he would apply the distinction of the classical school, between the rapidly fluctuating "market price" and the "normal value" which is based upon cost, to the commodity—labor. In the passage just cited he manifestly wishes to indicate the standard according to which the normal or long period position of wages is finally determined. But as it appears to me, he is not quite clear whether he would make the efforts and sacrifices of the laborer the ultimate standard (as his expression, "sufficient . . . for their efforts and sacrifices," would seem to indicate), or whether he would take the cost of rearing and maintaining human beings as the standard (as the expression "amount that corresponds fairly with the cost of production of human

* "Elements," Bk. vi., Ch. v, § 4, and corresponding place in "Principles."

beings '') would imply.   Doubt may also arise whether it is
his opinion that the *absolute height of wages* tends to an
equilibrium with the ''efforts'' or ''cost of production of
human beings,'' or that the differences in wages to which
these give rise are but variations from an average level, the
absolute height of wages being determined by other considerations.

If this last is Professor Marshall's opinion, then I am in
entire agreement with him in his conception of the value of
labor.   That differences in the pain of labor tend to bring
about corresponding differences in wages, I have already
admitted.*   The same influence, and for quite analogous
reasons, may be exercised by differences in the cost of producing human beings.

One Possible Meaning Of Marshall's Second Explanation Cannot Be Maintained. (1) The "Iron Law Of Wages" Is Not Accepted Now. (2) Reasoning In A Circle

If, however, the expression is to be interpreted in the
wider sense, that the absolute height of wages is finally determined by the pain of labor, or by the cost of producing
human beings, then, as it seems to me, Professor Marshall
has taken a position which cannot be maintained.   This, so
far as the pain of labor is concerned, I have endeavored to
show in a previous chapter.   In regard to the cost of producing human beings, a twofold objection suggests itself:
First, this statement is hardly verified by experience, for
modern economists are quite generally agreed that the '' iron
law of wages '' cannot be interpreted as meaning that the
necessary cost of maintenance is a fixed, definite amount,
toward which the wages of labor must in the long run tend.
On the contrary, they are agreed that the wages of labor
may permanently exceed that amount, which hitherto has
been regarded as the amount of the necessary cost of maintenance.   And when this excess of the wages of labor above
the cost of maintenance does disappear, it is really due to
the fact, that the better conditioned laboring population have
so accustomed themselves to the higher standard of life,
that much that before was a luxury is now a necessity.   **In**

*See foregoing p. 334.

an agreement between cost of maintenance and wages of labor obtained in this way it can hardly be said that the cost of maintenance is the determining, and the wages of labor the determined element.

Second, this last explanation is not satisfactory because it simply leads us around in a circle. According to this law of cost, the price of the means of maintaining the laborer (as bread, meat, shoes, coats, etc.), is to be explained by the value and price of the labor expended in the production of these commodities. If we start with this proposition, we can hardly continue, and say that the price of the labor is to be resolved into the cost or price of the means of maintaining the laborer. I have elsewhere dwelt upon the unsatisfactory nature of this explanation,* and so need not elaborate upon it at this point. Nor have I any ground for thinking that Professor Marshall and the other moderate representatives of the modern English school would accept the "iron law of wages" in any literal sense, with all the theoretic and practical consequences which this would involve.

Necessity, Therefore, Of Restricting Explanation To Marshall's First

Under these circumstances I do not believe it is possible to give a scientific explanation of the absolute height of wages, without some reference to that standard upon which, in the first of the above quoted statements, Professor Marshall seems inclined to base the market or demand price of labor. This is the marginal utility of the labor, or, otherwise stated, the value of the product of the last or marginal laborer. This explanation must, however, be supplemented in many and in part important details, by reference to the influence of the painfulness of labor and the cost of maintenance, though these can never entirely replace the above explanation. Even though for scientific purposes we were permitted to neglect the periods of short and moderate length, we could not explain those long periods to which we had limited ourselves without reference to other elements,

---

* In a paper, replying to Dietzel, on " *Wert, Kosten und Grenznutzen,*" in Conrad's *Jahrbücher,* third series, book iii, p. 332.

besides the painfulness of labor and the cost of maintenance.

But we are not permitted, even for scientific purposes, to
neglect these short and moderate length periods. On the
contrary, any serviceable explanation of the value of wares,
which could be included under the law of cost, must be based,
clearly and distinctly, upon the actual rates of wages during
the periods under consideration, periods which are really
long, though they may seem relatively short. The important point is that wages during these periods still come under
the influence of that determinant, to which Professor Marshall refers as the " demand price for labor."

What The Law Of Cost Describes, Namely, The Moderating Of Sharp Price Movements Into Oscillations. Self-Interest As The Basic Causal Factor

This point is just as important as it is simple. In order
to convince ourselves of its truth, we need only keep clearly
in mind what it is, that the law of cost really accomplishes,
in relation to the price of goods, and how this result is
brought about. The typical effect of the law of cost is to
change the chance and uncertain fluctuations which the price
of goods undergoes, into a regular oscillating motion like
that of a pendulum. In this motion the price always tends
to return to the cost as to an ideal resting-place. Though
the price seldom remains for any long time at this point, yet
in a general way this might be called the normal position
about which the price oscillates.

The wonderfully simple mechanism by which the law of
cost brings about this result is as familiar as the law itself.
It rests upon the very simple motive of self-interest. If in any
branch of production the price sinks below the cost, or in
other words, if the market price of the product is lower than
the value of the means of production, men will withdraw
from that branch and engage in some better paying branch
of production. Conversely, if in one branch of production,
the market price of the finished good is considerably higher
than the value of the sacrificed or expended means of production, then will men be drawn from less profitable industries. They will press into the better paying branch of

production, until through the increased supply, the price is again forced down to cost.

The Law Of Cost Changes The "Occupation Of Productive Power"

The law of cost operates, therefore, by changing the occupation of the productive power.* So long as the price tends to cause a change in the occupation of the productive power, it is itself not in a state of equilibrium. On the other hand, a condition of at least relatively stable equilibrium will be attained when in the different branches of production the price has so adjusted itself that the productive power does not tend to change its occupation. This would be the case, when, in all kinds of employment, equal labor received equal pay and unequal labor received proportionately unequal pay. Then the differences in pay could be regarded as a just equivalent for the special laboriousness or disagreeableness, or for the special skill or fidelity, etc., incident to certain occupations. Equal capital would everywhere receive the same rate of interest. Any excess above this could be regarded as a just equivalent for the greater risk, etc., incurred in that particular investment. We may, for example, assume that this point of equilibrium is reached, when in all branches of production the wages of an unskilled laborer are eighty cents, and the rate of interest on capital is five per cent.

The Rate Of Wages Does Not Necessarily Settle At The Subsistence Level

Under this supposition the normal price, toward which according to the law of cost the market price gravitates, should be such as would correspond with an average wage of eighty cents, and a rate of interest of five per cent. The price of a commodity that costs three days of common labor would, according to the law of cost, gravitate toward two dollars and forty cents (interest being ignored). This would be true, whether or not this equalized rate of pay of eighty cents corresponded to the minimum of existence. It may be

---

*The change of occupation is not always brought about by individuals abandoning the occupations in which they are engaged. When in any branch of employment the decrease from death, etc., is not offset by the number entering the same, we have a change of occupation. Those who make up the difference have gone into other lines. Though operating more slowly, the effect of this is the same as if individuals made a direct change.

that when the minimum of existence is only forty cents, the rate of wages will not remain at eighty cents. A generation later it may sink to sixty cents, or even to fifty cents. While this would show that there is no fixed and absolute normal price,* it does not alter the fact that at the present time the price of the commodity, according to the law of cost, gravitates toward that price, which would give the laborer a wage of eighty cents. When we examine this gravitating motion more closely, it is manifest that we cannot say that "the price gravitates toward the rate of eighty cents," because the laborer's cost of maintenance is forty cents. Instead we must say, that the price gravitates toward the rate of eighty cents, because the rate of wages which obtains throughout the whole field of employment is eighty cents. In other words, in explaining the oscillating motion of prices, according to the law of cost, we cannot avoid assuming as a basis, a certain average or normal rate of wages as the prevailing rate for the period under consideration.

Marshall's First Explanation Is The Only One That Is Acceptable; However, It Is Not Penetrating, And Appears To Move In A Circle

We will now repeat the question which was asked in the beginning of this chapter, a question which must be asked

---

* Professor Marshall has very correctly remarked that the use of the term normal is more or less arbitrary. A price which we would call normal, when we have in mind a period of a certain length, we would not call normal when considering a longer period ("Principles," Bk. vii., Ch. vi., § 4). Otherwise I would certainly insist that the real law of cost has to do with no longer period than is sufficient to allow the adjustment of the price of the ware to the equalized position of wages (and interest); the wider adjustment of the wages of labor to the cost of maintaining the laborer, which under certain circumstances might require a still longer period of time, is an entirely different problem. So far as this can be further maintained as a general law, it is in no sense an effect of the real law of cost, but should be regarded as the effect of another law—a law which has no actual connection with the real law of cost. It depends upon the action of quite different forces and in its results has but an external or non-essential similarity, which has led to the unqualified evil of confounding these two laws. The impelling motive of that law of cost, which really influences the price of wares, is usually a shrewd estimating of economic conditions, the striving for the greatest possible utility and the avoidance of harm. The motive of a pretended iron law of wages is on the one side the irresistibleness of sexual desire, and on the other the great mortality which results from insufficient food. But the effects of such natural forces can no more be credited to the vulgar economical law of cost than the aggregation of a great number of men in large cities can be credited to the law of gravitation, which of course, because of a similar play upon external analogies, has already been maintained by Carey.

if our explanation is to maintain a logical and coherent form :   Upon what does this average or normal rate of wages, prevailing at any given time, depend ?

We have already answered this question, or rather Professor Marshall has answered it, in the first of his explanations of the rate wages already quoted.   In this he has declared, and we must perforce agree with him, that the price of a day's labor depends upon the value of the pure product of a day's labor.   Or more correctly, upon the value of the product of the last employed laborer, in Professor Marshall's example the "marginal shepherds."*

This answer brings the whole doctrine of the law of cost to its final test.   Upon the one side, this analysis of cost practically abandons the attempt to show that disutility is the essential element of cost.   On the other side, the expression " value of the products of labor," makes manifest that we have not yet obtained the ultimate element, and that the analysis must be continued still further.   Finally, the explanation seems even more than before to continue in a circle.   In the name of the law of cost we explain the value of the product by the value of the labor expended in its production, and then explain the value of this labor by the value of the product.

There Is A Discrepancy Somewhere. A Gap In The Explanation Needs To Be Remedied

There is manifestly a great discrepancy somewhere in this explanation.   A discrepancy which the Austrian economists endeavor to avoid by a special interpretation of the law of cost.†   Their efforts, of course, will not receive much encouragement from those writers who do not recognize the existence of this discrepancy.   This includes the great

---

* I would not fail to mention that the position of wages which corresponds to or equals the " net product of the last employed laborer " is, according to Professor Marshall's views, in no sense a temporary market price, but a sort of "long period price," which requires for its development a more or less prolonged leveling process.   It is a sort of centre of gravity for the oscillations of the supply and demand of labor.

† In this attempt Wieser has taken a prominent part.   Compare his "*Ursprung und Hauptgesetze des Wirtschaftlichen Wertes*," 1884, page 139; and " *Der natürliche Wert*," 1889, page 164.   Compare also the excellent résumé by Smart, in the editor's preface to the English edition of the last named work.   London, 1893, p. xix.   [*Natural Value*, 1956.]

majority of those who hold, wittingly or unwittingly, that the explanation of the value of goods in accordance with the law of cost is firmly anchored upon the elementary factor, "disutility." That this is not the case, I have endeavored to show; and I will now attempt to bridge the gap in the explanation of value, which my investigation has revealed. On the one hand it is held, that in numerous cases the price of the product, according to the law of cost, oscillates about some normal rate of wages, which rate does not correspond either to the "disutility" of labor or the cost of maintaining the laborer. On the other hand, Professor Marshall, in common with many other English and American economists, admits that the normal rate of wages is adjusted according to the value of the product of the last employed laborer.

VI
What The Law Of Cost Really Means.
Final Result

A Simple Illustration Of Price Formation And The Resulting Wage For Labor

The existing productive powers, inclusive of the most original and important of all—labor—seek employment in the various opportunities for production that present themselves. Naturally, of course, they first engage in those branches of production that are most profitable. But as these are not sufficient to give employment to the whole productive power, some of this power must engage in successively less productive occupations, until finally all of it is employed. This gradual extension to less profitable occupations may be seen in the production at one and the same time, of more valuable goods, and of others, which from the very beginning were less valuable, because the demand for them was less urgent. But the important case of this gradual extension to less profitable employments is found elsewhere. In any branch of production which hitherto has been very profitable, the amount produced tends to increase. Hence, according to well known principles, we are compelled to market the increased product at a diminished price.

The demand arranges itself in strata that vary with the desire and purchasing power of the consumers. Let us assume that of a certain kind of commodity, thirty thousand pieces are produced by one hundred laborers with an outlay in labor of one day out of the three hundred working days in the year. Let us further assume that these are marketed at the price of eighty cents each. There will then be among the purchasers possibly one thousand to whom eight dollars per piece would not have been too dear, either because it satisfied some pressing want, or because their great wealth makes the value of the monetary unit exceptionally low in their estimation. Then come perhaps, five thousand more purchasers who, in case it is necessary, are prepared to pay two dollars. Another six thousand, who, in an extreme case, would pay one dollar and sixty cents. Another six thousand who would pay only one dollar and twenty cents. Again, another six thousand who, at most, will pay only one dollar, and finally, the last six thousand who are prepared to pay only eighty cents. Below these comes, perhaps, another group of six thousand who would be willing to pay sixty cents, but for whom the prevailing market price of eighty cents is too high, and who, therefore, must decline to purchase.

Assuming the conditions of this example, a product of thirty thousand pieces corresponds to a market price of eighty cents. But manifestly, if the productive power were less; if, for instance, the number of laborers was only eighty and the amount produced only twenty-four thousand pieces, the market price at which the whole product would be sold might be one dollar. It is equally clear that with one hundred and twenty laborers and a product of thirty-six thousand pieces, the market price might not exceed sixty cents. In other words, the value of the product of one laborer when eighty laborers are employed, would be one dollar; when one hundred are employed, eighty cents, and when one hundred and twenty are employed, sixty cents. In the same way, the market for the product of every additional laborer above one hundred and twenty must be found at a still lower point in the demand scale. Or at any given time there is a group of the least capable or willing buyers that corresponds to the last employed group of laborers. The valuation of this group of buyers determines, in the first instance, the value of the product of the last group of workers; and through this, since at the same time and in the same market, there can be but one price for the same product, the value of the product of every laborer in this branch of production.*

It even goes further than this, and determines the wages of the laborer. On the one side, no entrepreneur will, for any long period, pay his laborers more than he can obtain for the product of their labor. The value of the product will, therefore, be the upper limit of the rate of wages. Again, under conditions of free competition, he will not for any long time pay them less, for so long as the market price is in excess of the cost of production,† the entre-

---

* Professor Marshall, in his example of the marginal shepherd, has made a very useful application of this concept of the last employed labor, though in a somewhat different direction. The increase of product which results, when, without increasing the capital, we employ an additional laborer, he conceives to be the answer to the question, How much of the total product may be regarded as the product of labor, as opposed to product of capital? Professor Marshall also allows the last employed laborer to play a part in the question of the relation between the laborer and the capitalist, or in the question of the division of the price of their products; I, on the other hand, do not allow the last employed laborer to play any part in the question of the relation between laborer and consumer, or in the question of the determination of the height of the price of the product. Nevertheless, I believe there is no material difference in our positions. The truth is, that the "last employed laborer" in both cases plays the rôle ascribed to him. But since I have expressly excluded all factors of production except labor (see above page), there was no occasion for me to speak further of the division of the product between the laborer and the capitalist. In my book on "Capital," I have given special attention to this question. In our present discussion, we would not insist upon every point involved in that abstraction. (See foregoing p. 321.)

† I beg the reader not to forget that in this investigation we ignore all factors of production except labor, especially the so-called abstinence. If we did not do so, we would somewhat complicate our example. Besides the cost of labor, we would have to take account of the cost of abstinence, must then subtract this latter from the market price. Then all conclusions, which we have here developed for the relation between the total market price of the product to the wages of labor, would have to be developed, for the relation of the market price of the product, diminished by the other costs of production, to the wages of labor.

preneur obtains a profit; but he or his competitors will be tempted by this to increase their production, and so to employ more laborers, until the difference between the valuation of the last buyer and the wages of the last laborer disappears.

The Method Of Equalizing Wages In Different Industries

The same forces, which, in every branch of production, tend to fill the gap between the value of the product of the last employed laborer, and the rate of pay in this branch of production, tend also to fill another gap. Under conditions of perfectly free competition, there cannot, in the long run, be any serious difference in prices or wages in those branches of production, that are in free communication with one another. In the long run, the product of a day's labor and the labor itself cannot have a value of one dollar and twenty cents in the woolen industry, for instance, and only forty cents in the cotton industry. This would immediately give rise to a tendency in the productive forces to change their occupation, a tendency which would continue to operate until both of these branches of production, together with all others in communication with them, had been brought into a condition of equilibrium.

The Determination Of Equilibrium In Demand

But where will this point of equilibrium be? This must be decided within that general field of employment which includes all the freely communicating branches of production; and it must be decided upon the same grounds or reasons which we have found to be effective for a single branch of production. There is a total or aggregate demand for all the products of labor. This is as limitless as our desire for well being, for enjoyment or for the possession of goods, and is graduated according to the intensity of this desire. If our desire for any product is very intense, and our means of payment abundant, then to us the marginal utility of the product will be high, while the marginal utility of money will be low. In other words, we will be willing to pay a higher price for this product than we would if our desire for it or our ability to pay for it were less.

Hence, in the general, as in any special field of production, there may be several strata of demand. There may be one which in an extreme case would be willing to pay eight dollars for the product of a day's labor. Another might be willing to give two dollars, while others would find their limit at one dollar and sixty cents, one dollar and twenty cents, at one dollar, and at eighty cents. There may remain still others who desire to purchase, but whose wants are not sufficiently pressing or whose purchasing power is so limited that they either will not or cannot pay more than fifty, forty or twenty cents, and even less, for the satisfaction of that want to which the product of a day's labor would be devoted.

Significance Of The Limitation In The Labor Supply

To meet this practically unlimited demand we have a labor power which in comparison with this demand is always limited. It is never sufficient to satisfy all our desire; if it was we would be in paradise; we must, therefore, always choose which of our desires we will gratify. Under the influence of self-interest we will satisfy them according to the height or amount of the fee which we are willing to pay for their satisfaction. That stratum of the demand which is prepared to pay eight dollars for a day's labor will not suffer any inconvenience for lack of the desired commodity. So, too, that stratum of the demand which is willing to pay two dollars will not suffer any inconvenience. Nor will those suffer that are prepared to pay one dollar and sixty cents, one dollar and twenty cents, one dollar, etc. But the point must finally be reached where such satisfaction cannot be obtained. This point will, of course, vary with the circumstances or conditions of particular lands or times. Here eighty cents, there sixty cents, and elsewhere forty or even twenty cents, but such a point will always and everywhere be found. Let us assume a concrete case in which this point is at eighty cents. The existing productive power is here fully employed in the satisfying of those wants, for whose satisfaction we are willing and able to pay eighty cents for a day of common labor. In this case the stratum of the demand whose valuation is eighty cents is the last stratum for the satisfaction of whose desires the last laborer is active.*   It is the valuation of this stratum which determines both the value of the product and the wages of labor. All those desires for whose satisfaction we are either unwilling or unable to pay at least eighty cents must remain unsatisfied.   This on the one hand will affect some of the unimportant needs or desires of the well-to-do class, on the other, alas, it will affect many of the more important needs of those whose means are limited, whose entire purchasing power has been exhausted in providing for still more pressing wants.

Effect Of An Increasing Number Of Laborers

Let us now assume that, under otherwise unchanged conditions, there is an increase in the number of laborers entering into the problem, say through the sudden abolition of the standing army, or through a great influx of laborers from other lands.   The additional laborers must and will find employment in providing for a still lower and hitherto unsatisfied stratum of the demand, that stratum, for instance, whose valuation is only seventy cents.   This stratum is now the lowest for which the last laborer is active, and its valuation determines both the value of the product and the wages of labor.†

* The fact that there are always a number of laborers out of employment tells in no way against my contention; it is a result, not of an excess of labor force, but of those never-failing disturbances of the organization of the entire, yet insufficient, supply of the labor forces.

† For the sake of the critical reader I would here remark that I am well aware that if we assume an increase in the labor forces we cannot at the same time assume that the other conditions remain entirely unchanged.   The increase in product which results from an increase in the number of laborers will also bring with it an increase in the purchasing power or in the demand.   But if, as in the text, we assume that with an unchanged condition of capital and land, the labor alone is increased, the increase in the demand for labor and the products of labor would not be strong enough to completely compensate the increase in the supply of labor, for the increase in product thus obtained cannot be wholly applied to the indemnification of labor, some fractional part of it must be given as tribute to the other co-operating factors in production, Capital and Land, for these factors have, under our supposition, become relatively scarcer than the factor, Labor, and so are in a position to insist on the payment of this tribute.   It results from this, that this increased product of labor can no longer be taken up by that stratum of demand,

How The Necessary Function Of Determining What Should Be Produced Is Accomplished. The Market Trumpet

What, under these conditions (the statement of which I hope will meet the approval of my honored English and American colleagues), is the rôle played by the law of costs? An exceedingly simple one. It guarantees that the existing productive power shall be directed to the satisfaction of the existing needs, according to the height of the fee which they are able and willing to pay. It brings about for the productive power in an indirect way, just what occurs in the case of the finished product in a direct way, upon every open market the supply of the finished product goes as far as it will reach to the best paying of those who desire to purchase. The market price of the same ware, on the same market, at the same time, is uniform. This fixes, very clearly and definitely, the boundary between those who are willing and able to purchase at that price, and those who are willing to do so but not able. If, for instance, the market price is eighty cents, then all those to whom the money marginal utility (*Geldgrenznutzen*) of the commodity is eighty cents, or more, will provide themselves with the commodity, all those to whom the money marginal utility of the commodity is less than eighty cents must deny themselves this commodity. No one will intentionally reduce the price of his commodity, to those who are willing and able to pay one dollar and twenty cents, in order to favor those who will or can pay only forty cents.

This same function is performed for the productive power by the law of cost. The latter does not meet the consumers and their needs directly; it does not come in contact with them upon a common market; but it reaches the public through the money price which the public puts upon the finished product. This competition (*Werben*) is extended

which can pay eighty cents, but must find its market in a deeper, though it may be only a little deeper, stratum of the demand. I would also remark, that the question touched upon in this note is a most difficult and complicated one,—it contains, perhaps, the most difficult part of the difficult theory of wages,—and that I do not for a moment think that I have exhausted the subject with these rather brief, and I fear somewhat obscure remarks. I would only call attention to the fact that I have not lost sight of a difficulty, the complete exposition of which would lead us too far afield.

over as many parts of the general market as there are different kinds of products. But this competition, though widely diffused and indirect, eventually results in the establishing of a certain market price for the productive power. This market price of the productive power appears in each single branch of production as the cost of the same. It operates like a speaking trumpet through which the supply price in other and distant parts of the general market is made audible in the part where we are situated. Those interested in one part are notified of the conditions which obtain in the general market and are thus enabled to govern their actions according to these more general conditions.

How Different The Real Pricing Of Labor Is From The "Iron Law Of Wages"

Let us now return to our example. We will assume that, in the general field of production or employment, the market price of the product of a day of common labor, and thus the wages for a day of such labor is eighty cents. We will also assume that in some special departments, as cotton manufacturing, because of some unfavorable combination, the value of the product of a day's labor has fallen to sixty cents, while at the same time, the wages of labor being eighty cents, the cost of production is eighty cents. What is the meaning and effect of this rate of cost of eighty cents? It does not mean that the laborer cannot live on less than eighty cents; or that the labor involves a degree of disutility which he will not endure for less than eighty cents. It means, and that quite clearly, that there are enough people in the world who will give eighty cents for a day's labor, or for the product of the same, to keep all the productive power active, and therefore that it would be foolish to ignore this offer, and employ the productive power in the service of people who are able and willing to pay only sixty cents for a day's work.

Function Of The Law Of Cost — To Bring Prices Of Products Into Line With Each Other.
It Thereby Also Determines The Price Of Labor

Let us now assume, that in the woolen industry the product of a day's labor, through some favorable combination, is worth one dollar and twenty cents, while the cost is only

eighty cents. This is clearly nothing else than advice to
those interested, that in the general field of employment a
day's labor cannot obtain more than eighty cents, and therefore that it is wise to listen to the favorable offer that we
have been ignoring, namely, the offer of those people who
are willing and able to pay for the product of a day's labor
in the woolen industry, not indeed all of one dollar and
twenty cents, but something more than eighty cents. This
advice bears fruit through the action of the watchful self-
interest of the entrepreneurs. In obedience to the law of
cost it levels the abnormal prices of sixty cents and one
dollar and twenty cents, that prevail in different parts of the
general market, to the normal price of eighty cents. This
means nothing more than the bringing about of that disposition of the productive power, which insures that the best
paying wants shall always be satisfied first. At the outset,
according to our illustration, those needs whose money
marginal utility was eighty cents and sixty cents were satisfied, while those whose money marginal utility was between
eighty cents and one dollar and twenty cents remained
unsatisfied. Eventually a readjustment is effected so that
everywhere and in all branches of production, the productive power is employed in the service of the best paying
wants. This takes place successively from the highest down
to those whose money marginal utility is eighty cents. We
may conclude then, that in this and in all similar cases the
law of cost has no other function than to bring all products
of equal origin into line with each other. The self-evident
proposition that the same product, on the same market, at
the same time, must have the same value or price, is
extended by the law of cost a step further, and gives us the
proposition that products of like origin must have the same
value or price. But how high this value or price will be,
neither proposition informs us. The self-evident proposition,
that one bushel of wheat has the same value as another
similar bushel of wheat—gives me no starting point from

which I can determine the value of both bushels. In the same way, in the cases described, the law of cost gives me no starting point from which I can determine the absolute height of the price line; to which, according to that law, the price of all products of equal origin are brought. When we take a certain limited view of the question we do seem to get an answer. As when we confine ourselves to a single branch of production and think of the amount of the cost as something that we determine independently of our problem. But we might just as well argue, in the case of our two bushels of wheat, that according to our proposition, one of these bushels has just the same value as the other. We also *know* that number one is worth one dollar, therefore, according to our proposition, number two is worth one dollar. But the value of number one is just as much a subject for investigation as the value of number two, and hence, our answer does not give us the value of either. This is true of the height of the cost in every branch of production. We must, in every case, go back of the apparent answers until we find the real answer. In the case of the two bushels of wheat this answer lies close at hand, but in the case of costs in general, we must survey the whole field of production and finally find our answer in the following elementary proposition:

There is a certain limited quantity of productive power which at any given time, under the conditions set by the technical development of that time, can bring forth only a certain limited quantity of products. These products, through the action of certain leveling influences in the different branches of production, are disposed of in a regular order of succession, in each case, to the best paying purchaser. The satisfaction extends downward in the scale of wants until a certain equalization to the (money) marginal cost of production is attained, and it is this which decides the value of all goods that come under the dominion of that leveling influence. It determines the value of the products as well as the value of the productive power, which is represented by the cost.

Marshall's Illustration Of The Two Blades Of A Shears.
Its Inconclusive And Erroneous Character

The representatives of the English theory have chosen the figure of the two blades of a pair of shears, in order to show the opposition between the English and Austrian conception of the law of cost.   I gladly follow them in the use of this figure but with the conviction that the interpretation which my English colleagues have given to it, must be supplemented as follows:

In the case of freely reproducible goods, it is undoubtedly true that the price is fixed at that point where the money marginal utility of the commodity to those desiring to purchase it crosses the line of the costs.   In our example, the last purchaser of wool will be the one whose valuation will correspond with the amount of the cost, or with eighty cents. In this case it is entirely correct to say that utility (relative marginal utility for those desiring to purchase) and cost operate together in the determination of price, like the two blades of a pair of shears.

But now follows the unavoidable question: What determines the amount of this cost?   The amount of the cost is identical with the value of the productive power, and, as a rule, is determined by the money marginal utility of this productive power.   This, of course, has reference to the existing conditions of the demand for and supply of this productive power in the various branches of production.   If in the above formula we substitute for " cost " this explanation of cost, we would have the following: " The price of a definite species of freely reproducible goods fixes itself in the long run at that point where the money marginal utility, for those who desire to purchase these products, intersects the money marginal utility of all those who desire to purchase in the other communicating branches of production."

The "Cost" Of Marshall Is Really The Marginal Utility
Of "Production Related Goods," And, Therefore,
Also A Utility (And Not A Cost) Factor

The figure of the two blades of a pair of shears still holds good. One of the two blades, whose coming together determines the height of the price of any species of product, is in truth the marginal utility of this particular product. The other, which we are wont to call " cost," is the marginal utility of the products of other communicating branches of production. Or, according to Wieser, the marginal utility of "production related goods" (*productionsverwandten Güter*). It is, therefore, utility and not disutility which, as well on the side of supply as of demand, determines the height of the price. This, too, even where the so-called law of cost plays its rôle in giving value to goods. Jevons, therefore, did not exaggerate the importance of the one side, but came very near the truth when he said "value depends entirely upon utility."

Almost, but not quite entirely, for as I have endeavored to show, and as Jevons well knew, disutility plays a certain part in the determination of value. A part, however, which, in our actual economical conditions, is quantitatively unimportant. It occurs in full force only, in the case of the few and unimportant products of our leisure hours. For the great mass of products which are the outcome of our regular occupation, this disutility either does not appear, or is only a very weak and remote element in the complex standard that determines the "height of the cost."* If we were to put this roughly into figures, we might say that the ten parts of that blade which represents the demand consist entirely of *utility*, while of the blade which represents the "cost," nine parts are utility and only one part disutility. On the whole then value depends nineteen-twentieths on utility, and only one-twentieth on disutility.

Synchronously And Historically Reckoned Costs Will Yield Different Results

We must now consider a circumstance, which thus far in our argument we have intentionally ignored. Up to this point we have confined ourselves to those conceptions of the law of cost which come nearest to harmonizing with those of our opponents, namely, those which declare that there is a correspondence between the price and the historically reckoned cost, *i. e.*, the cost elements, labor and abstinence. It was only in this way that we could eliminate all those intermediate members, raw material, wear and tear of tools, etc.,

*See foregoing p. 334.

which in practice appear as part of the cost, and in common with most of our opponents, speak of labor and abstinence as the determining factors of cost.

We must not, however, forget that there is a second sense, in which the law of cost is susceptible of empirical demonstration, namely, the sense in which the law of cost asserts a correspondence between the price and the synchronously reckoned money cost of the entrepreneur.* When we carefully consider the historical and synchronous method of reckoning cost in their relations to each other, it is manifest, that while there is some connection between them, yet they are not entirely the same, either in their content or in the extent of their sway. The correspondence of the price with the historically reckoned cost involves the satisfying of much more severe and unusual conditions. The leveling feature, upon which both rules rest, must here operate unhindered through the whole of the complex system of production, down to the last elementary root. On the other hand, the gravitation of the price, toward the synchronously reckoned money cost of any particular stage of production, merely assumes that the leveling influence has free sway in this part of the productive process. The gravitation toward the synchronously reckoned cost is to a certain degree more readlly satisfied. For this reason it is more frequently operative, and hence there is a wide district, subject to its sway, which is not subject to the sway of the historically reckoned cost.

There are numerous instances in which the synchronously reckoned cost of a single stage of production is effective in determining the price of the product, although there may be no correspondence between the price and the historically reckoned cost. This may be due to the fact that the leveling influence may be temporarily inoperative through all stages of production, or though free for part of the distance, it may at some point be permanently hindered by some kind of a monopoly.

*See foregoing p. 325.

Illustration How Historically Reckoned Costs Are Overborn. The Sequence Of Cause And Effect

Let us illustrate this by an example. The production of one hundred weight of copper costs at a given time ten days of historically reckoned labor at eighty cents a day or eight dollars. This, of course, enters into the cost of all copper goods, and therefore into the price of copper wire, copper kettles, copper pans, etc. Now, because of a strong demand for electric wire the hundred weight of copper advances in price from eight to twelve dollars, nothing is more certain than that the coppersmith, the money cost of his material having risen, will advance the price of copper wire, etc. A copper kettle which weighs one hundred pounds and the production of which involved an expense of six dollars, had in the past a total cost of fourteen dollars; it now has an additional cost of four dollars and so must bring at least eighteen dollars, and this quite independently of the question, whether or not the historically reckoned cost of production has changed; whether ten or any other number of days of labor have been expended in its production; or whether we pay eighty cents or any other amount for a day's labor.

The fate of the " historically " reckoned cost will likewise depend upon a variety of considerations; difficulty may be encountered in producing the additional amount of copper which is necessary to supply the increased demand. It may be necessary to employ more miners, in which case it is quite probable that the wages of the miners will advance. Or, perhaps, though we can obtain a sufficient force of miners at eighty cents, it may be necessary to work poorer veins, in which a hundred weight of copper will cost not ten but twelve days' labor. In both cases the advance which first appeared in the money cost of a later stage of production, will be gradually transmitted, in a greater or less degree, to the elementary labor cost of the earlier stages of production. Finally, it is possible that we may be able to supply this increased demand for copper without any additional cost, or at the old rate of ten days of eighty cent labor to every hundred pounds of copper. In this case the increased demand for copper will eventually be satisfied at this rate of cost. The price of the copper, as well as that of the copper goods, will then have a corresponding return motion until it reaches the original price of eight dollars.

Types Of Synchronous Costs That Temporarily At Least Supersede Historical Costs

But in either event, it still remains true that the price of copper goods may be determined, at least temporarily, by other conditions than their historically reckoned cost. In practice numberless instances of this kind arise. Even though in the long run the elementary "historical" cost plays an important part, yet time is necessary for its influence to be felt through the whole of our complicated system of production. During this time the stages not yet effected by this leveling influence will follow the lead of their special "synchronous" cost.

Let us now take a few examples, in which this leveling influence is free to operate over a limited area of the process of production, and then at a certain point becomes permanently inoperative.

Take a chemical product, which we will assume to be sold at any given time, at its actual cost of production, say eight dollars. Let us further assume that some discovery is made by which the cost of this material is reduced to four dollars, and that the discoverer patents the process and allows others to use it for a fee of two dollars. The price of this product will now permanently adjust itself to a money cost of six dollars, which exceeds the elementary cost of four dollars by the amount of the patent fee or royalty of two dollars.

Let us take another case, and assume that a hundredweight of coffee, when admitted into a country free of duty, will sell at a price which is just sufficient to cover its cost of production, which we will assume to be sixty-five dollars. Let it now be subjected to an import duty of fifteen dollars. The price must, of course, be high enough to cover this additional cost, and, therefore, will rise to eighty dollars, an amount which exceeds the elementary cost by fifteen dollars.

Here we have two typical examples of price variations, which will be found to include nearly the entire field of price phenomena, for there are at the present time very few products in which some patented machine or process, or some import duty on raw or auxiliary material does not play a part.

Vague Explanations Of Prices, On The Basis Of Supply And Demand, Are Inadequate

It is now time to ask: What has our theory to say about the determination of these prices of copper kettles, chemical products, coffee, etc.?

It must offer some explanation of these facts, since they are of such frequent and general occurrence. It is also manifest that it cannot explain them in terms of the elementary cost of labor and abstinence, nor in terms of the value of these elementary factors of cost, nor by a reference to the disutility which may be associated with the same. The price of the copper kettle has advanced from fourteen dollars to eighteen dollars, and the price of coffee from sixty-five dollars to eighty dollars, not because, but in spite of the fact, that the elementary costs have remained unchanged at fourteen and sixty-five dollars. Again, in the case of our chemical product, if the price depended upon the elementary cost, it should not stop at six dollars but should sink to four dollars. It is equally clear that all these cases of price variations are subject to the law of cost and are actually effects of this law. It would, indeed, be a very serious sin of omission, on the part of economic science, to attempt an explanation why the present prices of the several commodities mentioned in our illustration are just eighteen, six and eighty dollars, without any reference to the characteristic circumstance that these prices represent the present cost to the entrepreneur, and instead, content itself, with a vague reference to the relation existing between the supply of, and demand for these commodities.

The same considerations which in the past have forced us to supplement the general law of supply and demand through the more exact law of cost, makes it necessary to so interpret the law of cost that it may include and explain the above variations in prices.

Both Synchronous And Historical Costs Should Be Retained

What now remains to be done? In our opinion, just that which the Austrian economists have endeavored to do.

The conception of a historically reckoned cost must be brought face to face with the conception of a synchronously reckoned cost, and due importance must consciously be given to each of the two conceptions. These two conceptions may, indeed, be put side by side, but are in no sense interchangeable. For the solution of different problems in our science, both conceptions are necessary. It is even necessary to distinguish between the different varieties of the "historical" cost. For certain explanatory and speculative purposes, it is well to have in mind the disutility of labor. In other cases (as in estimating certain technical advances in production), it is the quantity of labor that we must consider. In still others, it is the value of the labor that we must inquire about. There is not, as Professor Macvane thinks, only one "true conception" of cost. Professor Patten, although his limitations are not entirely satisfactory, comes much nearer the truth when he says that the competing concepts really belong to different branches of the theory, the one to the "theory of value" and the other to the "theory of prosperity."*

Increases In Prices, Apparently Caused By Increases In Costs, Are Really Disguised Increases In Utility

Again, we must not endeavor to find in the law of cost either more or less than the Austrian economists have found in it, namely, a universal law of leveling. And this is an influence which operates not merely upon certain final elements, but also at every stage of the productive process. There is a leveling or equating not merely of the final elements, labor and the disutility of labor, but also of productive goods and of utility with utility. This last takes place independent of, and ofttimes in direct opposition to the influence of the final elements. Why, in our example of the copper kettle, does the price rise from fourteen to eighteen

* "Cost and Expense," page 67. ANNALS, May, 1893.

dollars? Simply because through the common cost it can and must be leveled to the price of the other commodities produced from copper, *i. e.*, in this case to the price of the strongly demanded copper wire. But why have prices in the entire copper business advanced? Because, and in so far as, through the increased demand for copper, the marginal utility of this material has been raised. It is, therefore, an increase in utility and not in disutility, that here in the guise of cost dictates the advance of the price. The numerous instances of this kind which at once suggest themselves to the reader, confirm our earlier judgment of the important part which, under modern economic conditions, utility plays in the determination of cost.

Austrian Economists Are Not Neglectful Of Doctrines On Costs

It is a curious fact that the objection has been more than once advanced, that the Austrian economists have closed their eyes to the rich treasure of insight and knowledge which the great law of cost affords;* and that they have disdained to avail themselves of its help in the explanation of the phenomena of value. In reality as we have endeavored to show, the reverse of this is true. So anxious are we to coin the whole of this treasure, so strong is our desire not to neglect or discard one particle of the help which it offers us, that we object to a misleading interpretation of this law, an interpretation which would compel us to ignore the greater part of its influence. The character of the facts as well as the necessities of the science force upon us, as we believe, with equal imperativeness, the other universal concept, the concept which the Austrian economists have made their own, and whose essential features I will in conclusion recapitulate.

The Erroneous Definition Of The Second "Blade Of The Shears" Determining Prices

The variety of meanings that have attached themselves to the word cost have been the source of much confusion. There is, for instance, the cost, which, in the sense of the

---

* Compare for example B. Dietzel's writings, especially the paragraphs cited in my answer (Conrad's *Jahrbücher*), third series, book iii, page 327. See also Professor Edgeworth in the *Economic Journal*, June, 1892, pages 334, 337.

great empirical law of cost, operates as the determinant or regulator of price. To identify this either directly or indirectly with the personal sacrifice, laboriousness, pain or disutility that is imposed upon us by labor or abstinence, is an actual misunderstanding.

What Appears As "Costs" Are Really Levelling Factors Stemming From Competing Marginal Utilities

The "cost" of the law of cost is not the name of an elementary factor. It is a designation applied indifferently, according to the special circumstances of the case, either to sacrifice utilities embodied in goods, or to personal discomfort or pains, *i. e.*, either to utilities or to disutilities. The law of cost is always in the first instance a simple leveling principle. In order to determine what elementary forces are included under this title, we must inquire what it is, that under the name of cost, brings about this leveling. We then find that at first the marginal utility of one product is leveled to the marginal utility of other products, that are produced from the same cost good (raw material, machines, etc.), or it is a leveling of utility with utility. In most cases this leveling process not only begins but ends here. Only occasionally, under quite definite casuistic assumptions, is the leveling process carried a step further, and the utility of the good itself brought into equilibrium with the disutility endured by the producers. In this limited number of cases the general law of cost becomes a special law of disutility. The independent character of this law is shown by the fact, that while its domain is very limited, yet in one direction it extends beyond that of the classical law of cost.*

The Single Ultimate Standard Of Value Is "Human Well-Being"

What then is the "ultimate standard" for the determination of the value of goods, in the search for which, men have been as indefatigable during the last one hundred years, as they formerly were in their endeavors to square the circle. If we wish to answer this question in a single phrase, then we cannot choose any less general expression than "human well-being." The ultimate standard for the value of all goods is the degree of well-being which is dependent

*See foregoing p. 339.

upon goods in general.   If, however, we desire a more concrete standard, one that will give us a more definite idea,
just how goods are connected with well-being, then we must
take not one but two standards, which though co-ordinate in
theory are yet of very unequal practical importance, because
of the greater prevalence of the phenomena in which one of
them is operative; one is the utility of the good, and the
other is the personal sacrifice or disutility involved in the
acquisition of the good.   The domain of the latter is much
more limited than we usually think.   In the great majority
of cases, even in those in which the so-called law of cost
undoubtedly plays a part, the final determination of the
value of goods is dependent upon utility.

TO OBTAIN
COMPREHENSIVE ORIENTATION
IN NEOCLASSICAL ECONOMICS

If an economist asks himself in which of three schools of economic thought he has read least — whether Classical, Collectivist or Neoclassical — his answer will probably be, *Neoclassical*. Further reading of the writings of this school of thought should be rewarding.

(1) In time sequence, what is called Classical came first. In retrospect, it appears that the name was applied too early in the history of economic thought.

(2) Collectivist economics (socialist, communist, central planning, *dirigist*) is a hostile reaction to the Classical, which was basically rooted in freedom. The socialists discovered some of the fallacies of the Classicists, but the solutions of the socialists were aggravations of the errors of the Classicists. The socialists disagreed with the Classicists where the latter were right, and built their own socialist superstructure on the fallacies of the Classicists; the socialists in general rejected the good and kept the bad of the Classicists.

(3) The Neoclassicists (as their name indicates) are in the genuine tradition of the Classicists and they corrected ambiguities and errors of the latter. The writings of classicists as Adam Smith and David Ricardo are not effective today against collectivist economics. Those authors do not provide the help that the anti-collectivists need. It is the Neoclassical who are especially useful in this regard.

Several of the greatest Neoclassicists were Austrian nationals. They wrote in German. Only recently have translations or new books by them become available in the English language.

continued

LIBERTARIAN PRESS, South Holland, Illinois

(Page One of Six Pages)

The following three books constitute the main stream of Neo-classical thought:

(1) *Carl Menger*   PRINCIPLES OF ECONOMICS
The Free Press, Glencoe, Illinois, 1950 - 320 pages $ 6.00

(2) *Eugen von Böhm-Bawerk*   CAPITAL AND INTEREST
Libertarian Press, South Holland, Illinois, 1959
   I History and Critique of Interest Theories
   II Positive Theory of Capital
   III Further Essays on Capital and Interest
1248 pages   Three Volumes In One: $15.00

(See page four for reference to three-volume edition)

(3) *Ludwig von Mises*   HUMAN ACTION
Yale University Press, New Haven, Conn., 1949
899 pages $12.50

Libertarian Press will supply any of these books as long as they are in print.

Carl Menger

(1) *Menger*:
PRINCIPLES OF ECONOMICS

Menger's *Principles of Economics* is the earliest and shortest book in the series. It is also the easiest reading.

This book contains in simplest form the basic idea which constituted, in the 19th century, a "revolution in economics." (There is an Introduction by Frank H. Knight, which should be read *after* the Menger, Böhm-Bawerk and Mises books have been read.)

continued

LIBERTARIAN PRESS, South Holland, Illinois

(Page Two of Six Pages)

Böhm-Bawerk

(2) *Böhm-Bawerk:*
CAPITAL AND INTEREST

Marx and other socialists attacked *all* "unearned income," as exploitation of employes; they were grossly mistaken.

In opposition to that, pro-capitalism economists defended interest on the ground that it was not exploitation of the worker, but compensation for the productivity of the capital supplied; or they gave other reasons. But these arguments were fallacious, as both the socialists declared and Böhm-Bawerk has shown.

History and Critique of Interest Theories (Vol. I) is, figuratively, a graveyard of fallacious interest theories. *Positive Theory of Capital* (Vol. II) contains the most comprehensive analysis that has been made of capital and interest. This volume is an impressive superstructure reared on Menger's premises. *Further Essays on Capital and Interest* (Vol. III) supplements Volume II.

As an intellectual production, these volumes outrank anything published earlier in the science of economics.

Mises

(3) *Mises:*   HUMAN ACTION

Mises's major work is *Human Action.* It builds better, on and beyond, Menger and Böhm-Bawerk.

Human Action is the most comprehensive economic treatise yet written. (First 150 pages pertain to fundamental and difficult epistemological problems.)

Human Action shows where the cause for business booms and depressions must be sought, and what the policy should be to ameliorate that situation.

Mastering these books will be facilitated by reading them in the chronological order in which they were written; first Menger; then Böhm-Bawerk; then Mises.   *continued*

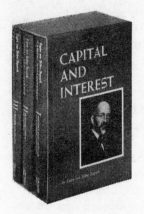

CAPITAL AND INTEREST: Böhm-Bawerk's main work is so large it has always appeared in more than one volume. In addition to the three-volumes-in-one edition, this text is also available in *three separate volumes,* boxed in a slip-case. 1959. I, 512 pages; II, 480 pages; III, 256 pages. $25 the set, plus postage.

In his review of this edition of CAPITAL AND INTEREST, Professor Ludwig von Mises wrote (see *The Freeman,* August 1959):

EUGEN VON BÖHM-BAWERK AND THE DISCRIMINATING READER

"*The publication* of a new English-language translation of Böhm-Bawerk's monumental work on *Capital and Interest* raises an important question. There is no doubt that Böhm-Bawerk's book is the most eminent contribution to modern economic theory.

"For every economist it is a must to study it most carefully and to scrutinize its content with the utmost care. A man not perfectly familiar with all the ideas advanced in these three volumes has no claim whatever to the appellation of an economist. But what about the general reader, the man who does not plan to specialize in economics because his strenuous involvement in his business or in his profession does not leave him the leisure to plunge into detailed economic analysis? What does this book mean to him?

"To answer this question we have to take into account the role that economic problems play in present-day politics. All the political antagonisms and conflicts of our age turn on economic issues.

"It has not always been so. In the sixteenth and seventeenth centuries the controversies that split the peoples of Western civilization into feuding parties were religious. Protestantism stood against Catholicism, and within the Protestant camp various interpretations of the Gospels begot discord. In the eighteenth century and in a great part of the nineteenth century constitutional conflicts prevailed in politics. The principles of royal absolutism and oligarchic government were resisted by liberalism (in the classical European meaning of the term)

continued

LIBERTARIAN PRESS, South Holland, Illinois

(Page Four of Six Pages)

that advocated representative government. In those days a man who wanted to take an active part in the great issues of his age had to study seriously the matter of these controversies. The sermons and the books of the theologians of the age of the Reformation were not reserved to esoteric circles of specialists. They were eagerly absorbed by the whole educated public. Later the writings of the foremost advocates of freedom were read by all those who were not fully engrossed in the petty affairs of their daily routine. Only boors neglected to inform themselves about the great problems that agitated the minds of their contemporaries.

"In our age the conflict between economic freedom as represented in the market economy and totalitarian government omnipotence as realized by socialism is the paramount matter. All political controversies refer to these economic problems. Only the study of economics can tell a man what all these conflicts mean. Nothing can be known about such matters as inflation, economic crises, unemployment, unionism, protectionism, taxation, economic controls, and all similar issues, that does not involve and presuppose economic analysis. All the arguments advanced in favor of or against the market economy and its opposites, interventionism or socialism (communism), are of an economic character. A man who talks about these problems without having acquainted himself with the fundamental ideas of economic theory is simply a babbler who parrot-like repeats what he has picked up incidentally from other fellows who are not better informed than he himself. A citizen who casts his ballot without having to the best of his abilities studied as much economics as he can fails in his civic duties. He neglects using in the appropriate way the power that his citizenship has conferred upon him in giving him the right to vote.

"Now there is no better method to introduce a man to economic problems than that provided by the books of the great economists. And certainly Böhm-Bawerk is one of the greatest of them. His voluminous treatise is the royal road to an understanding of the fundamental political issues of our age."

INVALUABLE PAPERBACK EXTRACTS
from CAPITAL AND INTEREST

1. "VALUE AND PRICE," 160 p., $2.00, 1960:

In his review, Mises goes on to write:

"The general reader should start with the second volume in which Böhm analyzes the essence of saving and capital accumulation and the role capital goods play in the process of production. Especially important is the third book of this second volume; it deals with the determination of value and prices."

continued

L'BERTARIAN PRESS, South Holland, Illinois

(Page Five of Six Pages)

2. "The Exploitation Theory," 97 p., $1.50:

Mises continues:

" . . . the reader should then turn to the first volume that gives a critical history of all the doctrines advanced on the source of interest and profit by earlier authors. In this historical review the most important part is the chapter that analyzes the so-called exploitation-doctrines, first of all the doctrine that Karl Marx developed in his *Das Kapital,* the Koran of all Marxians. The refutation of Marx's labor theory of value is perhaps the most interesting, at any rate the politically most momentous chapter of Böhm's contribution."

PLANNING FOR FREEDOM by Mises:

Trenchant essays, which constitute the easiest introduction to Mises. 1952. 174 pages. Paper $1.50.

Two of these essays are also available in pamphlet form:

"Middle-of-the-Road Policy Leads To Socialism," 24 pages, 25c.

"Profit and Loss," 55 pages, 75c.

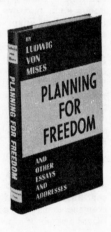

FIRST PRINCIPLES IN MORALITY AND ECONOMICS: A 32-page monthly for six years, 1955-1960. A hybrid publication covering ethics and economics, with the ethics Hebrew-Christian; and the economics, Neoclassical. The major emphasis is on ethics. Paperbound. Six volumes at $18. 384 pages each volume, size; 8½" x 5½".

LIBERTARIAN PRESS, South Holland, Illinois